Brain and behavior

Brain & Behavior

A TEXTBOOK OF PHYSIOLOGICAL PSYCHOLOGY

HUGH BROWN
University of Miami
and
Florida International University

New York   OXFORD UNIVERSITY PRESS   London   Toronto   1976

To My Father
Hugh Brown, M.D.

Preface

This book was developed from lectures presented in my physiological psychology course at St. Paul's College, University of Manitoba. The content is designed to help students with little or no background in biology see the relevance of some physiology to any study of psychology.

The book is organized into five parts. Part I represents an attempt to define physiological psychology and to put it in a context relative to its derivative sciences, primarily biology and psychology. Part II concerns aspects of the fundamental neurosciences necessary to a grasp of physiological psychology discussions. In Part III, the relation between the nervous system and behavior is dealt with. Part IV extends this relation to the social sphere, and Part V sums up contemporary opinion on the nature of the mind.

While the sequence is not strictly cumulative, it is recommended that the book be approached in the order presented; otherwise, a number of subtle but significant concepts may not be fully appreciated. Very frequent cross references to other sections of the book do, however, enhance the chances for meaningful outside reading.

One of the first things a prospective author comes to realize is that no one writes a book alone. The problem of thanking all those who contributed, however, is twofold: 1. finding words adequate to express appreciation and 2. being all inclusive, so as not to exclude any of the numerous, valuable contributors. With those limitations very much in mind, I want to express gratitude to the following. First, all the students of St. Paul's College who patiently listened to the lectures from which this book was developed, for their candor and enthusiasm at levels seldom seen in the classroom; their questioning and insight contributed mightily to articulation of my own views. The staff of St. Paul's College, particularly the cooperation and encouragement of Fr. Lawrence Braceland, S.J., a friend and Dean without peer. The staff at Oxford University Press, especially Bill Halpin, for faith and patience with a neophyte author. A special word for Dr. W. Lawrence Gulick of Dartmouth College, who reviewed the manuscript providing accurate and extensive comments; they not only improved the book significantly, they also provided me with an unparalleled learning experience. Consulting Editor Lee Edson applied his considerable talents to every word in this book. Editor Ruth Bounous whose objectivity provided clarity, focus, and organization. My mother, Helen, who applied the wisdom of her eighty-odd years to an incisive proofreading of all drafts. Last, but by no means least, my wife Louise who typed each of the many drafts the book went through—sometimes with patience and forbearance, sometimes not.

Miami, Florida   H.B.
February, 1975

Contents

I
The scope of physiological psychology

Part I defines and delineates the important role played by physiological psychology in resolving some of the basic behavioral problems and mysteries of modern life. Two major areas are discussed. The first chapter deals with the nature and domain of this pioneer branch of experimental psychology, discusses how it grew into an important science, and indicates how its experimental findings may shed new light on normal and abnormal behavior. The recent advances in physiological psychology also provide hope that the scientific study of man, in terms of the biological underpinnings of behavior, may resolve the ancient dualist puzzle of the connection between mind and body.

The second chapter looks at the development of physiological psychology in the long perspective of evolution. This chapter discusses the origins of behavior in terms of nervous system growth and explains how such knowledge aids in understanding present day human behavior.

This order of presentation serves two important functions. First the student is able to see the place of physiological psychology in the development of man's knowledge about himself. And secondly, it will lead to an understanding of why physiological psychology may create a new beginning in the understanding of man's own nature.

1 Physiological psychology in perspective

NATURE AND DOMAIN

Donald L. was a short, muscular, middle-aged man who was so violent he had to be restrained in the ward by a cover of heavy fish netting. Physicians who examined him found that if they came too close he would snarl, bare his teeth, and lash out. His frightened family told the physicians and the police that, for no reason at all, Donald had pulled a butcher knife and tried to kill them.

In subsequent study, psychiatrists found that Donald had first exhibited violent behavior six months earlier, at a time when he had complained of headaches and blurred vision. Since the symptoms went away, nothing was done until the butcher knife attack. Physicians examined Donald while he was sedated and found that his optic nerve was bloody and swollen, a condition that often results from pressures on the brain. Special x-rays with an apparatus that shows the brain in cross section confirmed that Donald had a tumor beneath a part of the brain called the right frontal lobe. This tumor was pressing on the front portion of another part of the brain, the temporal lobe. When the tumor was removed, the symptoms disappeared and Donald's behavior improved. Police charges were dropped and he went back to work. Donald was relatively lucky, and so were his victims. Several years later, an ex-GI named Charles Whitman climbed to the top of a tower on the campus of the University of Texas at Austin and started firing a rifle at random at people walking below (Figure 1-1). He killed fourteen people before he himself was killed by police. The autopsy showed that the reason for his bizarre criminal behavior lay in a tumor in the brain near a tissue known as the amygdala.

The cases of Donald L. and Charles Whitman are clear illustrations of the connection between the physical brain and

Figure 1-1.   After killing his wife and mother, Charles Whitman, shooting from the administration-building tower of the University of Texas, killed and wounded many others. He was subsequently found to have a brain tumor. (Wide World Photos.)

behavior, and thus can be considered to be part of the human clinical material that lies in the domain of the *physiological psychologist,* one who tries to explain scientifically how body structure and function, primarily the nervous system, can affect and control the overt and subjective behavioral characteristics of an organism. In Donald's case, the overt behavior consisted of taking a butcher knife to his family. The subjective behavior comprised the thoughts, fantasies, and drives that lay underneath his urge to kill. It is the basic task of physiological psychology, one of the oldest branches of experimental psychology, to establish the principles that clarify the structure-function connection.

The study of the relationship between the brain and behavior is enormously important in the contemporary world, not just in matters of disease and crime but in other areas as well. For instance, employers interviewing job applicants may want to know the connection between subjective thoughts and sweaty palms or blushing. Surgeons want to know whether an operation on the brain can change the behavior of a person for the better, and, if so, would society approve such a permanent change to the brain of a human being. The effect of drugs on the brain, of pills on learning ability, or the nature of neural and sensory circuits in the learning process play a part in everyday behaviors that are of utmost importance to the individual and his society.

Mind-body problem

Beyond such current concerns, the study of the relation between brain structure and behavior gives physiological psychology the unique mission of trying to resolve an old and basic puzzle of philosophy and science, often referred to as the "mind-body problem." Anthropological and historical evidence suggests that, from the time of his origins, man has had an abiding interest in the essence and source of his subjective experience, the regulation of his body reactions, and the identity of himself as a structural and functional unit. However, how these common elements of existence arose and how they are related to the body in which they are housed did not become a matter for formal philosophic examination until the time of Plato. Early Greek thinkers developed the contention that man as a living entity consists of two distinct beings: the material, physical, objective being—a body; and the nonmaterial, psychical, subjective being—a mind. This differentiation is called *dualism* (fully discussed in Chapter 16). Over the years, the mind-body dichotomy has become a much contested issue in philosophy and religion as various thinkers have attempted to build philosophies that advance one aspect of being over the other. Physiological psychology can be regarded as the first organized study that directly attempts the resolution of dualism, or the mind-body problem, through objective experiments designed to determine whether mind is a physical force emerging out of actions of the flesh or an independent entity arising out of the humanness of man.

As will be seen throughout this book, the mind-body problem centers on many specific questions which are as important today as they were at the time of the early Greeks. These questions involve such things as will (How does one voluntarily initiate activity?); feelings (What are the physical bases of one's emotions, attitudes, and motives?); knowing (What is the nature of the physical and neural events underlying awareness and consciousness?); and learning and memory (How do body processes serve in the acquisition, retention, and recall of information?).

To study these various mind-body issues is obviously to study the very nature of man. Expression of the action and content of mind is basic to all human conduct including that of the scientist (scientists, after all, are human too). Biochemical enhancement of learning, alteration of personality by brain lesions, modification of violent behavior by electrode implantation, hedonism as a viable source of motivation, drug-induced alteration of perception and cognition, hormonal regulation of emotions, and many other physiological psychology issues discussed in subsequent chapters have profound individual and social significance to both the contemporary and future state of mankind. The term "brain control" bandied about in modern rhetoric, with its connotations of a robot society run by a dictator, is a striking example of the importance of understanding physiological psychology in today's world.

But, despite their importance, the resolution of enigmas arising from the mind-body problem still remains one of the great puzzles for science. The brain is often spoken of as the final frontier of man's exploration, the last barrier to universal understanding. It is indeed paradoxical that while modern man has developed a technology that enables him to land on and explore the moon, he has not been able to unravel the secrets of the source of that technology, his mind!

Some observers feel that scientific elucidation of mind is close at hand, but maintain reservations as to man's capacity for constructively utilizing the applied benefits it will afford (Delgado, 1971). Others see little progress and despair of mind-body issues ever being resolved. Oatley, for instance, postulated that:

> It may be pointless trying to understand the brain. Its
> enormous complexity may defeat us. The only means we
> have for understanding it is our own brain and perhaps it
> would take a brain yet more complex to attain such com-
> prehension (1972, p. 8).

In any case, physiological psychology, by attempting to come to grips with mind-body relationships, remains both a dynamic contemporary social science and a historical study of man's efforts to understand and realize himself.

GROWTH AS A SCIENCE

Physiological psychology as a science grew from the attempt to find experimental procedures which would place the philosophical problems just discussed on an objective basis. It is one of the most recent experimental sciences to separate itself from philosophy and metaphysics. For years, after the heyday of the scientific renaissance that began with Galileo, scientists felt that behavior was beyond the measurable and, hence, beyond the experimental methods of "hard" science. The reasons most often cited for excluding behavior from experimental investigation were (and in some cases still are):
1. behavior has no "physical" dimensions comparable to mass,

length, time, in physics; 2. behavior is not obedient to natural law as is the physical universe, but is the individual product of a unique "free will"; 3. behavior is guided and controlled by a supreme Deity whose ways cannot be fully known to man.

These views as to the arcane nature of behavior delayed the application of scientific analysis to it until the latter half of the nineteenth century, 200 years after the physical and biological sciences had been well established. Even as late as the 1890s, Sigmund Freud, one of the founders of modern psychology, despaired of psychology ever becoming an exact science, one based on conclusions reached solely from so-called objective or publicly demonstrable experiments.

Early attempts to use the scientific method

Despite this pessimism, psychology and scientific method did eventually come together. In fact, the early proponents of the science of mind became preoccupied with efforts to emulate the methods of physics as closely as possible because physics was alleged to be "the most objective science."[1] Thus, the work of the German physician Gustav Fechner in 1860, which marks the rough beginning of scientific psychology (Chapter 5), was called *psychophysics* to demonstrate semantically, if not in reality, the "shotgun marriage" of the two disciplines.

Fechner introduced the law of stimulus and response as a way of describing the quantitative relation between the physical world (the stimulus) and an organism's reaction to it (the response). But his work was limited only to aspects of sensation and was not rigorous. The work was continued in the 1870s by Wilhelm Wundt, a German psychologist, who established the world's first experimental psychology laboratory in Leipzig and is credited with initiating the modern development of scientific psychology. Wundt, a *structuralist,* believed that the means to understanding behavior was to break down complex behaviors into smaller components, just as the chemists, enamored with the then new atomic theory, were doing

1. Though not all physicists hold this view (Popper, 1963). For a discussion of the problem of objectivity see Chapter 10.

with chemical compounds. Wundt's unit, however, was the sensation rather than the atom. He experimentally studied the relationship between physical stimuli, such as light and sound, and measurable responses, such as reaction time, with the kind of rigor found in physics. Thus, he laid the foundation for the subsequent biophysical contributions to the knowledge of sensation (especially vision) and learning.

It is interesting to note that in his experiments Wundt was concerned with the nervous system and its relationship to the particular behavior he was studying. But, in keeping with the prevailing bias toward physical objectivity, he avoided implying any kind of relationship between the nervous system and the operation of the mind. At the same time, he was apparently hopeful of breaking mind down into "atoms" of sensory experience. Wundt's contemporary, Alexander Bain, was not so reticent. He believed that mind was simply a breadboard of electrical circuitry. His most famous quote succinctly states: "No nerve currents, no mind" (1885). On the basis of such observations, Bain is generally considered the founder of physiological psychology.

New scientific theories and techniques

Since the time of Bain, physiological psychology has grown in capacity for experiment and exact measurement as it has enveloped the newest advances and techniques emerging from a variety of experimental disciplines, ranging from biology to zoology and from biochemistry to neurophysiology. The science of animal testing, developed in the United States by Edward Thorndike (Chapter 11), led in time to complex testing devices, such as T-mazes, shuttle boxes, and Skinner boxes, which allowed for even finer and more easily replicable experimentation. These devices are now the standard armament of the physiological psychology laboratory.

The development of methods for electrically stimulating the brain, beginning with the early work of Eduard Hitzig (Chapter 7), if not sooner, offered a special kind of experimental innovation to physiological psychology. The techniques were brought to refinement by the Swiss physiologist Walter Hess (Chapters 9 and 10) who developed methods of implanting fine electrodes in intact animals and laid the basis for a new method of measuring detailed behavior as a function of electrical changes in the brain and nervous system. These changes could then be correlated with the behavior resulting from the only previously available method of establishing brain-behavior relationships—*ablation,* or removal of parts of the brain. Hess, who shared a Nobel Prize for his work in 1946, contributed greatly to the mapping of the brain. The current advances in *electrophysiology,* as this discipline is called, even enlists the use of computers to record the myriad changes in the nervous system as a result of a variety of electrical stimulations in free-moving intact animals.

Physiological psychology has also embraced the techniques of the model building sciences, using the organism as a kind of "black box." Input or stimulus goes in, output or response comes out. The conditions of this action-reaction model are changed with a host of variables in order to predict behavior. To create models, physiological psychology today depends on contributions from molecular biology, chemical theories of synaptic transmission, genetic considerations, and chemical bond and valence theory. Electrolyte flux across a membrane is now as basic to the field of psychology as rat maze running. Many of these concepts will find their way into subsequent discussions of the neuron and the nervous system.

Brief mention must also be made of two lines of thought which influenced the development of physiological psychology. For one thing, the structural work of Wundt was quickly opposed by William James and other theorists, who proclaimed that it was impossible to learn about behavior through a study of structure alone. James' position, called *functionalism,* maintained that psychology should deal with the "why" of behavior rather than just the "what." He believed that psychology should be concerned with the relation between the organism and the environment rather than only the relation between body and mind. This paved the way for John B. Watson's *behaviorism.* Watson contended that mind was not observable and thus what could be studied was only the behavior itself (Chapter 10).[2]

2. One might note that in physics the atom is also unobservable, but no physicist seriously doubts its existence.

A second line of thought, a highly influential variation of behaviorism, brought a new dominant element into the field of measurement for physiological psychologists. This was the body of physiological and psychological work based on the conditioned reflex, which was introduced by Ivan Pavlov. Pavlov was basically a physiologist and so considered himself, although he has been adopted by American psychologists. Pavlov introduced the rigorous measurement of the conditioned reflex, which has cast its spell over many branches of psychological experiment, particularly learning (Chapter 12). However, the Russians consider reflex studies to be physiological experiments. Only outside of Russia are they regarded as learning studies and, therefore, a part of psychology. In Russian literature, conditioned reflex experiments are called studies of higher nervous activity and are interpreted in terms of cortical functioning rather than in terms of learning variables. Cognitions are simply *reflexes of the brain.* Regardless of how they are viewed, conditioned reflex experiments substantially increased the reliance of psychology on measurements of behavior and thus contributed to the scientific value of the field.

Many of the foregoing developments, which swelled the rivers of thought flowing into physiological psychology, have left a unified pool of scientific observation, testing, and theorizing, which is the inheritance of the physiological psychology student today. Whether the fundamental questions of the relation between body and mind are answered satisfactorily by physiological psychologists is up to the student to judge on the evidence presented.

SUGGESTED READINGS

Boring, E. G. *A History of Experimental Psychology.* New York: Appleton-Century-Crofts, 1957. A classic that is still the best simply because it remains the most readable of the history books.

Calder, N. *The Mind of Man.* New York: Viking, 1971. A fascinating "first-person" layman's description of contemporary physiological psychology.

Kantor, J. R. *Problems of Physiological Psychology.* Bloomington, Ind.: Principia, 1947. A difficult book to read but worth the effort because it is the only book which aptly describes the philosophical position of physiological psychology.

Oatley, K. *Brain Mechanisms and the Mind*. New York: Dutton, 1972. An elementary description of physiological psychology written in the provocative style of British science writers.

2 The phylogenetic emergence of behavior

Man is related by evolution to all of life and conceivably, in view of the commonality of chemical elements between them, to the world of nonlife as well. Human behavior, the product of man's inheritance interacting with environment, is as much the result of evolutionary pressures as of responses to short term challenges of the environment. The two are so well interconnected that they are often difficult to separate.

At what point in the long ascent of man did behavior begin? At what point did the nervous system, the most refined stimulus-response system yet devised, come into being and why? These questions are of considerable interest to the physiological psychologist because the answers enable him to view in perspective the nature of the physical structure which man has inherited and possibly to provide a new kind of insight into the nature of his mind.

To examine the role of evolution in the origin of behavior, it is necessary to recognize, as Manning points out, that "behavior represents the most highly integrated response to its environment which an organism can make" (1971). Nowhere else is the role of behavior shown more clearly than in the difference between plants and animals, the *autotrophic* organism versus the *heterotrophic* organism (Altman, 1966).[1] The

1. *Autotrophs* are organisms that can utilize inorganic compounds for their energy; *heterotrophs* need organic sources such as glucose. The terms, while most commonly used in reference to microorganisms, correctly apply to all life. All energy on earth originates as solar energy (sunlight). Autotrophs are the only organisms that can convert solar energy, by the process of *photosynthesis,* into forms other life can utilize.

activity of plants (autotrophs) is severely limited by their im-
mobility. The flower bends its stalk to follow the sun, or
changes occur within its makeup to accommodate a change of
external temperature. The Venus fly trap can even shut its
vegetable "jaws" when a palatable fly comes close. But that is
about all a plant can do.[2] Animals (heterotrophs), on the other
hand, can get up from a prone position, move about, seek
out new energy sources, and dash off to escape enemies. In
essence, heterotrophs exhibit mobility—behavior. To successfully recognize food, obtain it, and ingest it, or to recognize
an enemy and decide between "fight or flight" requires the
development of a system that provides sensitivity, motility,
and a means of integrating the two—a nervous system.

Some animals can, of course, do more than merely respond to needs by hunting or changing habitat. They can, to
some extent, manipulate their environment to suit their own
needs, and in that sense they share in the mechanism of natural
selection. The honeybee, for example, actively maintains the
temperature of the brood at 34–35° C and the worker bees have
elaborate behavior patterns which serve to correct any deviation (von Frisch, 1950). The beaver is a classic example of how
to build for the future. So, hopefully, is man. The long trail
to such complex behaviors can be traced back to primitive
forms of life.

SINGLE-CELLED ORGANISMS

The evolution of heterotrophic behavior patterns undoubtedly began at an extremely early time and with a single-
celled organism. Directive behavior is actually seen in such
one-celled animals as the amoeba, whose cytoplasm is composed of two interchangeable fluids: a peripheral, relatively
viscous area called plasmagel, and a central, more liquid portion called plasmasol. Manipulation of the interchange of these
fluids gives the amoeba its ability to move in a selected direction. For instance, when the amoeba moves, the cytoplasm

2. However, it has been recently postulated through a best selling book, *The Secret
Life of Plants* (Tompkins and Bird, 1973), that plants do have emotions (feelings)
and do communicate with each other and with humans.

flows either toward the peripheral or toward the central area, depending on the direction of the animal's movement. The viscosity of the cytoplasm changes to accommodate the selection of direction. The direction is not always aimless; the amoeba has receptor capacities which enable it to move in the direction of sources of stimulation, particularly food. That such movements are coordinated with the stimulation also indicates an integrative capacity. Perhaps, if it is not too far fetched to speculate, this is an example of the early beginnings of the simplest process that identifies one of the capacities of mind. A single-celled animal is simultaneously a receptor, conductor, effector, and integrator.

Besides specific localized changes in the viscosity of its cytoplasmic protein, the amoeba could conceivably be energized into movement in another way. The gelled protein could change to a fibrous or contractile protein which would cause motion during contraction. The system would be even more efficient if the contracting elements were joined to one another and oriented parallel to the axis of contraction. As just explained, the unstable cytoplasmic elements of the amoeba do not so change and are not so arranged; but other unicellular organisms, such as euglena and paramecium, do have what Maier and Schneirla (1964) call *permanent physiological gradients,* or fixed areas of cytoplasm with a specialized function (i.e., definitive body structures). Typical contractile structures are the flagella and cilia, which are respectively whiplike and hairlike appendages of the surface that provide a means to direct motion and allow retrieval of food and other floating objects. The protein molecules of these structures are arranged for maximal contractile efficiency in exactly the same pattern as the contractile elements of muscle fiber (see Chapter 6). This fact has given rise to the idea that these structures, which phylogenetically represent one of the first instances of structural specificity, may be the forerunner of the neuromuscular system in higher forms of life.

Another primitive protostructure is the eyespot, an area composed of granules that are selectively sensitive to photic stimulation and are probably the primitive ancestor of the eye. Such an area is found in the euglena, which, along with the mobile properties of the paramecium, also has the ability to move in relation to light. This property is useful to the tiny creature (which is classified as both plant and animal) to maximize its photosynthetic ability to manufacture foodstuff out of the interaction of sunlight and various elements.

MULTICELLED ORGANISMS

The next significant advance in structural correlates of adaptive behavior comes with multicellular organisms, which begin to show the rudiments of differentiation of cells that perform specialized functions. The most primitive of this group of organisms are the sponges, which have separate cells that carry out one or another of such functions as secretion, reproduction, and movement. Sponge cells maintain a high degree of autonomy and independence in the sense that there is no communication among individual cells. Among the various types of specialized cells in sponges, there are none designed to integrate the various functions.

Cells that function to pass a wave of excitation from one point to another, a process called *conduction,* first appear in coelenterates, the most familiar example being the jellyfish. Coelenterates need this intercellular excitation to withstand or attack objects that brush by in the water. These integrating cells in the jellyfish, called *protoneurons,* form a diffuse network so that, when any one cell is stimulated, the excitation spreads through the whole system until the entire system is activated by a kind of cell-to-cell domino effect. The network is not a maze with a preferred path, but a kind of crazy quilt array with many paths.

CELL SPECIALIZATION AND DIFFERENTIATION
Starfish

In slightly more advanced forms of life, such as the echinoderms (starfish), the beginnings of an organization of cells to serve as conductors of the stimulus, now called *neurons* (Chapter 3), are seen. The starfish neurons are grouped together, with their fiber processes projecting in a single direction. These groups are known as *plexuses*. The arrangement allows discrete rather than diffuse functioning; one section can be activated without the whole system responding. The organizing process is peripheral and local rather than general and, in its most primitive form, occurs only near the structure innervated. As a result, individual structures remain autonomous relative to the whole organism, but their cells are in communication with each other and the environment. Additional specialization provides a way for the action of individual parts to be integrated with the action of the rest of the organism to create greater adaptability to changes in environment. This begins to appear in clusters of nerve cells called *ganglia*.

Insects and mollusks

In another line of evolution, the clustering of cells to control specific types of activity begins to appear strongly in the arthropods (insects, crustaceans, and related organisms). If one cuts off the head of a wasp, for instance, it will continue to eat even though it has lost its abdomen. The praying mantis continues to copulate with the female while she devours him from the head down (Manning, 1971). Clearly, the ganglion controlling sexual reproduction operates independently of the rest of the body.

Despite the limitations of nervous control, insects have a remarkable repertoire of activity based on specialization. Ants, carrying eggs or grains of sand, can cross the lines of other ants without bumping, demonstrating some sort of signalling capacity (Sudd, 1967). Bees can retain internal maps which allow them to land on a particular strip on a flower which provides pollen. A bee can "tell"[3] the rest of the members of the hive the direction of sources of pollen relative to the sun (von Frisch, 1950).

Nonetheless, the limitations of evolution are shown in the inability of the insect to adapt to many environmental dangers. Moths will fly into a flame in decreasing orbits, without ever becoming aware that the flame marks them for death. A bee trapped in a room will batter itself to death on a window

3. Communication is actually accomplished with a series of body movements called a "dance."

pane while heading toward the light, although there is a way available to escape.

EARLY BRAIN

The first evolutionary step toward a true nervous system occurs in the flatworm, a tiny, black, hermaphroditic worm that has played an important role in psychology (Chapter 12). The flatworm, or planarian, has specific connections among neurons. For example, if a cut is made in one area, separating the neurons from the reacting muscle, that muscle will be paralyzed, but the rest of the organism will not be affected as would have been the case in animals with nerve nets.

Moreover, the flatworm exhibits the clustering of neuron cell bodies at the head end, the first instance of a brain. In conjunction, there are also neuron fiber processes, or *nerves,* which are arranged to carry signals from sensory organs to the brain, where they are integrated with muscle activity. Thus, the planaria show the beginnings of the synaptic type of nervous system that characterizes higher forms of life.

Behaviorally, planaria demonstrate habituation, a phenomenon in which the organism responds to a repeated stimulus by eventually disregarding it. If a planarian is touched with a glass rod, it will curl into a ball in response to apparent danger. After a while, if this action is repeated consistently, the planarian will no longer curl up. It will become habituated. Because of the planarian's capacity to do this, it has been studied extensively to determine whether its nervous system is the first to have developed to the point where the organism can learn—that is, whether it can modify its response to more efficiently accommodate an environmental circumstance. The experiments dealing with this phenomenon are discussed in Chapter 12 of this book.

MAMMALIAN BRAIN

The evolution of the large mammalian brain extended the centralization of the nervous system into the head region. This resulted in the development of a neural tube, the precursor of the spinal cord, and the development of a skeleton to protect it. The beginnings of these evolutionary changes can be seen in fish and amphibians and are carried through all vertebrate species into the mammals up to, and including, man.

As evolution continued beyond that, the brain became the primary focus of change. It increased in size, it became more and more dominant over the rest of the nervous system, and it became hierarchically organized by the addition of "higher" and "higher" parts (Jerison, 1973; Sarnat and Netsy, 1974).

Behaviorally, the trend in the evolution of mammalian heterotrophism has been in the direction of greater ability to responsively adapt to environmental change. Higher organisms have greater behavioral flexibility—the capacity to adjust behavior to circumstances. Many psychologists like to describe the progression from lesser to greater flexibility by dichotomizing behavior as innate or learned; the former being the more stereotyped reflexive behaviors characteristic of lower organisms, the latter being the more versatile behaviors characteristic of higher organisms. However, as with most natural phenomena, the real circumstance is undoubtedly much more complex than can be represented by a simple dichotomy, and the distinction has not had much conceptual utility (Bitterman, 1965; Hodos and Campbell, 1969; Lockard, 1971). The phylogenetic progression of behavior is not a case of learned behavior replacing innate behavior. Rather, higher organisms have greater control over the expression of their behavioral endowment in the sense of being able to utilize it more efficiently to adapt to their environment. Numerous examples, ranging from control of sucking responses to aggression, will be described throughout the rest of this book. Also, a detailed description of the mammalian nervous system and its development will be presented in the chapters which follow.

In summary, evolution has resulted in elaboration of a complex subsystem, a nervous system, specialized to facilitate the integration of the total living system into its environment. In that sense, the nervous system is the physical confirmation of heterotrophic behavior. As a consequence, any study of physiological psychology can only be meaningfully approached by beginning with a consideration of the neuron and the nervous system. From there, the task progresses to correlating those structural entities with overt and subjective organismic functions—to linking body and mind.

SUGGESTED READINGS

Altman, J. *Organic Foundations of Animal Behavior*. New York: Holt, Rinehart and Winston, 1964. The only definitive conceptualization of physiological psychology from the viewpoint of heterotrophy.

Jerison, H. J. *Evolution of the Brain and Intelligence*. New York: Academic Press, 1973. A detailed description of neural evolution as it relates to behavioral capacity; a relatively difficult book.

Maier, N. R. F., and Schneirla, T. C. *Principles of Animal Psychology*. New York: Dover, 1964. An updated re-issue of one of the first textbooks of comparative psychology, essential to a historical perspective on the development of conceptions of behavioral evolution.

Sarnat, H. B., and Netsy, M. G. *Evolution of the Nervous System*. New York: Oxford University Press, 1974. Somewhat theoretically biased and difficult in parts, but nonetheless compelling and up-to-date; very worthwhile.

II

Physiological, anatomical, and chemical aspects of nervous system functioning

Part II of this book describes the body components and bodily processes that comprise the physiological background of this branch of psychology. In Chapter 3, the neuron, the basic unit of the nervous system and the basis of the ability to adapt to the environment, is discussed. Chapter 4 examines the nervous system itself. How the sensory processes bring informational input from the environment to the nervous system is considered in Chapter 5. Chapters 6 and 7 deal with the nature of muscles and reflexes which represent, in behavioral terms, the responses of the body to stimuli.

It must be noted that, as marvelous as the human system is in its ability to adapt to the complexities of an ever changing environment, it cannot be assumed that the evolutionary process is complete. Man, as he is known today, may not be the "final product." The next two-and-a-half billion years of evolution may produce a being as far removed from modern man as man now is from the amoeba. Thus, this part of the book must be read with the sense of beginning a story rather than ending one.

3 Neurons

STRUCTURE AND FUNCTION

Neurons are cells structurally organized to function as conductors of chemical and electrical information. They can collect information, hold it, and then transmit it over the long distances of the body. They are, in effect, the communication units of the organism.

The structural arrangement of the neuron, shown in Figure 3-1A,B, is characterized by a number of projections, or processes, emanating from the cell body, which is sometimes called the *soma*. A group of neurons would typically appear as represented in Figure 3-1C. All of the projections are called *dendrites* except one, which is known as an *axon*. The distinction between dendrite and axon is not very clear in terms of function and structure. However, the axon is typically considered to be the projection that conducts information away from the cell body (*efferent*), whereas dendrites usually conduct information toward the cell body (*afferent*). As Katz (1966) points out, however, the term axon is frequently applied to all elongated neuronal processes, independent of the direction of conduction. Structurally, dendrites are not only shorter than axons but they are also more highly branched and are often referred to as dendritic trees. But, once again, there are enough exceptions in the nervous system to make that an inaccurate generalization.

23

Every neuron seems to exist as an independent unit having no apparent direct membranous connection with any other neuron. Communication between adjacent neurons occurs across contiguous gaps called *synapses* (Sherrington, 1947). The most-discussed synapse is the one between the end of an axon and a dendrite. It is known as the *axo-dendritic* synapse. *Axo-somatic* synapses, those between the surface of the cell body and the axon, are just as common. Not uncommon, but less frequent, are axon-to-axon or *axo-axonal* synapses (Stevens, 1966). Each of the 12 billion neurons in the human brain may have a thousand or more synapses and some cells in the cerebral cortex may have as many as 200,000, creating an astronomical number of interconnections—greater than the number of atomic particles in the universe.

The connections between neuron processes and other tissues are equally important to communication. These connections, which are also synaptic, are named according to the end organ involved (e.g., neuromuscular synapse). Any part of the neuron that is stimulated will conduct that stimulation through the whole neuron (*antidromic* conduction), but the excitation will only pass to another neuron from the termination of the axon. The synapse is a one-way conductor; its transmission is called *orthodromic* (Eccles, 1953). As a result, conduction through the nervous system takes place in only one direction, from the axon endings of one neuron to the membrane of another. This is known as the *law of forward conduction* (Sherrington, 1947).

INTERNEURONAL COMMUNICATION

Actually, the exact nature of interneuronal communication was a major controversy in the last half of the nineteenth century and still arouses occasional argument. One point of view, called the *reticular theory,* held that all nerve cells were connected to each other to form a network, or reticulum. The opposing notion, called the *neuron theory,* suggested that each nerve cell was a discrete unit with the axons and dendrites having free endings and that a gap, the synapse, existed between one neuron and the next.

The reticular theory was proposed by Joseph von Gerlach with the research support of the Italian physiologist Camillo Golgi, while the neuron theory was proposed by Heinrich

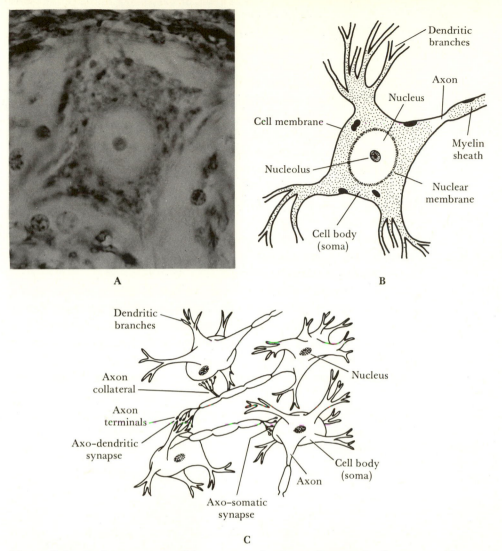

Figure 3-1. Basic structures of the neuron: **A,** photomicrograph of a neuron; **B,** cross section of a single neuron; **C,** schematic representation showing several neurons and their fiber processes. (Photograph courtesy of Dr. Ronald G. Clark, Department of Biological Structure, University of Miami School of Medicine.)

Waldeyer-Hartz with the research support of the Spanish physiologist Santiago Ramón y Cajal (Brazier, 1959). Cajal finally demonstrated the existence of the synaptic gap by using preparations of neural tissue made for microscopic examination with a silver staining technique developed by Golgi (see Figure 3-2 for portraits of Golgi and Cajal). Golgi never forgave Cajal for upstaging him with his own technique. Even when they shared the 1906 Nobel Prize, Golgi's acceptance speech amounted to a denunciation of the neuron theory (Eckstein, 1970). It is also interesting to recall that Sigmund Freud, in the early physiological phase of his career, carried out experiments on crab neurons that came close to providing definitive evidence for the neuron theory. Unfortunately, Freud did not fully understand the implications of his finding and dropped the work.

The synapse as a void between neuronal processes has stood as dogma in neurophysiology to this day. Even though some electron micrographs of neuroanatomical structures show evidence of the possible existence of a membrane between certain processes, the revival of such doubts (De Robertis, 1964) has not overthrown over-all faith in the doctrine of the neuron theory. Figure 3-3 is a typical electron micrograph of an axo-dendritic synapse showing different parts of the two processes and the structure of the synapse.

Verification of the neuron theory by Cajal led to another con-

Figure 3-2.   **A,** Italian physiologist Camillo Golgi (1844–1926) and **B,** Spanish physiologist Santiago Ramón y Cajal (1852–1934), opponents in the debate over the nature of neuron connections and co-recipients of the 1906 Nobel prize. (The New York Academy of Medicine Library.)

A   B

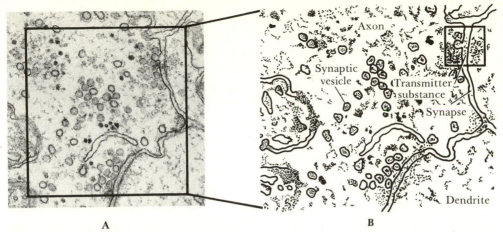

Figure 3-3. **A,** Electron microphotograph of a synapse (118,000X), showing basic features; **B,** schematic of synapse. (Photograph courtesy of Dr. Douglas E. Kelly, Anatomy Department, University of Southern California School of Medicine.)

troversy over the mechanism by which excitation is transmitted across the gap. Again, there were two opposing points of view. On one side, as will be discussed in detail later, the argument was that excitation generated in a neuron has electrical properties which, like current in a wire, simply jumped the gap. This is the theory of *electrical transmission* at the synapse.

The alternative notion, known as the *neurohumoral transmission* theory, is presently considered the best representation of synaptic events. It suggests that the transmission is chemical rather than electrical and that synaptic transmission occurs by liberation of a specific chemical substance from the axon terminal. The chemicals, called *neurohormones,* are thought to be stored in bubbles known as *synaptic vesicles* which are found near the ends of axons (Figure 3-3).

Definitive experimental demonstration of neurohumoral transmission was provided by Otto Loewi, a German physiologist, who received a Nobel Prize for his effort. The story has it (Eckstein, 1970) that the night before Easter, 1921, Loewi had a dream about the experiment. He awoke and made notes, but he could not decipher them the next morning. That night the dream came back. This time, however, he leaped from his bed, dashed to the laboratory, and carried out his famous experiment.

What Loewi did was to excise the hearts of two frogs and keep them viable by perfusion with a balanced salt solution, which passed from one heart to the other by means of a tube (see Figure 3-4). The contractions of the hearts were recorded. In one heart, which can be considered the donor, the primary controlling nerve, or vagus, was still intact. When it was stimulated by a slight electrical shock, the heart slowed immediately. Shortly afterwards the second, or recipient, heart slowed. Since the only connection between the two hearts was the perfusing solution, something must have been liberated from the first organ which slowed the rate of the second heart. Also, no effect occurred if the donor heart muscle, rather than the vagus nerve, was stimulated. Therefore, the substance had to come from the nerve. Loewi called the unknown substance *vagusstoff* (vagus substance).

At first there was difficulty in replicating Loewi's experiment because stimulation of the vagus sometimes resulted in increased, rather than decreased, heart rate. This was eventually found to be artifactual, a function of the season of the year. Once this influence was eliminated, the discovery was confirmed and extended to warm-blooded animals as well as to other nerve-organ combinations (Koelle, 1965). It was later established that vagusstoff is actually a chemical known as acetylcholine (Loewi and Navratil, 1926, see page 42).

Neurohumoral transmission has profound significance for physiological psychology because it is apparently the primary mechanism by which neural activity is regulated. As will soon become clear, the extent to which behavior is related to neural activity will involve, in large measure, chemical actions at the synapse. In that sense, the synapse has been viewed as the locus of the mind (see Chapter 15).

AXONAL TRANSMISSION

Since the chemical activity at the synapse is normally initiated by the electrical activity in the axon, it is first necessary to discuss the nature of this activity in more detail.

Discovery of animal electricity

The fact that living tissue is responsive to electricity was established late in the eighteenth century by Professor Luigi Galvani

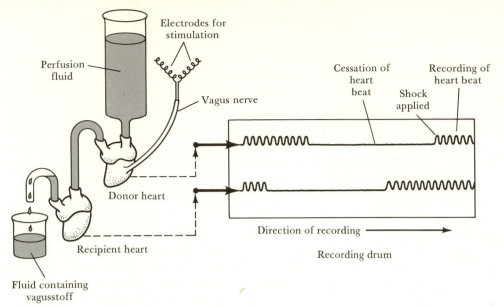

Figure 3-4. Diagram of Loewi's experiment demonstrating that electrical stimulation of the vagus nerve released "vagustoff," or acetylcholine.

and his wife Lucia. The Italian experimenters made their discovery by means of a series of experiments performed, among other reasons, for the entertainment of their house guests. In one such experiment, they placed a dissected frog on a table with a wire leading from its head to a metal rod on a balcony, and a wire leading from its foot to water in a well. The arrangement was established just before a thunder storm. When lightning flashed, the frog's muscles twitched, much to the amazed delight of Galvani's guests. It is easy to realize today that Galvani's metal rod on the balcony was simply a lightning rod grounded in the well water by way of the frog. At that time, however, the relationship between the lightning and the frog's muscles was regarded as somewhat of a mystery.

In a later, more profound experiment, Galvani excised a frog's leg muscle, leaving the nerve attached to it. He placed the nerve against the cut surface of another muscle. The second muscle twitched. Galvani concluded that something like the electricity from lightning was present in nerve tissue. He called it "animal electricity" and thus introduced what was to be one of the most important contributions in the history of physiology—the understanding of how a nerve functions.

Galvani also set into motion another classical debate in science. His opponent was physicist Alessandro Volta, who argued that the electrical current that caused the frog's legs to twitch arose not from animal electricity but from the contact of different metals. Galvani never conceded. He died in the belief that he had discovered a new form of electricity. But in 1800, a year after Galvani's death, Volta invented the battery, a device for generating electricity based on different metals immersed in an acid solution. This helped confirm Volta's contention that the source of electricity in some of Galvani's experiments was the contamination of dissimilar metals rather than the nervous system of the animal.

But that did not close the matter. Volta's discovery of the battery led to the development of the galvanometer,[1] a device for measuring current, named after Galvani. In 1848 Emil du Bois-Reymond, a German physiologist, used the galvanometer principle to show that it is indeed electric energy that flows through nerves, thus vindicating Galvani. In this curious, roundabout way of science, two battery scientists, a half century apart, closed an ancient argument and laid the basis for a new science, electrophysiology.

The nature of electrical flow through nerve fiber

Once it was established that it is electrical energy that flows through nerves, questions arose as to the nature of the electrical flow. Is the nerve fiber a battery (Figure 3-5)? Do currents flow through the body as they do through an electrical system? These questions, important in terms of understanding the later development of electrophysiology, were not answered until appropriate instrumentation was developed to measure the small amounts of electricity involved. However, the first explanations derived from analogies with the chemical battery.

1. The galvanometer is simply an electromagnetic device that measures electric current on the basis of movement of a conductor in a magnetic field. The principle is applied in an ammeter, which measures current in amperes, and in a voltmeter, which indicates how much electrical potential exists between two electrodes. For example, if a voltmeter is placed across the core and case of a flashlight battery, it will give a reading of 1.5 volts (Figure 3-5).

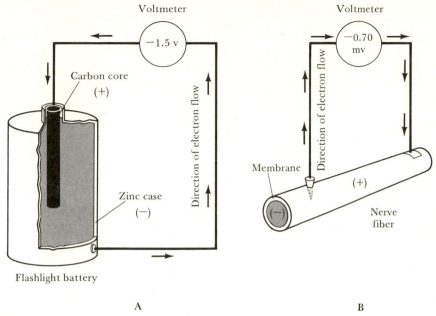

Figure 3-5. Is the Nerve Fiber a battery? **A,** Schematic of flashlight battery compared to **B,** nerve fiber with voltmeter attached to measure the voltage difference between the interior and exterior of the fiber.

The chemical battery and the nerve fiber A battery involves the arrangement of two metallic substances in a conducting medium in such a manner that *electrons* (or negatively charged particles) released from one of them, known as the negative electrode, or *cathode,* flow to the other electrode, known as the positive electrode, or *anode.*

The flow is called *current;* and it is important to distinguish this flow from the flow of individual electrons as such. The difference can be clarified by recalling that any conductor of electricity, such as a wire, contains loosely bonded electrons; the more of them it has, the better a conductor it is. Consider now what happens to the electrons in an electric wire. At first the electrons move about at random. When the wire is attached to a battery, however, the electrons move in a single direction. The electron in one end of the wire displaces a nearby electron, which in turn displaces another electron, and so on down the length of the wire, so that the last electron leaves the other end.

The energy in the current travels much faster than any individual electron. Electrons move at a rate of about 1 foot/hour, current at a rate of 186,000 miles/second. It is like a domino effect. Each domino moves slightly, but the wave of motion from the first domino to the last is rapid. The first electron that moves may not reach the end of the wire for a long time.

The tendency for current to flow between two points is the result of a difference in the number of electrons between them and is called *potential*; it is usually measured in volts (named after Volta). When two points have an unequal number of electrons, they are said to be *polarized* with respect to each other. Current will flow from the point with more electrons to the one with less, until the two sides end up in a state of *depolarization*, or equilibrium.

Following their substantiation of animal electricity, du Bois-Reymond and his contemporaries explained nerve conduction as analogous to current swiftly passing through an electric wire, a natural analogy to the then recently invented high-speed telegraph. They measured the voltage across a nerve fiber and found it came to −70 millivolts(mv). However, the analogy to a wire soon broke down when it was found that electrical current in nerves does not travel as fast as in wires. That is, it travels at a speed considerably less than 186,000 miles/second.

Membrane theory of nerve conduction In 1902 one of du Bois-Reymond's students, Julius Bernstein, opened up another possible explanation for the electrical activity of the nerve cell, without giving up the idea of the chemical battery. Bernstein formulated the *membrane theory of nervous conduction,* which stated that the membrane of the resting neuron or any other cell is polarized; that is, there is a potential or voltage across it. Specifically, the inside of the cell has more negative ions[2] than the outside medium and, therefore, is electrically negative relative to the outside medium. As has already been pointed out, there is a −70 mv potential between the inside and outside of a nerve; so that Bernstein viewed the neuron as a 70-mv battery not yet connected up, but ready to move current should the cell membrane allow it. This electrical state of a nonconducting nerve is now referred to as the *membrane,* or *resting, potential.*

2. *Ions* are electrically charged particles.

The resting potential seems to be maintained chemically by the difference in ionic concentrations between substances on the inside of the nerve and those in the surrounding fluid medium. Inside, there is a high concentration of positive potassium ions (K^+); outside, a high concentration of positive sodium ions (Na^+). The membrane of the resting neuron resists the inward passage of Na^+ ions, while K^+ ions pass out at a high rate, leaving the inside electrically negative relative to the outside. Eventually, an equilibrium is reached at which the K^+ ion diffusion is balanced by the difference in charge. This limit occurs when the inside of the nerve reaches a potential of -70 mv in relation to its surrounding medium.

The membrane theory further postulated that electricity was generated by a disturbance of the cell wall from some source of energy. This generation of current continued until another equilibrium occurred which resulted in depolarization of the membrane and in the resting potential falling to zero. The entire unit has been described as a potassium battery (Baker, 1966).

Experimental verification of Bernstein's theory did not come about until the 1930s, when two important methodological advances occurred. The first advance is represented by studies of the giant squid axon by Cole and Curtis (1939) in the United States and Hodgkin and Huxley in England (1939). The second advance is represented by Erlanger and Gasser's oscilloscope tracings of nerve conduction (1937).

Studies of the squid axon   The discovery in the mid-thirties that a tubular swimming structure in the squid, an aquatic animal common to Atlantic waters, was actually an axon was a particular boon to neurophysiological research. The axon of the squid was known to be the largest nerve fiber in the animal world, a thousand times larger than the largest human fiber. This axon allows the squid to propel itself backwards by sucking water into a cavity and then squirting it out under pressure through a funnel-like opening in front. Filled with pure cytoplasm known as axoplasm, the fiber provides an excellent laboratory tool for the investigation of nerve action.

In 1939 Cole and Curtis at Woods Hole, Massachusetts, and Hodgkin and Huxley at Plymouth, England, inserted elec-

trodes into the giant axon of the squid, the first time that electrodes had been placed inside an axon, and calculated the
potential between them while the fiber was "resting" in salt
water. The resting potential was found to be −45 mv in the
English experiment and −51 mv in the United States experiment. By adding potassium to the solution, the resting potential
dropped until depolarization set in, and the galvanometer read
zero. These findings suggested that Bernstein's membrane
theory was correct.

Development of the oscilloscope   The second important advance of this period was the development of the *oscilloscope* as a
tool of neurophysiology. The oscilloscope enables an investigator to measure and record changes in the magnitude of an electrical event as a function of time. This, as shall be seen, is particularly important in evaluating the Bernstein theory.

As shown in Figure 3-6, the oscilloscope employs a cathode
ray tube which consists, essentially, of an electron gun and a
luminescent face or screen coated with a substance that glows
when hit with electrons. Two vertical metal plates are aligned
on each side of the electron beam and affixed to a timing oscillator. At zero time, the oscillator circuit charges the left plate
positive relative to the right plate, causing the electron beam to
be attracted or bent to the left. The generator then reverses the
polarity on the plates, causing the electron beam to sweep to the
right. These events show up on the face of the tube as a horizontal line which represents a precise time base. Similarly, two
other plates are arranged above and below the beam. Changes
in their polarity are induced from the electrodes placed to
record a potential between two points, such as the inside and
outside of an axon. With an oscilloscope, it was possible for the
first time to trace precisely the electrical activity of a section (the
point under the tip of an electrode relative to a reference point)
of an axon over a period of time.

The source of electrical activity in nerve fiber

As mentioned earlier, the membrane theory predicted that
excitation would initiate depolarization—that is, the potential
would rise to zero and the membrane would repolarize when

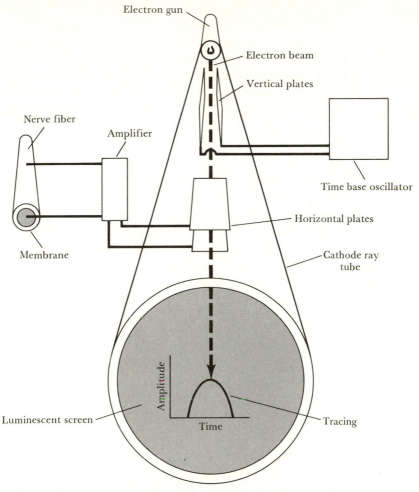

Figure 3-6. The oscilloscope is a major tool for recording changes in nerve potential.

the stimulation ceased. To the surprise of the early investigators, the potential generated by excitation, or the *action potential,* did not become zero, but reversed to become 40–50 mv positive in relation to the voltage of the outside medium. These events would appear on the oscilloscope as in Figure 3-7.

With a total change in potential of as much as 120 mv, it was immediately obvious that the resting potential alone was not sufficient to produce the action potential and send the new impulse down the nerve fiber; there had to be another energy source. The *sodium hypothesis* of Hodgkin and Katz (1949) provided what still seems to be the best explanation of this source. According to these experimenters, the concentration of the Na^+ ions in the neural medium holds the key to the change of potential. When they lowered the sodium content of this medium, the action potential decreased; when the sodium content was raised, the action potential increased. This suggested that the Na^+ ions were entering the resting axon through the membrane.

This was subsequently verified with radioactive tracers and proved to be the first phase of current flow across the membrane. In the second phase, the K^+ ions go out from the membrane to cause outward current flow. The nature of this "sodium pump" is not yet known, and the exact mechanism of its operation is still poorly explained. However, the present speculation is that enzymes facilitate trans-membrane Na^+ ion conduction (Gawronski, 1971; Woodbury, 1965). In any case, it seems clear that the so-called resting potential is actually an active energy-consuming process.

There is also some disagreement as to the exact mechanism involved in initiating the action potential. In some instances, it seems that stimulation temporarily renders the membrane highly permeable to Na^+ ions so that they pour into the axon in sufficient quantities to reverse polarity. In other words, the membrane would be a selective filter. In other instances, it appears that the sodium pump stops for an instant. The kind of mechanism in operation seems to depend on the specific type of neural tissue involved (Burn, 1963).

With this explanation of the localized action of nerve cell excitation, the propagation, or conduction, of an impulse along the length of the axon can now be considered.

Local circuits or electrical conduction in nerves

Bernstein's theory that conduction proceeds in small local circuits of current between resting and active areas of the nerve reconciled puzzling phenomena such as the speed of the nerve impulse. As Figure 3-8 shows, the reversed polarity of an excited axonal section sets up a local electrical circuit by disturbing the polarity of the resting part immediately ahead. In terms of

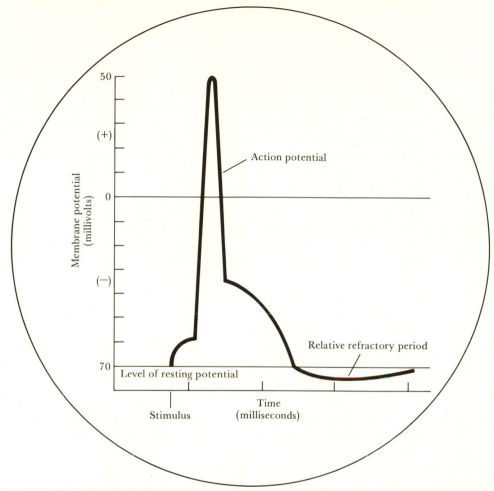

Figure 3-7. The action potential as it might appear on an oscilloscope screen. It can be seen that the entire process of initiating a neural impulse involves several variations of potential with time.

the sodium hypothesis, Na⁺ ions flow from the resting area to the excited membrane and enter at the permeable part. That, in turn, depolarizes the resting area, setting up a disturbance in the next resting axon and repeating the same action at the next adjacent section, and so on along the length of the axon. This movement is slower than that of electrical current moving directly along a wire. The speed of axonal conduction varies between 200 and 300 feet/second, depending on axonal diameter (Hodgkin, 1964). Even at top speed, axonal conduction is relatively slow (about 200 miles/hour), especially when compared with electric current passing along a wire (186,000 miles/second). Interestingly, the famous early German physiologist Johannes Müller was so convinced the two types of conduction were analogous that, in 1844, he maintained it would never be possible to measure the speed of nerve conduction because it was so fast. Six years later, Hermann von Helmholtz, one of Müller's students, successfully measured nerve conduction in a frog's muscle and found it to be surprisingly slow—50–80 feet/second.

As conduction of the impulse proceeds along the axon, the area immediately behind an excited section (the portion that itself was just previously excited) becomes temporarily *refractory*, or insensitive, to stimulation. Immediately after the current passes, there is a period of total inexcitability of that area. This is referred to as the *absolute refractory period*, during which time the area will not respond to any stimulus. The absolute refractory period is followed by a *relative refractory period*, during which time a greater than normal amount of stimulation is necessary to induce an action potential. In other words, the threshold for stimulation is higher than it is in the resting state. Following a slight supranormal period, the resting potential is re-established. All these events occur within a few milliseconds but are sufficient to keep the movement of the excitation unidirectional.

All or none principle

The existence of different refractory periods during the course of an impulse's travel down the nerve fiber does not imply that resting axons respond selectively to different levels of stimulation. The magnitude of the action potential, once initiated, is maximal. The nerve cell fires as hard as it can, and its action potential is independent of the amplitude of the initiating stimulus. Adrian (1914) called it the *all or none principle*, and it is one of the fundamental laws of neuron activity.

It should be evident by now that the conduction of excitation through an axon, the flow of biological current, is *not* similar to the passage of electricity through a wire. Electricity moves

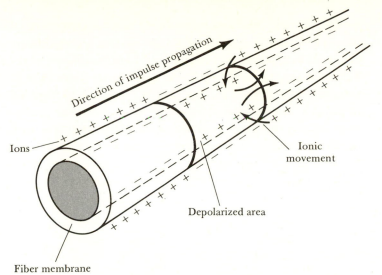

Figure 3-8. Principle of nerve energy conduction. The nerve, unlike a pipe, is not hollow. Nerve impulses move down the fiber in a spiral fashion. + indicates impulses on the outside of the fiber while − indicates impulses inside the fiber.

through a wire by the passing of energy from electron to electron. In a biological current, the ions carry the charge through the tissue. Thus, the action potential can be regarded as a flow of positive ions along a nerve membrane.

The membrane theory applies both to axons like that of the squid which are unmyelinated (not covered by a nonconductive lipid substance known as a *myelin sheath*) and to axonal fibers which are *myelinated*. In the latter case, there are regularly spaced intervals along the myelin sheath where the axonal membrane is exposed to the extracellular environment. These spaces are referred to as the *nodes of Ranvier*. In such fibers, the local current through the membrane simply jumps between adjacent nodes through the extracellular medium (Figure 3-9). The process is called *saltatory conduction*, and it is more efficient and faster than conduction in unmyelinated fibers.

SYNAPTIC TRANSMISSION

When the nerve impulse arrives at the synapse, a new form of transmission of information takes place. The events have been described by Koelle (1965) as occurring in four basic steps.

1. Release of the transmitter. As was pointed out previously, the transmitter substances are stored within the synaptic vesicles. During the resting or nontransmitting periods, the transmitters are continuously, but slowly, released in amounts ordinarily insufficient to cause post-synaptic excitation. It is only with depolarization of the axonal terminal that the contents of the synaptic vesicles are discharged and can affect the dendrite of the next neuron.

2. Combination of the transmitter with the postsynaptic receptors and initiation of the postsynaptic potential. The transmitter diffuses across the gap, or synaptic cleft, and combines with specialized chemical groupings called *receptors,* which are located on the surface of the post-synaptic cell membrane. Receptors are conceived of as molecular "cavities" on the membrane surface, shaped so the transmitter molecule will fit compatibly (Goldstein, Aronow, and Kalman, 1969; De Robertis, 1971; Durrell, Garland, and Friedel, 1969), like a key in a lock (Figure 3-10). As soon as contact is made, a localized, non-propagated potential called the *postsynaptic generator potential* develops. This potential may be one of two types. The first type

Figure 3-9. Propagation of neural energy through a myelinated axon. Note the segmented area—known as the node of Ranvier—where depolarization occurs.

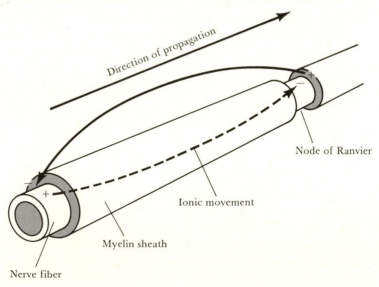

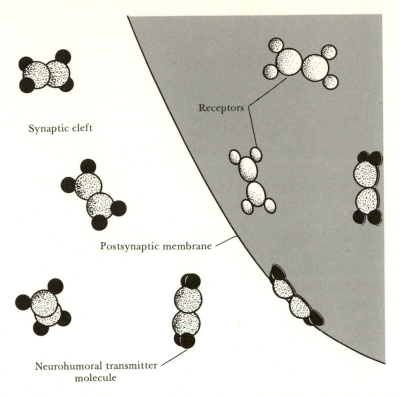

Synaptic cleft

Receptors

Postsynaptic membrane

Neurohumoral transmitter
molecule

Figure 3-10. Neurohumoral transmission across a synapse. Receptors are conceived to be molecular "cavities" on the surface of the postsynaptic membrane. Transmitter molecules are congruent with receptors on a lock and key principle. The combination results in the postsynaptic potential.

is the usual depolarization due to Na$^+$ ion disequilibrium, called an *excitatory postsynaptic potential* (EPSP). The second type involves hyperpolarization, an increase in membrane polarity and stability. Since this latter type raises the threshold for any immediately subsequent depolarization, it is called an *inhibitory postsynaptic potential* (IPSP).

3. Initiation of postsynaptic activity. If an EPSP exceeds the threshold value for the neuron, the usual type of action potential is initiated and conducted to the next synapse. An IPSP, as just implied, tends to oppose or block excitatory potentials initiated by adjacent neurons. As has already been seen, many axonal terminals converge on a single neuron. Whether a postsynaptic action potential will result depends on the algebraic summation of all the inputs active at a given time. This summation can be spatial, in that the local potentials are initiated synchronously in the same region; or they can be temporal, whereby local potentials arrive repetitively before the preceding ones decay.

From these facts, two important points emerge. First, synaptic transmission is orthodromic, i.e., in one direction only. Second, synaptic transmission is not all or none, but graded. It is because of these properties that the synaptic region serves a modulator (choice point) function by making further transmission conditional upon the relation between facilitatory and inhibitory influences. And that is why synaptic transmission has such profound significance to conceptualizations of neurobehavioral interaction.

4. Destruction or dissipation of the transmitter. Once the transmitter substance has completed its influence on the postsynaptic membrane, it is destroyed by enzymes so that the membrane can recover.

It should be remembered that this entire four-part sequence of events occurs within a few milliseconds. The sequence is diagrammatically summarized in Figure 3-11.

NEUROHUMORAL TRANSMITTERS
Acetylcholine

The nature and number of probable transmitter substances have not yet been definitively established. Of those known, the one best understood is Loewi's vagusstoff, or *acetylcholine*, which chemically consists of the merger of a B vitamin, choline, and acetic acid.

The synthesis of acetylcholine in the body is controlled by an enzyme, *choline acetylase;* and its catabolism is facilitated by another enzyme, *cholinesterase.* There are two types of cholinesterase enzymes. *Acetylcholinesterase* (also called specific, true, or e-type) is located only at synaptic junctions, where it carries out the destruction of transmitted acetylcholine by a hydrolyzing[3]

---

3. Removal of a water molecule.

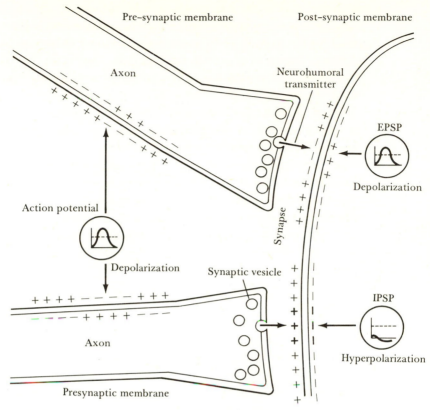

Figure 3-11. Electrochemical events at a synaptic junction: a nerve impulse (action potential) travels along an axon fiber until it reaches the presynaptic membrane, where the transmitter is released. The transmitter crosses the synapse and alters the permeability of the postsynaptic membrane, producing a flow of ions and effecting depolarization (EPSP) or hyperpolarization (IPSP).

action. *Butyrocholinesterase* (also called nonspecific, pseudo, or s-type) is found in many organs and in the bloodstream. It too hydrolyzes acetylcholine (Cooper, Bloom, and Roth, 1970).

Norepinephrine

Around the same time that Loewi was discovering vagusstoff in Switzerland, an American physiologist, Walter B. Cannon and his colleagues (Cannon and Rosenblueth, 1937) were working on the transmitter substance in other types of nerve fibers. Cannon found that stimulation of the hepatic nerve, which innervates the liver, also released a substance that increased heart rate. Here was another chemical transmitter. Cannon called the substance *sympathin*. It wasn't until the 1940s that a Swedish physiologist, Ulf von Euler (1946), identified sympathin as *norepinephrine* (also called *noradrenaline*). Norepinephrine is synthesized from an amino acid (phenylalanine) rather than from a B vitamin as is acetylcholine. For this discovery and other discoveries related to the functions of norepinephrine, von Euler received the Nobel Prize in 1970.[4]

Norepinephrine is an interesting substance. One of the intermediate products of norepinephrine synthesis is a chemical called *l*-dopa which is very effective in the treatment of Parkinsonism, a disease that causes incapacitating muscle tremors (see Chapter 13). In clinical testing, *l*-dopa also has shown evidence of being the first valid aphrodisiac in the history of pharmacology (McGeer, 1971).

A slight chemical alteration converts norepinephrine into *epinephrine,* or *adrenaline,* one of the two hormones secreted from the adrenal glands (Chapter 4). Epinephrine and norepinephrine have very similar physiological effects. However, norepinephrine is the one that appears to be primarily involved in synaptic transmission (von Euler, 1966).

The catabolism of norepinephrine is facilitated by two processes, each involving a different enzyme, either *catechol-o-methyltransferase* (COMT) or *monoamine oxidase* (MAO). In either instance, the process is slow relative to the speed with which acetylcholinesterase breaks down acetylcholine. It appears that, after transmission, norepinephrine diffuses from the synaptic junction into the bloodstream where the actual catabolism occurs.

Cholinergic and adrenergic nerves

With the validation of two distinct neurohumoral transmitters, neurons were differentially designated on the basis of which type was involved at the synaptic junctions. Those for which acetylcholine is the transmitter are called *cholinergic;* those in-

4. He was honored along with Julius Axelrod and Bernard Katz.

volving norepinephrine, *adrenergic*. So far, it has been definitively established that all the peripheral nerves outside the
autonomic nervous system, all the parasympathetic nerves, and
some of the sympathetic nerves of the autonomic system are
cholinergic; while other sympathetic nerves are adrenergic (see
Chapter 4). Among other things, adrenergic nerves function
in increases in heart beat, dilation of blood vessels, and stimulation of activity. They act as a balance to the cholinergic nerves
which tend to slow the organism down.

Other possible transmitters

In addition to acetylcholine and norepinephrine, other substances have been thought, at one time or another, to function
as neurohumoral transmitters (Buday, 1960). None has yet
been indisputably established as such, but a few have become
significant to physiological psychology. One of these is serotonin, also known as 5-hydroxytryptamine, *tryptamine*, or *5-HT*.
Many drugs that affect neuronal functioning, such as LSD and
other hallucinogens, also block the action of serotonin (see
Chapters 13 and 15). Both the catecholamines and serotonin
are often classed together as *biogenic amines*. All the biogenic amines have recently been implicated as the possible
biochemical substrate of many emotional and motor activities
(Chapter 9). *Gamma-Aminobutyric Acid,* or *GABA,* is an amino
acid which is involved in drug interactions in mammalian species, as well as being indisputably established as a transmitter in
invertebrate neurons (Kravitz, Kuffler, and Potter, 1963). *Substance P* is a complex compound found extensively throughout
the nervous system, especially where numerous synaptic junctions occur (Cooper, Bloom, and Roth, 1970). *Dopamine,* a
norepinephrine precursor, may also be a transmitter. Its significance is discussed in Chapter 13.

With the consideration of transmitter substances, a complete
description of neuron function has been provided. It is now
possible to go from there to a consideration of the communication system of multicellular organisms, the nervous system,
which is primarily an organization of neurons.

SUGGESTED READINGS

Cooper, J. R.; Bloom, F. E.; and Roth, R. H. *The Biochemical Basis of Neuro-pharmacology*. New York: Oxford University Press, 1970. The most concise and lucid description of neurohumoral transmission available.

Galambos, R. *Nerves and Muscles*. Garden City: Doubleday, 1962. Written by a scientist for the layman; brief and entertaining while at the same time accurate and informative.

Gardner, E. *Fundamentals of Neurology* (5th ed.). Philadelphia: Saunders, 1968. A standard text for many years, ideal for the neophyte.

Katz, B. *Nerve, Muscle and Synapse*. New York: McGraw-Hill, 1966. Somewhat more advanced and technical than Galambos' book, an excellent follow-up thereto.

McLennan, H. *Synaptic Transmission* (2nd ed.). Philadelphia: Saunders, 1970. A detailed up-to-date discussion that provides as much depth as current knowledge allows; not for casual reading.

Teitelbaum, P. *Physiological Psychology*. Englewood Cliffs, N.J.: Prentice-Hall, 1967. An excellent, unusually clear description of research methods and conceptions used to study the neuron.

4 The nervous system

THE NERVOUS SYSTEM

As multicellular organisms progressed phylogenetically, neurons became more specialized and better organized structurally and functionally to meet more efficiently the demands of the environment. The resultant organization of specialized neurons is called the *nervous system.*[1]

The process of neuron specialization appears in three forms: *differentiation, centralization,* and *encephalization.* Differentiation of neurons means that some came to function primarily as *receptors,* cells excitable by an energy source (chemical, electrical, mechanical, photic); others as *integrators,* cells that primarily conduct their excitation to other cells; and some as *motor neurons,* cells that activate muscles and glands. Centralization means that the cell bodies clustered together in bundles called plexus, ganglia, or nuclei,[2] and the axonal fibers organized as nerves or tracts.[3] Encephalization means that most of the ganglia are localized at one end of the organism.

Differentiation, centralization, and encephalization are

1. As well as neurons, the nervous system contains *glial cells;* in fact, they outnumber neurons five or ten to one. Aside from a few that form myelin (Chapter 3), their function is unknown (Galambos, 1961).
2. Nuclei generally refers to cell body clusters in the CNS, while plexuses or ganglia generally refer to cell body clusters elsewhere.
3. Tracts are fiber pathways in the CNS.

47

clearly evident at the evolutionary level of flatworms (Werner, 1948). As already discussed, earlier forms of animal life are characterized by a "nerve net," in which the nerves are spread over the organism like an umbrella. Any impulse arising from any point of stimulation is conducted through the whole system. The flatworm, by contrast, has two independently excitable fiber bundles and several encephalized ganglia. Further evolutionary development involves increases in the degree of differentiation, centralization, and encephalization (Figure 4-1). The study of the structures that resulted from such developments is called *neuroanatomy*.

Knowledge of the structure of the nervous system is quite old; one of the first known descriptions of the brain appears in the Old Testament (Levin, 1970). Generally, however, ancient people had poor ideas of the nervous system because they were hesitant to dissect cadavers and thus to violate strongly held beliefs in some form of post-mortem life. Aristotle and Hippocrates, despite their detailed discussions of anatomy, are believed never to have dissected a dead body (Singer, 1957). Emphasis on the experimental method was yet to come.

Ironically and grimly, the objection to dissection of the dead was circumvented to some extent by the sanction of dissection of the living. In Egypt, condemned criminals and slaves were used for vivisection but, for obvious reasons, not much detail of these experiments was recorded. Other fragmentary knowledge was obtained from early surgery. However, since speed in operating was important before the advent of anesthesia, little detailed knowledge of anatomy resulted.

The first accurate descriptions of the interior of the human body did not appear until the 1500s with the work of a succession of skilled anatomists, starting with Andreas Vesalius at the Italian medical school in Padua (Singer, 1957). There, the physicians collaborated with artists. They hired grave robbers to obtain cadavers and smuggle them into hidden basements. Their object, if they could avoid arrest, was to disseminate drawings which would foster a toleration of dissection among the enlightened citizenry of the day. In time this dedicated effort paid off in the accurate anatomical diagrams that have been hailed as artistic masterpieces. These diagrams are now regarded as cultural highlights of the early Renaissance

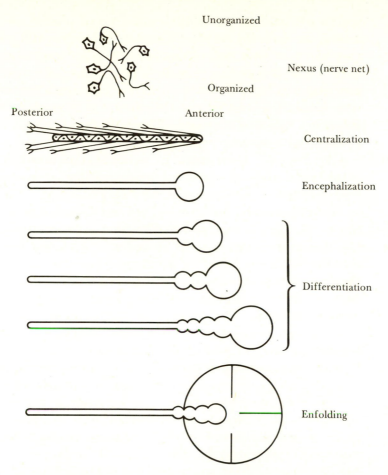

Figure 4-1. Evolution of Nervous System. Random nerve cells became organized when the cell bodies clustered (centralization) and congregated at one end (encephalization) where they divided into functional groupings (differentiation). These processes continued until the most anterior portion became so large it folded back over the other parts. The folds also defined structures. Individual nervous systems pass through similar stages of development.

period in Italy. A typical Renaissance anatomical chart is shown in Figure 4-2.

Similar progress occurred in most of Europe and in the Orient. However, in England anatomy was not considered a fit subject for medical study until the middle of the eighteenth century, when private extramural schools were established for teaching anatomy to medical students and physicians who felt a need for such knowledge. The rise of surgery made it necessary to know anatomy, although in England the surgeon was never regarded as highly as the medical man. To this day he is addressed as Mister, not Doctor. It was in the Colonies, at the new medical school of the University of Pennsylvania established in 1765, that anatomy finally became a recognized subject in an English-speaking medical school.

The rise of Darwinian evolutionary philosophy, which emphasized the continuity of animal from animal and man from animal, made comparative anatomy viable. The science continued to flourish to the extent that today most anatomists agree that gross anatomy is virtually a closed subject, with essentially nothing new to discover. Although microscopic anatomy (one example of which was seen in the discussion of the nature of the synapse) is still very much an open subject, most of the description that follows can be considered relatively undisputed.

The nervous system can be divided into parts according to location in the body. The encephalized portion and its contiguous caudal, or tail end, extension is called the *central nervous system* or *CNS*. The bulk of neurons at the rostral, or head, end is called the *brain;* the caudal extension is called the *cord.* Thus, the CNS consists of the brain and the cord, nothing more or less. It is totally contained within two major bony casings, the *spine* and the *skull.*

Everything (nerves, plexuses, ganglia) other than the brain and cord is called the *peripheral nervous system* or *PNS.* It includes the sensory neurons and receptors (Chapter 5), the axons of the final motor neurons (Chapter 6), and most of the autonomic nervous system (page 72).

The CNS and PNS are structurally and functionally integrated, and as will shortly be seen, it is difficult to discuss one without frequent reference to the other. The descriptive convenience of dividing the nervous system into parts, however, should not obscure the integrative aspects of nervous functioning. Any instance of behavior is the product of total neural integration. Having made that point, we can now follow the dictates of convenience and discuss each system in turn.

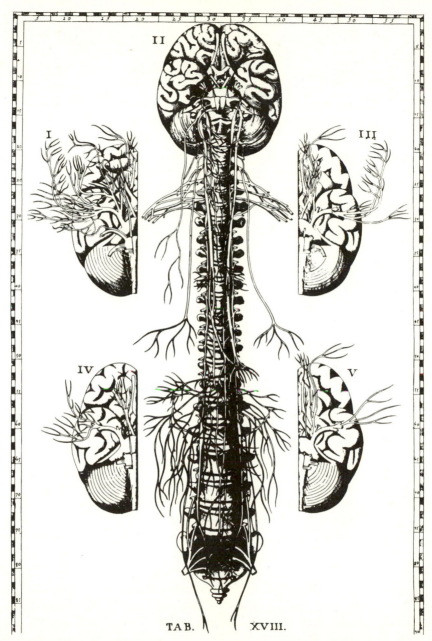

Figure 4-2. A typical Italian Renaissance anatomical chart of the sympathetic nervous system. The copperplate engraving is from the *Tabulae Anatomical,* assembled in 1552 by Bartholommeo Eustachio (after whom the Eustachian tube is named).

THE CENTRAL NERVOUS SYSTEM (CNS)

In the orientation of the CNS there is a fundamental difference between quadrupedal and bipedal organisms. The entire CNS of quadrupedal organisms is horizontal. In bipeds the brain is horizontal, but the cord is vertical. This difference leads to some confusion in nomenclature, as can be seen from Figure 4-3.

Spinal cord

Except for directly supplying nerves to the facial region, all incoming (afferent) fiber pathways and all outgoing (efferent) fiber pathways of the CNS run through the cord, which lies within the bony spinal column and is specifically referred to as the *spinal cord*. In man, the cord runs about three-quarters of the length of the spine and projects thirty-one pairs of *spinal nerves,* which pass through the spinal column at regular intervals along its length. Each spinal nerve innervates a small region of the body called a *dermatome* (see Figure 4-4).

Figure 4-3.   Central nervous system orientation nomenclature in **A,** quadruped and **B,** biped.

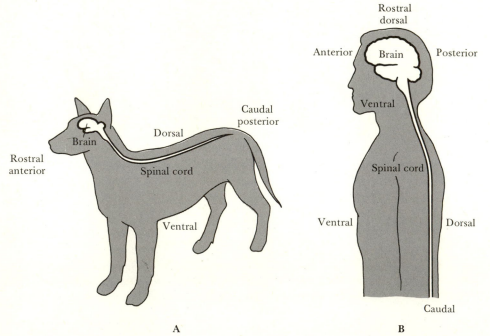

A

B

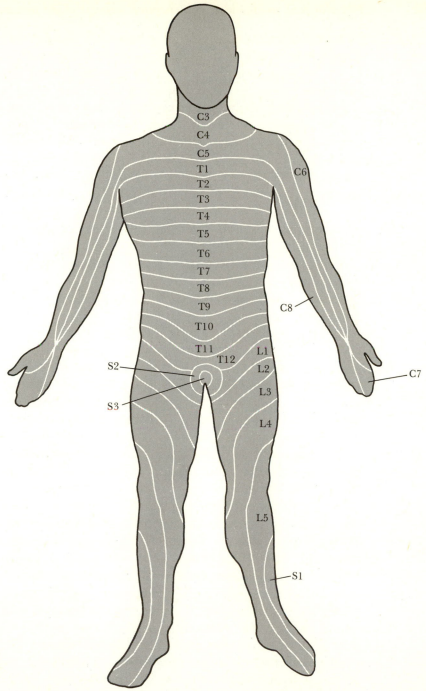

Figure 4-4. Map of human dermatomes, ventral surface. Each numbered area is innervated by a spinal nerve.

53

Spinal nerves, like any other nerves, are bundles of neurons. They each have two branches: a *dorsal* and *ventral root.* Some of the spinal nerve fibers arise from tactile, thermal, and pain receptors which receive impulses (afferent) from the skin, muscles, and joints. Others are motor fibers that carry impulses to the muscles (efferent). This fundamental distinction between the fibers that receive and those that stimulate arises from the *Bell-Magendie law,* which states that all ventral roots carry motor (efferent) impulses and all dorsal roots carry sensory (afferent) impulses. It should be noted that the spinal nerves involve every external body surface except the facial region, which is innervated by the cranial nerves originating in the brain (see page 58).

The cord is essentially a hollow tube, somewhat like an overly thick garden hose. Around it are three protective layers of tissue, called *meninges*. The outermost layer is known as the *dura mater,* or hard mother, because of its toughness. The next layer is a thick, flexible webbing called the *arachnoid,* or cobweb; and the innermost layer is a soft tissue called *pia mater,* or tender mother. The spaces between them are known as the *subarachnoid spaces.* They are filled with *cerebrospinal fluid* which acts as a nutritive and a shock absorber. Figure 4-5 shows the arrangement of the meningeal layers around the cord, while Figure 4-6 shows them over the brain.

The organization of the spinal cord can be appreciated from the cross sectional view shown in Figure 4-7. The exact relationship of the parts vary somewhat, depending on the level of the cross section, but Figure 4-7 can be considered prototypical. The most immediately noticeable feature is the central, butterfly-shaped, gray area called *gray matter,* surrounded by the white, peripheral area called *white matter.* The color difference is a significant clue to the manner in which the spinal neurons are organized. Neural tissue itself is gray; myelin, which covers the axons, is white. As microscopic examination would verify, the central region of the cord is composed primarily of cell bodies and unmyelinated axons. The peripheral area consists of axons of myelinated fibers that form tracts connecting one spinal level to another and/or to the brain. It can also be seen that the cord is bilaterally symmetrical, in that the two sides are identical or paired. The gray commissure

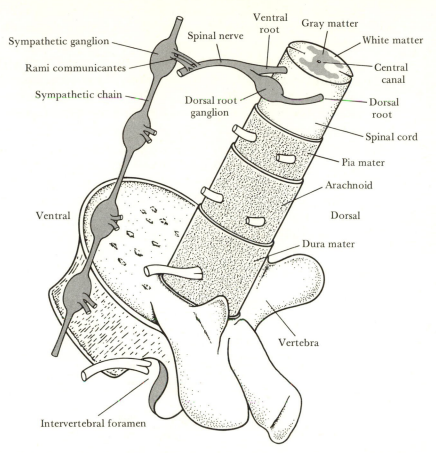

Figure 4-5. Spinal cord and ancillary structures. It can be seen that the cord is well protected from trauma by several layers of tissue and bone.

that joins the two sides contains the *central canal,* the interior space that makes the cord a hollow tube.

Just external to the cord, the spinal nerves branch into the dorsal and ventral roots. The dorsal root consists partly of afferent sensory fibers and the cell bodies of the sensory neurons, which constitute the *dorsal root ganglion.* The incoming fiber processes are functionally afferent and very long (up to three or four feet in man). Most of the dorsal root proper is taken up with the efferent process projecting from the cell body to the interior of the cord. This fiber is also relatively long, probably as long as the afferent processes in many cases. As a result, there is some confusion as to which of the long fibers is an axon and which is a dendrite. Generally, the issue can be avoided by considering the cells as *bipolar neurons;* that is, neurons having two long fibers, without concern as to relative function.

The efferent poles of the sensory neuron terminate in the dorsal horn of the gray matter, where they usually synapse with neurons that are totally within the CNS. These are called *internuncial neurons,* or simply *interneurons.*

Prototypically, the interneurons synapse with the cell bodies of motor neurons in the ventral region of the gray matter called the *ventral horn.* The axons of the motor neurons then leave the cord as the ventral root of the spinal nerve.

In actual fact, very few, if any, sensory-motor pathways are that simple. More typically, there are complex ascending, descending, and lateral internuncial relationships which can involve many synapses, cord levels, and brain neurons. As later discussion in Chapter 7 will reveal, many multisynaptic sensory-motor pathways do remain primarily at spinal levels, where

Figure 4-6.   Meningeal layers of the brain.

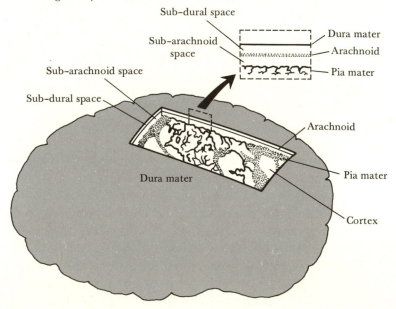

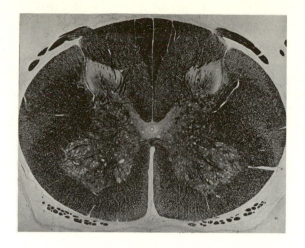

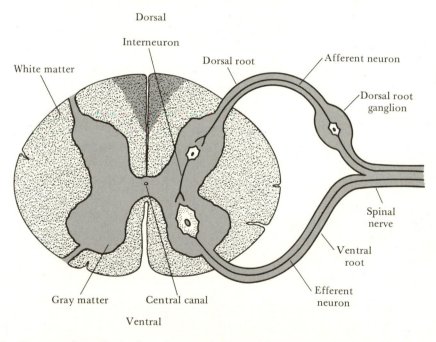

Dorsal

Interneuron

White matter

Dorsal root

Afferent neuron

Dorsal root ganglion

Gray matter

Central canal

Spinal nerve

Ventral root

Efferent neuron

Ventral

Figure 4-7. Cross section of spinal cord at cervical level, showing neuronal connections to a spinal nerve. The stain employed in preparation of the specimen for photography makes the white matter appear black. (Photograph courtesy of Dr. Ronald G. Clark, Department of Biological Structure, University of Miami School of Medicine.)

they represent the structural components of a number of functions called *spinal reflex arcs*. These arcs are the products of muscular and organ responses to stimuli that can occur without intervention of the brain. They represent the most basic functional unit of the nervous system, just as the neuron represents the most basic structural unit. To put it another way, fundamental behavior, stimulus → response (S → R), is physiologically represented by the sensory-motor pathway. This can be regarded as the first specific instance of a behavior-body relationship in the sense that a specific structural component, the sensory-motor pathway, is correlated with the occurrence of a specific behavioral sequence arising from the central nervous system.

Because this basic organization of the spinal cord is repeated thirty-one times (in man) with little variation, the cord is said to be *segmented*. The divergence from the segmented pattern occurs only at the anterior end of the cord where the cord becomes continuous with the brain. There is no sharp line of demarcation between cord and brain; the area in which they merge is known as the *brain stem*.

Brain

The brain can only be visualized by considering it in both frontal and lateral cross sections, since the marked encephalization and differentiation causes differences in structure at various levels. For this reason, a composite view of the brain must include several cross sections, such as shown in Figure 4-8.

The brain is organized into five divisions. In order of lowest to highest, or most posterior to most anterior, these are called *myelencephalon, metencephalon, mesencephalon, diencephalon,* and *telecephalon.* Each division contains several primary structures.

Myelencephalon   In the myelencephalon, the most significant structure is the *medulla.* This structure can be considered an extension and enlargement of the spinal cord, modified to serve the head region as the cord serves the body surface. The medulla contains several nuclei associated with some of the *cranial nerves,* which innervate the sensory receptors and muscles in the face and neck regions. The head, relative to the rest of the body surface, is unique in terms of both sensory and motor functioning. The head contains receptors specialized for photic, auditory, and chemical input. Also, it contains motor systems requiring highly specialized neural control, such as the systems involved in food and water intake, breathing, and speech. In man there are twelve pairs of cranial nerves. Their names and functions are listed in Table 4-1. All but the first five have their origin in bulbar[4] nuclei. In addition to the cranial nerve nuclei, the medulla contains areas concerned with various vital automatic functions, such as respiration, blood circulation, and gastro-intestinal activities.

Metencephalon   With the metencephalon, which lies in front of the medulla, the first true suprasegmental (above the cord) structure is seen. This is the *cerebellum*. While it lies dorsal to the main axis of the CNS, the cerebellum is directly connected to it by six large fiber tracts, three on each side. Cerebellar structure represents the first instance of the redistribution of

4. Bulbar is an adjective referring to the medulla which is, in fact, shaped like a bulb.

Table 4-1. Human cranial nerves

Number	Name	Origin	Function
I	Olfactory	Rhinencephalon	Smell (sensory)*
II	Optic	Thalamus	Vision (sensory)*
III	Oculomotor	Mesencephalon	Eye movement (motor)
IV	Trochlear	Mesencephalon	Eye movement (motor)
V	Trigeminal	Pons	Mastication (motor), face and tongue sensibility (sensory)
VI	Abducens	Bulbar	Eye movement (motor)
VII	Facial	Bulbar	Face movement (motor)
VIII	Auditory	Bulbar	Hearing, equilibrium (sensory)*
IX	Glossopharyngeal	Bulbar	Taste (sensory) swallowing (motor)
X	Vagus	Bulbar	Visceral sensitivity, muscle action (sensory-motor)
XI	Spinal accessory	Bulbar	Neck movement, visceral action (motor)
XII	Hypoglossal	Bulbar	Tongue movement (motor)

* I, II, and VIII also have efferent components that are involved in various feedback functions (Grossman, 1967; Kulikowski, 1971).

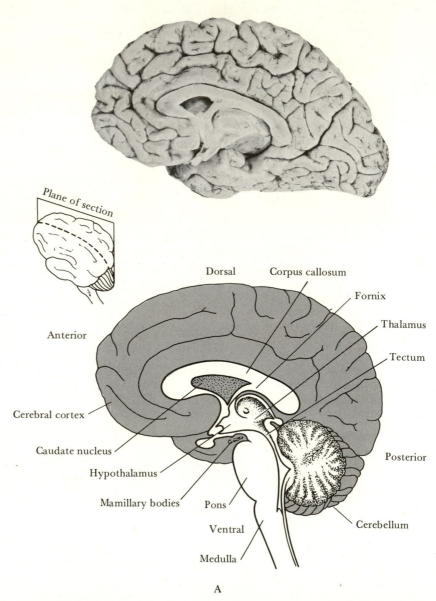

Figure 4-8. Photographs and drawings of **A,** lengthwise (medial) and **B,** crosswise (coronal) sections through the human brain showing structures important to physiological psychology. (Photographs courtesy of Dr. Ronald G. Clark, Department of Biological Structure, University of Miami School of Medicine.)

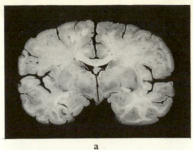

a

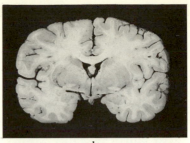

b

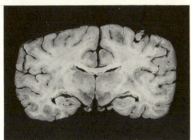

c

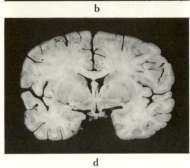

d

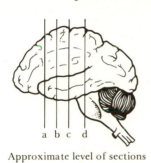

Approximate level of sections

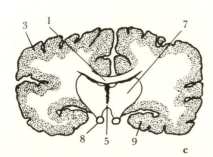

a

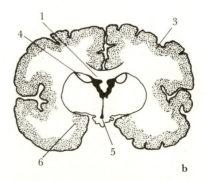

b

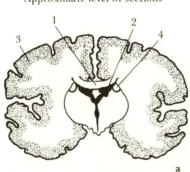

c

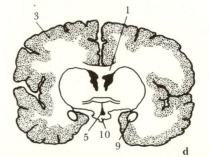

d

B

cell bodies and fibers characteristic of the rest of the brain—
the gray matter surrounding the interior white matter.

Since, as has already been implied, the nervous system
phylogenetically evolved in a caudal to rostral sequence, the
cerebellum represents an ancient structure. Indeed, it is present in its most rudimentary form in a primitive vertebrate, the
lamprey, and shows the greatest phylogenetic change up
through the birds. Later evolutionary development favored the
cerebrum (Maier and Maier, 1970). Since its primary function
involves motor coordination, the cerebellum will be considered
in considerably more detail when the motor system is discussed
in Chapter 7. Another metencephalic structure, the *pons,* is the
primary tract through which the two halves of the cerebellum
connect.

Mesencephalon   The mesencephalon, or midbrain (see Figure
4-9), is a relatively small division which seems to be primarily a
connecting link between the anterior and posterior parts of
the brain. Its ventral surface, the *tegmentum,* is composed
of sensory and motor tracts which go to and from other parts of
the brain. The tegmentum also contains a portion of the *retic-*

Figure 4-9.   Location of the reticular formation in the human nervous system.

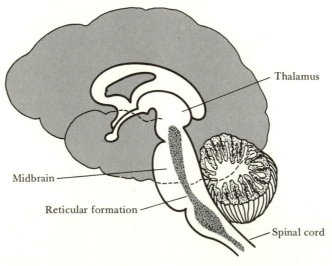

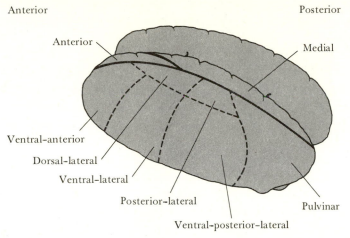

Anterior   Posterior

Anterior

Medial

Ventral–anterior

Dorsal–lateral

Ventral–lateral

Posterior–lateral   Pulvinar

Ventral–posterior–lateral

Figure 4-10. Approximate demarcation of the thalamic nuclei. The ventral-anterior nuclei have primarily subcortical connections, the ventral-lateral and ventral-posterior-lateral are primarily cortical relay nuclei, the remainder are association nuclei.

ular formation, which extends from the thalamus to the posterior medulla. The reticular formation is so named because it is a network, or reticulum, of cell bodies and fibers. It receives collaterals or branches from all sensory and some motor fibers. Fibers project from it to higher brain areas. The roof of the mesencephalon, called the *tectum,* contains the *colliculi,* which are synaptic centers for visual and auditory afferents.

Diencephalon The diencephalon, sometimes called the thalamencephalon, is noted for two significant structures: the *thalamus* and *hypothalamus.* These structures are in direct contact with the cerebral cortex by way of a large fiber tract.

Thalamus is a term derived from the Greek language, meaning bed or couch. It is an oval-shaped collection of nuclei which is often referred to as "the great relay station of the brain." Most sensory input, including that originating in the cranial nerves, goes through the thalamus. As shown in Figure 4-10, the thalamus is divided into three functional groups:

1. Sensory relay nuclei. These receive input from all the sensory fibers and transmit the messages to the cerebral cortex.

Sensory input can also reach the cortex indirectly by way of the reticular formation.

2. Association nuclei. They receive input from other fibers within the thalamus and project to the cerebral cortex.

3. Intrinsic nuclei. These nuclei project down as well as up in that they connect with other regions within the thalamus, with the reticular formation, and with the limbic system (described in the next section of this chapter).

The hypothalamus is a collection of nuclei that lie ventral to the thalamus. The hypothalamus projects to and receives input for many subcortical areas, especially those concerned with visceral autonomic activity. It is largely responsible for such things as control of the temperature and osmotic pressure of the blood. It is also, as shall be seen later, involved in certain motivational states such as hunger and fatigue.

Rhinencephalon   Intermediate between the diencephalon and the telencephalon is a structure or, more accurately, a group of structures known as the *rhinencephalon*. The term rhinencephalon, which literally means "smell brain," was initially applied to the olfactory parts of the brain. Eventually, it also came to include the structures around the brain stem which the French anatomist, Paul Broca (Chapter 11), described as the *limbic* lobe, from the Latin word limbus, meaning rim. Other names used to designate these structures are visceral brain, olfactory brain, and limbic system. Since it is phylogenetically older than the cerebral cortex, some authorities also call the rhinencephalon the *paleocortex*.

The structures that constitute the limbic system, shown in Figure 4-11, seem to be involved with the emotional and visceromatic functions that are related to such fundamental states as sexual arousal and hunger (McCleary and Moore, 1965; see also Chapter 8). In animals, a highly developed sense of smell is closely associated with sex and food, which accounts for the olfactory part. In man, smell gave way to vision as a tool for survival, possibly because man emerged from arboreal animals which needed a good sense of distance to escape from predators. However, man has not lost his other senses, and his

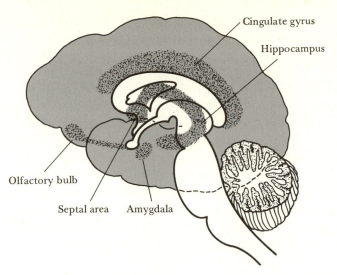

Figure 4-11. Locus of the principle structures that constitute the limbic system.

basic emotions, such as rage, fright, and fear—all needed for survival—are still tied to the limbic system. Interestingly, the limbic lobe is the same relative size in all animals (see Figure 4-12) and thus represents a common denominator in the brains of all animals.

Basal ganglia An important group of structures near the rhinencephalon are the *basal ganglia*. These structures (which should more accurately be called nuclei) are simply large clusters of cell bodies in the central part of the cerebral hemispheres, directly beneath the cerebral cortex. Phylogenetically, they are very old; they form a considerable part of the forebrain of lower vertebrates, particularly birds. The basal ganglia have functions that are primarily motor.

Telencephalon The telencephalon is the most advanced division of the brain. As shown in Figure 4-7, it is composed of the *cerebral hemispheres,* or *cerebrum,* which consists of the *cerebral cortex* or *neocortex* (gray matter) and the *corpus callosum* (white matter), a fiber tract that connects the hemispheres. The cerebrum is phylogenetically the most recently developed portion of the nervous system. In fact, in mammals it is the only part of the brain that changed substantially in size during phylogenetic development. In the human being, about one-half of the mass of the nervous system is cerebral cortex, and it contains 9 billion of the approximately 12 billion neurons in the human brain.

With the exception of the highly developed neocortex, the human brain is similar to any other mammalian brain (Figure 4-13). However, cerebral development and the assumption of man's upright bipedal posture resulted in several unique structural modifications. One is the bending of the neuraxis, so that the brain remained horizontal while the cord became vertical. Another is the development of folds like those of an accordion to accommodate the expanded neocortex in a small skull that would not be too heavy for upright carriage. To save space, the cortex also folded itself over the subcortical structures (Figure 4-14).

The surface of the cerebral cortex can be differentiated in

Figure 4-12. Coronal brain sections showing proportionate relationships of limbic cortex to neocortex in a variety of species. It can be seen that the amount of the limbic tissue remains relatively constant, the primary evolutionary advance being the increased neocortex.

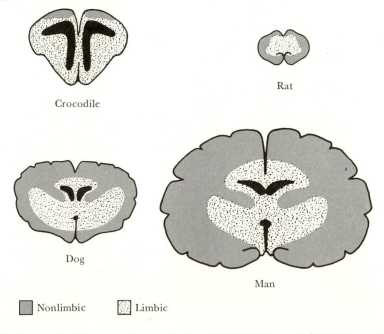

Crocodile

Rat

Dog

Man

■ Nonlimbic   ▨ Limbic

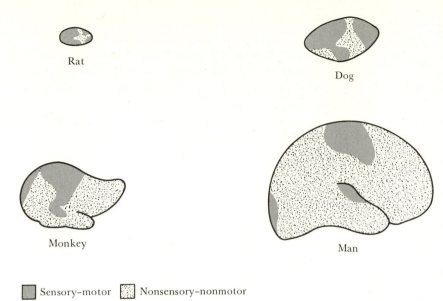

Rat

Dog

Monkey

Man

■ Sensory–motor   ▩ Nonsensory–nonmotor

Figure 4-13. Surface projection of the cerebral cortex of the brain of various species, showing that phylogenetic development has occurred primarily in terms of nonsensory-nonmotor or association cortex.

three ways. First, the major folds and wrinkles, *fissures* or *sulci*, are used as points of demarcation. Figure 4-16 shows the divisions of cerebral areas by these folds. Incidentally, since the cerebrum, with few exceptions, is bilaterally symmetrical, the descriptions of one side usually apply to the other. Names of the fissures and lobes usually follow the name of the skull bone beneath which they are located.

A second system of demarcation involves the *architectonic* structure of the neocortex. While, in a strict sense, the cerebrum is simply a large nucleus, it remains unique in regard to its large number of fiber connections between cells. In addition, the neocortex consists of six cellular layers, which can be divided into distinct areas (see Figure 4-15). A system of mapping the cerebrum on the basis of cellular structure was devised by the nineteenth century German anatomist, Korbinian Brodmann, who attached numbers to different areas in accordance with the differences in cellular arrangement. The areas, called *Brodmann's areas,* can also be seen in Figure 4-16. For instance, the occipital lobe, which is the cortical projection of the visual system, is Brodmann's area 17. Another area around the central fissure, called the motor cortex, is Brodmann's area 4. It should be noted that there are some areas of the brain which cannot be differentiated on the basis of cellular distinction.

A third system of differentiating the cerebral surface involves dividing it into *projection areas*. These areas are primarily regions which receive information provided by the sense organs. They are mapped electrically by either stimulating a sensory or motor pathway and observing where in the cerebrum a potential is evoked or, conversely, stimulating a part of the cerebrum and observing the organism's reaction. It appears that the cerebrum is topographically organized to some extent. That is, there are specific areas to which each sense projects and specific areas that correspond to motor control of specific body parts. A map of the projection areas is presented in Figure 4-16.

As shown, the surface is divided into several primary projec-

Figure 4-14.   Cross-sectional representation showing how overlapping and enfolding of the forebrain greatly increased the cortical area that could be contained in a fixed space.

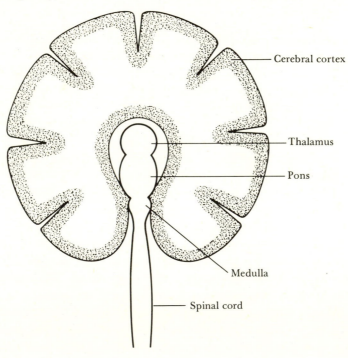

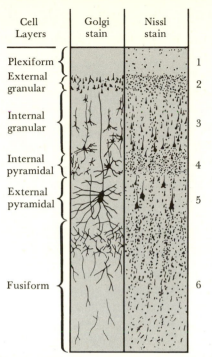

Cell Layers	Golgi stain	Nissl stain	
Plexiform			1
External granular			2
Internal granular			3
Internal pyramidal			4
External pyramidal			5
Fusiform			6

Figure 4-15. Schematic representation of a section of human cortex showing the six cellular layers as they might appear microscopically with different staining techniques. By observing how the distribution of these layers varied across the surface of the cortex, Brodmann was able to systematically number the areas.

tion areas. Some areas are involved in the neural representation of information relayed from the sense organs, and other areas act as distribution areas for outgoing motor impulses.

Information detected by the eye is projected onto a region in both occipital lobes. If one electrically stimulates the occipital region, the brain will "see" independently of the eye; the subject will have a visual experience. Similarly, if a lesion is made in the area, the subject will go "blind" even though the eyes are in perfect anatomic order. As well, there is a region of the cerebral cortex involved in representing sound, temperature, taste, touch, and various motor activities from licking the lips to blinking the eyelid.

While emphasis has been on the surface of the brain, it must not be forgotten that the brain, like the cord, is essentially hollow and filled with cerebrospinal fluid. The cavities of the brain are called *ventricles* (Figure 4-17). For many years they, rather than the cortical surface, were thought to be the functionally active areas (Chapter 11).

Blood-brain barrier

The CNS receives an abundant blood supply (Figure 4-18 shows the brain's vascular system), but the mechanism of material transfer from the blood stream has been under investigation for a long time. In 1885 Paul Ehrlich first noted that most tissues stained very rapidly when dyes were injected into the blood stream, with the notable exceptions of the cord and brain. Ehrlich suggested that a barrier between the CNS and the blood vessels prevented the diffusion of substances from the blood into the brain and cord.

The barrier is now called the *blood-brain barrier,* or *BBB.* A similar barrier prevents passage of substances from the cerebrospinal fluid into the brain; this barrier is called the *cerebrospinal fluid-brain barrier.* The structure of these barriers is still not known. Some investigators suggest that the barrier is the cell membrane of the glial cells which surround all the blood vessels of the nervous system and are present throughout the brain (page 47). Others think that the barrier involves the cells of the blood vessel walls. In any case, the barriers are extremely important for maintaining the chemical constancy of the CNS.

THE PERIPHERAL NERVOUS SYSTEM

As stated earlier, the PNS consists of three major components: the primary afferent fibers (those carrying incoming sensory impulses), the terminal efferent fibers (those carrying impulses to the muscles), and most of the autonomic nervous system. The first two are highly specialized and are covered in detail in the following three chapters. Thus, in this chapter only the *autonomic nervous system* (ANS) will be discussed. It is also referred to as the involuntary nervous system, to emphasize that it primarily involves reflex control of internal organs, such as heart, lungs, and genitals.

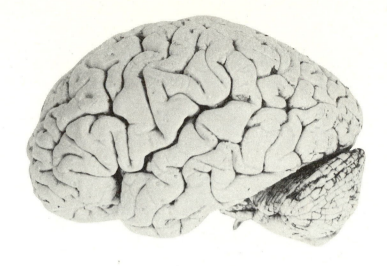

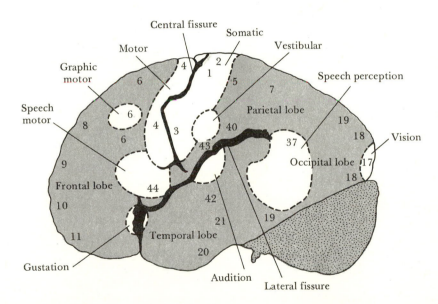

Figure 4-16. **A,** Photograph and **B,** drawing of the surface of a human brain showing the major demarcations, Brodmann's numbers, and topographical mapping. (Photograph courtesy of Dr. Ronald G. Clark, Department of Biological Structure, University of Miami School of Medicine.)

Autonomic nervous system

The functional nature of the autonomic nervous system was first described by Claude Bernard, perhaps the most famous of the mid-nineteenth century physiologists (Figure 4-19). Bernard, interestingly enough, began his career as a playwright who was mildly successful in local theatres. He was encouraged to bring one of his plays to a famed Paris drama critic for review. The critic gave the play one reading and promptly suggested to Bernard that, as a playwright, he should study medicine (Eckstein, 1970). Being a realist, Bernard took the advice and became a professor of physiology at the Collège de France, succeeding his famous teacher, Francois Magendie.

Bernard went on to make many ·significant discoveries in physiology, but he is primarily remembered for his conception of the internal constancy of the body. Bernard called it "la fixite du milieu interieur" (Bernard, 1858), the notion that the body is capable of maintaining a fixed internal environment regardless of external change. The internal environment con-

Figure 4-17.   Sketch showing the ventricular system of the human brain.

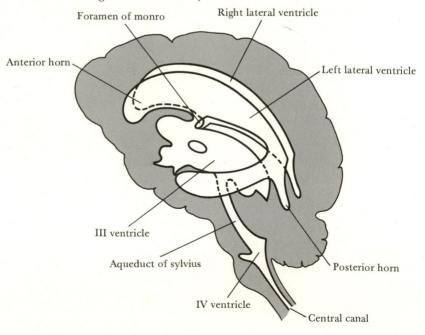

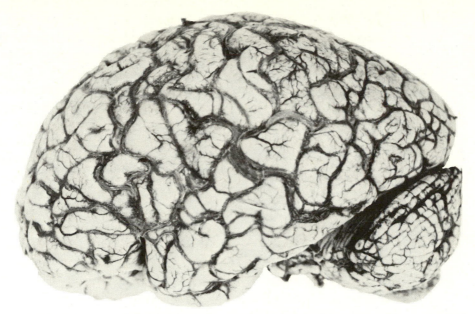

Figure 4-18. The vascular system of the brain. (Photograph courtesy of Dr. Ronald G. Clark, Department of Biological Structure, University of Miami School of Medicine.)

sists of fluids in which the cells are bathed; and such things as cell temperature, pressure, and salinity are kept constant by a kind of master control system. When the external temperature goes too low, the body calls upon adjustive devices, such as shivering and vasoconstriction, to provide more body heat. Similarly, when the body is too hot, vasodilation and perspiring occur to effect cooling. Walter B. Cannon later restated Bernard's notions as the concept of *homeostasis* and emphasized that it was controlled by the activity of the involuntary or autonomic nervous system (Cannon, 1929).

The autonomic nervous system can be divided into two broad parts that are structurally and functionally distinct. They are the *sympathetic* and *parasympathetic* nervous systems. Both are shown in Figure 4-20.

Structurally, the sympathetic nervous system, also called the *thoraciolumbar* system because its pathways to and from the cord are situated in that region, is organized to form a connected chain of ganglia that run parallel to the spinal cord. Fibers arising from these ganglia synapse with nerves that activate autonomic structures throughout the body. The parasympathetic, or *craniosacral* portion, is organized somewhat differently. The ganglion is near or in the organ being innervated; so the fibers are short.

The structural distinctions between the two portions of the autonomic nervous system, as already explained (Chapter 3), extend to the chemical transmitters across synapses. All the synaptic junctions of the parasympathetic nervous system are cholinergic, whereas some of the sympathetic system synapses are cholinergic and others are adrenergic. Figure 4-21 contains a diagram illustrating the types of synaptic connections involved in the peripheral nervous system. It should be emphasized that the peripheral system's synaptic sites are the only ones at which the specific neurohumoral transmitters have been positively identified. At all other synapses, especially those in the CNS, only indirect evidence exists regarding the chemical nature of the neurohumoral transmitters (Krnjevic, 1969; McGeer, 1971).

Functionally, the sympathetic and parasympathetic systems

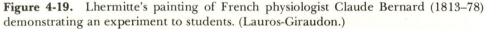

Figure 4-19.   Lhermitte's painting of French physiologist Claude Bernard (1813–78) demonstrating an experiment to students. (Lauros-Giraudon.)

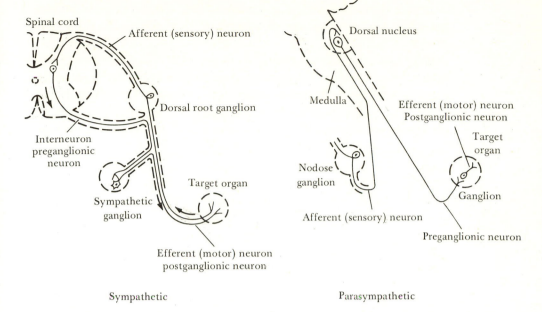

Spinal cord

Afferent (sensory) neuron

Dorsal root ganglion

Interneuron
preganglionic
neuron

Sympathetic
ganglion

Target organ

Efferent (motor) neuron
postganglionic neuron

Sympathetic

Dorsal nucleus

Medulla

Efferent (motor) neuron
Postganglionic neuron

Target
organ

Nodose
ganglion

Ganglion

Afferent (sensory) neuron

Preganglionic neuron

Parasympathetic

Figure 4-20. Diagrammatic representation of sympathetic and parasympathetic reflex arcs. It will be noted that only the motor portions are considered to constitute the autonomic nervous system. The nodose ganglion, indicated in the parasympathetic diagram, represents a type of ganglion found in various cranial nerve pathways, such as the vagus, that are analogous to the dorsal root ganglia of the spinal nerves. (The solid lines are fiber and the broken lines represent nerve and nerve tissue.)

are also easily distinguished. They are often spoken of as being antagonistic in effecting organs. To take some examples, activation of sympathetic fibers can result in contraction of arteries, acceleration of the heartbeat, inhibition of stomach contractions and secretions, and dilation of the pupils of the eye. On the other hand, parasympathetic nerve stimulation results in dilation of arteries, inhibition of the heartbeat, facilitation of stomach contractions and secretions, and constriction of the pupils of the eye. The sympathetic system tends to trigger all systems it innervates at once; the parasympathetic system acts in a more specific manner on target organs. The two systems are not, however, antagonistic; they work in unison to maintain maximal integrity of the organism at all times under all conditions.

HUMORAL INTEGRATION

A basic knowledge of the *endocrine system,* the system of ductless glands[5] that secrete chemicals known as *hormones* into the blood stream which affect behavior, is equally important to an understanding of the nervous system (Figure 4-22). The endocrine system is related to the nervous system in three ways. First, it too is a system of organismic communication, or integration, and regulation. The nervous system communicates rapidly, accommodating quick adjustments, while the endocrines communi-

5. Glands having ducts, i.e., do not secrete directly into the blood stream, are called exocrine. These include such organs as mammary and sweat glands whose secretions do not directly affect behavior.

Figure 4-21.   Schematic diagram of various peripheral efferent innervations, showing the types of synaptic connection involved. It will be noticed that all except the postganglionic sympathetic synapses are cholinergic.

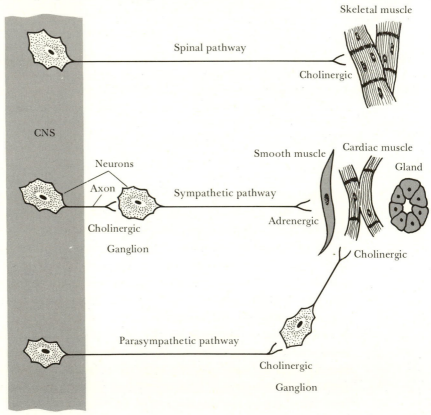

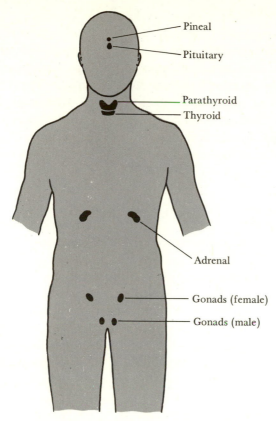

Pineal

Pituitary

Parathyroid

Thyroid

Adrenal

Gonads (female)

Gonads (male)

Figure 4-22. Endocrine glands in the human body.

cate more slowly, accommodating processes of longer duration. Second, the glandular system is closely regulated by the nervous system, primarily by way of the intimate connections between the hypothalamus and the pituitary gland. Third, since the axon terminals of neurons ductlessly secrete neurohormones (Chapter 3), they are, technically speaking, endocrines.

Some of the lower invertebrates, such as flatworms, produce hormone-like substances. However, it is not until the evolutionary level of the annelids (roundworms) is reached that distinct secretory cells are identifiable (Maier and Maier, 1970). The highest invertebrates (such as insects) possess well defined glandular systems (Scharrer, 1941).

In higher animals, including man, the endocrine system is functionally organized around the *pituitary gland,* or "master" gland, in the same sense that the nervous system is subservient to the brain. The pituitary, which regulates all endocrine secretion, is closely attached to the hypothalamus. This places it anatomically just above the nasal passages, which accounts for its name—a variation of the Latin for "nasal secretion." In naming it, Vesalius assumed that it discharged mucus.

Structurally (as shown in Figure 4-23), the pituitary is divided into an anterior portion, the *adrenohypophysis,* which is embryologically derived from glandular tissue, and a posterior part, the *neurohypophysis,* embryologically derived from neural tissue. Both the adrenohypophysis and neurohypophysis have neural and vascular connections with the hypothalamus.

Hypothalamic activity regulates the pituitary in the following way. When the hypothalamus is stimulated, by an emotion or by appetite, for instance, the neurosecretory neurons in various hypothalamic nuclei secrete chemical substances which influence pituitary secretion of hormones. Six hormones are involved. Four are adrenohypophysical: *adrenocorticotropic* hormone (ACTH) controls the activity of the adrenal glands, *thyrotropic* hormone controls the thyroid gland, *gonadotropic* hormone regulates the activities of the ovaries or testes, and *somatotropic* hormone regulates growth.

In addition, there are two neurohypophysical hormones: *antidiuretic* hormone (ADH) affects the renal tubules of the kidneys so as to minimize water loss, and *oxytoxin* stimulates uterine contraction and secretion of milk from the mammary glands. The various neurosecretory substances are directly released by the hypothalamic neurons and travel, by way of the vascular system, to the pituitary. Thus, the process, called *neurosecretion,* involves hypothalamic neurons in endocrine activity other than synaptic transmission.

The hormones secreted by the other endocrine glands perform various functions as detailed in Table 4-2. Many of them also affect the activity of the hypothalamus, thus establishing a type of control system known as a *regulatory feedback system.* For example, in response to physiological stress, the pituitary releases ACTH which, in turn, stimulates the adrenal gland to

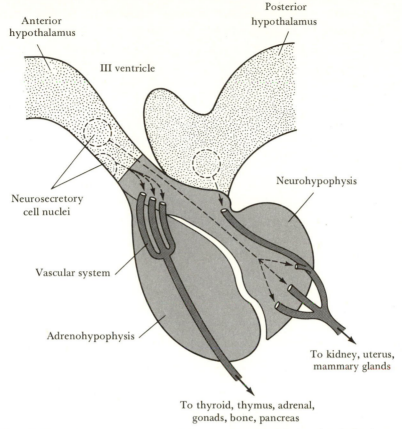

Anterior
hypothalamus

Posterior
hypothalamus

III ventricle

Neurohypophysis

Neurosecretory
cell nuclei

Vascular system

Adrenohypophysis

To kidney, uterus,
mammary glands

To thyroid, thymus, adrenal,
gonads, bone, pancreas

Figure 4-23. Schematic representation of the pituitary gland showing its intimate relation to the hypothalamus and the process of neurosecretion. Arterial blood to the
hypothalamus is monitored in terms of bodily functioning (water, sugar content, temperature, et cetera) by various receptor cells. These, in turn, regulate the output of the
neurosecretory cells which discharge substrates into the venous blood leaving the hypothalamus. The venous blood carries the substances to the pituitary where they effect
release of the relevant hormones into the blood.

release epinephrine and adrenal cortical steroids to activate
metabolism. As high blood levels of the steroids are reached,
however, they inhibit hypothalamic activation of pituitary
ACTH release. Thus, the system tends towards equilibrium,
thereby maintaining a viable organism.

Table 4-2.   Major human endocrine glands

Gland	Locus	Hormone	Target	Function
Pituitary	Base of hypothalamus			
Neurohypophysis		Antidiuretic	Kidney	Stimulates reabsorption of water
		Oxytoxin	Uterus	Stimulates contractions
			Mammary glands	Stimulates milk secretion
Adrenohypophysis		Somatotropic	Bone	Stimulates growth
		Thyrotropic	Thyroid gland	Activates thyroid secretion
		ACTH	Adrenal cortex	Stimulates steroid secretion
		Gonadotropic	Gonads	Stimulates secretion of estrogens and androgens
Thyroid	Neck, around pharynx	Thyroxin	Energy expending tissue	Regulates metabolism
Parathyroid	Thyroid gland	Parathormone	Blood	Regulates calcium and phosphate levels
Adrenal	On kidneys			
Cortex		Adrenal steroids	Cell membranes	Electrolyte balance
Medulla		Epinephrine	Cardiovascular system	Increases blood flow
Pancreas	Below stomach	Insulin	Energy expending tissues	Stimulates glucose absorption
Gonads	Sex organs	Estrogens (ovaries) Androgens (testes)	All tissues	Sex arousal, primary and secondary sex characteristics
Pineal	Third ventricle of brain	Melatonin	Gonads	Inhibits gonadal secretions

SUMMARY

In this broad description of organismic integrating systems, emphasis has been placed on the nervous system, which is dominant over the endocrine system in the sense that humoral integration is closely regulated by neural activity.

The anatomical organization of the nervous system can be summarized as follows:

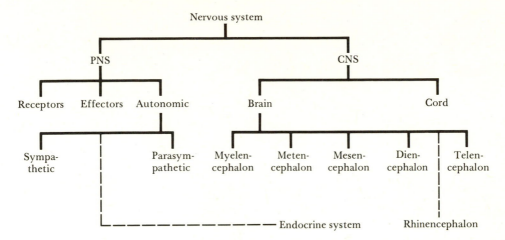

The receptor and effector aspects are very complex and specialized facets of neural structure and function, and require further elaboration. They will be considered separately in the following three chapters, as a continuation of the discussion of the PNS.

SUGGESTED READINGS

Anthony, C. P. *Basic Concepts in Anatomy and Physiology: A Programmed Presentation.* (2nd ed.) St. Louis: Mosby, 1970. A highly efficient and effective way for the beginning student to quickly develop a fundamental knowledge of anatomy.

Burn, J. H. *The Autonomic Nervous System.* Philadelphia: Davis, 1963. A short, clear description of the autonomic nervous system from a pharmacological perspective.

Netter, F. H. *Nervous System.* The Ciba Collection of Medical Illustrations, vol. 1. Summit, N.J.: Ciba, 1962. These large colored illustrations drawn by a physician from actual specimens are the best visual aids available short of the real thing.

5 Sensory processes

Organisms are aware of the world around them through their senses. Without sensory mechanisms, there would be no experience and no basis for an orderly relationship between organisms and their environment. In fact, the world and self are defined in terms of what one senses. To recast Descartes' familiar quotation, "I sense, therefore I am."

Not always, however. Many sensory phenomena which come into the purview of the experimenter seem to relate to an ultra environment—occasionally to what one might call a pseudo or fabricated world, created entirely out of internal experiences. For instance, there is the familiar phenomenon of the "phantom limb" wherein an amputee still feels pain, indeed excruciating pain, in a nonexistent arm or leg. Some 30 percent of amputees report pain after amputation. For most of them, the pain goes away in time. Five percent, however, feel severe pain that never leaves (Melzack, 1970). Why the brain reports sensation from a limb that is not there remains an unanswered question.

The basic problems of sensing for physiological psychology to resolve are: How do the mechanics of sensory reception become experience? What processes guide the sensory input from the environment to the brain? What processes then underlie their perception and creation into a portrait of the world in terms of myriad shapes, colors, and odors, or a portrait of an unreal world with its own set of characteristics? More importantly, how do sensory phenomena correlate with the organism's behavior? This chapter describes how some physiological psychologists have attempted to answer these questions. The emphasis will be on a discussion of sensing as a general neural phenomenon, rather than on each individual sensory modality.

THE SENSORY MECHANISM

All living cells respond to external influences through their membranes, which can be affected by a variety of sources in such a way that *irritability,* or disruption of the cell's ionic equilibrium, occurs. As was mentioned earlier, cells specialized for responding to the environment in this manner are called receptors. The source that creates the effect is known as *stimulation*. Present conceptions correlate stimulation with one or another type of physical energy.

Receptors

The more primitive receptors are generalized; they respond indiscriminately to any type of energy source. These are referred to as *common receptors*. Some investigators believe that the skin receptors in man are of this type. Indeed, even "visual" reception through the fingertips has allegedly been demonstrated. Youtz (1968) reports that a blindfolded woman subject could identify different colors through fingertip touch alone. Most of the receptors of higher animals, however, tend to be specialized to respond to one specific energy source. A smell receptor, for instance, is sensitive only in terms of odor and will not respond in terms of sound or touch. These are called *differentiated receptors.*

Functionally, receptors are *transducers,* mechanisms that change one form of energy into another. A familiar transducer in the communications world is the microphone, which transforms sound waves into electrical energy. In the organism, photic, mechanical, chemical, or thermal energy is transduced by the various receptors into the bioelectrical energy that initiates neuron activity in the nervous system. It should be remembered that, while energy input to the receptors varies, all output from them to the nervous system, irrespective of the nature of the original energy source, is electrochemical and remains so within the entire nervous system. How these electrochemical impulses come to be experienced as light, sound, heat, touch, and taste is a primary target of sensory process research.

Sensory structures

Before this problem can be dealt with, it is necessary to know something about the sensory structures themselves. In higher animals, individual receptor cells are often organized into special organs—the major five being skin, nose, tongue, eyes, and ears. All these sensory structures have three components: 1) *accessory structures* which are nonsensory but facilitate energy input to the receptors, e.g., the cornea and lens of an eye, the lobe of an ear; 2) *transducer structures,* or the receptors proper, e.g., the retinal rod and cone cells of an eye and the hair cells of the inner ear; and 3) *conducting structures,* the afferent fibers that are part of, or synapse with, the receptors and conduct impulses to the CNS, e.g., the I (optic) cranial nerve.

When a sense organ responds to a stimulus, a bioelectric potential is developed by the receptor. This potential, which is called the *receptor generator potential,* is similar to the post-synaptic generator potential discussed in Chapter 3 in that it, too, is local and graded—that is, its amplitude is a function of the intensity of the applied stimulus. The receptor generator potential also must exceed a threshold value before an action potential will be transmitted through the nervous system. It is important to emphasize at this point that in sensory systems, as in any other neural system, there is a relatively constant, spontaneous level of electrical activity which is not ordinarily experienced by the organism. Thus, "exceeding the threshold" in a sensory system involves not only nerve discharge, but also overcoming the existing level of electrical activity. Barlow (1956) describes this situation in terms of signal-noise ratios, as in communication circuits.

SENSORY CODING

Both the amount of bioelectric energy going through the nervous system and the changes in the patterns of the energy levels are essential to code the incoming signals in such a way that they can be properly translated by the nervous system and then converted into perceptions. Moreover, since the magnitude of the stimulation is coded as an analogue of the magnitude of the potential in the nervous system, the type of transduction involved is referred to as analog coding. In conformity with the all or none law, the threshold values in the conducting neurons convert the analog code into a digital code.

Sensory coding has long been a fascinating problem for physiological psychologists. Even though all sensory input reduces to a bioelectric potential, an organism is capable of differentiating (perceiving) various forms of experience as light, heat, sound, or whatever and of discriminating among different qualities and quantities of these sensations, such as brightness, intensity, loudness, color, pitch and smoothness. How are these experiential qualities and quantities derived from essentially identical electrical impulses? How does the nervous system distinguish between and direct the appropriate response to a Swiss steak, a Beethoven sonata, or a bikinied playgirl on the beach? Such questions have been the basis of a good deal of research.

Qualitative differentiation

An attempt to answer the question of how nerves produce qualitative differentiations was made as early as 1826 by Johannes Müller (Figure 5-1). Müller found that, while all sensory nerves appeared to work alike, they are actually different because of their sensory connections. Their power or quality lies in what they are, rather than in what is used to excite them. In short, one's sensory reaction depends on *which* nerve is stimulated, rather than on *how* it is stimulated, each sensory nerve being "awakened" to a given response. Müller called this finding the *doctrine of specific nerve energies*, and it has stood the test of time. Stevens recently described the notion quite well as follows:

In the year 1800 Volta assembled a large battery of his newly invented cells and connected the total array to a pair of metal rods inserted in his ears. When he closed the switch he felt a jolt in the head, followed by a noise like the boiling of thick soup. Goaded by a similar curiosity some years later, E. H. Weber persuaded his brother to submit to electrodes in the ears. Brother Weber said he heard nothing, but he saw a light that seemed to pass right across his head. Since those heroic days, many experimenters have confirmed the specificity of the sensory system: however we excite them, they do their separate things. Sensory quality, depends, it seems, on which nerve is actuated and where in the brain it leads (1970, p. 1043).

In the middle of the nineteenth century, von Helmholtz (Figure 5-1), who was a student of Müller, extended the doctrine of specific nerve energies to include intrasensory qualities. He postulated the existence in the nervous system of specific receptors for such things as specific colors, tones, tastes, and odors. Indeed, he suggested the remarkable idea that the diversity of human sensation can be traced to just a few basic receptors in each sense modality. Many such correlations have since been experimentally established and the development of the sensory process explicated. Some are reviewed here.

Vision   To analyze the physiological aspects of seeing, researchers have attempted to sequentially trace the impulse initiated by light striking the *retina*—a complex structure composed of several cell layers, which lines the interior surface of the eyeball (Figure 5-2)—through the brain. Retinal cells vary from the photoreceptors proper, called *rods* and *cones*, to *ganglion cells,* the fibers of which become organized as the I (optic) cranial nerve. It should be noted that the sensitive rods and cones in the eyes of most organisms are at the back of the retina, so that incoming light must pass through all the other layers before reaching them.[1] The outermost retinal layer is composed of ganglion cells.

A single ganglion cell receives input, via the other cell layers,

1. Retinal reversibility, which is characteristic of all but a few lower species of animals, seems to be an artifact of the manner in which the retina develops directly from the brain.

A   B

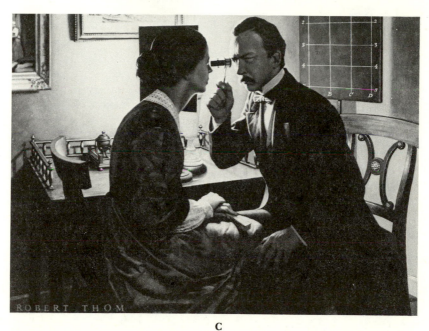

ROBERT THOM

C

Figure 5-1. **A,** German physiologist, Johannes Müller (1801–58) formulated the doctrine of specific nerve energies and coined the phrase *nemo psychologus nisi physiologus* (no one can be a psychologist unless he is a physiologist). (The New York Academy of Medicine Library.) **B,** Ernst Weber (1795–1878), German physiologist and discoverer of the psychophysical principle now known as Weber's Law. (The New York Academy of Medicine Library.) **C,** Robert Thom's painting of Hermann von Helmholtz (1821–94), German physiologist and pioneer researcher and theorist in sensory processes. (Courtesy Parke, Davis & Co., © 1961.)

from several rods and cones lying immediately adjacent to each other. They delineate a discrete area of the retinal surface, approximately circular in shape, called a *receptive field*. Kuffler (1953) has shown that receptive fields are, in fact, organized concentrically in a center-surround mode. In some, the central area of the field produces increased ganglion cell activity when stimulated by light; while the outer ring, when stimulated, inhibits activity. Other receptive fields function in the opposite manner, having "off" centers and "on" surrounds. The result

Figure 5-2.   Drawing representing the various layers of cells in the retina. Notice the relation between the path of light and the position of the rods and cones.

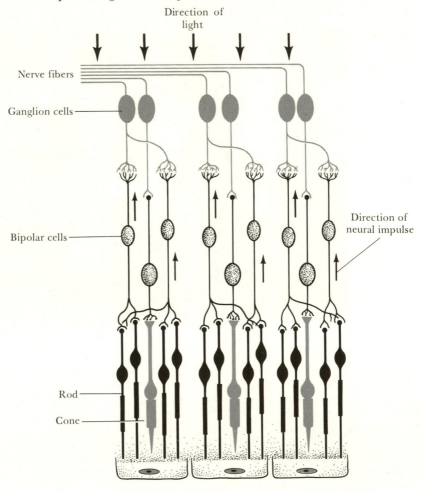

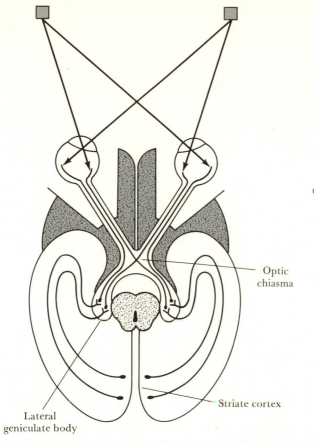

Figure 5-3. Schematic representation of the neural pathway involved in vision.

is an adversary relationship in which variations in light, such as might be caused by a dark edge on a light field, allow the retina to respond to the edge.

The bioelectrical impulses generated in the retina are conducted by the I (optic) cranial nerve to a site which is known as the *lateral geniculate body* (Figure 5-3). Here, complex synaptic connections result in the retinal impulse being subjected to various excitatory and inhibitory influences and to intensify changes which bring about further coding.

The impulses are then conducted to the visual cortex in the striate area of the occipital lobe, where still further and even more complex coding occurs. Within the last few years, Hubel and Wiesel (1959, 1962, 1965) have begun to decipher the electrical code in the visual cortex. Using cats as subjects, they implanted microelectrodes into individual neurons in the visual cortex. Next they placed the animals before a screen onto which various pictures and geometric designs were projected. The electrical activity of the individual cortical neurons was then measured in conjunction with specific projected images.

They found that there were functionally distinct types of cortical cells, hierarchically organized. The geniculate impulses first reach *simple cells,* which respond to specifically oriented slits, bars, contours, and edges in their own receptive fields (Figure 5-4). The *complex cells* receive input from a number of simple cells which further process the impulse before it reaches the *hypercomplex cells,* where still further refinements are added. The cells also appear to be structurally organized, beginning with the simple cells near the surface and progressing sequentially down into the cortex, with the hypercomplex cells being deepest. Each cell group seems to add more generality so that the primary visual pattern which reaches the cortex becomes modified by other sensory and memory information, presumably to give rise to the percept. What occurs beyond the hypercomplex cells is not yet known.

In addition to shape and form, color vision has also received research attention in regard to its neurophysiological correlates. Of the numerous color vision theories that have been proposed over the years, the one known as the *Young-Helmholtz theory*[2] has the most compatibility with research findings.

The Young-Helmholtz theory proposes that there are three kinds of color receptors in the eye; one kind for each of the primary colors red, green and blue. Other color perceptions arise from neural mixtures of the inputs from these three basic receptors.

Although the theory is more than a century old, experimentation to determine if there are indeed three color receptors in the eye was not possible until the 1950s, when relevant research techniques became available. It was long known that stimulation of the rods alone only gives rise to monochromatic vision;

2. The theory was first proposed by Thomas Young in 1807 and expanded by von Helmholtz in later years.

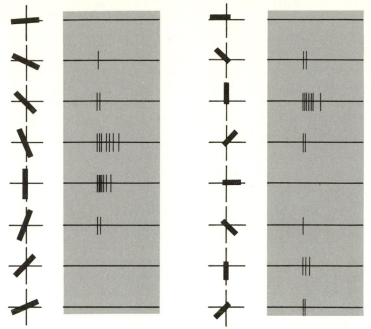

Figure 5-4. Drawing of Hubel and Wiesel's records from single simple visual cortex cells. The line on the left was presented to the cat in various orientations. The cell, as shown by the recorded spikes, would only discharge at a specific orientation.

i.e., the cones are necessary for color vision. It was also long known that the rods contain a pigment called *rhodopsin*, or *visual purple*, which absorbs light and becomes bleached by it, and that the bleaching somehow electrochemically creates the receptor generator potential leading to vision.

Thus, it seemed logical that the three kinds of color receptors postulated by the Young-Helmholtz theory may, in fact, be three types of photosensitive cone pigments. Two recently available techniques have established that this is so.

Retinal densitometry involves measuring a beam of light reflected from the eyeball surface behind the retina. The amount of light absorbed during its double passage through the retina will vary as a function of the concentration of photosensitive pigments in the receptors being illuminated. Rushton (1958) used the method on single-colorblind subjects (such as red-blind). He selectively illuminated the fovea of their eyes, an area that contains only cones, with lights of different colors and found they lack pigments that normal sighted people have.

MacNichol (1964) utilized a technique called microspectrophotometry to confirm and extend Rushton's findings. The method allows measurement of light passing through a single cone. Such measurements indicate that there are definitely three cone pigments, with peak sensitivities of 445 mμ (blue), 540 mμ (green), and 557 mμ (yellow-red).[3] The Young-Helmholtz theory thereby enjoys physiological verification.

Nonetheless, these discoveries do not resolve such questions as how the presence of color specific pigments in the cones relates to color specific neurons known to exist in the lateral geniculate body and cortex (DeValois, 1965). That is, the neural parameters of color vision have not yet been traced in the brain, but the foregoing studies do represent enormous progress in delineating one part of the sensory processes underlying the perception of color.

Audition   The ear is capable of discriminating many aspects of sound, including pitch, intensity, direction, and tonal pattern. But, as with vision, the diversity of sensation has its origin in rather simple, basic, mechanical impulses. Also like vision, the elucidation of the neurophysiological correlates of hearing has been the subject of many experimental investigations over the years.

The ear consists of three parts: the external, middle, and inner ears (Figure 5-5). The external ear, or *pinna,* collects the sound waves (which are essentially differential air pressures) and funnels them through the *external auditory canal* where they cause the *tympanic membrane* (or ear drum) to vibrate. A series of articulated bones conducts the vibration to the middle ear.

The middle ear contains a coiled, tubular, fluid-filled structure, the *cochlea*, which is divided into three compartments separated by membranes (Figure 5-6). One of the membranes, the *basilar membrane*, supports the *Organ of Corti*, which contains the *hair cells*, the basic receptor of hearing. When the sound waves (now translated into minute oscillations, or waves, of fluid) pass the membrane, the cells are stretched and com-

3. Wavelength, measured in millimicrons (mμ) of length, is the physical aspect of light that corresponds to the experiencing of color by organisms.

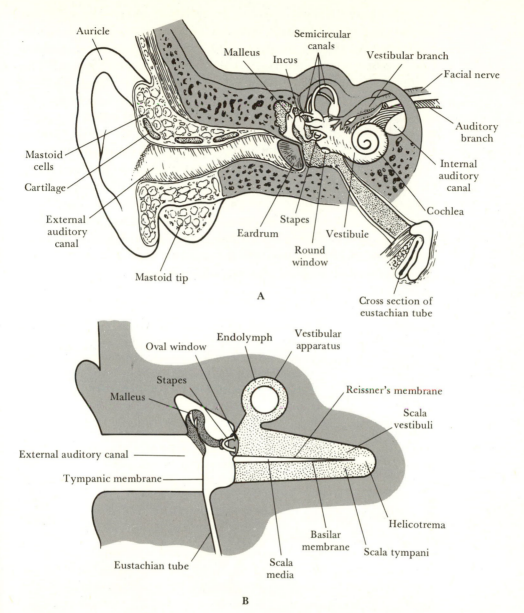

Figure 5-5. Anatomical representation **A,** and schematic diagram **B,** of the human ear showing its major parts.

pressed against the membrane. The distortion causes a receptor generator potential which may, in turn, elicit an impulse in the VIII (auditory) cranial nerve. The resultant impulse is carried into the brain by a highly complex neural route (Figure 5-7).

George Von Békésy (1960), who won the 1961 Nobel Prize for his effort, demonstrated how the hair cells act to code the sensation of pitch. Using microelectrode techniques, he measured the response of the basilar membrane to sounds of various frequencies. He found that, up to 60 cps,[4] the entire membrane vibrated at the frequency that corresponded to the frequency of the sound. Above 60 cps, however, the basilar membrane vibrates unequally over its entire surface because of the difference in thickness. The maximum deflection for each region depends on the frequency of the sound stimulus. The basilar membrane is, thus, a frequency analyzer. Similar research has been done to show how the intensity of sound waves is coded

4. Cps stands for cycles per second, the measure of the number of sound waves as a function of time.

Figure 5-6.   Cross section representation of the cochlea showing the major membranes and ancillary structures.

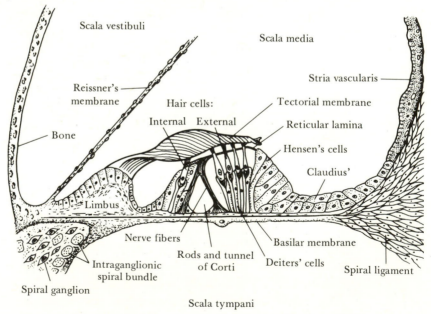

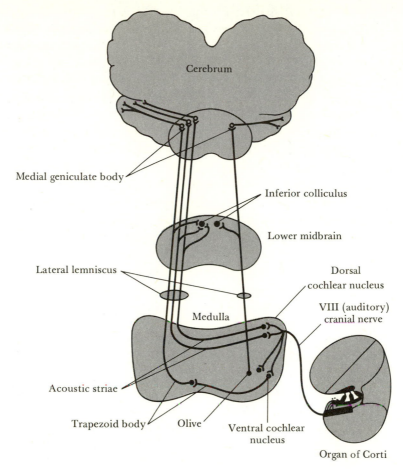

Figure 5-7. Schematic representation of the neural pathways involved in hearing.

at the basilar membrane. How the ability to discriminate pitch or loudness is subsequently reflected in the cerebral cortex has not yet been established.

Olfaction As noted earlier, smell plays an important role in the behavior of organisms, more so in lower animals than in man. Nonetheless, the ability to detect and identify odors is an important sense in human beings, as anyone who sits down to the aroma of a charcoal broiled steak can testify.

The smell receptors are located in the nasal cavity and respond to the molecules given off by odor-producing substances.

The fibers from the olfactory receptor cells lead to the olfactory bulb in the brain. Odor molecules cling to the receptor cell surface, producing depolarization and a consequent receptor generator potential. Electrode studies of the olfactory bulb of the frog show that this organ can neurally differentiate several types of odor (O'Connell and Mozell, 1969).

How are odors coded in the CNS? To answer this question, Amoore (1962) postulated the existence of seven different types of basic odor—camphoraceous (moth balls), floral (roses), putrid (rotten eggs), pungent (vinegar), musky, pepperminty, and ethereal (dry cleaning fluid). These seven odors form the basis from which the variety of odors in the world are neurally created. Amoore suggested that the size and shape of the molecule involved in each odor is congruent with the configuration of molecules in the olfactory receptors.[5] Five of the seven odors seem to fit the theory, while two of the odors (pungent and putrid) seem more dependent on the electric charge of the molecule. Nonetheless, compound odors are thought to be the result of combinations of the primaries. In fact, the theory has been used to predict the odor of a new substance on the basis of the size and shape of the molecules involved.

Taste The sense of taste has been under considerable study by Carl Pfaffmann (1959) and his colleagues. Pfaffmann, in fact, is known as "the father of taste neurophysiology," because he has been able to measure specific neuron responses to taste stimuli. But little is well defined concerning the actual mechanism by which chemical contacts result in subjective taste reactions.

Classically, taste has been considered a function of the tongue and its buds and is thought to be manifested in four modalities: salt, sweet, bitter, and sour. Physiological maps of tongues have been based on the view that the tip of the tongue contains receptors that are sensitive to salt, the sides to sour, and the middle area to sweet; while bitterness is the province of the receptors in the posterior third of the tongue. Henkin, Graziadei, and Bradley (1969) have challenged this concept by experiments which show that the role of other oral structures—the

5. This is similar to the lock-and-key arrangement postulated for synaptic receptor sites (Chapter 3).

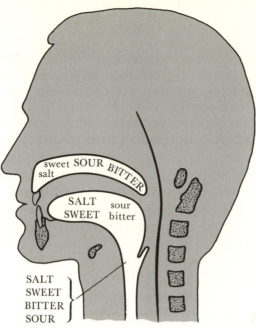

Figure 5-8. A schematic representation of taste localization on the tongue, palate and pharynx of normal man. Capital letters indicate more sensitive taste acuity, small letters less sensitive taste acuity (Redrawn and modified from Henkin, Graziadei, and Bradley, 1969).

palate, pharynx, and larynx—are as important as the tongue in localizing taste qualities. The relationships of these parts in the taste sensation are shown in Figure 5-8. Note that, contrary to the earlier view, the palate is the most sensitive anatomical area for the tastes of sour and bitter.

Experiments involving microelectrode recordings of the activity of single taste neurons in the chorda tympani[6] of the rat demonstrate that the taste pathways to the brain are more complex than believed earlier. Erickson (1963) recorded the electrical activity of gustatory neurons to verify whether stimuli that have an identical effect on these neurons send the same message to the brain. If they do, they should be indistinguishable. He found that neuron firings from related chemicals were similar and predicted that the animal would not be able to find

6. This is a branch of the VII (facial) cranial nerve, which innervates the tongue.

much difference in taste. This proved to be so. Subsequently, Frank and Pfaffmann (1969) observed that such neurons are responsive to stimuli of different quality, though the number of fibers responsive to given parts of stimuli (say bitter and sweet) could be predicted if the four basic modalities are randomly distributed among the nerve fibers.

Cutaneous senses   Touch (pressure), temperature, and pain sensations, along with experiences involving various combinations thereof (such as tickles, itches, and smoothness), arise from stimulation of receptors in the skin (Figure 5-9). The neural fibers from these receptors are organized as the dorsal roots of the spinal nerves, each of which innervates an area of skin surface called a dermatome (recall Figure 4-4). The fibers from similar receptors in the face region are carried by the V (trigeminal) cranial nerve. By way of any of several complex routes, impulses generated in skin receptors eventually project on the somatic areas of the cortex—S1 in the postcentral gyrus, S2 in the Sylvian fissure.

Because the skin receptors and the related fiber pathways are so intimately interwoven, their differentiation and elucidation have required unusually heroic experimental methods. The British physiologist Henry Head (1920)[7], in conjunction with a surgeon and psychologist, had two nerves in his forearm severed so he could determine the loss and recovery of cutaneous sensation. In 1916, Boring replicated Head's experiment, and Lanier (1934) did similar studies by injecting forearm nerve tracts with 95 percent alcohol. Bazett and his colleagues (1932) used dulled fishhooks to suspend preputial skin so they could determine the depth of thermal receptors therein!

By and large, these efforts were fruitful in clarifying the neural nature of touch and thermal sensations. The physiological aspects of pain, however, remained rather ill-defined until more recent times. This is because, relative to other sensations, pain experiences are more susceptible to a host of situational and perceptual feedback influences. As Murphree expressed it:

In the elementary case of a hammer striking a thumb, variables include the mass and velocity of the hammer, whether the blow is glancing or direct, how free the thumb

7. He was also involved in a theory of emotional behavior (Chapter 9).

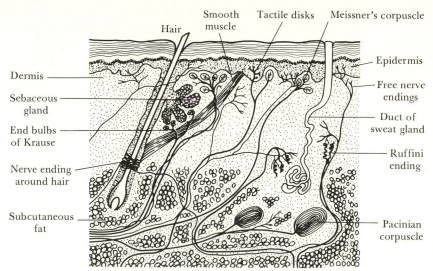

Figure 5-9. Anatomical depiction of a section of human skin showing the major receptors.

is to move with the blow, and so on. Other imponderables include whether the blow was self-inflicted, whether it was deliberate or not, whether it was consciously or accidentally done (1966, p. 15).

For example, Melzack (1961) points out that regarding child-birth as a painful experience seems largely a cultural artifact. He describes cultures in which pregnant women continue working until the instant of birth, show virtually no distress during birth, and return to work almost immediately afterwards. Yet, while the mothers are bearing the children, the fathers go to bed and moan and groan in pain. Afterwards, they stay in bed with the baby for several days to recover from the ordeal.

It would appear, then, that the impulses generated by pain receptors are highly subject to modification in the CNS. Melzack and his colleagues (Casey, 1973; Melzack and Wall, 1965) have proposed a theory, the *gate hypothesis,* which attempts to neurally define how pain is perceived. They point out that there is a continuous flow of impulses from skin receptors to the spinal cord. Some of the fibers carrying these impulses (those having a larger diameter) continue directly to appropriate sensory brain areas without synapsing. Others (those having a smaller diameter), synapse in the spinal cord with what are called *transmission* or *T neurons.* T neuron fibers project to brain areas which are responsible for pain phenomena, and it is in conjunction with them that gating occurs. If the gate is open, T cells will be activated and pain will be experienced; if the gate is closed, no pain will be experienced.

Two circumstances control the gate. First, as implied above, two sizes of fibers carry cutaneous receptor impulses. If more small fibers are activated, and that usually occurs only after intense stimulation, the gate is open; when the reverse holds, the gate is closed. Second, impulses conducted through efferent pathways from the brain can open or close the gate. These fibers, originating in the reticular formation and projecting to the spinal cord, are activated by attitudes, cognitions, perceptions, motivations, emotions, et cetera. Pain, then, perhaps even more so than is the case with other sensory processes, results from an interaction of peripheral and central influences. It is not a mere passive consequence of receptor activation.

Internal senses   Besides having sensory awareness of the external environment, organisms also sensorily monitor several aspects of their internal state. These sensations are often referred to as "feelings." The modalities involved are as follows:

1. *Kinesthesis and propioception* refer to the sense of body motion or awareness of the spatial location of body parts which arise from sensations originating in muscles, tendons, and joints. The receptors, pathways, and functioning of the kinesthetic senses are fully discussed in Chapters 6 and 7.

2. *Labyrinthine* senses are concerned with the maintenance of balance and equilibrium, keeping organisms in a proper posture relative to gravity and surface. The receptors for the labyrinthine senses are located in nonauditory portions of the cochlear canals of the inner ear. There are two kinds, *semicircular canals* and *vestibular sacs* (Figure 5-10).

There are three semicircular canals, one for each major plane of the body. They contain a fluid called *endolymph,* which shifts position or circulates in response to tilting, rotation, or

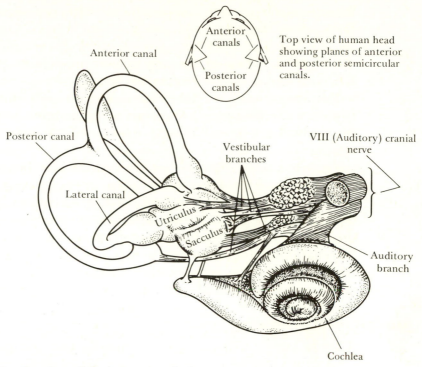

Figure 5-10. Drawing of the human vestibular apparatus.

other motions. The movements of the endolymph activate hair cells located in the enlarged ending of each canal called the *ampulla,* giving rise to a receptor generator potential.

The vestibular sacs also contain hair cells which have crystals of calcium carbonate suspended above them. These appear to load the hair cells so they can respond to gravitational pull; i.e., the inertia of the crystals following motion of the body bends the hair cells to effect a receptor generator potential.

The fibers from the hair cells in both structures pass into the brain as the vestibular component of the VIII (auditory) cranial nerve. Although there is some projection to the cortex (Andersson and Gernandt, 1954), most vestibular input is to the vestibular nuclei in the medulla, where they function in the reflexive postural adjustments discussed in Chapter 7.

3. *Organic* senses are those involved in awareness of tissue deficits and experienced in such feelings as hunger and thirst. These are discussed in Chapter 8 since they are an important aspect of motivation.

This brief review of the major sense modalities verifies, as stated earlier, that the doctrine of specific nerve energies has indeed stood the test of time. One test of the applicability of any hypothesis is the amount of research it generates—as was seen, the doctrine of specific nerve energies fully passes in that respect.

Yet, while sensory modalities are discrete physiologically and in the production of sensations, their integrative nature must not be forgotten. Even the most basic of behaviors involves a dynamic interaction of several senses. A simple walk across the room, for instance, is not just a function of kinesthetic and labyrinthine sensitivity; vision and cutaneous sensing are every bit as important to the successful accomplishment of the act.

Quantitative differentiation

The doctrine of specific nerve energies and the subsequent correlation with receptor areas, while giving some insight into qualitative manifestations, still did not totally answer the question of the quantitative aspect of sensation. How can an organism differentiate between such different quantities of stimulation as twice as loud, half as bright, or not salty enough?

Fechner's law An answer started to develop in 1850 when Gustav Fechner became interested in experimental sensory physiology, especially vision, during which study he became nearly blind from looking at the sun through colored filters. In addition, he suffered a "nervous breakdown," which Watson (1968) characterizes as a "neurotic depression with pronounced hypochondriacal features." He then made a "miraculous" recovery and, in the process, began to realize there is both a body and a state of mind. Thus, Fechner was converted from a mechanistic monist to an anti-mechanistic dualist.[8] After this

8. See Chapter 16 for a distinction between dualism and monism.

conversion, Fechner attempted to find a quantitative unity (or mathematical relationship) between body and mind. His conclusions were first presented in *Zend-Avesta: On the Things of Heaven and the Hereafter* (1851), and then in textbook form, *Elements of Psychophysics* (1860).

Fechner's work resulted from his interest in some observations reported by his colleague, the physiologist Ernst Weber (the same individual mentioned by Stevens). As an experimentalist, Weber had devoted considerable effort to the study of discrimination, specifically, the ability of an observer to detect changes in the intensity of stimulation. He was concerned in particular with the so-called muscle sense, the ability to discriminate between two different weights when they are successively or simultaneously lifted. He attempted to measure the smallest difference between the two weights that could be discriminated, a value referred to as the *just noticeable difference* (j.n.d.). On the basis of many trials with numerous subjects and a variety of pairs of weights, he found that the just noticeable difference in one weight relative to the other maintained a constant ratio, independent of the actual values of the weights. Stated differently, the j.n.d. represented a constant fraction of the level of stimulation to which it was being compared.

As Fechner described it (1860), the significance of Weber's data came to him just before he got up on the morning of October 22, 1850. As he lay in bed, he realized that Weber had, in effect, provided a lawful relation between body and mind, which can be quantitatively expressed in terms of proportional changes between the action of the body and the resultant experience. Fechner thereupon launched a ten year research program to replicate and extend Weber's studies. From his data, Fechner expressed the ratio as a general equation applicable to any sense modality. The statement is known as *Weber's law*.[9]

Fechner mathematically modified Weber's Law to show that perception changes arithmetically as the physical stimulus changes geometrically. Today, this is known as *Fechner's law*.[10] Fechner's law marks a significant event in the history of psy-

9. Mathematically stated, $K = \Delta R/R$. K is the constant value, ΔR is the change required to effect a j.n.d., and R is the magnitude of the existing stimulus.

10. Mathematically stated, $S = K \log I$. The perceived intensity of a stimulus, S, changes as the logarithm of the physical intensity of the stimulus, I.

chology, the first major attempt to quantify mind-body relationships.

Stevens' power law   As an explanation of the quantitative aspect of sensory experience, Fechner's law stood as dogma for decades. While several theorists occasionally questioned it, not until the 1960s, when the American psychologist S. S. Stevens presented his paper "To Honor Fechner and Repeal His Law," was serious attention paid to its possible limitations. Stevens cited a number of reasons why Fechner's law had remained unchallenged for so long and based his criticisms of it on a number of points. To him, the main difficulty was the assumption that relative j.n.d.'s were psychologically equal throughout their entire range. Numerous findings (in Fechner's own time and since), using more refined experimental methods, also suggested that perceived stimulus magnitude increases or decreases geometrically rather than arithmetically. In effect, it seems that the perceived ratio, not the perceived difference, is what remains constant.[11] In other words, the perceived change in intensity (the psychological magnitude) is proportional to changes in the intensity of the physical stimulus (stimulus magnitude) raised to a certain power. Today the statement is called *Stevens' power law*. Where Fechner's law produces a different ratio for each sensory modality (such as 1/64 for brightness, 1/10 for loudness, 1/50 for weight), Stevens' law has a different exponent for each modality (such as 0.33 for brightness, 0.67 for loudness, 1.45 for weight).

Experiments seeking physiological correlates to psychophysical laws   The controversy over which mathematical law correctly describes the relation between physical stimulus and psychical experience is of concern to sensory physiology. The problem has been to determine whether the same kind of relation as exists between physical stimulus and experience holds with stimulus and neural response. In 1931, Matthews performed a very simple experiment. He systematically added weights to an isolated frog muscle and recorded the changing rate of impulse

11. Plotting the data from such experiments results in an S-shaped curve, rather than the linear curve that a logarithmic function would produce. Stevens suggested that a curve of this type is better fit by a power function, $S = K I^n$.

generation in a single nerve fiber conducting from a stretch receptor (see Chapter 7 for a description of stretch receptor mechanisms). The results, graphically represented in Figure 5-11, show that the relation is clearly linear, and the curve is best fitted by a log function. In 1932, Hartline and Graham performed a somewhat similar experiment using single optic nerve fibers and light flashes to the eye of the horseshoe crab, *Limulus*. As Figure 5-12 shows, they also obtained a linear curve.

In 1963, Mountcastle and his colleagues carried this work further by employing chronically implanted electrodes to record from single thalamic neurons in the brains of monkeys. The neurons were innervated from stretch receptors stimulated by bending the monkey's knee at various angles. Tension on the stretch receptors was increased or decreased by simply rotating the knee joint.

As with other studies, such as that of Matthews (1931), the greater the stretch, the greater the tension on the receptors, and the higher the number of impulses. The Mountcastle study was unlike the earlier ones, however, in that: 1) the recordings were made from third-order rather than first-order neurons, and 2) they were from a live intact animal rather than from an isolated nerve-muscle preparation. The result, as seen in Figure 5-13, is a curve best fitted by a power function.

Stevens (1971) recently reviewed these and related studies. He concluded that recording a single, peripherally generated signal (such as the receptor generator potential) may result in a logarithmic function; but the final input to the CNS (from which the perception is presumably formed) is the result of a comparison of several signals, and combined logarithmic functions can result in a power function. Besides, Stevens demonstrated that the data from the log function studies can also be readily accommodated by a power function.

Thus, much of the experimental data are compatible with Stevens' hypothesis. However, Stevens (1971, 1972) quite correctly indicates that his contention must remain hypothetical until more definitive parametric data are provided. Most particularly, much more needs to be known regarding synaptic modification of neuronal potentials and central sensory mechanisms, since (as was seen earlier) the neuron impulse is changed in its path through the nervous system.

It should not be overlooked that, in all the experiments described and in many others like them, intensity coding (altering intensity of stimulus) is related to the frequency of impulse conduction, not to the magnitude of the impulse. The primary sensory neuron, when discharged, obeys the all or none law; but the frequency of its discharge varies as a function of the magnitude of physical stimulation. Therefore, there is no change in the size of the neural impulse relative to sensation.

Moreover, as was mentioned earlier, a sensory experience does not arise from a single input, but from a spatial/temporal combination of inputs which can involve several modalities providing simultaneous input and/or feedback from the CNS itself (there are descending systems which modify ascending sensory signals; see Livingston, 1959). It is a long way from a flash of light into a crab eye to the reaction of a living organism to its milieu.

In summary, there are numerous factors to consider in understanding the process of sensation. Increasing evidence, such

Figure 5-11.   Graph of Matthews' (1931) data from two of his experiments (solid and broken line). Both show a clear linear relation between increases in stimulus magnitude and neural activity measured at the receptor level (Redrawn and modified from Matthews, 1931).

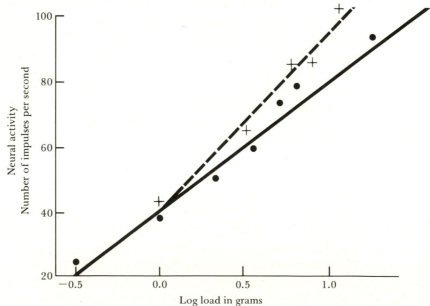

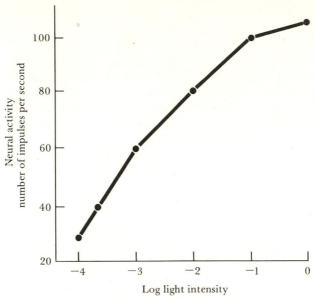

Figure 5-12. Graph showing the relationship between intensity of illumination and neural activity at the receptor level. (Redrawn and modified from Hartline and Graham, 1932).

as presented in this chapter, indicates that there is indeed a psychoneural unity, or meeting of mind and body. Nonetheless, the precise quantification of the mechanisms of sensation suggested by this research should not tempt one into "man as machine" conclusions. While the neural formation of sensations may be rigidly lawful, the step from sensation to perception is nebulous. As was explained several times earlier, in the formation of percepts sensory data are modified by many influences, such as cognition, memories, motivations, and emotions, which vary from instant to instant. As well, the sensation-perception transformation is, to an extent, a function of each individual's unique experience. Any conception of sensory processes, whether it be a doctrine of specific nerve energies or a power law, must therefore accommodate both generality and individuality. As Luce has aptly indicated:

. . . man—and any other organism—is, among other things, a measuring device, in function not unlike a spring balance or a voltmeter, which is capable of transforming many kinds of physical attributes into a common measure in the central nervous system.

107

But:

> . . . as compared with man made, special-purpose devices, higher organisms are both complex and flexible measuring devices; their overall behavior does not clearly suggest the nature of the recoding signals; some responses depend on peculiar nonlinear processing of the sensory information; and each individual within a species is calibrated somewhat differently (1972, p. 96).

HOW MANY SENSES?

Most people would say there are five senses and, if one is "tuned into" parapsychology, perhaps a sixth sense, "psi." Actually, the number of distinct receptors or senses one can enumerate depends on how they are classified. In 1906 the famous neurophysiologist Charles Sherrington (Chapter 7) proposed a classification scheme that is still widely employed. He organized the sensations with regard to the source of physical stimulation and the location of the receptor in the organism. From that scheme, four categories emerged. 1. *Teleceptors* receive input from sources spatially distant to them; these are the organs of vision, hearing, and olfaction. 2. *Exteroceptors* receive input from sources in direct contact with the surface of the organism; these are the organs of gustation and the skin senses—pressure, pain, warmth, or cold. 3. *Interoceptors* receive input from "inside" the organism; these are the organs of the visceral senses (hunger, thirst, nausea, pain). 4. *Propioceptors* receive input from muscles, tendons, joints (kinesthetic organs), and balance organs (vestibular organs); propioceptors are involved in senses such as balance, motion, and spatial orientation.

Another commonly employed designation emphasizes the energy source to which the receptor is most specific. From this system, *chemoreceptors*, *photoreceptors*, *thermoreceptors*, and *mechanoreceptors* are differentiated. In this scheme, Sherrington reserved the term *nociceptors* for pain, because these receptors seemed to directly respond to high intensities from any energy source. As was explained earlier, more contemporary theories of pain render Sherrington's contention simplistic by emphasizing the neurological and perceptual complexity involved in

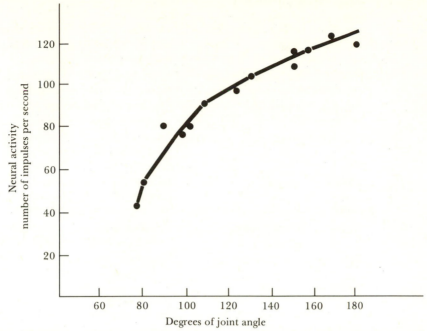

Figure 5-13. Graph showing the relationship between joint articulation in monkeys and neural activity at the thalamic level (Redrawn and modified from Montcastle, Poggio, and Werner, 1963).

pain production (Kast and Collins, 1966; Melzack and Wall, 1965; Murphree, 1966). However, the term nociceptor is still frequently used.

Ruch and his colleagues (1965) offer a classification based on neurological symptoms. They designate: 1. special senses served by the cranial nerves—vision, audition, gustation, olfaction, vestibular; 2. superficial or cutaneous senses—touch-pressure, warmth, cold, pain; 3. deep senses—muscle, tendons, joints (vestibular); and 4. visceral senses—hunger, nausea, pain.

Table 5-1 presents a summary perspective of the various human senses. It can be seen that, by any classificatory scheme, the range of sensing is finite. The exact number of distinct senses, however, depends on how they are classified. But, regardless of exact number, it is apparent that higher organisms have a variety of specifically differentiated receptors that facilitate heterotrophic commerce with the environment and also permit the organism to retain its biological integrity.

Table 5-1.　Major Human Senses

Sense	Energy Source	Organ	Receptor	Neural Substrate
Vision	Radiant (light)	Eye	Rod and cone cells in retina	Optic nerve, visual cortex
Hearing	Mechanical	Ear	Hair cells in organ of corti	Auditory nerve, auditory cortex
Olfaction	Chemical	Nose	Olfactory cells in nasal epithelium	Olfactory nerve, rhinencephalon
Gustation	Chemical	Tongue	Gustatory cells in papillae, mouth, and throat	Trigeminal and glossopharyngeal nerves, somatic cortex
Balance and motion	Mechanical	Ear	Hair cells in semicircular canals	Vestibular fibers of auditory nerve, cerebellum
Spatial	Mechanical	—	Cells in joints, tendons, muscles	Afferent spinal pathways, cerebellum
Pressure	Mechanical	—	Free nerve endings in skin	Afferent spinal pathways, somatic cortex
Temperature	Thermal	—	Free nerve endings in skin (separate for cold and warmth)	Afferent spinal pathways, somatic cortex
Pain	Any which results in tissue damage	—	Free nerve endings	Varies with locus of receptors
Organic (hunger, thirst, nausea, et cetera)	Chemical, mechanical	—	Free nerve endings in organ, hypothalamic receptors	Afferent fibers related to the autonomic nervous system

Although a dominant part of physiological psychology for many years, the study of sensory processes is not exclusive to it. To the contrary, sensory processes are more usually considered a separate psychological discipline in themselves and a significant part of the revitalized area of experimental aesthetics. In both of those instances, considerable emphasis is placed on the physiological mechanisms of each of the specific senses.

SUGGESTED READINGS

Berlyne, D. E. *Aesthetics and Psychobiology*. New York: Appleton-Century-Crofts, 1971. A brilliant discussion of the relation between sensation and experience.

Christman, R. J. *Sensory Experience.* Scranton, Pa.: Intext, 1971. An intermediate level, up-to-date discussion of the major sensory modalities.

Cohen, J. *Vision.* Sensation and Perception, vol. 1. Eyewitness Series in Psychology. Chicago: Rand-McNally, 1969. A well-organized presentation of the psychobiology of seeing.

Geldard, F. A. *The Human Senses.* (2nd ed.) New York: Wiley, 1972. The latest edition of the most definitive reference on sensing; cites nearly 700 references.

Gregory, R. L. *Eye and Brain: The Psychology of Seeing.* (2nd ed.) New York: McGraw-Hill, 1973. Another book by the scientist for the layman; written in the whimsical style characteristic of British science writers.

Mueller, C. G. *Sensory Psychology.* Englewood Cliffs, N.J.: Prentice-Hall, 1965. A brief, concise, simple overview of the major senses.

6 Muscles

The significance of the effector systems was recognized from the very beginnings of psychology, even before it was called such. In 1863, the Russian physiologist Ivan Sechenov (remembered as the person from whom Pavlov drew his inspiration regarding conditioned reflexes) maintained that all external manifestations of brain function could be reduced to muscular movement. More recently, Thompson succinctly pointed out, "Since psychology is the study of behavior, it is really the study of muscle movements" (1967).

Clearly, this is true up to a point. Even though most psychologists would like to think that behavior is more than a muscular phenomenon, the data from many, some would even say all, psychological experiments involves some record of motor activity. Most certainly, an elementary knowledge of muscles is useful in order to understand many behavioral processes. Interestingly, the brain itself was once regarded as analogous to a muscle. Educators quickly supported this notion by including Greek and Latin verb conjugation in the curriculum as exercise to keep the brain fit.[1]

As implied in Chapter 2, animative activities are not possible without systems that can transduce biochemical energy (the energy from food and other outside sources) into me-

1. This point of view is common to faculty psychology.

112

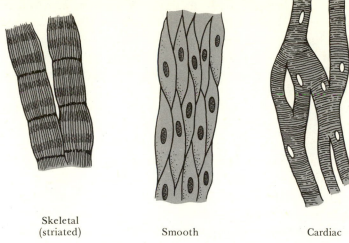

Skeletal
(striated)   Smooth   Cardiac

Figure 6-1.   The three types of muscle cell.

chanical energy (the energy of behavior). This transduction is accomplished by contractile proteins capable of reversible shortening and lengthening when stimulated. With the phylogenetic advent of multicellular organisms, specific cells became specialized for this kind of contraction and expansion. The tissue composed of such cells is called *muscle*. Since contraction is initiated by a nerve impulse, the muscular and nervous systems are intimately associated as the *neuromuscular system,* which can be regarded as the behavioral control system of the body.

Muscle is generally considered to be of three distinct types: *striated* (or *skeletal*), *smooth,* and *cardiac* (Figure 6-1). Striated muscle is innervated by the somatic effector nerves, smooth and cardiac by the autonomic nervous system. It should be pointed out, however, that these distinctions are not always clear. Control of the bladder, for instance, seems to be voluntary but the muscle involved is a smooth muscle. On the other hand, heart rate, once regarded as the involuntary action of cardiac muscle, can be controlled to some extent by the will.

STRIATED MUSCLE

Striated muscles are attached to the skeleton and move the different parts of the body. The most familiar are muscles of the

113

arms and legs. Individual striated muscles are organized from *muscle fibers,* which are not anatomically distinct cells. Each fiber may have several nuclei and bundles, or columns of *fibrils.* Each fibril, in turn, is composed of *filaments* (see Figure 6-3). Individual filaments consist of one of two protein macromolecules, *actin* or *myosin.*

The filaments differ in size. The thicker ones, composed of myosin, are each surrounded by six thinner ones, which are composed of actin. Two such sets are arranged so that when contraction occurs they telescope into each other. The filaments do not shorten, but the muscle as a whole does.

It should be noted that striated muscle is striated (striped) in appearance both longitudinally and transversely. The longitudinal striations are due to the arrangement of the fibrils. The transverse striations, called *bands,* are due to differential coloration and are anatomically designated by letters. All the types of bands are indicated in Figure 6-3.

Muscle fibers contain numerous mitochondria, which are the loci of the metabolism that energizes contraction. The primary energy source is *adenosine triphosphate* (ATP), a high energy containing substance formed from the oxidation of glucose or other carbohydrates. In muscles, ATP is formed from glyco-

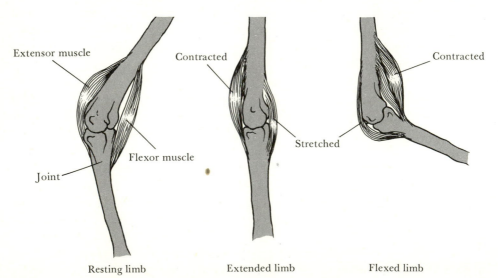

Figure 6-2. Articulation of a joint showing the reciprocal relationship between the paired muscles that control its movement.

gen, a glucose complex. ATP is an intermediate between the direct release of energy, resulting from carbohydrate catabolism, and the release of the energy to perform mechanical work. In a manner of speaking, it holds the energy. Thus, it is often referred to as "the body's storehouse of energy." When ATP is hydrolized to adenosine diphosphate (ADP), the stored energy is released. ADP can be restored to ATP by again entering the carbohydrate oxidation process.

In addition to carbohydrate oxidation, muscle ATP can be formed from glycogen by an anaerobic (nonoxidative) process, but this yields lactic acid as an end product. Lactic acid can be oxidatively metabolized only in the liver, where it is reformulated into glucose and then into muscle glycogen. The recycling process, called the *Cori cycle,* is summarized as follows:

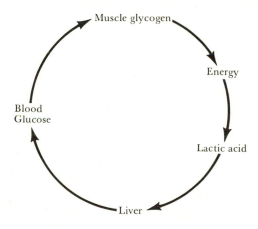

It accounts for the so-called *oxygen debt,* commonly experienced as hard breathing after running. A sprint, for instance, may take only twenty seconds, but the muscles used require hours to complete the chemical changes needed for recovery to normal. Yet the muscles continue to put out the work involved in running. They are said to go into debt for the oxygen and act on the assumption that it will be available. The heavy breathing is an attempt of the body to supply the oxygen more rapidly. Creatine phosphate, a compound present in muscle, can also contribute to ATP formation by a nonoxidative process.

The muscle fiber is to the muscular system what the neuron is to the nervous system. It is the basic structural unit which carries on all the physiological functions essential to the system's ability to carry out organismic functions.

There are two basic types of striated muscles: holding, slow, or red muscles and moving, fast, or white muscles. The former increase tension or tonus without changing in length. The process is called *isometric contraction*. Such muscles contract slowly and can hold the contraction for a long time. They function primarily to maintain posture. The red color that characterizes them is due to high concentrations of myoglobin, an oxygen storing compound similar to the hemoglobin of blood. The moving muscles change in length but not in tonus. This is referred to as *isotonic contraction*. They contract and relax quickly to facilitate movement.

The striated muscles are attached at both ends to their accessory structures, usually bones, by tendons. The effect of a muscle contraction depends on the nature of the attachments. When a muscle is connected across the joint of two bones in such a way that contraction results in straightening or extension of the joint, it is called an *extensor* muscle. Those attached so that contraction induces bending or flexion are called *flexor* muscles. Joint articulation is controlled by both. The muscle that initiates the movement by contracting is referred to as the *agonist*. The muscle that would move the joint in the opposite direction becomes the *antagonist;* it relaxes and is stretched. The stretching eventually causes the antagonist to contract in opposition to the action of the agonist. (The mechanism is described in detail in Chapter 7.) Each skeletal muscle attachment, then, consists of a set of muscles that act in opposite directions. The arrangement is referred to as *reciprocal organization* (as shown in Figure 6-2). It is the basis of muscular co-ordination. Other muscles may facilitate the action of the prime mover, resulting in *synergistic action.*

THE NEUROMUSCULAR JUNCTION

As has already been stated, muscle contraction is initiated by impulses from nerve fibers, specifically, efferent nerves. The efferent fiber originates in the cord or brain and is carried to the muscles as the motor component of a spinal or cranial nerve.

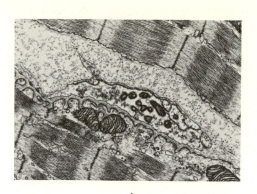
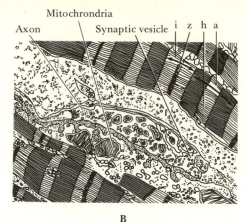

Mitochrondria

Axon   Synaptic vesicle   i z h a

A   B

Figure 6-3. **A,** Electron microphotograph and **B,** drawing of a neuromuscular junction (27,000 X). The elongate profile in the center is the termination of an axon which contains synaptic vesicles and mitochondria. The longitudinal sections (sarcomeres) contain actin and myosin filaments. The letters in the sarcomeres designate the different bands. (Photograph courtesy of Dr. Douglas E. Kelly, Anatomy Department, University of Southern California School of Medicine, and Dr. M. A. Cahill, Department of Biological Structure, University of Miami School of Medicine.)

As it nears the muscle, the efferent axon branches and innervates several muscle fibers. Thus, one motor neuron has control of a number of muscle fibers. A motor neuron and its associated muscle fibers constitute a *motor unit*. The extent of the motor unit varies over a range from three muscle fibers per neuron (in eye muscles) up to 150 muscle fibers per neuron (in large limb muscles), depending on body location. The larger the innervation ratio, the grosser the contraction; the smaller the ratio, the finer or more precise the movement.

This type of innervation of contracting elements, called *α-innervation,* constitutes about 70 percent of skeletal muscle innervation. The rest is called *γ-innervation,* (see Chapter 7). The α-efferent fibers are classified according to degree of myelination and fiber diameter:

Myelinated

Group I	12–20 microns diameter
Group II	6–12 microns diameter
Group III	1–6 microns diameter

Unmyelinated

Group IV

The region where efferent fibers and muscle fibers come together is called the *motor end plate* (Figure 6-3). It is, in effect, a neuromuscular synapse. The efferent neuron action potential, upon reaching the motor end plate, establishes a graded electrical potential called the *end plate potential*. If the end plate potential exceeds the threshold of the muscle fiber membrane, the *muscle action potential* is initiated. It involves a Na^+ and K^+ ion shift similar to that in neurons (Chapter 3), but the recovery of equilibrium is somewhat different.

It is not presently clear how the muscle action potential brings about contraction. It is known that the concentration of potassium (K^+) and magnesium (Mg^{++}) ions must be within a certain range and that there must be an absence of calcium (Ca^{++}) ions. From these facts, some investigators conclude that the muscle action potential causes an inorganic shift similar to the Na^+ and K^+ ion shifts involved in the generation of nerve action potentials. However, several studies have shown that contraction begins too soon to be produced by a substance diffusing inward through the muscle membrane (Granit, 1970; Woodbury, Gordon, and Conrad, 1965). Consequently, others have suggested that the Z-band (Figure 6-3) is actually a transverse membrane which acts as an electrical conductor that temporally facilitates the ion shifts (Woodbury, Gordon, and Conrad, 1965). The result, in any instance, is ATP breakdown and muscle contraction.

The fact that neuromuscular transmission at the end plate is humoral was demonstrated as early as 1858 by Claude Bernard. He employed the South American poison *curare* whose effect is paralysis, total loss of muscle tonus and function. One hind leg of a frog was ligatured (tied off) to impair blood circulation. The primary motor nerve, the sciatic, leading to each leg was exposed so that it could be stimulated electrically. After injection of curare, the frog became paralyzed in every part of its body except the ligatured leg. Electrical stimulation of the nerve in the unpoisoned leg produced some muscular contraction, while the poisoned leg was unresponsive when its sciatic was stimulated. However, the muscle in the curarized leg contracted when directly stimulated, and the nerve conducted impulses when stimulated. Thus, the drug had to be acting at the neuromuscular junction. Discovery of the exact nature of the transmission and identification of the transmitter substance as acetylcholine came with Loewi's studies in the 1920s (Chapter 3). Nonetheless, the basic principle had been clearly elaborated by Bernard some seventy years earlier.

NONSTRIATED MUSCLE

Smooth and cardiac muscle are not organized and integrated like striated muscle; the individual fibers are not aligned with each other. There is reciprocal functional organization and the cells are held together by connective tissue.

Smooth muscle occurs in sheets of cells that line the walls of body cavities, such as the arteries, the tubes of the urinary tract, and the digestive tract. They are usually in circular rings; so the bore, or interior, of the cavity can be changed by contraction or relaxation. Cardiac muscle is exclusive to the walls of the heart, where it accomplishes blood pumping by a similar mechanism of cavity-size changes.

Both smooth and cardiac muscle, as mentioned, are innervated by fibers of the autonomic nervous system, which typically are unmyelinated and synapse with some, but not all, of the cells in the muscle. The contraction is initiated in the innervated cells and transmitted from them to the adjacent noninnervated ones. Enervation of smooth muscle does not lead to paralysis as it does with striated muscle, because smooth muscle can also be activated or deactivated by humoral mechanisms.

The membrane potential is lower in smooth muscle (50 mv) than in striated muscle (90 mv). Smooth muscle has a lower internal K^+ ion concentration and its membrane is more permeable to Na^+ ions. As a result, the membrane potential is unstable. In fact, smooth muscle sometimes depolarizes spontaneously. Membrane stability, expressed as muscle relaxation, is increased when the efficiency of the sodium pump is increased. Epinephrine produces the increased efficiency, simultaneously relaxing smooth muscle and contracting skeletal muscle where it facilitates depolarization (Burn, 1963).

So the physiology of muscle action represents an important aspect of overt behavior. Regardless of how efficiently the nervous system may function, its activity will only result in overt behavioral expression to the extent that muscle action allows it.

Heterotrophic adaptation, then, is not possible in any sense without an efficiently functioning muscular system. To see how this system relates to the deeper complexities of behavior one must first examine the role of the reflex, which is described in the next chapter.

SUGGESTED READING

Granit, R. *The Basis of Motor Control.* New York: Academic Press, 1970. A comprehensive, up-to-date review of neuromuscular system research by a Nobel laureate.

7 Reflexes

REFLEXES

The discussion now turns from structure to function, from neurons and muscles to the reflex, the fundamental functional unit of the nervous system. It is important to examine the reflex because of the help it provides in understanding the operation of the motor system. The motor system cannot be meaningfully considered as merely a nerve-muscle network unit. Muscles do not twitch randomly following any nerve stimulation; their action is integrated with sensory input to achieve purposive functioning of the organism. Thus, the present chapter on reflexes provides a transition between the presentation of basic neurobiology and the actual subject matter of physiological psychology, the functional correlates of structure, which will be discussed in the remaining parts of this book.

ORIGIN OF THE CONCEPT OF REFLEX

The word *reflex* comes directly from the Latin verb meaning to reflect. When applied to behavior, the term reflex usually refers to automatic actions that are reflected in an activity of the nervous system, just as a face is reflected in a mirror. Some common reflexes are the blink of an eye, the knee jerk resulting from a tap, and laughter brought on by tickling.

René Descartes, the famous French philosopher (Chapter 16), who was interested in geometrical optics at the time, first used the expression *esprits refléchis*. He defined it as the automatic, neural-based, soulless action of animals as contrasted to the voluntary, rational, spiritually-based behavior of human beings. Soon after Descartes, a number of investigators, including the English physician Thomas Willis and the Scotch neurologist Robert Whytt, suggested, in opposition to Descartes, that humans also perform some things automatically and that, on the other hand, animals are capable of voluntary, willful, or directed behavior. Willis was fond of citing vomiting as an example of automatic human behavior. Whytt, who lived in the eighteenth century, went on to do experiments comparing automatic body reactions in intact and decapitated animals. He made some important observations on salivary discharge which, he suggested, was also an example of a human automatic reaction. Whytt called these activities "vital motions" and explained that they were so instantaneous there was no time for the exercise of reason. As it turned out, his remarks were precisely in the context of Pavlovian conditioning, although preceding Pavlov by a hundred years.

In 1850 the British physiologist, Marshall Hall, proposed the concept of the *reflex arc* as the anatomical correlate of reflexive behavior. He defined the reflex arc as:

. . . its existence in *Anatomy and Physiology* of a continuous *Diastaltic Nervous Arc* including an *Esodic Nerve,* the *Spinal Center* and *Exodic Nerve* in essential relation and connection with each other (1850, cited by Brazier, 1959, p. 35).[1]

Hall placed the seat of reflex action in the spinal cord. He called it the "spinal brain" and suggested it might be superior to the volitional brain in the head because it never slept while the head brain did. Hall came to this conclusion from his observations of the behavior of a beheaded snake. He noted that the headless snake would writhe when on the ground, transferring motion from one segment to the next; but it would not wiggle when free of the ground. He concluded that the contact with the ground caused the series of reflex actions in the

1. His arcane terminology, according to Brazier, arose from a neological tendency; fortunately most of it did not come into wide usage.

spinal cord which, in turn, led to writing. In short, the spinal cord acted as an initiator of action, a brain.

Hall's concept of the spinal brain ran into enormous controversy, particularly among theologians. In the nineteenth century the soul was considered to be located in the brain. The thought of two brains, with conceivably two souls, was too much for many leading theologians to accept. One argument was that the spinal action was simply reflex action in the cord and was soulless and mechanical. Others suggested that there were indeed two souls, one for the brain and one for the spinal cord.

In any case, whether he meant to or not, Hall's conception of the reflex nature of the spinal cord led to the development of the notion of reflex arcs as isolated structural and functional units. An organism was considered to be essentially a collection of reflexes independent of each other. That is, there was no significant integration or other influences of the CNS.

The Russian reflexology of Sechenov's and Pavlov's successors and the neobehaviorism of American psychologist B. F. Skinner are contemporary reflections of this early concept. Russian reflexology takes its cue from Lenin's philosophy that mental phenomena are reflections of the material and external. This notion, which dominated Russian neurophysiology in the 1930s, satisfied the Marxists because it led to the belief that man's behavior could be understood only through the conditions in which he lived and worked, and thus, behavior could be altered through changes in those conditions.[2] Skinner's philosophy, that man is conditioned by his environment into what he is and thus can be reconditioned through changes in that environment, is a similar approach to the influence of environment in changing human behavior. Both philosophies have their champions and critics.

In 1906 Sir Charles Scott Sherrington (Figure 7-1) challenged the notion that reflexes operate in isolated arcs. Sherrington thought that reflexes must be regarded as integrated actions of the total organism. His best known book, *The Integrative Action of the Nervous System,* describes how an arc acts like

2. For a specific example, see the discussion in Chapter 11 concerning Luria's notion of brain function.

the nervous system as a whole: gathering sensory signals and passing them through the CNS, which responds by activating or inhibiting corresponding muscles. His emphasis was on the fact that various neural signals pursue a path through a number of reflex arcs that work together to create an integrated organismic response.

To grasp this idea, which proved to be one of the most important in contemporary neuroscience, consider one of Sherrington's best known experiments, that of causing a decerebrated dog to scratch an artificial flea bite. Sherrington devised an electric flea—a small pin which could be energized with slight electric current. When he inserted this pin into the dog's skin and sent a current through it, the dog started to scratch.

> . . . in the dog a feeble electric current applied by a minute entomological pin set lightly in the hair-bulb layer of the skin of the shoulder brings the hind paw of that side to the place, and with unsheathed claws the foot performs rhythmic grooming of the hairy coat there. If the point lay forward (toward) the ear, the foot is directed thither, if far back in the loin the foot goes thither, and similarly at any intermediate spot (1947, pp. xi–xii).[3]

Simply, dogs scratch where fleas bite. They have the ability or means to direct their scratch reflex to where it will be most effective. The behavior is integrated with, or purposively directed to achieve, the comfort of the total organism.

Sherrington continued to perform one experiment after another with this artificial flea device and to draw important conclusions about the nervous system. He discovered, for instance, that it took more than one flea bite, or impulse of current, to cause the dog to scratch. In fact, it took a summation of several stimuli which acted on a nerve near the spot where the scratching took place. He also found that the scratch reflex will give way to a higher priority reflex, such as that involved in balancing on one foot when the dog steps on a

---

3. The quote shows that Sherrington, along with many other early physiologists, is at times a difficult writer to read. As a professor of physiology, he had the reputation of also being a difficult lecturer to follow. He would sometimes stop in the middle of a lecture, make some notations on the blackboard, then absent-mindedly resume the lecture on an entirely different subject.

Figure 7-1. Sir Charles Sherrington (1857–1952), British neurophysiologist who elaborated the concept of integrated reflex activity. He was recipient of the 1932 Nobel prize. (The Bettmann Archive.)

tack with the opposite foot. Sherrington went on to study other reflex actions.

In Sherrington's words:

Milk placed in the mouth is swallowed; acid solution is rejected. Let fall, inverted, the reflex cat alights on its feet. The dog shakes its coat dry after immersion in water. A fly settling on the ear is instantly flung off by the ear. Water entering the ear is thrown out by violent shaking of the head . . . (1947, p. xvi).

Sherrington, who is the "father of neurophysiology," allegedly developed his interest in the nervous system from a visit to Cajal (who was working in Spain) in 1885. When Cajal later visited England, he lived with the Sherringtons and it is said he secretly pursued his microscopic investigations for the neuron theory in the Sherringtons' guest bedroom. Sherrington regarded Cajal's neuron theory as important to an under-

125

standing of his own contributions. He devised the term synapse (from the Greek word meaning to clasp) to identify the junction between nerve cells that Cajal had revealed. For his numerous contributions, Sherrington was awarded the Nobel Prize in 1932. He died twenty years later at the age of ninety-four.

To study reflexes, Sherrington primarily used cats and dogs in a preparation called a spinal animal, in which the cord has been surgically separated from the brain. These animals were still alive and could demonstrate behavior directed entirely by spinal mechanisms, without interference by brain activity. To focus on particular reflexes, Sherrington discovered how to eliminate uninvolved peripheral nerves and deal only with the nerves involved in the reflex functions in which he was interested. Sherrington thus devised what has been called a "living wheelwork animal, a live Cartesian puppet." The principles of reflex action that he derived from this work are today considered classic.

TYPES OF REFLEXES AND THEIR CHARACTERISTICS

Functional classification

Reflexes are classified both structurally and functionally. In functional terms, reflexes can be regarded as a series of functional synaptic connections, having three basic features (Butter, 1968).

1. Adaptiveness. Reflexes are not just random sensory-motor actions; they specifically facilitate the interaction of the organism with the environment. For example, *approach reflexes* bring all or part of the organism into contact with such essentials as food, water, and sexual partners. *Withdrawal reflexes* remove all or part of the organism from contact with noxious aspects of its environment.

2. Coordination. Reflexes involve patterns of action; they are not merely isolated muscle contractions. For example, the contraction of flexor muscles also involves the relaxation of extensors and may also involve the cooperation of other muscles known as synergists (Chapter 6).

3. Adequate stimulus. This Sherringtonian term means that each reflex is evoked by only one particular stimulus or class of stimuli. For example, the adequate stimulus for reflexive scratching in dogs is tactile stimulation in the class of flea biting. That type of stimulation will never elicit any other reflex.

Structural classification

In the structural method of classification, reflexes can be grouped according to the number of synaptic junctions. In *monosynaptic* connections, sensory and motor neurons synapse directly with each other as, for example, with the knee jerk reflex. In *polysynaptic* connections, sensory neurons synapse with internuncial neurons which results, for instance, in the flexion reflex—the quick withdrawal of a finger from a hot stove. These interneurons, in turn, may then synapse with motor neurons or other interneurons, which may again do likewise.

With polysynaptic connections it is possible to have a long series of neurons forming a reflex chain. The laterality of the final synapse relative to the sensory neuron results in a distinction between *crossed reflexes,* where the synaptic junction is contralateral (on the opposite side) to the sensory neuron; and *uncrossed reflexes,* which occur when the synaptic junction is ipsilateral (on the same side).

Spinal reflexes

When the levels of the CNS are considered, a distinction is made among three types of spinal reflex. *Segmental reflexes* are those wherein all synaptic junctions occur in the same segment of the cord. *Intersegmental* or *supersegmental reflexes* occur when sensory or internuncial fibers ascend or descend to other segments before synapsing. *Suprasegmental* (or *supraspinal*) *reflexes* involve neurons in the brain.

In view of the complexity of environmental stimuli, there are many more afferent fibers to the CNS than there are efferent fibers from the CNS. A single spinal motor neuron, for instance, may have as many as 1400 different sensory and/or internuncial and/or brain motor neurons (see page 133) synapsing with it. This numerical disparity again emphasizes the point that reflexes do not exist as independent units in the sense that each behavior has its own pathway. Any one motor unit can and does take part in many reflexes. Therefore, many different reflexes must ultimately funnel their final motor impulse through the same primary motor neuron. Sherrington referred to this as the *final common path.*

With such a crowded circuit, the question of path sharing becomes significant. What happens, for instance, if the neural impulses for two reflexes arrive simultaneously at the primary motor neuron synapse? There are two possibilities: inhibition or facilitation.

If the two reflexes are antagonistic, they compete for the final common path. In Sherrington's words, one will generally win a "total victory" over the other, depending on the strength and significance to the integrity of the organism. Other things being equal, the stronger of the two, in terms of the magnitude of the evoking stimulus, will come out ahead.

On the other hand, one reflex can be more important than another to the integrity of the organism even if it is weaker than its competitor. This factor will influence final common path precedence. For example, nociceptive reflexes (those involved in responses to pain, see Chapter 5) are usually dominant over all others. They will gain total victory even when of lesser strength than an antagonistic reflex. If two reflexes are not antagonistic, they may alternately share the final common path. This is called *successive induction;* the reflexes involved in walking are an example.

THE STRETCH REFLEX

To examine the various neuropsychological aspects of reflex action, one need only look at one of the simplest: the *stretch, lengthening*, or *myotatic reflex*. This reflex is segmental and monosynaptic. Working in close conjunction with the stretch reflex is a protective response to excessive extension of a joint, which is called the *clasp-knife reflex.*

Figure 7-2 diagrammatically represents the stretch reflex, showing the neuronal impulse pathway between the stretch receptors in the skeletal muscle fibers and the spinal cord. The

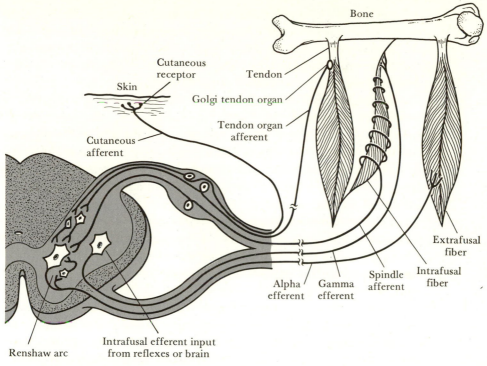

Figure 7-2. Diagram of the stretch reflex.

movement of an impulse along this pathway results in automatic contractions of the muscle when it is stretched.

Structural aspects of the stretch reflex

Before seeing how this happens, several points should be noted about the structural aspects of the neuromuscular system involved in the stretch reflex. First, there are two distinct kinds of fibers in striated muscle. *Extrafusal fibers,* as was discussed in Chapter 6, are the actual contracting elements and are innervated by α-efferents. *Intrafusal fibers* are randomly intermingled among the extrafusals, but are always aligned parallel to them. Intrafusals contract very weakly, contributing nothing to the pull of the muscle. They are innervated by the other type of motor fiber, previously designated as γ-efferents.

Secondly, the diagram in Figure 7-2 indicates that, before emerging from the ventral root, the α-efferents give rise to a collateral fiber that synapses with an interneuron in the ventral horn of the spinal cord. This interneuron in turn synapses with the α-efferents, setting up a loop known as the *Renshaw arc,* after the investigator who first described it (Renshaw, 1940). The interneurons are called *Renshaw cells.*

The importance of the Renshaw cell is that it produces an inhibitory postsynaptic potential (IPSP) on the α-efferent membrane and apparently acts as a damping mechanism to prevent over-contraction of the muscle. The process is referred to as *recurrent inhibition.* All evidence for the existence of the Renshaw cell is indirect since it is based on changes in the action potential of the motor neuron and various synaptic events. There is no question as to the presence of recurrent inhibitory influences on motor activity. However, some investigators (Weight, 1968) feel that such influences can be more parsimoniously accounted for by the looping back of the collateral process itself (Figure 7-3).

The Renshaw arc is significant for another reason. It is the only CNS site where relatively direct evidence has been accumulated regarding the specific neurohumoral transmitter. Eccles (1957, 1964, 1969) referred to *Dale's principle* (Dale, 1934), which states that whatever the neurohumoral transmitter is for a given neuron, it will be the same at all synaptic junctions of that neuron. Since the transmitter at the neuromuscular junction is acetylcholine, Dale's principle would make this chemical the transmitter at the collateral process—Renshaw cell synaptic junction. Curare blocks activation of the Renshaw arc and anticholinesterase drugs prolong its activity; so the contention is pharmacologically valid.

The third important feature of the stretch reflex that can be seen from Figure 7-2 is the existence of three sensory aspects of the reflex: 1. the cutaneous receptors—touch, pain, thermal; 2. the spindle organs (stretch receptors) in the intrafusal fibers; and 3. the *Golgi tendon organ,* which, being in the tendons, responds to pressure when the attached muscle contracts or is passively pulled (e.g., as when antagonistic muscles are contracting). The endings of the spindle organs are of two types, primary (or annulospiral) and secondary (or flowerspray). Both innervate the intrafusal fibers. Unlike the Golgi tendon organ, which is connected in series with the muscles, the spindle

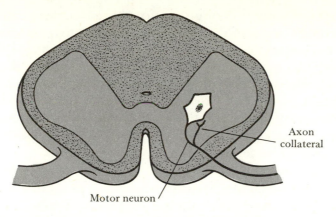

Axon
collateral

Motor neuron

Figure 7-3. Renshaw arc, as described by Weight (1968).

organs are connected in parallel so that tension on them is reduced when the muscle contracts. Thus, relative to their spontaneous firing rate, impulse generation decreases with contraction but increases with stretch. As a consequence of their differential arrangements, the various receptors code the state of a muscle in terms of comparative discharge rates.

Operational description of the stretch reflex

Now it only remains to consider how these structures set up the myotatic or stretch reflex. To take an artificial but common example, a physician taps a patient's knee with a mallet, causing the familiar knee jerk. Actually, the physician taps the tendon, causing it to stretch. That, in turn, stimulates the attached extensor intrafusal muscle fibers to stretch and activates the spindle organ receptors, whose output becomes the sensory component of automatic reflexive muscle contraction. Behaviorally, the leg extends. When the extensor muscle contracts, its intrafusal fibers relax, while the ones in the antagonistic flexor muscle are stretched. The result is decreased activity in the spindle organs, deactivating the reflex. The extensors relax and, behaviorally, the leg returns to the resting position.

The contraction of the muscle, of course, has stretched the tendons which are attached to them and to the bone. If the

131

stretch were severe enough to exceed the relatively high threshold of the Golgi tendon organs, the clasp-knife reflex arc would become activated. The action of this polysynaptic reflex is inhibitory; its activation is reflected in relaxation of the extensor muscles. In addition, the antagonist flexor muscles which are stretched by the extensor contraction also reflexively contract, providing further opposition to the extensor action. As a result of these inhibitory actions, the over-all tendency of the system is to resist contraction.

Comparing the reflex action to a control system, Patton (1960) described the spindle organs as providing a positive feedback because their activation leads to further activation. The Golgi tendon organs provide negative feedback because their activation results in decreased activation. The total result of the various actions is precise muscle control by the neuronal system. Characteristically, the stretch reflexes function to support the organism against the pull of gravity and, thus, are called antigravity reflexes. Behaviorally, this means that the stretch reflex is responsible for man's upright posture.

The activity of the *fusimotor,* or γ-efferent, system is also involved as a limiting factor in the stretch reflex. As has been explained earlier, γ motor neurons can innervate the intrafusal muscle fibers and cause them to contract. That, in turn, stimulates the spindle organs (stretch receptors) in these fibers to generate neural impulses.

The γ-efferents are activated (in conjunction with muscle contraction) at either spinal or supraspinal levels. Their contraction does not contribute to the contraction of the muscle; they only activate the intrafusal fibers which normally tend to relax when the muscle contracts. With tension maintained on the spindle organs while the muscle is contracted, the intrafusal fibers are prevented from becoming completely relaxed. As the muscle continues to contract, the γ-efferents cause the intrafusal fibers to take up their slack, thus maintaining the threshold of sensitivity of the spindle organs. Without such a mechanism, the muscle could not contract any further even though additional stretch was imposed on it. Thus, the γ-efferents adjust the stretch reflex to varying degrees of stretch, independent of the contraction state of the muscle. In control system terms, such a scheme is referred to as a *biasing,* or *gain control, mechanism.*

The foregoing description of one of the simplest reflexes, the stretch, emphasizes that spinal reflexes are peripheral loops of positive and negative feedback systems. Both facilitatory and inhibitory mechanisms are utilized to achieve precise muscle control, which is reflected as directed behavior.

BRAIN INVOLVEMENT IN EFFECTOR ACTIVITIES

Most knowledge of reflexes comes from experiments with spinal animals, which remain inert until stimulated externally. Such specimens are quite different from the normal, intact animal which is far from a passive responder to stimuli. A significant amount of intact animal behavior appears to be spontaneous, self-determined, purposive, conscious, inner-activated, or voluntary, just to mention a few of the descriptive terms that have been applied to behaviors carried out in apparent independence of external stimulation. On the other hand, spinal reflexes occurring as a direct result of observable stimulation are referred to as involuntary, unwilled, unconscious, or externally elicited. Some observers have even sought to categorize all behavior as belonging to one or the other of the two types. Some maintain most behavior is basically conscious and purposive, while others say most activity is unconscious and involuntary.

What seems to make the difference between these two types of behavior is brain activities which compete with and modify the functioning of spinal reflexes. The muscle units involved in such brain-directed behaviors are the same as those for spinal reflexes; recall the concept of final common path. Which of the two types of behavior predominates depends upon the source of the input to the primary motor neurons. With conscious, purposive behavior, the source of the input is neurons originating in the brain, rather than from primary receptors, and terminating in the spinal effectors.

Cortical control over movement

That there are cells in the cortex capable of activating movement was established as early as 1870 by the pioneering electrical brain stimulation experiments of Fritsch and Hitzig on dogs. They maintained that the front, or anterior, half of the brain contained motor cells, whereas the posterior portion contained sensory cells. They also showed that stimulation of one side of the anterior part caused movements in the opposite side of the body. It is now known that the brain neurons which control movement mostly lie in the prefrontal and parietal areas of the cortex, although others are scattered here and there in various other areas of the cortex.

The amount of representation of motor parts in the cortex is proportional to function rather than to the structural mass of the body area. The hands, for example, have several times the representation of the trunk. This relationship is often represented by a homunculus, which is a drawing of a figure with its body parts represented in proportion to the amount of motor cortex they involve (Figure 7-4).

Wilder Penfield (1958), a Canadian physician, has been among those responsible for developing the homunculus of man through electrical stimulation of the brains of patients undergoing brain surgery. Such surgery is typically conducted with local anesthesia since the brain itself has no pain receptors and is impervious to pain. Penfield simply applied electrical stimulation to an area of the exposed brain and observed the behavior or asked the patient to describe his experience. He found, among other things, that the human brain has motor areas similar to those of lower mammals.

Pyramidal motor system   The fibers that descend along the cord from the motor neurons in the cortex define two motor systems: the *pyramidal* and the *extrapyramidal*. The pyramidal system is an axon tract that descends directly from the cortical motor neurons to the primary spinal neurons. There are few, if any, synaptic junctions and interneurons. The system is called pyramidal because the fibers pass through large pyramid-shaped fiber bundles in the medulla. While projecting directly on the primary motor neurons, the fibers also project numerous collaterals to various subcortical levels of the brain, particularly the reticular formation.

As they descend through the medulla, about half of the fibers cross or decussate contralaterally, while the other half decussate in the cord at their level of exit. Some of the fibers originate from large pyramid-shaped neurons in the cortex called Betz

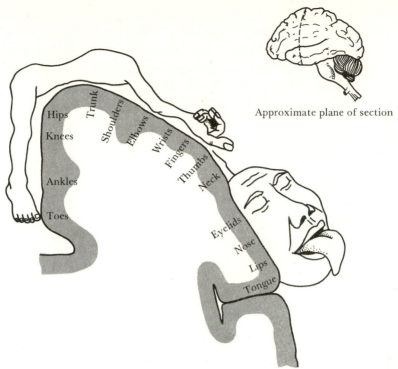

Approximate plane of section

Hips
Knees
Trunk
Shoulders
Elbows
Wrists
Fingers
Thumbs
Neck
Ankles
Toes
Eyelids
Nose
Lips
Tongue

Figure 7-4. A homunculus superimposed on a section of motor cortex to show the proportionate relationship between body parts and amount of cortical representation.

cells, other fibers emanate from other types of cortical neurons. About 40 percent of the cells contributing pyramidal fibers are located in other than primary motor areas. Phylogenetically, the pyramidal tract is a recent innovation; it is found only in the nervous systems of mammals and is most developed in primates. Mammals in general, but man most of all, are uniquely capable of exerting direct influences on primary motor neurons by way of direct pathways from the brain. That is, the pyramidal system is primarily executive in function.

Extrapyramidal motor system   The extrapyramidal system is not very systematic. It overlaps the pyramidal system, but its pathways do not pass through the pyramids in the medulla. It consists, in effect, of all brain motor tracts other than pyramidal. The extrapyramidal pathways are frequently interrupted synaptically throughout the subcortical regions. The function of the extrapyramidal system is essentially inhibitory or integrative, rather than executive. The motor systems of animals below mammals have structures homologous with those in the mammalian extrapyramidal system. This suggests that the extrapyramidal system is phylogenetically the older motor system.

Cerebellar control over movement

The oldest motor structure, it will be recalled (see Chapter 4), is, in fact, the oldest definitive brain structure, the cerebellum (shown in Figure 7-5). Structurally, the cerebellum is composed of two principal subdivisions. The posterior *flocculonodular lobe* is phylogenetically the more primitive subdivision, being found in lower animals. The anterior *cerebellar cortex* is nonexistent in lower animals but well developed in higher animals. The cerebellar cortex, in turn, is divided into two phylogenetically dif-

Figure 7-5. Dorsal perspective of the surface of the cerebellum differentiating its various lobes.

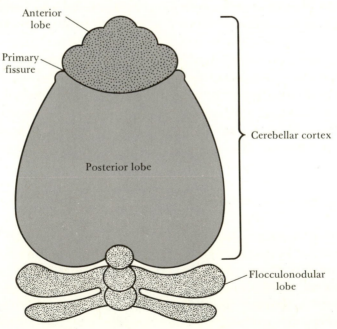

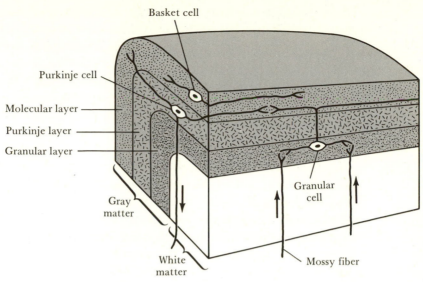

Figure 7-6. Cellular arrangement of the cerebellum.

ferentiated parts, the older *anterior* (or paleocerebellar) *lobe* and the newer *posterior* (or neocerebellar) *lobe*.

The interior cellular organization of the cerebellum is uniform throughout its mass and phylogenetically constant from reptiles to man. As Figure 7-6 shows, there are three cell layers of gray matter covering a central mass of white fiber tracts. The inner layer consists of numerous small cells, known as *granular cells.* Above them are the *Purkinje cells,* which are efferent cells that terminate at various nuclei in the brain. The upper layer of cells comprises a group of cells, known as *basket* or *star cells.*

The informational input to this complex neuronal architecture is transmitted along two sets of fibers, known as *mossy* and *climbing.* The mossy and climbing fibers (named for their bushy latticework of dendrites) project from the cord and various parts of the brain. They synapse with the granular cells and basket cells, which are interneurons. The latter cells synapse with the Purkinje cells. Unlike the mossy fibers with their rambling through the granular layer, each climbing fiber innervates only one Purkinje cell to make one impulse. Every sensory and motor system of the body is represented at least once in the cerebellum, and there is a continuous flow of information, with

137

the cerebellum acting as a kind of traffic coordinator. The result is the complex interplay of muscle movements that make the organism capable of responding to the infinite variety of environmental changes.

Cerebellar damage in man produces difficulties in muscular movement—notably in its force, rate, direction, and steadiness. Relatively well-coordinated behaviors, such as touching a moving target, are markedly impaired and accompanied by *intentional tremors,* tremors that occur only when the limb is in movement. To put it more generally, cerebellar damage causes a dysfunction of coordination between adjustment of movement and changing sensory input. In control system language, the cerebellum shows the same kind of malfunction that appears in any servomechanism when there is interference with its feedback loops. Figure 7-7 is a control system diagram of brain function.

Neuraxial transections

It should be clear from the foregoing that the complex interactions that occur when the brain becomes involved in movement are experimentally difficult to specify. This difficulty is what led Sherrington to employ spinal animals, which remain basic to the study of motor functions. The spinal animal, however, is only one of a series of possible experimental preparations, collectively called *neuraxial transections.* That is, instead of simply separating the cord and the brain, it is surgically possible to sever the CNS at other levels and to determine the relation of each CNS level to function. Table 7-1, as adapted from Cobb (1958), lists five such preparations and summarizes their effects on various motor functions.

It can be seen that in spinal animals all segmental and intersegmental reflexes are still present but somewhat exaggerated, possibly due to the removal of higher inhibitory influences. Decerebellate animals at rest display *cerebellar hypotonia,* a state in which the striated muscles are flaccid, lacking tonus Movement is characterized by *cerebellar ataxia,* or staggering, and loss of coordination. In addition, decerebellate animals display prolonged reaction times, poor control over range of movement (dysmetria), intention tremors, and rhythmic eyeball

Table 7-1. Motor effects of various neuraxial transections

cerebrum
basal ganglia
midbrain
cerebellum
medulla
cord

Functions	Intact	Preparation Spinal	Decerebellate	Hindbrain	Midbrain	Hypothalamic
1. Volitional behavior	+	–	+	–	–	–
2. Reflexes:						
Conditioned	+	–	+	–	–	–
Emotional	+	–	+	–	–	+++
Locomotor	+	–	I	–	++	++
Righting	+	–	I	–	++	+
Respiratory	+	–	+	+	+	+
Neck	+	–	+	++	+	++
Spinal	+	+	+	++	++	++
Anti-gravity	+	+	I	+++	++	++

Code:

    – = absence of function
    + = normal function
   ++ = increased function
 +++ = greatly increased function
Shaded = extirpated area
    I = incoordinate

Note: Adapted and modified from Cobb (1958).

oscillations (nystagmus). The hindbrain, midbrain, and hypo-thalamic preparations are collectively referred to as *decerebrate animals.* They differ only in the level of transection. While each shows important differences in motor activity, they have one outstanding feature in common—sustained contraction of all the extensor, or antigravity, muscles. In effect, there is an exaggeration of all the stretch reflexes. The condition is called *decerebrate rigidity.* With few exceptions, the lower the transec-tion the greater the rigidity.

Suprasegmental reflexes

The role of the brain in the control of movement can also be studied through the suprasegmental reflexes. These involve most facial activities that are reflected by spinal reflexes. As well, the suprasegmental reflexes include those concerned with spatial orientation, the postural reflexes. The two main types of postural reflexes are: 1. *tonic reflexes,* which control the attitude of the parts of the body in relation to each other, but not in relation to gravity; and 2. *righting reflexes,* which maintain the body in a constant orientation relative to gravitational forces. Both are experimentally studied in animals with de-cerebrate transections.

Tonic reflexes   The tonic reflexes function primarily to main-tain the body in proper orientation with the head. When the head is moved, the tonic reflexes effect postural adjustments that bring the body into proper alignment with the head's new position. Two reflexes are synergistic in accomplishing such

Figure 7-7.   Brain function as a servomechanism. Note the feedback role of the cerebellum.

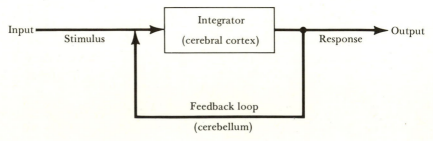

Figure 7-8.   The "fencing position," frequently seen in sleeping or unconscious infants.

adjustments: the *tonic neck reflex,* which is elicited by stimulation of neck muscle receptors; and the *tonic labyrinthine reflex,* which is evoked by the vestibular apparatus of the ear (Chapter 5).

Evaluation of the operation of the tonic neck reflex can be made independently of its interaction with the labyrinthine reflex by surgical removal of the vestibular apparatus or transection of the vestibular branch of the VIII (auditory) cranial nerve. With animals in that condition, rotation of the head elicits extension of the limbs on the side towards which the head, or even just the jaw, is rotated, while the limbs on the other side relax. Lowering the head elicits extension of the forelimbs and relaxation of the hind limbs.

With allowance for labyrinthine influences, the tonic neck reflex can be seen in newborn humans. When the head of an infant is turned to one side, the limbs assume what is called the "fencing position" (Figure 7-8), one limb being outstretched as though ready to lunge. Another instance of the tonic neck reflex seen in the infant is the so-called Moro reflex, which occurs when the baby's head falls backward. The baby immediately stretches its arms outward and then brings them over the chest as though grasping something.

To evaluate the labyrinthine reflex independently of the tonic neck reflex, animal experimenters sever the first three spinal nerves which innervate the neck. When an animal so prepared is placed in a supine position, extensor tonus is minimal, the muscles staying flaccid. At intermediate positions, the tonus is proportionally intermediate. The animal is able to stand upright if placed in that position, but it cannot right itself if placed on its back.

With intact animals (in which the neck and labyrinthine reflexes are viable), the pattern of tonus for any given position of the animal is the sum of the individual reflexes. If the head of a prone animal is ventrally flexed, that is, bent toward the belly, the fore-limbs will relax and the hind-limbs will remain unchanged. This attitude of the muscles will remain as long as the position is held.

Righting reflexes   For observing the righting reflexes, the neuraxial transection is made above the thalamus, constituting a *thalamic preparation*. Such a preparation has two advantages over other experimental decerebrate animals: 1. there is no decerebrate rigidity, and 2. the animal can restore itself to the upright position when it is on its back.

There are four types of righting reflexes: *labyrinthine, neck, body,* and *optic*. The labyrinthine righting reflex is activated by way of the vestibular apparatus and functions to maintain the head in an upright position. It is typically absent in newborn infants but develops early in the first year, when it is reflected behaviorally by the ability to raise the head. The neck-righting reflex orients the body to the position of the head. Head movement stretches neck muscles, which evoke the reflex-activating muscles to bring the body into line with the head position. The body-righting reflex operates so that when the organism comes into contact with a surface, the head is brought into a normal position relative to the surface. The reflex is elicited by stimulation of the touch receptors. The optic-righting reflex is unique to higher mammals, whose spatial orientation of the head depends on visual cues. Even labyrinthectomized animals can orient their heads if they have visual cues.

As the name implies, the righting reflexes function together to maintain the organism in an upright position. It should be noticed that the head leads the rest of the organism in achieving this position. When the animal is disoriented, the head assumes the vertical position first by way of the visual, vestibular, proprioceptive, and tactile righting reflexes. Then the body aligns itself with the position of the head in a head-to-tail sequence of motions. The sequence represents an instance of a chain reflex.

SOME DEVELOPMENTAL ASPECTS OF HUMAN REFLEXES

In the development of human infants, changes in reflex activity follow a definite sequence. The newborn, for instance, is so cerebrally immature that it remains relatively inert until external stimulation is applied. This behavior, as Delgado (1971) notes, is similar to that of a spinal animal, or a brain stem or midbrain preparation.

Newborn reflexes

Stimulation of a newborn elicits various reflexive behaviors (Figure 7-9) that can be analyzed in terms of approach and withdrawal reflexes. Approach reflexes are most noticeable as a chain reflex called the *rooting reflex.* Tactile stimulation of the facial region of a newborn human, for instance, elicits head movements towards the stimulation. The infant attempts to take the stimulating object into its mouth and, if successful, commences sucking. That this behavior is completely automatic is clear from observations that even a sleeping or comatose infant will so respond. The behavior is adaptive because of its obvious relationship to feeding and drinking.

The *grasping reflex* is another very noticeable approach reflex. Tactile stimulation of the palm or sole evokes closure of the hand or foot. The resultant grip is great enough for an infant to support its whole body weight.

The withdrawal reflexes involve various avoidance or escape movements in response to aversive or noxious stimulation. Common examples are eye closure to a bright light, rejection of bitter substances from the mouth, and removal of an extremity from painful stimulation. All these behaviors are present in newborn infants.

Fully developed reflexes

As an infant develops, individual reflexes tend to become integrated into more complex behaviors. Rooting becomes selective in regard to the properties of the stimulus and is accompanied by reaching, hand-grasping, and hand-mouth coordination. In fully developed humans, newborn reflexes seem to have disappeared. Obviously (and thankfully!) tactile stimulation of the cheek or chin of a normal adult does not elicit the rooting reflex. The reflexes do not actually disappear, however; their elicitation is simply rendered more selective by integration with other actions and by experience. Kimble and Perlmuter speak of:

. . . a developmental sequence by which the individual
first acquires voluntary control over initially involuntary
responses and then with extended practice allows these
responses to retreat from consciousness and attention and,
in that sense, to become involuntary (1970, p. 382).

For them, this sequence represents the basis of volition.

Physiological psychologists consider the sequence as occurring in parallel with cortical development. As the cortex matures, it acquires the ability to inhibit a number of reflexes. This conception is supported by observation of adults who have suffered cortical damage (e.g., clinical reports such as Denny-Brown, 1958; Denny-Brown, and Chambers, 1958; Williams, 1970). As an example, if the cheek of a patient with frontal lobe damage is touched, the approach reflexes are released. The stimulus sets up a complete rooting reflex—orientation of head, contact, and sucking. The patient is surprised and embarrassed but unable to stop his movements. The same reaction occurs with the grasping reflex. Patients are unable to release their grip on objects such as doorknobs.

On the other hand, damage to the parietal lobes results in release of the withdrawal reflexes. Simply touching the patient with parietal lobe damage, for example, produces an exaggerated withdrawal pattern that may become so extreme that the patient actually loses sensory awareness and is affected by "psychological anesthesia." In instances of unilateral parietal damage, a condition called "unilateral neglect" may result. Williams describes such cases:

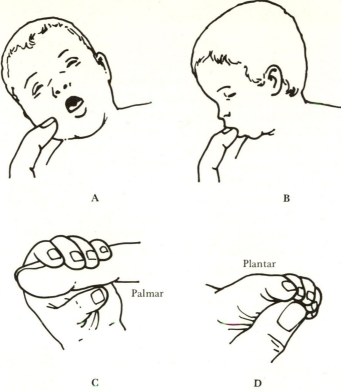

A   B

C   D

Figure 7-9. Reflexes in human development. The rooting reflex arises when the face of an infant is stroked; **A,** the head turns and **B,** a stimulating object is sucked or ingested. The grasping reflex, which is elicited by tactile stimulation of the **C,** palm of the hand or **D,** sole of the foot.

> A patient . . . will sometimes ignore one side of his body—or fail to carry out commands with it. When asked to lift his arms, he lifts one arm only. When dressing, he puts on only one shoe or combs only one side of his hair. This condition can be demonstrated by the "glove test." The examiner tosses a pair of gloves into the patient's lap, telling him to put them on. The patient puts on only one . . . leaving the other aside (1970, p. 74).

She points out that the neglected half of the body still functions (e.g., in the glove test, the neglected hand will be employed to put the other glove on) and that there is little concern about the condition because, for such patients, the neglected side does not exist conceptually.

145

REFLEX ASPECTS OF VOLITION

So far this discussion has covered cortical control over reflexes, the motor pathways from the brain to the primary spinal motor neurons, and initiation or inhibition of movements by activation of these cells. But what initially excites the brain motor neurons? Is the impulse involuntary or is it voluntary and controlled? Can thinking give rise to motion?

As might be expected, these questions can be answered quite differently, depending on whether one is a monist or a dualist.[4] Monists regard the nervous system as merely a passive transmitter of impulses because it cannot act until activated by some source of stimulation from the outside. Volition is no more than an internal aspect of physical happenings in the nervous system, and everything the brain does is predetermined. Dualists, on the other hand, view the nervous system as active because it can initiate motor behavior within itself in the absence of external stimulation. To put it simply, the brain can tell the finger to point or to move the muscle that pulls the trigger, and do it as an act of free will.

Sherrington's position in this argument is interesting. Sherrington tried to resolve the question of volition by conceiving of the motor cells in the cortex as part of a reflex arc. He considered them to be internuncial links between the afferent input from the distance receptors (teleceptors) and the primary motor neurons. Sherrington then maintained that the actions of the individual were impelled through the stimulation of this nerve circuitry. He went further and declared that "the cerebrum itself may be indeed regarded as the ganglion of the distance receptors" (1947).

From such statements, it would appear that Sherrington took a monistic point of view, very similar to the "reflexes of the brain" tenets of Russian reflexology, in which the brain is regarded as a mirror of outside forces. However, at the same time Sherrington went beyond monistic reflexology by contending that there was another type of integration operative in the body. "Integration," he wrote, "has been traced at work in two great systems . . . the physical which is merely a collection of

4. See Chapter 16 for a discussion of monism and dualism.

organs and the psychical which creates a percipient thinking and endeavoring mental individual" (1947).

This statement seems to identify Sherrington as a dualist. However, the British physiological psychologist apparently did not want to be labelled a monist or a dualist. He went on to say that the probability that there was only one fundamental element of being was just as great as the possibility of two. This is the way Sherrington related to the mind-body dichotomy. How other physiological psychologists have attempted to come to terms with this issue will be seen in subsequent chapters.

SUGGESTED READING

Sherrington, C. S. *The Integrative Action of the Nervous System*. New Haven, Conn.: Yale University Press, 1947. An undisputed classic, a "must" reading adventure for any student of behavior.

III

Physiological-behavioral correlates

The heart of physiological psychology lies in the body of experiments and observations that attempt to relate behavior to underlying physiological mechanisms. Much of the behavior of an organism arises from the demands of survival. The various neural substrates, subcortical and cortical, are alerted and mobilized in highly ingenious ways to facilitate the organism's capacity to satisfy its needs and repel its enemies.

Subcortical structures are involved in three major survival mechanisms: motivation, emotion, and consciousness. These mechanisms are states of body and mind familiar to everyone. Expressions of motivation in everyday language include terms such as drives, wishes, and desires—the last two being intentions that may mask basic drives. The intimacy of body and mind is more sharply pointed up by everyday expressions of emotion. In the expressions "She's sad and broken-hearted" or "He's afraid, he hasn't any guts," body conditions are clearly descriptive of feeling states. The individual's awareness of the physiochemical state of various body tissues, such as the state that gives rise to hunger, results in behavior directly related to satisfying that state and maintaining the integrity of the body. Thus, these behaviors lead to direct involvement with the environment. Consciousness is a more subtle survival mechanism. Consciousness has to do with the states of awareness and attention, which involve selection and interpretation of incoming stimuli. Both these states give evidence of the relationship between body and mind.

After a consideration of motivation, emotion, and consciousness, the balance of Part III is concerned with physiological-behavioral correlates that involve the higher areas of the brain. Correlations between the frontal lobes and localization, the cortex and learning, and biological details of personality are examined.

8 Motivation

Physicist Robert Oppenheimer, the late head of the World War II A-bomb project, once remarked: "There are no secrets in nature, only in the motives of man."

Puzzling out motives from behavior has always been a hazardous but fascinating pastime, not only for psychologists but for people in all walks of life. "What is he after?" is a common everyday question. Physiological psychology attempts to get behind the motives of individuals, to see how tissues change in relation to an individual's needs. Motivation, in the sense of preparing the organism to get what it needs from the environment when it needs it, represents the most basic aspect of heterotrophic functioning.

The prime importance of motivation to purposive behavior is further evidenced by the attention paid to it in the development of psychological thought. For example, Freud, in his elaboration of psychoanalytical theory, emphasized that all behavior has antecedent causes. He explained that any instance of behavior is not the mysterious consequence of some omnipresent nonsecular force but the result of definable variables in oneself and in the environment. Freud further maintained that these variables can be studied and understood. The leading behaviorist spokesman, Skinner, who is often labeled as an anti-Freudian, emphasized and supported Freud's contention.[1]

1. In an interview, Skinner said: "Freud made some very important contributions. As a determinist he convinced many people that things formerly believed to be accidental were really lawful and I think he was right on that point" (Evans, 1968, p. 5).

DEFINITION OF MOTIVATION

Freud, who was trained as a physician and oriented toward the physiological basis of disease in conformity with the medical science of the day, devised a biological definition of motivation which is still used by physiological psychologists.

However jealously we usually defend the independence of psychology from every other science . . . we stood in the shadow of the unshakable biological fact that the living individual organism is at the command of two intentions, self preservation and preservation of the species which seem to be independent of each other, which so far as we know at present, have no common origin and whose interests are often in conflict in animal life. Actually what we are talking about . . . is biological psychology, we are studying the psychical accompaniments of biological processes (Freud, 1965, pp. 95–96).

In other words, *motivation* is the change in the biological state of the organism that relates to behaviors directed at self and species preservation.

Such a definition of motivation, of course, seems broad enough to include all behavior. But, in general practice, psychologists use the term in a more restricted sense. Actually, Freud (who wrote in German) used the term *Treiben* (drives), which has been translated as "instincts," in discussing motivation. This confused his exact meaning for many English-speaking persons. Whatever the semantics, Freud believed that motivation arose from tissue disturbances or imbalances caused by a deficiency in an essential substance, such as oxygen, water, or food. A deficiency of water or food, for instance, results in an irritation which motivates the organism by thirst or hunger to seek a way of removing the deficiency. Freud also tried to fit sexual behavior into the same scheme. In fact, he contended that all behavior was ultimately initiated at the biological level. The organism perceives a biotic deficiency as a feeling of need which then results in behavior directed to reducing the deficiency and its resultant feeling of irritation.

Of course, the lexicon of modern psychology contains many drive states that are classified as secondary, or learned, rather than biological or innate. Such drives as the need to achieve and obtain success or the need to maintain self-esteem are said to be the products of cultural factors. Still other drives, some maintain, are both innate and culturally influenced, such as togetherness and the urge for flocking in groups. Many of these secondary drives, it is suggested, can be more powerful than a biological drive. The need to achieve a particular goal, for instance, may cause a person to go hungry for days and even months at a time.

Physiological psychologists have attempted to prevent any possible overgenerality of the concept of motivation by using the term *consummatory behavior* to describe the actions of seeking and consuming to achieve satisfaction of a physiological need. Thus, some behaviors arising from hunger, thirst, and sex would be examples of consummatory behavior. Many physiological psychologists have been concerned with tracing the biologic basis of these drives and working out the relation of body and mind involved in the process of satisfying them.

HUNGER DRIVE

To illustrate the nature of a drive and how it results in behavior, one need only to consider the most studied of the innate drives—hunger. The connection of body and mind in hunger was noted thousands of years ago. Deprivation of food results in two feeling states: when pleasant, it is known as appetite; when unpleasant, as hunger. Despite this awareness, the part of the body involved in these feeling states was not really defined until the third century B.C., when the Greco-Roman physician Galen maintained that the stomach and its contractions were involved in hunger. This notion prevailed through the years. The eighteenth century physiologist, von Haller, said:

We are induced to take food, both from the sense of pain which we call hunger, and from that of the pleasure imparted by the sense of taste. The first of these proceeds undoubtedly from the folds of the stomach, which possess great sensibility, being rubbed against one another by the peristaltic motion, and by the pressure of the diaphragm and abdominal muscles, so that naked nerves being rubbed against naked nerves excite an intolerable degree of pain. Thus man is both effectually admonished of the dangers

of abstinence and excited to procure food by his labors
(1765, cited by Teitelbaum, 1964, p. 464).

By the beginning of the twentieth century, complications in
this idea started to appear. The notion of regulation, as derived
from the internal constancy concept of Bernard (Chapter 4),
was applied to water intake (André Mayer, 1901) and then to
food intake (Gasnier and André Mayer, 1939). André Mayer
(known, among other things, for the invention of the gas mask
in World War I) found that animals adjust their food intake not
simply to satisfy hunger but as a function of such factors as
bodily activity, environmental temperature, and the energy
value of the food. Elaboration of Cannon's (1929) concept of
homeostasis further emphasized the validity of the interactions
in food consumption. The emphasis switched from simply
identifying the physiological origins of hunger sensations to
discovering the physiological mechanisms which regulate food
intake.

Early studies of food intake regulation

Despite this new emphasis, the search for regulatory mechanisms remained initially in the context of peripheral nervous
system theories (that is, minimal CNS involvement). During
those years, reflex concepts were prominent in both physiology
and psychology; so the resolution of the problem seemed to
be merely a question of isolating the reflex arcs involved in
the regulation of food intake. The famous Cannon and Washburn (1912) studies are indicative of the attempted experimental advocacy of such an approach. Human subjects swallowed a
balloon that was then inflated in the stomach, and changes in
stomach contracture due to the pressure were recorded pneu-
mographically. At the same time, the subjects were asked to
report any feelings of hunger. As it turned out, the presence or
absence of hunger pangs did indeed correlate with increases
and decreases in stomach contractions. This demonstrated, it
seemed, that stomach contractions are the basis of hunger and
of the regulation of food intake.

Unfortunately for the tenability of such a concise causal
relationship, reports of conflicting evidence soon followed.
Wangensteen and Carlson (1931), for instance, reported the

case of a surgical patient who ate normally and reported a normal desire for food even though his stomach had been totally removed and his esophagus was attached directly to the intestinal tract (a relatively common surgical procedure nowadays). This remained as an unnoticed clinical finding in the literature until 1938 when Tsang found that rats with total gastrectomies could learn food-rewarded behaviors as readily as normal animals. Thus, there was experimental verification that hunger and stomach contraction had less to do with one another than was thought. In fact, animals whose stomachs were totally enervated maintained normal food consumption (Bash, 1939). Adding to this, Wilder and Shultz (1931) found that stomach contractions could be inhibited by anticholinergic drugs, which in themselves have no effect on feelings of hunger, yet hunger remained.

Other attempts, most notably those dealing with blood sugar, were made to define the sensory component of the food consumption reflexes. Luckhardt and Carlson (1915) reported, for instance, that the transfusion of blood from starved dogs to satiated dogs induced stomach contractions in the latter animals. Further, the increase in those contractions correlated with a decrease in blood sugar levels suggesting that changes in blood sugar was the sensory component (Bulatao and Carlson, 1924). However, in 1948 Grossman and Stein cast some doubt on this conclusion when they demonstrated that insulin injections (insulin lowers blood sugar) caused feelings of hunger in human beings whose stomachs were enervated.

Nonetheless, the blood sugar idea did not die completely. During the 1950s, Jean Mayer postulated the existence of hypothalamic receptors that monitor glucose levels (Mayer and Thomas, 1967). Mayer's work not only implicated blood sugar but also revived interest in the central nervous system theories of hunger regulation.

The idea that the CNS might somehow be involved in the regulation of food intake was not new. As far back as 1826, Magendie postulated the existence of a center in the brain that gave rise to hunger sensations. In 1840 Mohr observed that a lesion in the area of the hypothalamus resulted in overeating. Around the turn of the century, Alfred Froehlich, a Viennese physician, reported a correlation between obesity and pituitary tumors, a condition now known as *Froehlich's syndrome.* In 1939 Hetherington and Ranson reported that Froehlich's syndrome could be produced in animals by hypothalamic lesions. Brobeck (1948) noticed a relationship between food consumption and ambient temperature; organisms ate more when cold, less when warm. He concluded that regulation of food intake involved monitoring of the temperature of the blood in the brain.

Hypothalamic lesions and food intake regulation

These and similar findings made it seem reasonable to concentrate on the role of the hypothalamus in the regulation of food consumption. Brobeck and his colleagues (Anand and Brobeck, 1951*a, b;* Brobeck, Tepperman, and Long, 1943) verified the earlier findings relevant to Froehlich's syndrome in rats. But it was also discovered that lesions in the upper distal (lateral) part of the hypothalamus produced the opposite effect, refusal to eat even to the point of death from starvation. They suggested that there may be two antagonistic feeding centers, a distal or lateral excitatory area which induces food intake and a ventromedial inhibitory center which discourages it. To this picture, Stellar (1954) added the thought that the hypothalamus acted as the integrating center for all factors related to food intake. Figure 8-1 shows the location of the feeding centers of the hypothalamus and Figure 8-2 shows the feedback loops involved in the consummatory response.

Figure 8-1.   Cross section of a rat's hypothalamus showing areas allegedly involved in regulation of food consummation.

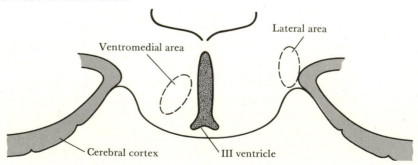

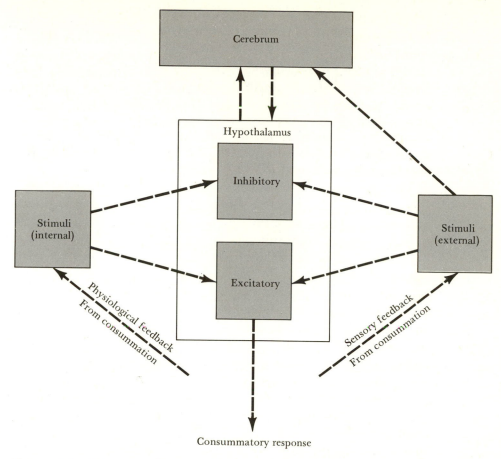

Figure 8-2. Schematic diagram of factors influencing a consummatory response. (Redrawn and modified from Stellar, 1954.)

Stellar's contention influenced much of the subsequent research directed towards elucidating the physiochemical nature of the hypothalamus in relation to the hunger drive. By way of example, Teitelbaum (1964, 1966, 1967) extensively investigated hypothalamic lesions in the rat in relation to the regulation of food intake. He found that destruction of the ventro-medial region produced overeating, or *hyperphagia,* in distinct stages. Immediately following surgery and for a few days afterwards, the lesioned rats ate two to three times as much as normal and gained weight very rapidly. This period is the dynamic phase of hyperphagia. Once the animals reached a certain level of obesity, they returned to near-normal levels of food consumption, eating just enough to maintain the higher weight level.

If the hyperphagic animals were then starved until their body weight returned to presurgical levels and were once more given access to food, they again overate and returned to their obese level. Thus, the leveling off at obesity was not due to the lesion's "healing" or to food consumption, but more likely to a shift in the optimal level of homeostasis, analogous to turning up the thermostat.

This was further verified by injecting the hyperphagic animals with insulin, force-feeding to a super obese condition, and letting them return to their own regulation. Instead of retaining the new condition of fat, they reassumed the normal obese level for hyperphagic rats. In contrast, normal rats will overeat and get fat when injected with insulin, but as soon as the insulin injections are stopped they will cease eating until their body weight returns to normal.

In a series of experiments with lateral hypothalamic lesions in rats, the behavioral changes that occurred included *aphagia,* abstention from eating, and *adipsia,* abstention from drinking. The course of events was multiphasic, following a pattern called the *lateral hypothalamic syndrome.* In the first stage, which lasted about twenty days, the animals actively turned away from food, pushed it away, and would not swallow it even when it was placed directly in their mouths. The second stage, during the next ten days or so, was characterized by *anorexia,* decreased appetite. The rats would eat moist and highly palatable food (e.g., milk chocolate) but not in a quantity sufficient to maintain body weight, and they were still adipsic. They no longer actively avoided food in that they would approach and explore it. The anorexia ended abruptly, initiating the third stage in which the animals ate copiously, regaining and maintaining normal body weight. However, even though they would only consume a wet diet, they still would not drink water. If they were force-fed water they would eat dry food, suggesting that dehydration prevented normal eating and emphasizing the intimate relation between eating and drinking (Verplanck and Hayes, 1953).

The final stage was recovery, at about sixty days postsurgery. The recovery was not total. The rats did regulate food intake in relation to ambient temperature, just as normal animals would. However, when injected with insulin they would not increase food intake to counteract the lowered blood sugar. It was concluded from these findings that the lesion destroyed both thermostatic and glucostatic receptors, with only the thermoreceptors eventually recovering. The partial recovery of capacity was sufficient to induce a full behavioral recovery. In learning situations and latency tests where rate of food approach was measured, recovered rats maintained significantly enhanced approach responses compared to both intact and ventromedial lesioned rats. After recovering, their motivation was apparently increased (Davenport and Balagura, 1971).

As Teitelbaum (1967) notes, the stages of recovery are similar to those seen with motor reflexes following damage to the motor cortex. That is, the recovery sequence follows the ontogenetic development of the behavior. Initially, the approach reflexes were absent. When they returned, regulation still was not present. It was only after a considerable period of time that any degree of voluntary eating and regulation of intake returned. The notion that eating is a reflexive action integrated by the hypothalamus can thus be considered to be in conformity with established concepts of reflex development.

Hypothalamic stimulation and food intake regulation

Electrical and biochemical stimulation of the hypothalamus have tended to complement the effects observed with lesions. Delgado and Anand (1953) found that lateral hypothalamic stimulation with electricity in cats elicited immediate gnawing, biting, and other eating-like responses, but had a delayed effect on food intake. Starting the day after stimulation, the animals displayed a marked increase (70 percent) in solid food consumption that lasted about two days. Milk consumption increased as much as 300 percent for as long as five days poststimulation. It was later found (Anand and Dua, 1955) that such stimulation initially effects increases in blood sugar; so the consumption aspects were masked until the blood sugar decreased. However, stimulation of specific points in the lateral hypothalamus of rats elicited immediate eating behavior (Miller, 1957). The behavior was *stimulus-bound,* meaning that it started and stopped immediately with the onset or termination of the stimulus. In fact, the animals instantly stopped other behaviors and commenced eating when they were stimulated. Even a food-satiated but water-deprived rat would stop drinking and start eating.

Biochemically, Grossman (1960) reported that administration of norepinephrine directly to the lateral hypothalamus of rats, by way of a chronically implanted cannula, resulted in marked increases in food consumption; while acetylcholine produced markedly increased drinking. The effect is dose-dependent and can be antagonized by adrenergic and cholinergic blocking drugs[2] (Milner, Nance, and Sheer, 1971; Weiss and Strongman, 1969). The implication is that both eating and drinking areas exist within the same hypothalamic locus, with the difference being one of chemistry rather than anatomy. This contention was recently given further validity by Berger, Wise, and Stein's (1971) demonstration that the anorexic effects of lateral hypothalamic lesions in rats could be immediately reversed by intraventricular norepinephrine injections. While such evidence suggests the existence of adrenergic and cholinergic synapses in the CNS, this evidence is still indirect. The only possible definitive exception which still remains is the Renshaw arc (Chapter 7). In any instance, it has recently been demonstrated that elevated brain calcium concentrations induce eating irrespective of satiation level or the pharmacologic state of the hypothalamus (Myers et al., 1972).

Integrative aspects of food intake

Until recently, the case for localization of the structural components of food consumption regulation in the hypothalamus seemed relatively well established, even to the extent of acquiring dogmatic overtones. But in 1970, as a result of some of their own research, Valenstein, Cox, and Kakolewski expressed some reservations because of possible bias in the hypothalamus experiments. Valenstein and his colleagues found that other behaviors could be regulated by the same hypothalamic areas, i.e., that the areas are nonspecific. In one series of experiments, eating responses were elicited in rats by hypothalamic

2. These facts imply that the effect is directly due to the chemical intervention.

stimulation. Then the food was removed without discontinuing the electrical stimulation. The result was that other behaviors, such as drinking, gnawing on wood, sexual behavior, preening, and sand digging, emerged as a direct function of the external stimuli. When food was again introduced, hypothalamic stimulation elicited these other behaviors as frequently as eating. The finding has been replicated by several investigators in a variety of species.

Even more recently, Schachter (1971), who has worked with human subjects, emphasized that in certain cases external stimulus conditions, (such as taste or food cues), more than the power of any specific anatomical site or physiological motivation, are the critical determinants in the regulation of food intake. In his experiments, he found that normal weight people ate more after being deprived of food for several hours than they would under their usual dietary regime. In contrast, obese people ate more when they were already sated than when they were deprived, suggesting that obese individuals, unlike normal weight individuals, are not primarily influenced by internal physiological events independent of the environment. Schachter concluded that obese people are externally controlled. One implication of this research is that notions about the hypothalamus need revision.

So, again, the conclusion about hunger and food intake is clear. Food consumption involves many complex variables at all levels of life, from the molar extraorganismic (such as visual cues) to the molecular intraorganismic (such as blood sugar). These variables are somehow brought together in the hypothalamus which integrates the entire operation so as to maintain a viable organism. As Stellar puts it:

. . . hunger and feeding are under multifactor control. Many sensory factors, both learned and unlearned, contribute, in an additive way, to the arousal of hunger and to the development of satiation: taste, smell, gastric contractions, and gastric distension to name some major ones. Added to these are powerful influences from the internal environment, including both osmotic and specific chemical changes . . . all these factors are integrated in the central nervous system, particularly the hypothalamus . . . (1967, pp. 105–6).

OTHER PRIMARY DRIVES

There have been similar but less extensive attempts to specify structural and/or biochemical loci in regard to other motivated behaviors such as thirst (e.g., Anderson, Gale, and Sundsten, 1964; Gilbert and Glaser, 1961); sexual behavior (e.g., Beach, 1947; Lisk, 1962; Vaughan and Fisher, 1962); and numerous other related behaviors such as attack, vocalization, and nesting (e.g., Roberts, 1970; von Holst and von St. Paul, 1960). The same principles relevant to food consumption probably also hold in these instances.

For example, Beach (1947, 1969) has found that the neural organization of male and female brains are somewhat different in regard to sexual behavior. Damage to male cortex brings about a greater diminution of sexual activity than in females similarly ablated. The hypothalamus also seems particularly important to male sexual arousal in that appropriate lesions can totally stop mating (Phoenix, 1961), while direct electric stimulation of the same areas produces increased sexual behavior (Vaughan and Fisher, 1962). Further, Schreiner and Kling (1953) have implicated various limbic structures (such as the amygdala and hippocampus) in the expression of cats' sexual behavior.

Similarly, von Holst and von St. Paul (1960) demonstrated sex-specific regulation of mating behavior in common barnyard chickens. Appropriate brain stem stimulation of roosters elicited many aspects of the courtship sequence, such as seeking nesting sites, calling the hen, and attacking intruders. Likewise, hens could be induced to assume nesting postures compatible with incubating eggs or "expressing relief" after the exertion of "laying" (a characteristic relaxation behavior).

INTRACRANIAL SELF-STIMULATION

To complete the story of consummatory behavior, one aspect should be mentioned in detail because it confounds generalization. This is the so-called *Intracranial Self-Stimulation* or *ICSS*. In the early 1950s, James Olds and Peter Milner, at McGill University in Montreal, were experimenting with electrically stimulating the reticular formation to determine whether it would act as a negative stimulus to cause a rat to avoid some areas of a maze which it associated with the stimulation.[3] While routinely testing the electrode placement in a single rat, much to their surprise, they obtained an effect opposite to what they had been led to expect. Whenever the rat was stimulated while running the maze, it would stop and go back the way it had come. The investigators decided that the animal was searching for the place in the maze where it had received the stimulation in the apparent hope of getting more. Instead of being negatively affective, the stimulation seemed to be positively rewarding.

To test this impression, Olds and Milner set up a new series of experiments. They first x-rayed the brain of the rat and found that the electrode had been implanted not in the reticular formation, but in the septal area. (Inaccurate electrode placement is not unusual; it is at best an inexact procedure that always necessitates postexperimental verification.) The investigators then deliberately implanted electrodes in the septal area and provided the animals with a lever which would produce stimulation when it was pressed. The rats learned to press the lever to stimulate their own brains and eventually maintained very high response rates, up to 7000 responses per hour. It was concluded that intracranial self-stimulation, as it came to be called, was rewarding; that some sort of "pleasure center" had been found in the brain. Olds and Milner summarized their findings as follows:

It is clear that electrical stimulation in certain parts of the brain produces acquisition and extinction curves which compare favorably with those produced by conventional primary reward (1954, p. 426).

Although to this day the implications are still somewhat unclear, this finding was very exciting and had a profound effect on the psychological world. It was seen as a possible way of understanding neural control of reward and punishment which is the basis of all drives and thus the key to behavior.

To gain some insight into ICSS, it is helpful to maintain a conservative perspective which is obtainable from a precise statement of Olds and Milner's findings. They demonstrated that electrical stimulation of certain subcortical areas can result

3. Personal communications, 1972.

in a repetition of the behavior that just preceded the stimulation. In some respects, the characteristics of that behavior correspond to behavior maintained by primary rewards, such as food and water.

Subsequent research, however, has revealed some differences between the two types of behavior (Milner, 1970; Olds, 1958, 1962). These are:

1. Animals rewarded with ICSS never achieve satiation. They continue to respond until totally exhausted.

2. ICSS takes precedence over all primary rewards. Hungry animals given a choice of food or ICSS, and thirsty animals given a choice of water or ICSS, always choose ICSS. Rats would cross a highly charged electric grid to obtain ICSS, a grid they would not cross to obtain food after being food-deprived.

3. Termination of ICSS brings about a very rapid extinction (cessation of responding) rate which is unlike the pattern seen with positive rewards. Typically, there is an initial increase in response rate following removal of food and water, and then a gradual decrease with occasional spontaneous bursts of responding. Removal of ICSS results in a very rapid and permanent decline in response rate. The animal emits two or three responses, and then stops completely.

4. Similarly, schedules of reinforcement[4] or running complex mazes cannot be developed for rats with ICSS as the reward, although in some instances they will work if the animals are also food-deprived.

There is a definite but unclear interaction between ICSS and food and water rewards. Brady (1958a) found that thirsty rats preferred ICSS to water but stopped responding to ICSS when they became satiated with water. Similar relationships hold for food (Hoebel and Teitelbaum, 1962) and sex (Prescott, 1966). Such findings suggest that ICSS involves more than mere activation of a "pleasure center." Again, there appear to be integrating aspects.

4. An experimental procedure in which access to reward can be obtained only after some temporal or spatial sequence of responses are completed (e.g., only every fifth lever press will result in reward).

As a consequence of these studies, which run contrary to the view of ICSS as a unique kind of positive reward, a number of alternative theories have been proposed. The differing points of view center around whether the ICSS stimulus is serving a rewarding function (and if so what kind) or a cue function.[5]

It would seem that the most direct way to determine what is taking place during self-stimulation would be to implant electrodes in the hypothalamus of human beings. This has been done with patients suffering from various neurological, psychiatric, or terminal physical disorders (Bishop, Elder, and Heath, 1963; Delgado, 1971; Delgado and Hamlin, 1956; Heath, 1963; Sem-Jacobson and Torkildsen, 1960). The results were almost universally positive; nearly every subject reported feelings of pleasure, optimism, joy, and happiness. Some subjects described their feelings as comparable to those they experienced just before sexual orgasm. Individuals provided with an opportunity to stimulate themselves pressed the levers or buttons quite readily. Heath (1964) reported using the technique in the case of a homosexual patient who was given stimulation while looking at pornographic movies. As a result of this association, Heath reported that the patient was able to obtain and enjoy a heterosexual experience.

Not all such stimulation is pleasurable. Delgado, Roberts, and Miller (1954) and, independently, Olds and Milner (1954) found that stimulating some centers of the brain causes an animal to try to avoid the effect or to escape. They thus revealed the existence of pain centers in the hypothalamus. Hungry animals can be trained to avoid food by stimulation of such regions.

One fascinating outcome from the discovery of the centers of pleasure and pain is the new view it provides of motivation from the physiological perspective. In the past, starting with the early conceptions of Freud, motivation was generally considered to be a process of reducing tissue needs, which are experienced as feelings of discomfort. Motivation was considered to be unidirectional. That is, organisms behaved to reduce the effects of deprivation, and pleasure was the success-

5. The status of research relevant to the dispute is reviewed adequately by Milner (1970) and Hokanson (1969).

ful accomplishment of this (a point of view referred to as *drive-reduction*). Behavior that occurred for the sake of pleasure alone, the *hedonistic* point of view, was considered untenable from the standpoint of the underlying physiological mechanisms that were then known. That has changed. There is now a physiological basis for the idea that people are motivated toward pleasure. The discovery also does injury to the Calvinist ethic, which opposes behavior conducted solely for pleasure-seeking. Instead there is now a scientific basis for the contemporary emphasis on pleasure and the joys of leisure.

SUGGESTED READINGS

Grossman, S. P. *A Textbook of Physiological Psychology.* New York: Wiley, 1967. The chapter on motivation is exceedingly thorough, detailed, and heavily referenced.

Hokanson, J. E. *The Physiological Basis of Motivation.* New York: Wiley, 1969. A comprehensive discussion of the concepts and research relevant to motivational theory.

Milner, P. M. *Physiological Psychology.* New York: Holt, Rinehart and Winston, 1970. Chapters on ICSS are the best available discussion of "the pleasure centers of the brain."

9 Emotion

The word *emotion* derives from the Latin *emotus,* which some writers maintain can be translated as "stirred up." In that sense of the word, psychologists become very emotional when it comes to defining emotion. The term predates the science of psychology, having come to it from the lay language where the distinction was made between emotional and passionate acts on the one hand and rational and voluntary acts on the other. Everybody from the Greeks forward seemed to understand what that meant, and it was a useful distinction in law and in the everyday counseling of human affairs.

Psychologists, for two reasons, have had a difficult time trying to incorporate the distinction between emotional and rational into their conceptions of behavior. First, they have tended to categorize any behavior that did not fit anywhere else as emotional, "a wastebasket category of behavior" as Millenson (1967) described it.

Second, as with many other aspects of the mind, there is no way to observe emotions directly since they are feeling states and, hence, totally subjective. The typical psychologist's answer to this problem has been to define emotions only in terms of their overt, observable, behavioral consequences. Unfortunately, this solution confuses the question of the nature of emotion. It results in a distinction between *emotional behavior* and the *emotion*, or feeling state, proper.

167

DARWIN'S THEORY

That solution has had a long history, however. In 1872 Charles Darwin's famous book, *The Expression of the Emotions in Man and Animals*, described facial expressions and body postures as indicators of emotional states and considered them in terms of their evolutionary significance. Specifically, Darwin emphasized the importance of overt indicators for communicating feeling to other organisms. For example, dogs show hostility by baring their teeth, growling, arching their backs, and raising their hair and tail. Darwin called these activities the indicators of withdrawal. Conversely, tail wagging, barking, and jumping about, he said, communicate feelings of friendliness or approach. Such behaviors promote species survival. The show of hostility frightens off enemies or competitors. Approach behavior facilitates social interaction.

Darwin also examined the survival value of emotions in terms of their motivating aspects. Fear, he thought, maintained the species by motivating the animal to caution, while anger motivated it to remove obstacles that stood in the way of survival. Darwin's formulation is relatively succinct behaviorally. An external stimulus event gives rise to a feeling state, the emotion, which then effects (motivates?) a response:

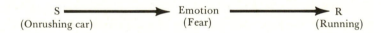

JAMES-LANGE PERIPHERAL THEORY

A few years after Darwin, the pioneer American psychologist, William James (1890, 1894), suggested that feeling states were primarily physiological in origin. He maintained that emotion arose from the person's perception of physical changes in the state of various internal organs, such as changes in stomach contraction, heartbeat, respiration, and dilation and contraction of blood vessels. In other words, physiological changes mediated by the autonomic nervous system. Unlike Darwin, James did not regard these changes as the cause of the overt behavior, but rather as the result. That is, James maintained that "we feel sorry because we cry . . . not that we cry . . . because we are sorry . . ." (1890 II). He insisted that bodily changes follow an exciting event and that the immediate perception of those changes constitutes the emotion.

It is traditional at this point to state that the Danish physiologist, Carl Lange, independently proposed the same theory as James. As a result, the concept is often referred to as the *James-Lange theory,* and the original papers of each were published together as a book, entitled *The Emotions* (Lange and James, 1922). While the two points of view are similar in that both are peripheral theories, Lange's formulation was, in a sense, narrower than James'. Lange considered only changes in blood circulation as involved in emotion while James included all the internal organs. Specifically, Lange contended that emotion was localized in the vasomotor system, which controls the contraction of the blood vessels. When this system is stimulated, he said, a person experiences feelings. Therefore Lange concludes:

We owe all the emotional side of our mental life, our joys and sorrows, our happy and unhappy hours, to our vaso-motor system. If the impressions which fall upon our senses did not possess the power of stimulating it, we would wander through life unsympathetic and passionless, all impressions of the outer world would only enrich our experience, increase our knowledge, but would arouse neither joy nor anger, would give us neither care nor fear (Lange and James, 1922, p. 80).

Further, Lange globalized his concept by postulating that awareness of changes in the diameter of blood vessels is the basis, not only of emotion, but also all behavior. So, his theory, while physiologically more restricted than James', is psychologically much broader.

The James-Lange peripheral theory of emotion, like Cannon's peripheral theory of motivation, was compatible with the thinking of the psychologists and physiologists of the time. Indeed, it became the dominant point of view among psychologists. For years this theory was regarded by them, as Dunlap notes, ". . . as the basis for the study of the emotional life." (1922).

CRITIQUE OF THE JAMES-LANGE THEORY

Despite its position in contemporary thought of the early 1900s, the theory did not escape unscathed. Sherrington, in 1900, attempted to refute it by demonstrating that dogs manifested rage even after the spinal cord was severed. In 1927, Cannon wrote an extensive review article covering all the experimentation and observation on emotion to that time and concluded that the data offered little to support the James-Lange theory. He defined five major objections.

1. Total separation of the viscera from the CNS does not alter emotional behavior. Cannon removed the sympathetic ganglia in cats and found, as Sherrington had in dogs, that it did not eliminate rage responses. Cannon also offered as evidence against James and Lange the famous clinical report of Dana (1921) concerning a forty-year-old woman who broke her neck in a fall from a horse. She was quadriplegic and anesthetic from the neck down. Yet, for the year that she lived, she was reported as having expressed every emotion in a manner similar to the way she behaved before the accident.

In such cases there is not necessarily a total separation of visceral feedback to the CNS. Besides, James and Lange did not claim that the ability to express emotion depended on such pathways, but only that the ability to experience emotion did.

2. The same visceral changes occur in very different emotional states and in nonemotional states. This involves the fact that such changes as acceleration of heart rate, dilation and contraction of blood vessels, lowered blood sugar, sweating, and variances in respiration rate can occur without giving rise to emotion under many relatively nonemotional conditions, such as exercise, exposure to extreme temperatures, and injections of drugs. Also, the same organic changes occur with quite different emotions.

3. The viscera are relatively insensitive structures. Compared to somatic sensory innervation, there are few afferent fibers originating from the internal organs. The fact that one is usually unaware of such activities as stomach contractions or liver and spleen pulsations illustrates the point.

4. Visceral changes are too slow to be a source of emotional feeling. Smooth muscle, as implied earlier (Chapter 6), has a comparatively long latency. In some instances, there can be several minutes between activation of an organ and a resulting afferent potential. In view of these facts, it seems highly dubious that emotion comes out of the viscera.

This "inferiority" of the autonomic nervous system has been challenged lately. It has been found that the temporal relations between visceral sensations and one's awareness of them occur rapidly enough to be readily conditioned (Bykov, 1957; Miller, 1969; Razran, 1961; and see Chapter 10).

5. Artificial induction of the visceral changes typically related to strong emotions does not produce emotion. The contention here is that pharmacological activation of the autonomic nervous system should produce emotional feelings. The classic study, cited by Cannon, was done by Marañon (1924). He injected 210 individuals of diverse ages and backgrounds with epinephrine to induce sympathetic nervous system arousal. He then asked each person to report how he felt. Most of the subjects (71 percent) reported some physical symptoms, such as flushing, warmth, pounding heart, and tremors, but with no associated emotional aspects. The remainder reported an emotional experience, but most of them were what Marañon called "as if" emotions. That is, the subjects reported, "I feel as if I were afraid, as if I want to cry, as if I were happy," rather than "I am afraid, sad, happy." It was possible with some subjects to obtain a "real" emotion if they were confronted with a situational circumstance, such as the presumed death of a loved one. Marañon described it thus:

One must suggest a memory with strong affective force but not so strong as to produce an emotion in the normal state. For example, in several cases we spoke to our patients before the injection of their sick children or dead parents and they responded calmly to this topic. The same topic presented later during the adrenal commotion, was sufficient to trigger emotion. The adrenal commotion places the subject in a situation of "affective imminence" (1924, pp. 307–308).

The relationship between artificial inducement of visceral changes and emotion has been subsequently elaborated by Schachter and his colleagues. In one instance (Schachter and Wheeler, 1962), they injected one group of human subjects with epinephrine; another with the adrenergic blocking drug, chlorpromazine; and a third with saline (the solvent for the drugs). All the subjects were shown a humorous film and laughing responses were recorded. Relative to the saline-treated group, the epinephrine-treated subjects laughed the most and the chlorpromazine-treated subjects laughed the least. In another study (Schachter and Singer, 1962), epinephrine-treated subjects mimicked the emotional responses of stooges (experimenter assistants acting as subjects) more than undrugged control groups.

CANNON-HEAD CENTRAL THEORY

After offering these objections to the James-Lange theory, Cannon proceeded to offer an alternative central theory of emotion involving the thalamus. Ironically, this was a central nervous system theory of emotion despite the fact that Cannon had been an advocate of the peripheral approach to motivation. Initially, Cannon based this theory on clinical observations reported by the British neurologist Henry Head (see Chapter 5), and at first the theory was known as the *Cannon-Head theory* of emotion.

Head (1920) had described several cases of unilateral thalamic lesions in which the patients reacted excessively to very slight stimulation. If the stimulus was mildly disagreeable, such as a pin prick or chill, the patient manifested extreme discomfort. If the stimulus was mildly agreeable, such as music or warmth, the patient manifested extreme delight, often to the point where the delight was itself unbearable. It felt so good the patient could not stand it! From these observations, Head concluded that the lesions released the thalamus from cortical inhibition.[2]

Citing other clinical data, including his own as well as Sherrington's (1900) neuraxial transection studies mentioned

2. The inhibitory role of the cortex in the regulation of emotion is a basic tenet of neurology, espoused by John Hughlings Jackson and explained in Chapter 11.

earlier, Cannon concluded that the thalamus was the integrating center for emotion. He said that "the peculiar quality of the emotion is added to the simple sensation when the thalamic processes are roused" (1927). The paradigmatic representation would be as follows:

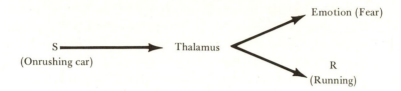

CANNON-BARD THEORY

In subsequent years, Philip Bard, an American physiologist, provided much experimental evidence to support Cannon's notion. As a result, and because of his more specific implication of the hypothalamus, the present form of the theory is referred to as the *Cannon-Bard theory*. Bard (1928, 1939) implicated the hypothalamus in emotion by demonstrating, with systematic neuraxial transections, that an intact hypothalamus is necessary for integrated emotional behavior. He found that fully developed rage, reflected by such behavior as hissing, scratching, biting, and attack, could be elicited by pinching a cat's tail, even with all brain tissue above the hypothalamus surgically removed. Once the hypothalamus itself was ablated, however, only certain components of the rage response could be obtained. Specifically, these were the components mediated by the autonomic nervous system, which involved such behavior as snarling, spitting, tail lashing, piloerection, increased blood pressure and heart rate, and sweating. Bard called this response syndrome *sham rage*, not to imply that the rage was false in any sense, but rather to emphasize that no subjective aspects were involved. The rage behavior was not part of a fully integrated pattern of directed attack. The animal was angry, but not angry at anything.

These ablation studies were later complemented by electrical brain stimulation studies. Hess (1954), using chronically implanted electrodes in the brains of intact cats, found that the hypothalamus, like the autonomic nervous system, was functionally organized into sympathetic and parasympathetic divisions. The posterior portion is organized as a sympathetic integrating center, which Hess called the *ergotrophic zone*. Stimulation of it increased heart rate and blood pressure. Behaviorally, the animals became alert, aroused, and, if the stimulation persisted, aggressive to the point of attack. The anterior portion, which correlated with parasympathetic functioning, Hess called the *tropotrophic zone*. Stimulation resulted in decreased heart rate and dilation of peripheral blood vessels. Behaviorally, the cats became calm and drowsy and eventually went to sleep if the stimulation was maintained.

PAPEZ-MACLEAN THEORY

At the time when Cannon and Bard were performing their ablation experiments on cats, James Papez, an American neuroanatomist, was also looking into the neural aspects of emotion. He had noticed the relation between lesions in a number of subcortical structures and changes in emotional behavior. In rabies, for example, Papez noted that:

> . . . the essential lesions of rabies, or hydrophobia, have their site of predilection in the hippocampus and the cerebellum and since the disease is characterized by intense emotional convulsive and paralytic symptoms, there seems to be offered an important clue to the probable location of the emotive mechanism. The prodromal symptoms—insomnia, irritability and restlessness—usher in the stage of excitement and profound emotional perturbation. There is extreme hyperesthesia to all forms of stimuli, such as light and sound, and every stimulus situation provokes great apprehensiveness and paroxysms of fear. The patient presents the appearance of intense fright and of mingled terror and rage (1937, p. 735).

Augmenting these observations on patients, Kluver and Bucy (1937) reported that lesions to many of the subcortical areas and the temporal lobes in the brains of monkeys produced profound emotional changes. The animals became passive, docile, and unemotional, even when provoked. They also showed changes in motivated behavior, such as hypersexuality, and

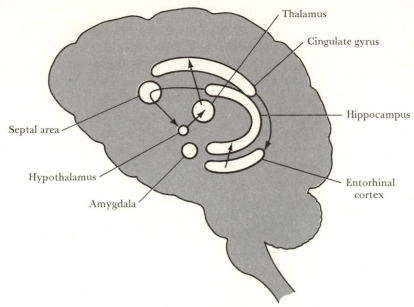

Figure 9-1.Thalamus

Cingulate gyrus

Hippocampus

Septal area

Hypothalamus

Amygdala

Entorhinal cortex

Figure 9-1. Papez circuit (*shown by arrows*). Note that it involves all the structures of the limbic system.

a compulsive mouthing of even inedible objects. This behavior pattern is known as the *Kluver-Bucy syndrome*.

By combining such comparative anatomical findings with the clinical evidence, Papez postulated a cortical-subcortical system or series of pathways in the brain, known as the *Papez circuit,* to explain the origin and regulation of emotion. In this circuit, (see Figure 9-1) sensory impulses, such as sound and sight, travel to the thalamus and hypothalamus which act as relay stations and regulators. Here, the impulses are joined by those from the cortex via the hippocampus. The cortical contribution stimulates the hypothalamus with what Papez calls "psychic activity" (such as thought and imagination). Then the confluent impulses stream into the cingulate gyrus, which gives rise to the experience known as emotion. Papez singled out additional circuits which, he felt, tied the operation of the cortex and the subcortex together in "an attempt to allocate specific organic units to a larger organization dealing with a complex regulatory process" (1937).

MacLean (1949) elaborated upon Papez's theory by suggesting the addition of the limbic system (Chapter 4), or "visceral brain," as he called it, to the Papez circuit. In doing so, MacLean emphasized the integrative aspects of the system by correlating emotionality with motivationally-oriented, sensory-motor components (e.g., the sight of a gun and fear-motivated flight). Starting in the early 1950s, Brady and his colleagues (Brady, 1960, 1962; Brady and Nauta, 1953, 1955; Brady, Schreiner, and Geller, 1954; Schreiner and King, 1953) verified the limbic system involvement in emotional behavior by means of a large number of animal experiments. They demonstrated that various parts of the limbic system have inhibitory or facilitory effects on emotionality. But, perhaps, more significantly, the studies revealed that the changes in emotional behavior brought about by brain manipulation will occur only under certain external environmental conditions, that is, when a relevant outside stimulus is present.

CONTEMPORARY CONCEPTIONS

The trend today in defining the physical correlates of emotion remains CNS-oriented despite a recent suggestion (Fehr and Stern, 1970) that a more comprehensive approach should be attempted. As with many other attempts at localization (Chapter 11), the emphasis has become biochemical rather than anatomical. Mason and his colleagues (Mason, Brady, and Sidman, 1957; Mason et al., 1961), for instance, have found a relationship between emotionality and the blood levels of various biogenic amines, such as epinephrine and norepinephrine, and ACTH. Wolley and van der Hoeven (1963) have also implicated serotonin in the expression of emotions. However, other authors stress that a biochemical explanation of emotion is not enough. The integration of body, mind, and environment are crucial to an understanding of human emotion. For example, Schildkraut and Kety point out:

It is not likely that changes in the metabolism of the biogenic amines alone will account for the complex phenomena of normal or pathological affect. Whereas the effects of these amines at particular sites in the brain may be of crucial importance in the regulation of affect, any comprehensive formulation of the physiology of affective state will have to include many other concomitant biochemical, physiological, and psychological factors ... the intricate ... environmental and psychological determinants of emotion ... must be stressed (1967, p. 28).

SUMMARY

To emphasize again, there are no areas of behavior in which body and mind are so intimately related as in motivation and emotion. This is so because both take on a meaningful relationship to the maintenance of the fundamental integrity of the organism, primarily in terms of the environmental conditions under which emotion and motivation occur. Also, these behavioral characteristics, like any other integrated behavior, cannot be physiologically localized in any one area of the body because of the interplay of these multifarious aspects.

SUGGESTED READINGS

McCleary, R. A., and Moore, R. Y. *Subcortical Mechanisms of Behavior*. New York: Basic Books, 1965. Superior introductory description of the physiological substrates of emotion and motivation.

Smythies, J. R. *Brain Mechanisms and Behavior*. New York: Academic Press, 1970. A somewhat more advanced and up-to-date discussion of research concerned with subcortical mechanisms.

10 Consciousness

WHAT IS CONSCIOUSNESS?

Consciousness is a familiar word these days. Thanks to a variety of social liberation movements and to books such as William Reich's *Greening of America* (1970), the word consciousness, once used to designate the knowledge a man shares with himself, is used in everyday language to describe an awareness of one's values and role in society. Reich's facile grouping of levels of awareness as Consciousness I, II, and III gives some common understanding of the term's usage to represent one's inward view of his relationship to his family, to the generations, and to the world around him.

The lack of precise definition and the diverse application of the term consciousness in day to day language usually presents no special problems. But, psychologists, as has already been seen, need empirical or conceptual specification of a behavior before they can proceed to investigate it. Thus, for psychology, precise definition of consciousness becomes an issue and, as usual, there is a large variety of opinion. This chapter will begin with a discussion of psychology's attempts to define the concept of consciousness. That will be followed by a consideration of attempts to specify a physical locus for the various behavioral states one or another theorist considers an aspect of consciousness.

PSYCHOLOGICAL DEFINITIONS OF CONSCIOUSNESS

Psychologically, the term *consciousness* was originally defined as self-awareness of one's knowledge and thought. Over the years, the definition has broadened to embrace awareness of all experience, including sensations, perceptions, emotions, desires, and volition (the topics discussed throughout this book). So pervasive did this latter definition become that William James defined psychology as the "study of consciousness" (1890). This concept remained fashionable until Freud's treatment of consciousness. Freud postulated what amounts to three levels: active awareness (consciousness), relative unawareness (subconsciousness), and total unawareness (unconsciousness). Most relevant to the present discussion is the fact that Freud viewed consciousness as something that could be observed and measured through analysis (Figure 10-1).

However, with the advance of behaviorism and its subsequent domination of American psychology, any conception of consciousness was rendered untenable as a scientific construct. John Watson, who, as was pointed out (Chapter 1), is generally considered to be the founder of behaviorism, stated in the first account of his then new philosophy that:

The time seems to have come when psychology must discard all reference to consciousness and need no longer delude itself into making mental states the object of observation (1913, p. 163).

To Watson, consciousness was nothing more than a term applied to subtle responses to stimuli. Thought, for instance, was only the covert, silent movement of the vocal cords. Watson's 1913 declaration fitted in well with the desire of many psychologists of his time, especially the comparative psychologists, to become more "scientific," that is, more methodological and nondualistic. The elimination of the need to deal with consciousness allowed comparative psychologists to extrapolate from animal behavior to human behavior.

This behaviorist denigration of the role of consciousness—indeed, the denial of its existence—is not accepted everywhere. For example, Burt states that ". . . without it observation which every scientist, including the behaviorist, automatically postulates would be impossible" (1962). Opponents of the behaviorist point of view maintain that attempts to ignore or to call consciousness by some other name do not in any way change the fact of its existence. The cognitive psychologists argue that the conscious mind is not a passive receiver of impressions but that it actively processes information and utilizes it in new ways. For instance, Sperry (1969)[1] postulated that consciousness has a directive role which determines the flow of cerebral excitation.

In response to such arguments, the behaviorists initially attempted a form of methodological circumvention. They emphasized the need for objective analysis, thereby limiting observations of behavior only to overt or public events. Thus consciousness could not exist unless there was a behavioral correlate or a physiological component in action. Under this stricture, consciousness could not be defined in terms of one's own awareness of himself (introspection) but only in terms of one's awareness of the awareness of others as expressed through their behavior!

The current tendency in behaviorism is to regard consciousness as a covert response (Lichtenstein, 1971). In paradigm form, $S \rightarrow R$ is regarded as $S \rightarrow R_1 R_2$, where R_1 is the perceptual response and R_2 the reporting response. R_2 is obviously dependent on R_1 and is the actual data that psychologists obtain and study. For example, R_1 is the personal visual experience of seeing green, R_2 is the verbal report "I see green."

Thus contemporary behaviorism has attempted to modify Watson's absolute rejection of consciousness. But the damage has already been done. Behaviorist domination of experimental psychology over the years, while markedly improving methodological rigor, has also contributed to the retreat of the field from a viable interdisciplinary science.[2]

If consciousness is to be restored to psychology, physiological psychology will have the enormous task of defining its physical basis. Can this be done? The solution has frequently been attempted with the typical experimental approaches, notably,

1. See Chapter 16 for a full account of Sperry's position.

2. As Eccles recently indicated "There has been over the last decades a distortion of psychology into a purely behavioural psychology of a strictly deterministic and so-called objective character. . . . We suffer today from the unjustifiable violence done by psychologists to the science of psychology when they reject from its subject matter all conscious experiences" (1970, p. 3).

A

B

Figure 10-1. Sigmund Freud (1856–1939), Viennese physician and founder of psycho-analysis. Freud's theories influenced many modern conceptions of behavior such as the nature of consciousness. **A,** Drawing by Jean Cocteau, *c.* 1923 (The Granger Collection), **B,** Photograph taken in the office of his Vienna home, *c.* 1930. (The Bettmann Archive.)

ablation and electrical stimulation of the nervous system. However, none of these approaches has yet proven to be completely successful.

DIFFICULTIES IN DEFINING THE PHYSICAL BASIS OF CONSCIOUSNESS

In the early days, the cerebral cortex was targeted as the seat of consciousness, but while many experiments showed that damage to the cortex can result in paralyses, anesthesias, and defects in memory, learning, and personality, none demonstrated the production of unconsciousness. Conversely, electrical stimulation of the cortex also failed to pinpoint a cortical center of consciousness.

Evolutionary theory has not been much help either, mainly because it is not clear at which point in the ascent of man consciousness arose, or even to what extent animals other than man possess this quality. Rose (1973) poses the question this way: "Let us assume that stones, for example, or viruses or bacteria . . . do not possess consciousness, but how about sea anemones, or flat-worms, or octopi, or frogs, or dogs, or chimpanzees?"

Rose goes on to suggest that there is a hierarchy of consciousness which is identifiable, or at least correlative, with the number of cells in the brain and the size of the neocortex and its association areas. A formula that relates level of consciousness with these factors would place man at the top of the list and show the enormous qualitative jump between man and the next species in line. This might be another way of indicating that consciousness is primarily a human affair, which may have evolved as a uniquely flexible strategy for survival. However, it leaves the question of how to prove, other than by a plausible process of elimination, that the physical parameters of consciousness are confined to the cortex.

Despite such difficulties, one external measure consistently correlates with the behavioral level of consciousness, from sleep to alertness (or, in Freudian terms, from unconsciousness to consciousness), and gives hope that a physiology of consciousness might be established. This is the electrical activity of the brain as recorded and measured by the *electroencephalograph*

(EEG), a device that measures electric brain activity from electrodes attached to the scalp. Most physiological work with consciousness has been done with the help of the EEG.

Some caveats should be noted, however, before considering the relationship of EEG waveforms and consciousness. For one thing, the EEG does not provide a measure of consciousness as a whole nor does it come to grips with the essential integrative mechanism behind the concept. Moreover, there is a problem in making clear distinctions among the states of consciousness based on overt behavior and on EEG traces. The immediately aware state, for instance, is behaviorally detected in animals through an orientating reflex—called by Pavlov the "What is It?" reflex—in which the animal gives a sign, such as ears up or a movement of the head, that shows it has received and is attending to an outside stimulus. Attention in the animal is, thus, a behavioral indicator of consciousness. A human being, however, may be inattentive and yet be perfectly conscious. How often does a person perform an action such as buttering bread or switching gears while his basic attention is directed elsewhere? Similarly in the case of the subconscious state, some awake brain processes are subconscious and so are some sleep brain processes (that is, dreaming), making the category difficult to define exactly. As will be seen, EEG traces can show differences among these conditions, more so than direct observation; and, to the extent that they do, scientists can begin to understand the physiology of consciousness.

USE OF THE EEG TO STUDY CONSCIOUSNESS

The existence of spontaneous, continuous, electrical activity in the brain was first reported in 1875 by Caton, who recorded from electrodes laid directly on the exposed brains of dogs. Some years later, Hans Berger, a German psychiatrist, demonstrated that this type of activity could be recorded from intact organisms without exposing the brain, and the modern EEG was born. The first published description of the EEG of man (Berger, 1929) involved a differentiation of EEG patterns as a function of the level of consciousness of the subject (Berger's son, Klaus).

EEGs, like any other bipotentials, are recorded in voltage-frequency values. To a certain extent, the states of consciousness correlate with these values (Figure 10-2). In some periods of sleep, for instance, the voltage changes are relatively large, but they occur infrequently to form a pattern characterized as a *high-voltage slow wave,* or *HVS*. This pattern is also often referred to as the *synchronized* pattern. At the other extreme of consciousness—the awake, alert, and fully aware state—the voltage changes are relatively small, but frequent. Alert awareness is characterized by a *low-voltage fast wave,* or *LVF*. Berger called this pattern the *beta-wave;* it is also referred to as the *desynchronized* or *activation pattern.* Intermediate between these extremes, Berger designated a region of *alpha-waves* (medium voltage, medium speed) to characterize an awake but calm, relaxed organism (see Chapter 12). Contemporary electrophysiologists, having the advantage of computer aids, tend to describe EEG recordings in terms of frequency or amplitude

Figure 10-2.   EEG tracings showing various patterns and their correlated behavioral states.

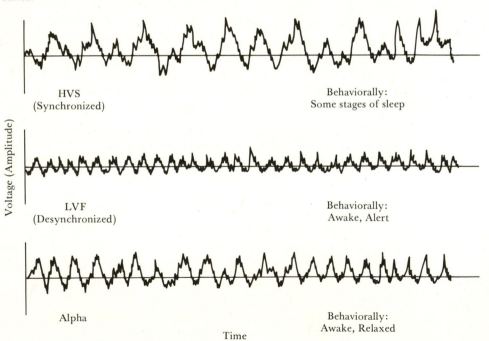

HVS
(Synchronized)

Behaviorally:
Some stages of sleep

Voltage (Amplitude)

LVF
(Desynchronized)

Behaviorally:
Awake, Alert

Alpha

Behaviorally:
Awake, Relaxed

Time

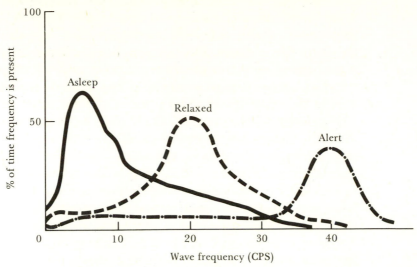

Figure 10-3. A frequency analysis of the EEG showing the relative percentages of the various frequencies present during different behavioral states of consciousness.

analysis (such as shown in Figure 10-3), rather than in wave patterns (Goldstein and Beck, 1965). Analytical efficiency is thereby greatly enhanced.

A Belgian physiologist, Frederic Bremer (1935), applied the new EEG technology to the study of states of consciousness in cats. Bremer used two neuraxial preparations (see Figure 10-4), a transection of the brain stem just posterior to the medulla and below the reticular formation, which he called an *encephale isolé* (isolation low on the brain); and a transection above the reticular formation directly through the thalamus, a *cerveau isolé* (isolation high on the brain). Despite somewhat different terminology, the preparations were identical to the neuraxial transections discussed in Chapter 7. The only significant difference is that the motor system studies were concerned with the activity of the caudal portion of the CNS independent of the rostral portion, while Bremer's studies were concerned with the opposite activity. In both cases, he recorded the animals' behavior along with their EEGs.

Bremer's results were the first to show a systematic relationship between EEG, behavior, and levels of consciousness. The encephale isolé animals were almost totally paralyzed but some behavior was still observable, and the EEG trace showed normal patterns of sleeping and waking activity. The cerveau isolé preparation resulted in totally unconscious animals, which at the same time showed continuously synchronized EEG patterns. These results appeared in conformity with the notion, prevalent among psychologists of the period, that sleep was simply due to a decrease of sensory stimulation to the brain. The cerveau isolé sectioned off all afferent cranial nerve input, except olfactory and visual, and all motor output, with its accompanying propioceptive feedback, except in regard to eye movement. It was concluded that, with the eyes closed, there was simply insufficient sensory support for maintaining wakefulness. Considering that olfaction is probably the primary sense for cats (as vision is for man), this conclusion was at best dubious. But the spirit of the times was against any change in the prevailing view, and Bremer's work did not stimulate further research interest.

SUBCORTICAL SYSTEMS AND CONSCIOUSNESS

Nowadays, it seems clear—the Russian reflexological viewpoint (page 194) notwithstanding—that the cortex is not directly involved in consciousness. Such physiological substrates as do seem to be involved are all subcortical: the reticular formation, the pons, the thalamus, and the hypothalamus. The influence of these areas lies, however, in their interaction with the cortex.

Reticular formation

In those same years that Bremer was working with the EEG, Allen (1932) published his conclusion that the reticular formation has something to do with the control of brain activity and, in fact, went on to suggest that the reticular formation might be the locus of consciousness. He employed a comparative anatomical analysis, pointing out that the reticular formation consists of cells "left over" after the sensory and motor systems were formed and that it receives input from all sensory and some motor systems. Despite the fact that Bremer's transections suggested a linkage between unconsciousness and the

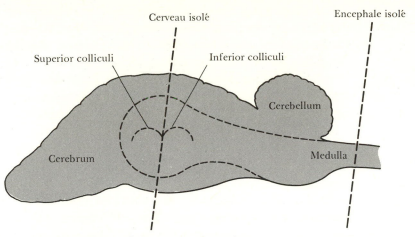

Figure 10-4. Levels (*dotted lines*) of Bremer's transections.

reticular formation, Allen's contention received scant attention from his contemporaries.

It was not until 1949, with the research of Moruzzi and Magoun, that the reticular formation received serious consideration. These scientists were monitoring the EEGs from an anesthetized cat in whose reticular formation electrodes were implanted. To their surprise, they found that when they stimulated the reticular formation the cat awoke, and its EEG waveform pattern shifted from high-voltage slow to low-voltage fast, the characteristic pattern of arousal from sleep. Other studies (Lindsley, 1958; Lindsley, Schreiner, and Magoun, 1949; Lindsley et al., 1950) demonstrated that organisms with lesions limited to the direct sensory pathways maintained normal sleep-wake behavior and EEG patterning, while those with only reticular formation lesions became comatose. It seemed clear that the reticular formation—not, as had been thought, sensory input per se—was critical to consciousness. The reticular formation was identified as the site of the *reticular activating system,* or *RAS* (see Figure 10-5), which is now conceived to be the basic arousal mechanism of the brain.

Functional interaction between the reticular formation and the cortex, as in any other cortical connection, is through the thalamus (Chapter 4). Unlike the "classical" systems, however,

187

which are topographically represented in discrete cortical areas, the reticular formation is represented in all of the neocortex. Consequently, the pathways are referred to as the *diffuse* or *non-specific thalamic projection system*.

It was discovered some years ago (Morison and Dempsey, 1942) that stimulating the thalamic nuclei, which receive reticular fibers, produces a cortical response that increases in a systematic way over time. This is called *cortical recruitment*, or the *recruiting response*, because it suggests that more and more neurons are being recruited into the activation initiated by the thalamic stimulation.

At first some observers felt that the recruiting response resembled the synchronized EEG characteristic of slow-wave sleep and that the diffuse thalamic system might be an antagonist of the reticular activating system. That is, the diffuse thalamic system might depress cortical excitability and induce sleep. However, the fact that certain thalamic lesions abolish the recruiting response but do not affect behavior, and the fact that some cortical areas have a lower rather than higher threshold during recruitment has rendered the notion untenable. A more plausible postulation is that the two systems interact to provide maximal behavioral adjustment. The diffuse thalamic system is sensitive to even slight changes in environmental stimuli and, thus, finely tunes the input from the rectricular system, which is capable of only gross differentiation among stimuli (Sharpless and Jasper, 1956).

The pons and hypothalamus

Hess (1954), in his studies of hypothalamic stimulation, found that a cat will curl up and go to sleep when the area along the midline of the thalamus is stimulated. He identified the region as a sleep center. Moruzzi (1954), on the other hand, described an area of the pons that, when ablated, induced cats to stay awake. These cats gave 20 percent of their day to sleep rather than the normal 65 percent. Thus, there appeared to be antagonistic sleep-wake centers similar to those for food consumption (Chapter 8). The connection between the hypothalamic areas, the pons, and the reticular formation in producing the states of consciousness and unconsciousness is still not clear.

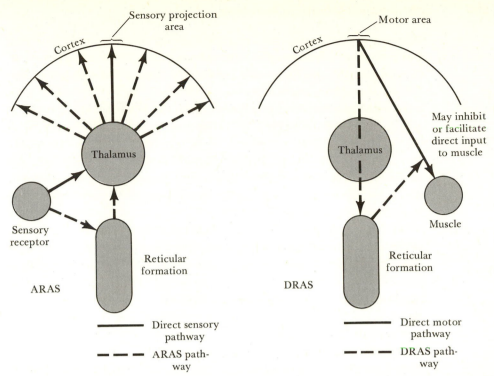

Figure 10-5. The ascending (ARAS) and descending (DRAS) reticular activating system. All sensory input to the cortex is represented in both the discrete sensory areas of the cortex and in the reticular formation. The latter arouses the whole cortex to a state of wakefulness, the former specifically identifies the sensory input. Impulses arising from cortical motor neurons provide input to muscles and to the reticular formation which may, in turn, modify the direct input to the muscle.

LEVELS OF UNCONSCIOUSNESS OR SLEEP

Just as there are different levels of consciousness, so too there are different levels of sleep. The notion of different levels of sleep is apparently very old; it is mentioned, for example, in ancient Hindu tales. Only recently, however, with the help of the EEG, has the existence of such levels been given experimental credibility. Kleitman (1963) and his colleagues (Aserinsky and Kleitman, 1955; Dement and Kleitman, 1955; 1957) recorded EEGs and eye movements of sleeping human infants and adults and observed that they went through several levels or stages, which alternated from periods of restless or active sleep to periods of still or quiescent sleep. The latter were characterized by *rapid eye movements*, or *REM*, and correlated with

189

reports of dreaming. Interestingly, some of the quiescent sleep periods were also characterized by a desynchronized EEG, that is, the pattern of an awake, alert person! Appropriately, the state was named *paradoxical sleep* because the fast brain waves indicated an alert rather than a sleeping individual.

Michel Jouvet, a French physiologist, and his colleagues have extensively studied the sleep of cats (Jouvet, 1967a, b; 1968) and found that many physiological changes accompany the shifts in sleep state. Besides EEG and eye movement changes, there are changes in heart rate, blood pressure, breathing, and muscle tone. Compared to slow-wave sleep, paradoxical sleep occurs in conjunction with decreased heart rate, lower blood pressure, lower muscle tone, and decreased respiration. In the sense that these vital bodily functions are more depressed, paradoxical sleep is a deeper sleep. In addition, much more intense stimulation is necessary to awaken an animal from paradoxical sleep than from slow-wave sleep.

Cerveau isolé or anesthetically induced sleep is completely of the slow-wave type associated with active sleep, yet behaviorally the organism is so unconscious that it cannot be aroused by any stimulation. The cortex is involved. It appears that the cerveau isolé transection severs the cortico-thalamic pathways, preventing activation of the cortex by input from the thalamus. Anesthetics are believed to act in the same way. Consequently, it would seem that the cortex must be activated before paradoxical sleep can be achieved. However, decortication produces only paradoxical sleep. In order to understand how these last two statements could both be true, Jouvet searched further for mechanisms of sleep and arousal.

Jouvet (1967b) discovered two interesting facts about neurochemicals in the brain which led to a more complete understanding of paradoxical sleep. He determined that the wakeful area of the brain was a part of the brain stem known as the *nuclei of raphe,* which contained a heavy concentration of serotonin; a nearby area, the *locus coeruleus,* contained norepinephrine. These areas are shown in Figure 10-6. When ablated, the locus coeruleus abolished paradoxical sleep. Putting these findings together, Jouvet postulated the existence of a biochemical system that regulates sleep. He suggested that sleepiness occurs when the serotonin levels of the Raphe nuclei pass a

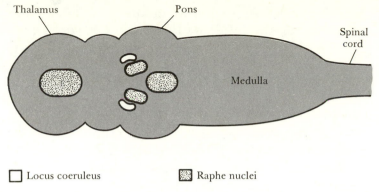

Thalamus　　　　　　Pons

Spinal
cord

Medulla

☐ Locus coeruleus　　　　▨ Raphe nuclei

Figure 10-6. Schematic representation of a dorsal view of the brain stem showing the areas involved in sleep.

threshold level. The increased serotonin causes decreased input to the cortex from the ascending RAS, thus decreasing cortical activity and eye movement and inducing slow-wave sleep. At the same time, locus coeruleus norepinephrine works to antagonize the descending RAS, decreasing muscle activity. Meantime monoamine oxidases have deactivated the serotonin, reactivating the ascending RAS, but not to the extent of affecting behavioral sleep. The result: paradoxical sleep. Figure 10-7 diagrams the biochemical changes just described.

DRUGS AND SLEEP

Understanding the chemical mechanisms of sleep is not only important in developing a full picture of the physiology of consciousness but has profound significance for the pharmacological understanding of sleep-producing drugs, such as sedatives and anesthetics. But, from a pharmacological perspective, Jouvet's contentions offer what might at first appear to be neurohumoral incompatibilities. For example, although he considers only biogenic amines, there are cholinergic aspects to sleep. Bradley (1958) reported that systemically administered atropine, an anticholinergic drug, results in a strongly synchronized EEG in rats, with a complete absence of concomitant behavioral sleep. Even very intense stimulation could not produce an EEG arousal pattern, and the animals readily

191

learned avoidance, discrimination, and maze-running tasks while under the effect of the drug. Conversely, Hernandez-Peon and Brust-Carmona (1961) found that the hypothalamic sleep center could be activated by implantation of acetylcholine. Recently, Jasper and Tessier (1971) reported increased acetylcholine release from the cortex of cats during paradoxical sleep.

The apparent disparity between these biochemical sleep mechanisms can probably be resolved easily because the adrenergic and cholinergic systems are not mutually exclusive. In fact, it is well established that they are often synergistic in regard to the behavioral effects they induce (Chapter 15). As well, caution must be exercised in assuming a direct relation between the effects of systemically administered drugs and the neurochemical substrates of a given behavior. A systemically administered drug may have other effects, or may undergo metabolic changes in the organism to become another substance altogether. The biogenic amines, it will be recalled from Chapter 9, are also said to be involved in emotional arousal.

STUDIES OF THE SUBCONSCIOUS

Freud differentiated between the state of awareness and unawareness in an awake organism; the latter state is sometimes called preconsciousness but, more often, *subconsciousness*. One of the popular early criticisms of psychoanalysis was directed at this differentiation because the subconscious had not been experimentally verified. This has changed. In recent years, the state of awake unawareness has been subjected to experimentation with positive results.

In a typical experiment, Hefferline and Perera (1963) rewarded several subjects with money for pushing a key with their thumbs at the sound of a bell. By means of a recording electrode, the thumb muscle of each subject was made to activate the bell circuit without the subjects knowing it; indeed, they did not even feel the muscle twitch. The subjects pressed the key every time the bell rang and did not stop even when the sound level of the bell was gradually decreased until it was no longer ringing. The investigators concluded that the subjects had learned to respond to the muscle twitch, not to the bell, and had done it subconsciously.

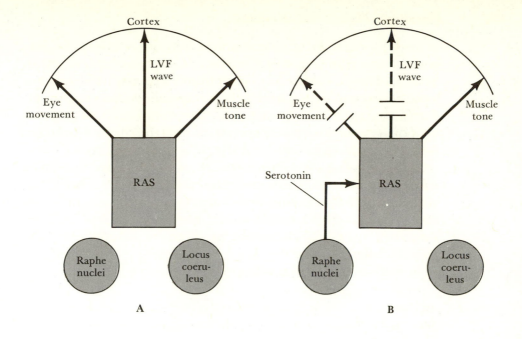

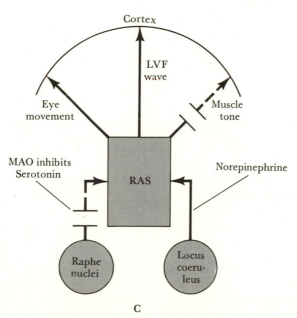

Figure 10-7. A diagrammatic representation of biochemical changes during the passage from wakefulness to slow-wave sleep to paradoxical sleep; **A,** wakefulness is transformed into **B,** slow-wave sleep; this becomes **C,** paradoxical sleep when the serotonin level is reduced by MAO inhibitors and norepinephrine from the locus coeruleus supplants it and effects reduced muscle tone.

Examples of learning that occurs subconsciously have also been reported in connection with interoceptive classical conditioning. Here, stimulation of, and/or responses by, various internal organs are utilized in the classical conditioning paradigm[3] (Bykov, 1957). In humans, for example, a conditioned dilation response of the blood vessels in the arms was established by a simple but unusual stimulus—pumping warm water through a balloon swallowed by the subject (Razran, 1961). After a number of pairings of heat applied to an area of the arm (causing vasodilation) with warm water in the stomach, the latter alone could cause vasodilation of blood vessels in the arm. Data from these types of studies verify that subconsciousness is a real process.

Such results are interpreted thus:

It is from this point of view we think, that we should consider the single physiological mechanism of the origin of those phenomena diverse in physiological character, which are termed "conscious" and "subconscious." Subconscious stimulation is a real process, accomplished in the cerebral cortex, which may become perceptible and present, depending on the character of the intercentral relations in the given current behavioral act. Any stimulus from the internal and external milieu, depending on its physiological and biological intent and the functional state of its address, may become subconscious or be immediately transformed in a conscious one. (Airapetyantz and Bykov, 1945, pp. 592–593).

In this type of analysis, consciousness, subconsciousness, and presumably unconsciousness, are construed to be merely different levels of attention. All stimulation of the nervous system is "registered," and the part which is "utilized" to maintain the integrity of the organism represents consciousness. The remainder is subconsciousness. Since the cerebral cortex is the locus of the integration of the internal and external sensory inputs with the motor system, it can be considered the seat of consciousness. Such a position displays overtones of reflex doctrine and Sherringtonian constructs which are due to its development within Russian reflexology. Proponents of the view have had difficulty rendering it compatible with the rela-

3. See Chapter 12 for a definition of classical conditioning.

tively well elaborated functions of the reticular formation as described earlier (see Anokhin, 1961).

STUDIES OF SUPRACONSCIOUSNESS

Scientific psychology has, in recent years, started to deal seriously with some altered states of consciousness that heretofore were regarded as artifactual. The various states are behaviorally and physiologically dissimilar, except for being collectively considered "above" the more usual levels of consciousness (i.e., as representing instances of *supraconsciousness*).

Transcendental meditation

Transcendental meditation, which is a process of achieving a higher plane of consciousness through continued concentration on an object or sound, represents another instance of behavioral-physiological paradox. The so-called high or trance that practitioners achieve is behaviorally sleeplike; while the physiological picture is one of relaxed wakefulness, including prominent EEG alpha-waves (Wallace, 1970; Wallace, Benson, and Wilson, 1971). The state is apparently induced by self-imposed reduction (biofeedback, Chapter 12) of body activities mediated by the parasympathetic nervous system—such as decreased heart rate, blood pressure, and oxygen consumption. In that sense, the transcendental state is the direct opposite of the more familiar emotional arousal mediated by the sympathetic nervous system (Chapter 9).

Subjectively, the meditative state involves consciousness expansion or increased sensory awareness. Devotees report sensory, perceptual, and cognitive experiences beyond those possible by the usual neural functioning. The state closely resembles that achieved with hallucinogenic drugs, and meditation is often advocated as a substitute for such drug use—the "drugless high."

Hypnosis

Hypnosis, an artificially induced, sleeplike state in which there is increased responsiveness to suggestions and commands, resembles neither sleep nor meditation physiologically. The physiological parameters of a hypnotized subject parallel whatever emotional state has been suggested by the hypnotist (Barber, 1965; Hilgard, 1973; Sheehan, 1973), whether it be suggestions designed to alter the functioning of organs directly or to produce byproducts of affective changes. Thus, the suggestion of fear could produce acceleration of heart rate, and the suggestion of a hot branding iron on the skin could actually produce blisters. The well-known increase in physical endurance in hypnosis is said to be due to selective anesthesia, or inhibition of the expectation of pain or fatigue (Schneck, 1953).

Hypnosis is currently drawing research attention in two respects. There is still skepticism on the part of some observers as to whether the hypnotic state is "real." That is, does it involve an actual consciousness alteration (trance) or is it merely a state of decreased resistance to suggestibility (nontrance)? Despite numerous and highly complicated experimental attempts to expose any artifactual aspects in hypnosis-induced behaviors, the issue remains unresolved (Hilgard, 1973; Sheehan, 1973).

Hypnosis is also gaining interest in terms of clinical application. It is consistently valuable in the management of pain of all types, ranging from phantom limbs to migraine headache. There are also reports of its effectiveness in the management of a host of clinical conditions ranging from allergies to drug addiction (Hilgard, 1974).

Acupuncture

Acupuncture, the ancient Chinese practice of inserting needles in the body to control pain, has been of marked interest to Western medicine in the last few years (Chaves and Barber, 1973). Acupuncture is used both to relieve painful diseases, such as arthritis, and as a surgical anesthesia.[4] That it works is indisputable; how it works remains a mystery. The needles are commonly inserted only a few millimeters into the skin, often in physiologically innocuous areas and usually remote from the site of pain. For example, analgesia for gastric surgery is accomplished with needles inserted in the ear lobe. After insertion the needles are constantly rotated or electrically vibrated.

4. It has even been successfully employed in the treatment of drug addiction (Wen and Chung, 1973).

The traditional theory maintains that acupuncture works by restoring balance between the two forces (Yang and Yin) of life energy. Modern conjecture centers on Melzack and Wall's (1965) gate hypothesis of pain (described in detail in Chapter 5). This hypothesis, it will be recalled, maintains that the experience of pain depends on the relative neural activity between larger and smaller diameter fibers. Since the former type conduct impulses arising from nonpain stimuli and close the spinal gate, acupuncture needles are presumed to work by stimulating their activity. In contrast, Chaves and Barber (1973) suggest acupuncture is essentially placebo therapy (see Chapter 15).

Extrasensory perception

Extrasensory perception (ESP), which includes *telepathy, clairvoyance, precognition, reterocognition,* and *psychokinesis,*[5] is just beginning to enjoy scientific respectability (Tomkins and Bird, 1973; Watson, 1973). Consequently, there has been little research regarding its physiological aspects. Schmeidler (1969) succinctly states, "Good research on physiological determinants of ESP has been so sparse that it would be dangerous to offer anything more than tentative generalizations."

Asimov (1972) suggests that some ESP phenomena may represent endogenous self-stimulation of the cortex, similar to the kind of sensory and cognitive experiences Penfield (1958) provoked when he electrically stimulated cortical areas of patients undergoing brain surgery. Dean and Nash (1967) and Tart (1963) imply that the autonomic nervous system is somehow involved. Sympathomimetic drugs do indeed alter ESP capacity; drugs such as the amphetamines increase the variability of the subjects' ability to receive transmitted thoughts (Cadoret, 1953; Huby and Wilson, 1961; Rogers and Carpenter, 1966). Ullman, Krippner, and Vaughan (1973), using the EEG/REM measure of dreaming, demonstrated the receipt of telepathic messages by sleeping subjects. Specifically, an individual could transmit elements of pictures he was concentrating on into the dream content of sleeping subjects. Once the sleeping subject

5. See the Glossary for definitions of these terms.

showed REM sleep (and, hence, was dreaming), he would be awakened and asked to describe his dream. The content of the pictures and dreams correlated significantly. Interesting as these studies are, synthesis and a conceptual model of the physiological correlates of ESP is a long way from fruition.

Psychic healing

Psychic healing is said to bring about a remission of pathology by an act of will on the part of a healer, rather than by any sort of medical intervention. From ancient primitive shamans to backwoods Bible Belt faith healers, some form of the laying-on of hands has been a cure for almost any illness. Psychic healing has enjoyed a revival in recent years, and numerous clinically verifiable cures, up to and including remission of cancerous tumors, are said to have been accomplished (Newsweek, 1974).

At the present time, the mechanisms of the mind-body relationships involved remain vague. LeShan (1974) maintains that the process involves helping the patient achieve a level of consciousness where his self-healing mechanisms become highly mobilized. LeShan himself has learned to do this and has effected cures; he contends anyone can develop the technique and that physicians and nurses should. Even without going that far, psychic healing will have made a significant contribution if it does nothing more than move medical practice back to a less mechanistic, more humanistic, position.

SUMMARY

In this chapter, a number of psychological definitions of consciousness have been discussed. A strict behavioristic definition, which limits the study of consciousness to objective observation alone, seems far removed from a full examination of the content of the mind. In preference, the Freudian categories of consciousness, subconsciousness, and unconsciousness have been used as the organizing basis for understanding what physiological psychologists have accomplished thus far in their search to explicate the physical basis of consciousness. Although some of the research holds promising possibilities, the present understanding of consciousness is minimal. Moreover, if psychologists are to fully understand the content of the mind, they will need to utilize a broader approach than presently used. In Heath's terms, there is a need for both the inspective scientific methods of anatomy, physiology, chemistry and electronics; and for the introspective approach which depends on a person's reporting of his subjective state of consciousness (1962). Only by correlating data from the two methods can a better understanding of consciousness be obtained.

SUGGESTED READINGS

Boring, E. G. *The Physical Dimensions of Consciousness*. New York: Dover, 1933. A classic, an outstanding discussion of the philosophical basis of scientific psychology.

Foulkes, W. D. *The Psychology of Sleep*. New York: Schribner, 1966. Comprehensive overview of research and concepts concerning sleeping and dreaming.

11 | Localization and frontal lobe functions

The three previous chapters have been concerned primarily with subcortical structures as they relate to behavior. The next few chapters will be concerned primarily with the role of the cerebral cortex and the so-called higher brain functions in relation to behavior. Basic to concepts of higher brain functioning is the issue of *functional localization*. What are the specific areas or centers of the nervous system which are the physical basis (or physiological cause) of specific behaviors? The topographical mapping of cortical sensory and motor areas in Chapter 4, as well as the attempted specification of hypothalamic feeding centers in Chapter 8 and reticular sleep centers in Chapter 10, are examples of functional localization.

EARLY CONCEPTIONS OF BEHAVIORAL CENTERS IN THE BRAIN

The notion of control centers of behavior in the brain is as old as the anatomical understanding of the nervous system. Hippocrates, the early Greek physician, is said to be the first to associate mental activity with the brain. In later years, according to Murphy, you could always find "a bold medical practitioner . . . who would lock memory in one lobe of the brain, fantasy in another, and will in a third . . ." (1949). Throughout the Middle Ages and the Renaissance, this approach to a file cabinet view of the brain fitted well with the burgeoning studies of the nervous system and with the observations of changes in the movement of muscles due to cranial injuries.

Leonardo da Vinci's definitive anatomical studies of the brain in the sixteenth century led to the postulation that three of the fundamental faculties of human mental activity were localized in the ventricles. The anterior ventricles, or *cellula phantastica,* were considered the center for the faculties of sensation and imagination; the second ventricle, or *cellula rationalis,* was the center for thought; and the third ventricle, or *cellula memorialis,* was the center for memory. The material substance of the brain, even though it was subdivided and its parts named by anatomists, was considered to act as a unit. The destruction of one part, they thought, did not result in loss of a function because another part simply took over.

Gall's theory of functional localization

This tripartite view of the busy spaces of the brain was not seriously questioned until the beginning of the nineteenth century, when a Viennese anatomist named Franz Joseph Gall attempted to compartmentalize various kinds of moral and intellectual faculties in different areas of the brain. He maintained, for instance, that the faculty of speech was localized in the frontal lobes just above the eyes, basing the claim on his boyhood observation that excellent orators had prominent eyes. Their frontal lobes, he thought, being extraordinarily developed, pressed the eyes outward.

Gall began to study the cranial development of exceptional people with the intent of localizing the various faculties contributing to their behavior. Initially, he studied criminals and inmates of asylums in terms of "bumps" or protuberances on their skulls which, he declared, corresponded to the shape of the brain. Gall believed that the shape was molded by the qualities of the brain. Thus, insight into an individual's character could be obtained by studying the shape of the skull. For example, a "bump" directly above the ears, which was assumed to correlate with acquisitiveness, was characteristic of pickpockets. Gall referred to his theory as *physiognomy* and began teaching it.

He was joined in 1800 by Johann Kasper Spurzheim, one of

his pupils. Spurzheim attempted to improve the scientific reception of Gall's idea by calling it *phrenology* (which literally means "science of the mind") and persuading Gall to consider and deal with the more positive aspects of human behavior. Spurzheim succeeded in popularizing phrenology so much that it grew into a worldwide movement. Figure 11-1 shows a typical phrenological chart used by Gall, Spurzheim, and their followers.

Phrenology was not, of course, universally accepted; in fact it was disapproved by the Austrian government, the church, and the scientific community. One accusation led to another, and in 1805 the government, at the insistence of the church, ordered Gall and Spurzheim to stop teaching phrenology. Defiant but helpless, they fled Vienna in 1807 and settled in Paris. Again, they were accepted by everyone except the government, the church, and the scientific community. On one occasion, Gall and Spurzheim were proposed for membership in the French Academy of Sciences on the basis of their research, and a committee was formed to examine their applications. However, Napoleon intervened and the applications were denied.

Over the years, Gall's notions have been vigorously opposed by neuroscientists (e.g., English and English, 1958). But, considered in a contemporary perspective, he pioneered several important psychological concepts. Gall was among the first to consider mind-body relationships empirically, contending that the philosophizing of the then dominant British empiricists, such as Locke, was not empirical at all. He suggested that psychology should be divorced from speculative philosophy and become the special study of the naturalist and physiologist. In pursuit of this goal, Gall can be considered a founder of physiological psychology along with Wundt and Bain (Chapter 1). More specifically, and directly relevant to the present discussion, Gall firmly established the concept of functional localization in the brain.

Unfortunately, Gall was also antiexperimental, preferring instead to use the naturalistic method of data acquisition, that is, to obtain data by direct observation and classification. While that has been his undoing in many circles, it should not detract from his contribution. Gall inspired a generation of investiga-

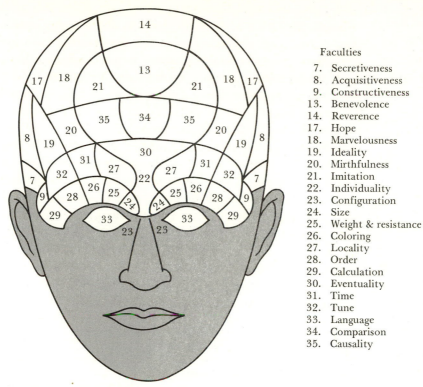

Faculties

7. Secretiveness
8. Acquisitiveness
9. Constructiveness
13. Benevolence
14. Reverence
17. Hope
18. Marvelousness
19. Ideality
20. Mirthfulness
21. Imitation
22. Individuality
23. Configuration
24. Size
25. Weight & resistance
26. Coloring
27. Locality
28. Order
29. Calculation
30. Eventuality
31. Time
32. Tune
33. Language
34. Comparison
35. Causality

Figure 11-1. Portion of a phrenological chart. The numbers on the head correspond to the faculties listed at the right. A "bump" in any numbered area would indicate that the person has the corresponding faculty.

tors to view the brain as a biological object. Thus, if characterization is necessary, Gall's contributions are protoscientific, not, as some maintain, pseudoscientific.

Flourens' theories

The early controversy over the merits of Gall's phrenology, and indeed of localization in general, involved another nineteenth century anatomist, Jean-Pierre-Marie Flourens, a permanent secretary of the French Academy of Science, grand officer of the Legion of Honor, national deputy, member of the French Academy, and professor at the Collège de France. Flourens had also been attempting to correlate behavior and the brain and came to the conclusion that much of the brain acted as a homogeneous unit. In contrast to Gall, he emphasized direct observation in carefully executed experiments on animals. To Flourens, method was of utmost importance. As he put it, "A new method leads to new results; a rigorous method to precise results; a vague method can only lead to confused results" (1842).

Flourens' emphasis on the experimental method was directed mainly to the nature of the ablation to be used in determining the relation of the brain to behavior. He carried out precise experiments on birds, for instance, which showed that many functions recovered to the same degree no matter which brain part was destroyed. He thereupon argued that one area took over to fill the gap left by the area that was removed, and thus he held firm to his case for the unity of the brain.

Flourens' ablations did indicate, however, that certain parts of the brain correlated with specific functions. His findings regarding cerebellar function still stand as accurate. He reported:

I made a lesion in the cerebellum of a young and healthy dog, by means of incisions which extended deeper and deeper. The animal gradually lost the power of ordered and regular movement and when the midregion of the cerebellum was reached he could only totter along with a zigzag motion . . . (1824, cited by Stevens, 1971, p. 37).

Flourens determined that the cerebellum coordinated the movements of locomotion.

Being a strict Cartesian dualist,[1] Flourens objected to Gall's division of the mind into faculties since, as he took pains to emphasize, the Cartesian soul is unitary and cannot be compartmentalized like the body. Flourens could not conceive of entering the mind experimentally and simply excluded the cerebrum from his experiments on the nervous system. As Young points out:

Although he localized different functions in different parts of the nervous system, he considered the hemispheres a unitary organ. Thus, he was an advocate of localization in the brain but not within the hemispheres themselves (1970, p. 69).

1. See Chapter 16 for a definition of Cartesian dualism.

and

Flourens was not prepared to submit human character, the mind, or its organs to analysis. Their unity was a necessary basis of his beliefs about man's dignity and freedom. On the other hand, he was prepared to subject sensory-motor functions to close analysis as long as the organ of the mind was kept entirely separate from his analysis (1970, p. 74).

From his experiments, Flourens concluded that the nervous system had two clearly separated functions: an *action propre,* or specific function, and an *action commune,* or holistic function. While it may be true that Flourens' methods were more important to scientific progress than his findings were (Young, 1970), the action commune concept re-established an alternative to strict localization of faculties in the brain and gave encouragement to those who thought of the brain as something more than a set of sensory-motor circuits.

Flourens' notions, unlike Gall's, agreed with the temper of the times; the contemporaries of these men tended to be non-cerebral localists. Two of Flourens' colleagues, who were also experimentally oriented, have already been mentioned: Magendie and Müller. Magendie's most significant contribution was the experimental demonstration of the distinction between the sensory and motor pathways of the dorsal and ventral spinal roots. This relationship was simultaneously developed by Sir Charles Bell, a British anatomist, and as was pointed out earlier (Chapter 4), is known as the Bell-Magendie law. Müller is most directly remembered for his doctrine of specific nerve energies, also discussed earlier (Chapter 5). However, with regard to extending the doctrine into the cerebrum, Magendie and Müller, along with Flourens, were adamant in refusal.

BRAIN LESION-BEHAVIORAL CORRELATIONS

Because brain and spinal surgery was still a new technique (not many investigators had Flourens' skill) and since anesthesia was not yet in use (although Flourens pioneered the use of chloroform), many investigators had to rely for their data on what are known as "nature's experiments." Williams, from a contemporary vantage point, maintains that such experiments have unique merit:

It has long been recognized that mental functions which cannot be studied selectively under laboratory conditions in the healthy individual may break down in a circumscribed manner as a result of brain injury or disease. Nature herself performs the experiment and its consequences are open to scientific scrutiny. The study of mental disorders as they are manifested in the clinical setting can, therefore, provide valuable information about the working of the healthy mind . . . (1970, p. 11).

Essentially, the method and approach is the same as Gall's, but instead of correlating particular behavior patterns with cranial protuberances, they are correlated with brain lesions.

The birth of the orthodox conception of cerebral localization is usually considered to have occurred in 1861. At that time the French surgeon, Paul Broca,[2] conducted postmortem studies of patients who had suffered brain damage and correlated his findings with the observed behavior of the patient while he was alive. In one case, Broca reported his results from a postmortem examination of the brains of two hemiplegic patients who had been paralyzed on the right side and had lost the ability to speak (motor aphasia). He found that both had lesions in a small area of the left inferior frontal gyrus, now known as *Broca's area.* Assuming speech to be a motor activity, Broca concluded that the vocal cords were controlled from that region of the cortex. Broca's area has been regarded as one of the brain's speech centers ever since.

A few years later, a British physician, John Hughlings Jackson, derived a more extensive picture of cortical localization from studies of epilepsy, chorea, and various defects of blood circulation in the brain that result in paralyses.[3] Jackson concluded from numerous case histories and postmortem examinations that there was a primary functional organization, or localization, of the cerebral cortex. In this arrangement, all

2. Broca is also remembered for designating the limbic lobe (Chapter 4).

3. Jackson, who became known as the "father of neurology," was not well educated by the standards of his day, having been graduated from the small, obscure York Medical College as one of a class of nine. He was, however, an avid reader and taught himself a good deal of advanced medicine and physiology.

sensory functions were located posterior to the central fissure and all motor functions were anterior. In effect, Jackson extended the Bell-Magendie law to the cerebrum. The same notion, it will be recalled from Chapter 7, was almost simultaneously proposed by Fritsch and Hitzig (1870).

Jackson's proclamation that a continuity existed between the lower and higher portions of the CNS was contrary to the currently accepted neurophysiology based on the findings and conclusions of Flourens, Magendie, Müller, and other dualists. Jackson, however, had the benefit of two other influential scientific figures of the day, who helped strengthen his argument. At York College, Jackson's colleague, physician Thomas Laycock (regarded as somewhat of an authority) believed that the brain was subject to the laws of reflex action and was no more than a complicated ganglia. Jackson quoted Laycock often in his speeches and writings.

Also, early in his medical career Jackson had been influenced by the views of the British philosopher, Herbert Spencer, to such a degree that at one point he had considered giving up medicine to study philosophy. A major point of Spencer's philosophy was the descent of man by evolution, which he had proposed several years before Darwin. He differed from Darwin in two ways. Spencer applied evolution broadly to all types of behavior, social systems, and the solar universe, as well as to species structure. Also, he proposed inheritance of acquired characteristics, rather than natural selection, as the evolutionary mechanism.

Jackson mastered the concepts of both men and applied them to the brain. By regarding the brain simply as a structural elaboration of the nervous system and by considering the nervous system to be hierarchically organized in terms of its evolutionary development from lower forms to higher ones, Jackson was able to interpret his clinical findings as being in support of brain localization of lower functions.

Jackson also suggested that the higher parts of the nervous system are endowed with more generalized functions than the lower parts. He was the first to speak definitively of neural inhibition as the most significant function of the higher centers. He compared this function to that of government in keeping down and controlling the lower echelons. Once the government fails, the lower levels of command begin to dissolve, going down in the order of level. Jackson felt the same process obtained in a patient with brain damage.

Among the higher generalized activities of the nervous system Jackson included volition, which he placed at the head of a spectrum of activities. The nervous system, he said, is not sharply divided between the automatic and the voluntary. It is a continuum of degrees of automation, going from the most automatic in the lower centers to the least automatic in the highest centers.

Jackson's views had a profound effect on neurology. Indeed, practitioners of that medical speciality still maintain the Jacksonian tradition by providing all types of brain lesion-behavioral correlations and giving them appropriate names—e.g., disturbances of visual perception, *optic agnosia*; loss of the ability to perform objective actions, *apraxia*; disturbances of arithmetic skills, *acalculia*; writing skills, *agraphia*; reading skills, *alexia*; musical ability, *amusia*; constructive activity, *constructive apraxia*.

Such correlations sound disturbingly phrenological because they retain the flavor of a system of psychology based on compartments or faculties of the brain. Although experimental and clinical precision was established in regard to brain structure,[4] no standardized descriptive behavioral terminology or method of systematically measuring behavioral changes was similarly developed. But, vague behavioral descriptions did not impede a trend towards strict localization, which became the predominant neurophysiological concept at the turn of the nineteenth century.

In 1898, Edward L. Thorndike, an American psychologist, published his famous puzzle box studies in which he had trained cats, using food as a reward, to lift a latch to escape from a box. These studies, generally considered as marking the beginning of experimental animal psychology, also allowed further study of cerebral localization. Previously, accurate measures of behavior had been restricted to observation of sensory and motor changes. More complex behaviors, such as learning, intelligence, or desire, were construed as faculties and

4. Two outstanding examples are Ferrier's (1886) techniques for diagnosing and precisely locating brain lesions, and Horsley and Clarkes' (1908) development of stereotaxic methods of implanting electrodes.

outside the possibility of precise measurement. Thorndike found he could measure these behaviors in his puzzle boxes. Soon others began to publish findings that related them to parts of the brain.

THE SILENT OR ASSOCIATION AREAS OF THE BRAIN

Unfortunately for strict localizationists, extirpation or stimulation of certain large areas of the cerebrum of many animals did not result in any observable change, sensory, motor or otherwise. Since these areas had no demonstrable function, they came to be called *silent areas,* and, as will presently be seen, they were to play an important role in modifying localization theory.

Lashley's theory of mass function

In 1902, Shephard I. Franz, another American psychologist, used the new techniques of testing animal behavior to study one of the silent areas, the *frontal lobes.* Franz found that, following removal of the frontal lobes, cats and monkeys lost recently acquired behaviors (not older ones), but that they could be quickly re-established. In effect, localization of frontal lobe function did not appear exact. As Boring described it:

By 1912, Franz was poking fun at the belief in exact localization, calling it "the new phrenology." "We have," he said, "no facts which enable us to locate the mental processes in the brain any better than they were located fifty years ago" (1957, p. 685).

Soon after, Franz began attempts to empirically refute the established concepts of sensory-motor localization.

In 1917 Franz was joined by Karl S. Lashley, a colleague of, and advocate for, the ideas of Watson. Lashley (who devised more efficient and refined techniques for studying vision and learning in animals, primarily rats) initially had wanted to establish the cortical basis of stimulus-response connections, just as the paths of simple reflexes had been traced through the spinal cord. But, as it turned out, Lashley could not do it. He reported that:

The experimental findings have never fitted into such a scheme. Rather they have emphasized the unitary charac-

ter of every habit, the impossibility of stating any learning
as a concatenation of reflexes . . . (1963, p. 14).

Lashley had found that localized cortical lesions per se may
not necessarily affect a specific learned response.[5] Specific behaviors dependent on sensory input were seriously affected by
major extirpation of the relevant sensory projection areas. But,
on the other hand, most learned behaviors were affected in
proportion to the *extent* of cortical destruction in the silent
areas. The more difficult the problem learned by the animal,
the greater the influence of extirpation; and the greater the
extirpation, the greater its influence on the process of learning
(Figure 11-2). From these results, Lashley concluded that the
more the amount of silent cortex available, the more rapid and
accurate the learning. This means that any silent cortical area
can assume any function; it is equipotential. Lashley called his
conclusion the *theory of mass function.* In Lashley's words:

The term "equipotentiality" I have used to designate the
apparent capacity of any intact part of a functional area to
carry out, with or without reduction in efficiency, the functions which are lost by destruction of the whole. This
capacity varies from one area to another and with the
character of the functions involved. It probably holds only
for the association areas and for functions more complex
than simple sensitivity or motor coordination.
. . . the equipotentiality is not absolute but is subject to a law
of mass action whereby the efficiency of performance of an
entire complex function may be reduced in proportion to
the extent of brain injury within an area whose parts are
not more specialized for one component of the function
than for another (1963, p. 25).

Lashley thus defined a middle ground between the extremes of
strict localization and holism. His view represented a modern
counterpart of Flourens' action propre-action commune.

Simultaneously with Lashley's animal experiments, mass
function was receiving clinical support. A German-American
physician, Kurt Goldstein (1939, 1963), who was concerned
with visual, learning, and intelligence defects, undertook the
study of former World War I veterans who had suffered brain

5. For details, see the collection of Lashley's papers edited by Beach et al. (1960), and
Chapter 12 of this book.

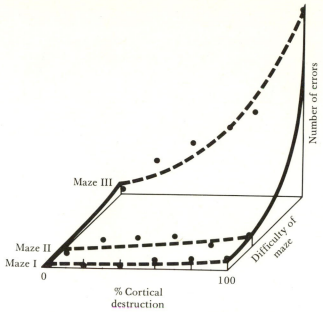

Figure 11-2. Lashley's graph showing the relationship between extent of cortical destruction and the difficulty involved in learning various mazes. It can be seen that even massive (in excess of 50%) cortical ablation had only insignificant effects on performance (number of errors) in the simpler mazes, but profound influence on performance in the complex (Maze III) maze. (Redrawn and modified from Lashley, 1963.)

injuries in combat. Goldstein reported that individuals with impairment of the visual cortex compensated quite readily by reorganizing their percepts to regain familiar (normal) vision. Similarly, individuals with damaged silent areas adjusted to the environment by reevaluating their behavioral capacity in terms of their reduced ability to cope intellectually. An equipotentiality concept is obvious in these analyses. Goldstein saw mass function as clinically significant. Speaking of permanent damage, he said that ". . . the only goal of the physician is to provide the patient with the possibility of existing in spite of his defect" (1963). Goldstein declared that any symptom has to be looked at in terms of the total personality.

More recently, the Russian neuropsychologist, Alexander R. Luria (1966*a, b;* 1970; 1973*a, b*) has developed his own antilocalization theory of brain function, based on an equipotentiality-like concept. Emphasizing voluntary motor actions and language (primarily writing), Luria concluded that it was use-less to look for localized function centers. He allows that while certain specific parts of the nervous system, such as receptors and their pathways, do have specialized functions, most of it functions as a unit in adapting the entire organism to its environment. The cortex is seen as an integrating center for reflexes, somewhat in the Sherringtonian sense (Chapter 7). Luria's concept is analogous to a telephone circuit in which the switchboard (the cortex) acts as the integrating center for telephone calls (sensory-motor connections).

This point of view, compatible with Russian reflexological constructs, is monistic because the adaptability and plasticity of human behavior can be accounted for within a basic reflex arc context. The theory, like all Russian reflexology, as has been pointed out, is also compatible with Marxist dialectical materialism, which maintains that mental processes are a product of material processes. Luria is quite explicit:

Among the more important achievements of Soviet psy-chology . . . are the introduction of the historical method into psychology and the confirmation of Marx's statement that the human mind is the result of the social form of life and that the formation of the five external senses is the work of basic processes of world history . . .

The behavior of an animal, however complex, is the result of two factors: inborn tendencies on the one hand, and indirect, individual experience, formed in the course of conditioned reflex activity, on the other. In contrast to this, the conditions in which human behavior is formed include yet a third factor beginning to play yet a decisive role in the development of human faculties: the assimila-tion of the experience of mankind in general, which is incorporated in objective activity, in language, in the prod-ucts of work, and in the forms of social life of human beings.

This social experience not only forms the methods of human work and operations with objects in the external environment, but it also creates complex and plastic meth-ods of controlling the individual's own behavior and the wide range of generalized images and ideas composing human consciousness (1966*b*, p. 21–22).

Thus:

Human psychological processes must therefore be understood, not as elementary properties or primary faculties,
but as systems with an *historical origin* and a complex *functional* structure . . . (1966*b*, p. 25).

These quotations point up the irony of using a scientific finding to advance a particular philosophy. Luria's view of the social
influences that play on the brain may be useful to those who
espouse dialectical materialism. But it is no more than a modern representation of Flourens' holistic action commune concept, which itself was influenced philosophically by Descartes'
dualist point of view, the direct opposite of materialism.

So, cortical organization can be conceived of from both the
structural (localization) and functional (mass function) points
of view. The distinction is relative, not absolute, since there is
obviously some localization and some plasticity, an action
propre and an action commune. The latter, however, is most
significant to an understanding of the physical basis of heterotrophic functioning; recognition of that point was one of
Lashley's major contributions. Discussing Lashley's 1933 paper
on the issue, Boring said:

It was now clear that the mind-body problem had come to
be integration, not localization. There never was much
meaning to localization as a theory anyhow. You assign a
function to a spot in the brain, and what then? What does
that tell you about how it works? Why is it there? What
else might happen if you changed the conditions? It is at
best a remnant, not merely of phrenology as Franz said in
1912, but of the philosophy that demanded a seat for the
soul (1960, p. xiv).

Early localizationists' view of the silent areas

For a number of years, those scientists who believed in strict
functional localization in the brain were attempting to extend
their ideas of localization to include the silent areas. Early
localizationists had been confounded by the effects of extirpation in monkeys of the nonsensory or nonmotor areas of the
cortex. According to Ferrier (1886), there was a definite alteration in the monkeys' character and behavior, although the pre-

cise nature of the change could not be stated. He nonetheless went on to attempt describing the monkeys whose silent cortices were destroyed, calling them "apathetic," "dull," and "listless." From such observations, Hitzig (1884) concluded that the silent areas were specific to intelligence or abstract thought in that they were the areas where memories, experience, and knowledge became "associated." Hence, the silent areas became known as the "association areas," a terminology which is still in use today.

As late as 1936, despite attempts to present further supportive data, the notion of association area localization did not receive the acceptance accorded sensory-motor localization. In one challenge Loeb contended:

> The assumption of "centers of association" is just as erroneous as the assumption of a center of coordination in the heart. Association is, like coordination, a dynamical property . . . Associative processes occur everywhere in the hemispheres (and possibly in other parts of the brain) just as coordination occurs wherever the connection between two protoplasmic pieces is sufficient (1900, p. 275).

Moreover, the early associative position assumed *horizontal* transcortical projection (transfer of information from one part of the cortex to another). This was soon experimentally and anatomically compromised (Clark, 1941; Lashley, 1948, 1950) when it became obvious that transcortical projections are primarily *vertical,* by way of the thalamus. The association nuclei of the thalamus project to the association cortex (Chapter 4).

Frontal lobes and their functions

The behavioral role of the association areas started to emerge with some clarity as early as 1902 with the above mentioned experiments of Franz, which were primarily concerned with the frontal association areas.[6] The frontal area is but one of three areas of association, which are also called *granular* or *homotypical cortex.* These areas can be seen in Figure 11-3. As pointed

---

6. The frontal association areas are also called the frontal lobes, prefrontal lobes, prefrontal areas, orbitofrontal cortex, or any combination thereof.

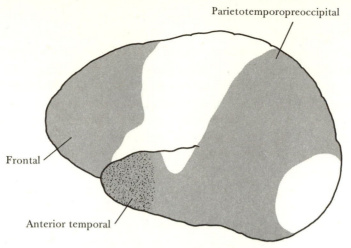

Parietotemporopreoccipital

Frontal

Anterior temporal

Figure 11-3.   Association areas of the human brain (side view).

out, Franz's major finding was that recently learned behavior is lost when the frontal lobes are removed.

Memory and frontal lobe functioning   Jacobsen (1936), using different behavioral observations, was not able to confirm Franz's finding. But, he did find that delayed responding, involving short term memory, was impaired following frontal lobe extirpation. Jacobsen's experiments involved making lesions in the frontal area of monkeys and then giving them a learning task to do. Monkeys without lesions could learn the task and would respond, even after a delay in presenting the cue that was to elicit the response. In contrast, lesioned monkeys could not perform the task if a delay of several seconds occurred between the time the cue was presented to the animal and the time permitted to carry out the response. Apparently, the animal's short-term memory had been affected by the lesion in the frontal area. Many subsequent replications have tended to establish that impairment of delayed responding is a primary behavioral result of frontal lobe ablation in animals. It should be noted, however, that other behavioral effects do occur when the frontal lobe is removed. For instance, in one experiment (Jacobsen, 1935) a chimpanzee was unable to perform because she got emotional when placed in the testing situation. After removal of the frontal lobes, she became docile and cooperative and performed without distress.

215

Delayed responding, however, was the measure most often used to gauge the effect of frontal lobe ablation. To take a typical example, French and Harlow (1962) trained monkeys to perform a simple delayed response task in their Wisconsin General Test Apparatus (WGTA; see Figure 11-4). At the start of a trial, an opaque screen was placed between a monkey and the tray. The screen was raised while a peanut was placed under one of two identical cups. The screen was then immediately lowered. Five seconds later, the tray was made available to the monkey for its selection of a cup.

Intact monkeys quickly gained 100 percent competence in the selection of the proper cup. Immediately after recovery from bilateral ablation of the frontal lobes, performance deteriorated to chance levels, but was usually re-established with prolonged retraining.

Numerous other variations of delayed responding, with a variety of animals and lesions, have been performed in an attempt to specify the mechanism of the impairment. As just implied, Jacobsen's notion was that it was a memory deficit. But, Malmo (1942) and Finan (1942) found that the deficit was contingent on the absence or presence of distraction during the delay. The distraction hypothesis, which states that impairment occurs only when some stimulus intervenes to distract the animal's attention while it waits for the test trial, remains the more viable one since most subsequent studies support it (see Pribram and Luria, 1973; Warren and Akert, 1964).

Personality and frontal lobe functioning   Frontal lobe function has not been significantly clarified by human studies. The original and still classic case report of human frontal lobe damage is Harlow's 1869 description of the tamping iron accident of Phineas P. Gage, a railroad construction worker. In 1848 he was laying gunpowder explosives with a tamping iron. One charge accidentally exploded, driving the four-foot long, fourteen-pound iron into the area above Gage's left eye, up through the frontal lobes, and out the top of his head. The anterior portion of the frontal lobes was extirpated.

Amazingly, Gage was a bit stunned but otherwise apparently unaffected. He simply went to his room and lay down for

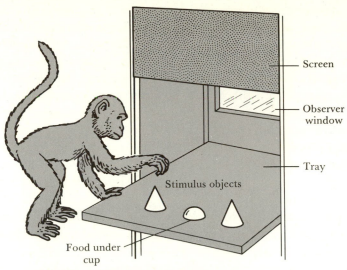

Screen

Observer
window

Tray

Stimulus objects

Food under
cup

Figure 11-4. Wisconsin General Test Apparatus.

awhile. But his subsequent behavior showed marked personality changes. As Harlow described them:

> He is fitful, irreverent, indulging at times in the grossest
> profanity (which was not previously his custom), mani-
> festing but little deference to his fellows, impatient of
> restraint or advice when it conflicts with his desires, at
> times pertinaciously obstinate yet capricious and vacillat-
> ing, devising many plans for future operation which are
> no sooner arranged than they are abandoned in turn for
> others appearing more feasible (1869, pp. 13–14).

Gage drifted from Chile to San Francisco. He spent some time
as a Barnum Circus exhibit and died in convulsions thirteen
years after the accident. The tamping iron and Gage's skull,
which are shown in Figures 11-5, are permanent exhibits of
the Warren Museum at Harvard Medical School.

The behavior changes Gage manifested, usually considered
under the rubric "personality," are characteristic of humans
with frontal lobe damage. Such individuals are usually highly
distractable, lack foresight, are unable to plan and anticipate
future events (i.e., utilize past experience), and display *Witzelsucht*, "a tendency towards frivolous and sometimes stupid and
tedious joking, often at the expense of others" (Ruch, 1965).

217

Psychosurgery   Jacobsen's report of the effect of frontal lobe removal on an emotional chimpanzee influenced Egas Moniz,[7] the Portuguese neurologist and diplomat, who reasoned that the personality decompensations of mental illness might be due to faulty frontal lobe functioning (1956). In 1936 he put the hypothesis to a direct test by injecting alcohol into the frontal lobes of an incurable asylum patient, then severing the fiber connections between the frontal lobes and the rest of the brain. Like Jacobsen's chimpanzee, the intractable patient became docile, cooperative, and unemotional. Moniz called the operation a *leucotomy.* For this work, he shared the 1949 Nobel Prize with Walter Hess.

The leucotomy procedure became quite popular in America and Great Britain. The operation was simple enough to perform and could be done in a psychiatrist's office. The patient would be lightly anesthetized, then an ice-pick-like instrument, the leucotome, would be driven with a mallet through the bone of the upper corner of the eye, swept from side to side, and withdrawn. This variation, called a *transorbital lobotomy,* could easily be accomplished twenty to thirty times a day. In Britain alone, between 1942 and 1954, 10,365 patients were so treated (Tooth and Newton, 1961). Of these, 46 percent were said to have improved, 25 percent unchanged, and 5 percent became worse.

More careful studies, using stringent experimental control procedures and long-term follow up (McKenzie and Kaczanowski, 1964; Robin, 1958) failed to find advantageous effects of any kind arising from lobotomy. To the contrary, many of the patients were found to have developed the undesirable personality characteristics of frontal lobe damaged humans. In short, the operation turned loose thousands of Phineas P. Gages—individuals with blunted creativity, intellectual retardation, and other deleterious features. Thus, being both practically and morally questionable, lobotomies of the kind practiced in the 1940s and 1950s are seldom performed today.

It must be pointed out, however, that other kinds of psychosurgery are currently being practiced in a number of countries, including the United States (Brown, Wienckowski, and Bivens,

7. This name was the pseudonym of Antonio Caetino de Abrew Freire.

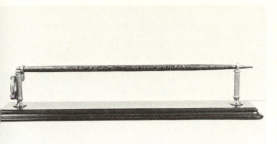
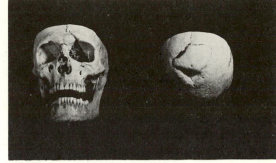

A   B

Figure 11-5. **A,** Tamping iron which induced Phineas P. Gage's frontal lobe lesion.
B, The skull of Phineas P. Gage. (Photographs courtesy of Mr. David L. Gunner, Warren
Anatomical Museum, Harvard Medical School, Boston, Massachusetts.)

1973; Pines, 1973; Pool, 1973). These new procedures, capable
of more accurately pinpointing certain targets in the brain, are
being used for the relief of intractable pain as well as for the
alleviation of severe phobias, compulsions, anxieties, and ob-
sessions. The procedures are directed at deep and medial fibers
of the frontal lobes and at limbic system structures, particularly
the amygdala and cingulate gyrus. Although the surgeons claim
these operations are beneficial, long-term followups are still
required. Moreover, there is a need to deal with serious ethical
questions regarding such issues as the right of society to force
social deviants to undergo behavior-modifying surgery (Chorover, 1974).[8]

Intelligence and frontal lobe functioning   Another area of human behavior that has been considered in relation to frontal
lobe function is intelligence. It seems that frontal lobe damage
has no adverse effect on many types of intelligence measurements, particularly I.Q. (Ghent, Mishkin, and Teuber, 1962;
Hebb and Penfield, 1940; Weinstein and Teuber, 1957). To the
contrary, Freeman and Watts (1950) reported that patients who
underwent psychosurgical lobotomies showed improved intelligence. They concluded that the effect was an indirect result of
lowered anxiety.

8. Indeed, the whole of psychotechnology—mind altering drugs, electrode implantation, et cetera—also has to be similarly regarded.

219

When patients are confronted with abstract situations, however, particularly those requiring improvising, a defect becomes apparent (Luria and Homskaya, 1964; Milner, 1964; Nichols and Hunt, 1940; Teuber and Mishkin, 1954; Teuber, 1959). Milner (1963), for example, found the Wisconsin Card Sorting Test to be a very sensitive indicator of frontal lobe damage. In the test, the patient is presented with a set of cue cards and a pack of response cards. His task is to sort the pack of response cards according to one cue (such as color, shape, or position) for ten consecutive responses, after which another cue becomes appropriate for the next ten responses, and so on. Patients with frontal lobe lesions make *perseverative errors;* that is, they continue with a cue after it is inappropriate. In delayed-response paradigms, human deficits are similar to those seen in animals (Milner, 1964; Teuber, 1959).

Temporal lobe functioning

Turning now to the posterior regions of the association cortex, one of the commonly found effects of temporal lobe lesions is *psychic blindness.* That is, pattern and color discrimination are affected while object recognition and visual acuity are unaffected. The deficit was first reported by Kluver and Bucy (1937; see Chapter 8), and has been verified many times (Blum, Chow, and Pribram, 1950; Meyer, 1958; Riopelle and Ades, 1951).

The most specific behavioral effect of temporal lobe lesions, however, involves performance in learning set situations (Chow, 1954; Meyer, 1958; Riopelle et al., 1953). Learning sets are usually demonstrated with monkeys in the WGTA. The animal is trained to perform in a two-cue discrimination. When the first discrimination is acquired, another problem involving two different cues, but otherwise of the same type, is introduced. When that discrimination is acquired, the process is repeated, and so on. Eventually, when the monkey is presented with a new problem, it will learn it in one trial. Thus, it has not learned a single problem, but rather a general approach to solving all problems of a given type. It has developed a "set" for solving new problems.

Monkeys subjected to bilateral temporal lobe lesions before training in a learning set sequence do not show the subsequent improvement in problem-solving ability. If the lesion occurs after training, however, retention is only temporarily affected.

Stimulation of the temporal association areas facilitates learning. Spinelli and Pribram (1966) affixed miniature stimulators to the skulls of monkeys, with electrodes leading into the temporal lobes. The result was a continuous low level of stimulation over a period of several weeks. Animals so prepared learned visual discrimination problems significantly faster than control animals.

The effect of temporal lobe damage in humans is somewhat more specific (Milner, 1954; Penfield and Rasmussen, 1950; Ruch, 1965; Schiller, 1947). Damage to the left temporal lobe (in the region of Broca's Area) produces aphasia, while damage to the right temporal lobe impairs complex visual discrimination. In addition, lesions in either lobe may cause uncinate fits (unpleasant olfactory sensations), tinnitus (unpleasant auditory sensations), narrowed peripheral vision, and "dreamy states" (periods of arrested consciousness accompanied by visual and auditory hallucinations).

SUMMARY

The search for localized areas or centers of the brain that control the different behaviors of an organism has intrigued numerous philosophers and scientists over the years. Hippocrates first suggested the brain was the locus of mental activity. Da Vinci divided the ventricles of the brain into centers of imagination, thought, and memory. In the nineteenth century, Gall and Spurzheim made the idea of functional localization so popular that it grew into a cult known as phrenology, based on the idea that bumps on the head are clues to the quality of the brain. Although phrenology fell into disrepute, Gall left a legacy of psychological interest in relating regions of the brain to specific activities. With the advances of anatomical technique and precision in lesioning of the brain, there was a spurt of research directed toward correlating specific brain components with behavior. Flourens', Jackson's, and Broca's role in this research and in introducing the modern view of cerebral localization remain milestones in physiological psychology.

Localization theory has been compromised by numerous discoveries that lesions in the nonsensory-nonmotor areas of the cerebrum result in no specifically consistent changes in behavior. These puzzling areas of the brain, which came to be known as the silent, or association, areas, were the targets of a good deal of research aimed at determining their true function. It now appears, as a result of psychosurgical investigation and animal experiment, that the frontal lobes may have something to do with short-term memory and with personality, but the connections are not clear.

In retrospect, it is evident that the functions of the association areas are diverse and vague, not yielding to localization except in the poorest behavioral sense of faculty psychology. The greatest challenge for advocates of localization remains with the association areas. Until their function can be specified, localization remains a compromised doctrine. With contemporary research emphasizing other areas as being the ones in which associations might be made (e.g., the hippocampus; see Blakemore, Iversen, and Zangwill, 1972), the silent areas have returned to silence.

SUGGESTED READINGS

Warren, J.M., and Akert, K., eds. *The Frontal Granular Cortex and Behavior.* New York: McGraw-Hill, 1964. A collection of papers describing modern research studies of the frontal lobes.

Williams, M. *Brain Damage and the Mind.* Harmondsworth, Middlesex: Penguin, 1970. Concise, elementary discussion of the clinical aspects of brain damage.

Young, R. M. *Mind, Brain and Adaptation.* New York: Oxford University Press, 1970. An inspired, insightful, critical review of nineteenth century brain research; far and away the best source available.

12 Learning

DEFINITION OF LEARNING

One major feature that characterizes heterotrophic life is the ability of an organism to integrate its motility with environmental dynamics. That is, the organism has a capacity to efficiently and adaptively move about and manipulate the environment for its own benefit and survival. This flexibility varies phylogenetically from the very rudimentary to the very complex (McConnell, 1966; Munn, 1971; Chapter 2), but in all animals there seems to be some ability to modify response capacity to accommodate to changing environmental circumstances. In turn, this ability depends to a large extent on previous interactions with the environment; that is, on experience with related circumstances. The processes, whatever they may be, by which earlier experiences come to influence subsequent adaptations constitute what is often called *learning*.

Beyond this point, the definition of learning becomes very much a matter of opinion (Verplanck, 1957). A large number of constructs have been developed, particularly in American psychology, which are designed to incorporate the various classes of behavior that are known as learned. For instance, during the early part of the twentieth century Ivan Pavlov (1927) discovered the type of learning which came to be called *conditioning* and attempted to demonstrate that all learning was based on this construct. Pavlov introduced the notion of conditioning with his famous experiments on dogs, in which the animal was made, by pairing the sound of a bell with presentation of food, to salivate at the sound of the bell alone (Figure 12-1). Normal salivation, which occurs at the sight or taste of food, Pavlov called the *unconditioned response*. Salivation made to occur with a formerly neutral stimulus he called a *conditioned response*. (In fact, the original term was conditional response, but in the translation from Russian the terms got mixed up and conditioned response has been used ever since.)

The basic mechanism of conditioning was thought to be the creation of some sort of association between the neutral (*conditioned*) stimulus and something that satisfies a basic need (*unconditioned stimulus*). The sound of a bell or the footstep of a keeper will make the animal salivate if it is repeated enough times while the animal is given a food reward. After a while, the animal associates the food with the sound of the bell alone and starts to salivate. Likewise, if an animal is given a shock often enough until it associates pain with a neutral stimulus it will learn to fear that stimulus. This latter process is known as *aversive conditioning*.

Watson based his behavioristic concepts on Pavlovian conditioning and experimentally demonstrated that the process also occurs in human beings. His best-known experiment (Watson and Rayner, 1920), was done with an eleven-month-old child named Albert who was aversively conditioned to fear a white, furry rat by repeatedly striking a gong whenever the child tried to touch the rat. The noise was so frightening to the child that he not only came to fear the rat but generalized the fear to other white, furry objects, including Santa's beard.

Skinner later expanded the work of Pavlov and Watson and laid the basis of modern behaviorism by elaborating a new form of conditioning known as *operant conditioning*. Henceforth, Pavlov's and Watson's conditioning became known as *classical conditioning*. In Skinner's conception, the subject plays a role in his own conditioning experience. An animal—for example, a pigeon—learns to peck at an illuminated button (key) to get a food pellet (a reward) or learns to avoid pecking a key if doing so results in an electric shock (punishment). The animal can thus learn to "operate on" the environment and can be condi-

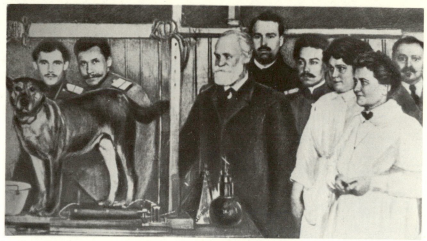

Figure 12-1. Ivan Pavlov (1849–1936), Russian physiologist who discovered conditioned reflexes. He is shown here with visitors in his laboratory at the St. Petersburg Medical Academy. (The Bettmann Archive.)

tioned into complex behaviors on the basis of this system of rewards and punishments.

Although numerous other notions of learning have developed over the years (Bush and Mosteller, 1951; Guthrie, 1959; Hull, 1943; Kohler, 1925; Spence, 1956; and Tolman, 1966; to name just a few), the methodological rigor and empirical convenience of behaviorism attracted the more scientifically oriented psychologists, including many physiological psychologists. The influence of conditioning theory becomes noticeable, for instance, in physiological psychology's efforts to delineate the physiochemical substrates of learning. These studies have been carried out in terms of conditioning paradigms to such a great extent that many physiological psychology textbooks find it necessary to devote several chapters to learning and/or conditioning (Deutsch and Deutsch, 1973; Grossman, 1967; Milner, 1970; Morgan, 1965).

Unfortunately, the quantity of information has not begotten quality because, not only has the term learning been subjected to numerous definitions, it has also been claimed that learning, especially conditioning, is a totally objective process. That contention has given rise to confusion between what is observed (the performance) and what is inferred (the learning). In actual fact, learning presently must remain a process whose existence is assumed from observation of a behavioral change. That in no way diminishes its conceptual utility; but, as will soon be seen, meaningful analyses can only be developed if the distinction between observed and inferred events is prudently maintained.

Even with this distinction kept in mind, there is no universal agreement on the nature of learning. How permanent does a change in behavior have to be before it is considered to be learned? One second? Three hours? Ten days? A lifetime? How much of a change in behavior has to occur? Is the modification of a threshold level, called sensitization (the lowering of response threshold as a function of prior stimulation), sufficient evidence of learned behavior, or must there be development of a so-called new response, such as key pecking?

With such latitude of conceptulization each investigator has gone his own way, totally compromising any attempts at a conceptual synthesis that would unify the numerous behaviors labeled as "learned." For example, arguments rage back and forth over whether or not amoebae and other unicellular organisms can learn (Gelber, 1964; Jensen, 1965), largely because of individual definition of what constitutes a learned response (Bitterman, 1965; Kimble, 1967; McConnell, 1966). For that matter, it is equally difficult to find agreement on a definition of response (Verplanck, 1957).

Although these ambiguities also plague physiological studies of learning, William James did establish a basic proposition by which physiological psychology has approached learning by postulating the concept of *plasticity* as the underlying mechanism that explains how organisms learn. Plasticity refers to the nervous system's capacity to change under the influences of environment. As James put it:

Plasticity, then, in the wide sense of the word, means the possession of a structure weak enough to yield to an influence, but strong enough not to yield all at once . . . Organic matter, especially nervous tissue, seems endowed with a very extraordinary degree of plasticity of this sort; so that we may without hesitation lay down as our first proposition the following, that *the phenomena of habit in living things are due to the plasticity of the organic materials of which their bodies are composed* (1890 I, p. 105).

ELECTROPHYSIOLOGICAL STUDIES OF LEARNING

Stimulus-response connections in the nervous system

If the brain is plastic, there must be some physiological change in the brain that shows the effects of learning. Under that assumption, early investigators attempted to localize stimulus-response connections in the nervous system and thus represent a structural base for learning. An example is the work of Loucks (1933, 1936, 1938) who used direct electrical stimulation of the sensory cortex in dogs as the conditioned stimulus instead of the usual peripheral exteroceptive sensory input (light, bell, or whatever). Loucks found that a conditioned response could be developed from sensory cortex stimulation but not from the motor cortex, even after hundreds of pairings. These data were taken to suggest that conditioned response-unconditioned response connections must occur somewhere between the sensory and motor cortex. In those days the logical place, it was thought, was the association cortex (Chapter 11). This is no longer considered to be true because, as mentioned earlier, it is now known that the relevant transcortical projections are primarily vertical; that is, they involve subcortical structures, and that massive, in some instances even total, decortication does not impair all learning (Hernández-Peón and Brust-Carmona, 1961; Lashley, 1963).

Changes in brain electrical activity and conditioned responses

During the 1930s, however, the cortex was the only structure considered as the possible base for recording the changes due to learning, and a good deal of experimental study was focused on it. This "cerebrocentrism" was reinforced by Durup and Fessard's (1935) demonstration that certain types of brain activity can be modified by conditioning, much like a motor response. Employing Berger's then new EEG technique, the investigators attempted to condition the appearance of *alpha-blocking*, the shift from alpha to beta waves as a function of

behavioral alerting (response to a new stimulus), in human subjects. The method was to expose the subjects to a camera shut-
ter click (the unconditioned stimulus) which was paired with
a light flash (the conditioned stimulus). Since the sudden light
flash itself would produce the phenomenon of alerting, it was
necessary to have a preconditioning phase of habituation training, in which the light flash was presented so often the subjects
no longer responded to it. Once this happened, responding to
the light could be re-established after pairing it with a click.
Durup and Fessard also reported that subjects could change
their alpha rhythm when they heard a habituated auditory
stimulus that had been associated with a novel light stimulus.

Durup and Fessard's finding was accepted as a conditioned
response by numerous other investigators who replicated the
experiment with both animals and humans. More contemporary studies suggest that individuals can even be conditioned to
discriminate alpha and nonalpha in terms of subjective experience (Kamiya, 1968).[1]

In any case, some critics do not consider alpha-block conditioning proof of a physiological change due to learning
because the process is no more than what they call pseudo-
conditioning, or false conditioning. They maintain that the
experiments only demonstrate instances of sensitization; that is,
whenever any strong unconditioned stimulus is presented first,
any subsequent conditioned stimulus will result in some type of
startle response. So right away, with some of the very first experiments in conditioning cortical activity, the "nitpicking" over
the definition of learning came up. Completely ignored in the
debate over semantics was the fact that relatively significant
and permanent changes in cortical activity, and presumably
underlying structure, were induced by experience. Whether
those changes are to be called sensitization, learning, conditioning, or whatever is not highly relevant to that fact.

Over the years, many studies, instead of using the EEG

---

1. Conditioning individuals to produce alpha waves is a major type of biofeedback
therapy; commercial monitoring devices are sold to the public. The state of mind of an
individual who can be so conditioned has been described as: "calm; alert; relaxed;
open to experiences of all kinds; pleasant in the sense that to be serene is pleasant, as
opposed to the hassle of American life. It's akin to the good feeling that comes from
taking a massage or sauna bath—a relaxed, put-together sort of feeling. It's receptive
as opposed to a getting, forcing frame of mind . . ." (Pines, 1973, p. 63).

changes as a conditioned response, simply monitored the EEG while regular conditioning was taking place. These experiments almost universally showed changes in EEG activity that correlated with the progress of conditioning. During the earlier stages of conditioning, there was apparently an over-all arousal of the whole cortex. As conditioning progressed, the arousal usually became limited to relevant areas, such as the auditory cortex if an auditory conditioned stimulus was involved (John and Killam, 1959).

Looked at in perspective, the EEG studies of learning have provided a mass of data but little knowledge. In a recent review, Thompson, Patterson, and Teyler concluded:

We had hoped that the large amount of research in the area . . . would allow us to compile a behavioral stereotaxic atlas of brain activity accompanying learning. This has not been possible (1972, p. 85).

Yet, even more recently, Olds (1974; Linseman and Olds, 1973) used multiple electrodes to record single unit potentials from various areas of rats' brains while the rats were learning to approach food at the sound of a tone. The procedure allowed Olds to "map" the brain parts that were active during different stages of the learning. Early in the training, when the tone elicited no overt behavior, the hypothalamus was active. When the rats started attending the tone, the reticular formation was primarily active. Initial approach responses correlated with high extrapyramidal activity, later approach with sensory cortex activity and asymptotic performance with frontal cortex activity. So perhaps a brain-learning atlas will be possible afterall.

While the results of attempts to find electrical correlates have strongly implied the existence of specific structural modifications due to experience, the primary contribution of these studies has been to sway speculation away from localization of a learning center. They have implied that learning is a whole nervous system, not just a discrete cortical area process.

THE SEARCH FOR THE ENGRAM

During the 1940s and 1950s, a few investigators began to focus on brain microstructure, primarily the individual neurons, as the site of physiological change due to learning experiences.

They speculated, as did the early Greeks, that an *engram,* or memory trace, a relatively permanent physical or chemical change in tissue resulting from some sort of repeated stimulation, was formed.

A leading modern figure in the search for the engram was Lashley who, as mentioned in Chapter 11, devoted thirty years to the pursuit of this elusive trace in rats and chimpanzees. In Lashley's experiments the animals were trained in various ways. Then parts of the brain were removed. The animals were finally retested to see what effect this surgery had on learning.

Lashley tested thousands of brains, systematically extirpating brain tissue to the point of demise of the animal. He found that it was the amount of brain material removed, and not the place in the brain structure from which it was removed, that determined the ultimate behavioral change (see Figure 11-2 and Chapter 11). Even though it was clear from physical analysis that various transient functional modifications, such as changes in membrane polarity and release of neurohormones, did occur with the learning input to the nervous system, the affected system apparently re-establishes stability as fast as possible. Lashley could find no permanent neural change that could be attributed to experience.[2]

The development of consolidation theory

Despite Lashley's fruitless hunt, many psychologists remained convinced of the existence of a physical correlate to memory and learning, and some experimental evidence has accumulated in support of the neural process by which an engram would be formed. The Canadian psychologist Donald Hebb called the process *consolidation* (1949) because it represents a kind of storage of experience which shows up in structural changes of a relatively permanent nature. Consolidation somewhat revives the notion of the reflex arc (Chapter 7) as the neurostructural basis of reflex action. In the instance of consolidation, the pathway is laid down by the neural consequences of environmental, rather than genetic, actions. Hebb explained:

2. In 1950, Lashley looked back on his extraordinary accumulation of data and concluded somewhat ruefully, "I sometimes feel, in reviewing the evidence on the localization of the memory trace, that the necessary conclusion is that learning just is not possible. It is difficult to conceive of a mechanism which can satisfy the conditions set for it." (p. 477).

One important fact is that newly acquired learning must be left undisturbed for some time if it is to last. The synaptic changes must be allowed to mature, as it were, much as raw whisky must be left to sit awhile in its oaken barrels if it is to be fit to drink. Whisky takes a year or more; learning needs something between 15 minutes and an hour or thereabouts. The maturing process is known as *consolidation* . . . From our present knowledge one may guess that the consolidation process is either or both of two things; a structural change at the synapse, or a biochemical change in the two neurons concerned (1966, pp. 122–124).

Memory loss and convulsive shock   The line of reasoning and subsequent experimental evidence leading to consolidation theory derived primarily from convulsive treatment of psychiatric disorders. The various methods employed to induce convulsions, from dosing with camphor (the original technique, first developed in the early 1930s) to electroshock, had in common one consistent behavioral modification other than therapeutic. The treatment almost always induced memory impairment for events immediately preceding the treatment, an impairment known as *retrograde amnesia*. Some degree of recall did return with time, and in a definite temporal pattern; the closer the event was to the actual convulsion, the longer it took to recall it. For events immediately prior to the seizure, however, memory loss was often permanent.

The definite time period involved suggested to proponents of consolidation theory that short-term memory pathways were destroyed by the convulsive activity inflicted upon the brain. That is, the neural activity induced by a memory-generating experience was interrupted before it could effect permanent structural changes in the brain. The older memories were unaffected by the convulsions since the structural changes had already occurred.

To test this hypothesis, Duncan (1949) trained eight groups of rats to avoid painful shock in a shuttle box with a light as the conditioned stimulus. The conditioned stimulus-unconditioned stimulus interval was ten seconds. The animals underwent one learning trial a day for eighteen consecutive days, with each rat receiving an electroconvulsive shock (ECS) after each day's trial. The time interval from the end of the trial until the electroconvulsive shock treatment varied for each group, ranging from twenty seconds to fourteen hours. A ninth group of rats served as a control, receiving a sham electroconvulsive shock.

Duncan plotted the animals' performance in terms of the number of anticipatory runs through the shuttle box (An anticipatory run is one which the animal makes from memory and thus reflects the effect of previous experience.) as a function of the trial-to-electroconvulsive shock interval (Figure 12-2). He found that the effectiveness of the electroconvulsive shock in obliterating the memory of the learning experience varied with the time between the learning trial and the convulsive shock. The closer the convulsion to the learning experience, the less the influence of previous experience and the fewer the number of runs. It looked as though the shock disrupted a short-term functional trace before it could turn into a long-term structural effect. The data suggested that it took somewhere between fifteen minutes and one hour for the structural modification to set.

These experiments have been replicated numerous times with electroconvulsive shock and with other types of brain function-disrupting operations, including drug-induced convulsions, comatose states, hypoxia, and hypothermia (Jarvik, 1970; 1972). The results are startlingly consistent.

Yet, while the different methods of convulsive shock are reportedly effective in one or another type of learning impairment, electroconvulsive shock itself does not destroy retention of all learned behaviors. Even allowing for the critical time intervals, Brady and his colleagues (Brady and Hunt, 1951; Geller, Sidman, and Brady, 1955) have not found any electroconvulsive shock-induced impairment of rat lever pressing in the conditioned emotional response paradigm. In their experiments, rats, trained to press levers for food, were periodically administered an unavoidable foot shock which had been preceded by a long warning signal. Typically, when the warning signal was sounded, the animals would stop lever pressing and freeze until the shock was applied and the signal ceased. This behavior constituted the conditioned emotional response. Rats administered electroconvulsive shock treatment, however, lost their conditioned emotional response and continued to press the lever despite the signal. Their "anxiety" was reduced by

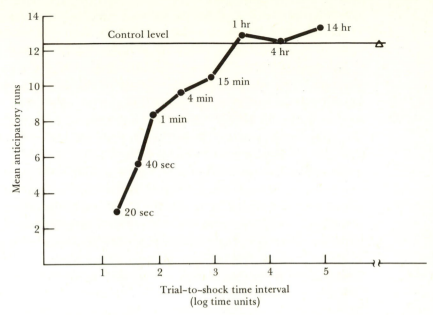

Figure 12-2. Effect of electroconvulsive shock (ECS) on retention of learning in rats. (Redrawn and modified from Duncan, 1949.)

electroconvulsive shock, but the lever press was in no way impaired.

Recently, Meyer (1972) offered the alternative notion that electroconvulsive shock impairs retention by destroying, not the engram, but the capacity to retrieve it. Of course, as he points out, there still remains the question of "retrieval from where?"

Learning and drug-induced neural activity It occurred to some investigators that, if disruption of experience-induced neural function impedes learning, facilitation of this function should enhance learning. Nonseizure level increases in neural activity can be produced by various drugs in proper dosage. These drugs include strychnine, pentylenetetrazol (metrazol), and picrotoxin which, at subconvulsant doses, stimulate both overt and neural activity. Nonconvulsants, such as the amphetamines and caffeine, are also neural and behavioral stimulants.

In 1917 Lashley reported that subconvulsant doses of strychnine facilitated learning of a circular maze by rats, while caffeine inhibited it. Strychnine-treated rats reached the criterion in fewer trials than control animals, while rats treated with caffeine needed more trials. But Hull (1935) found that caffeine facilitated the learning of nonsense syllables by normal humans. The obvious interpretation of these disparate results would center around the contention that different kinds of learning are involved. However, all that is beside the point. The primary issue is that, in these experiments and others like them (e.g., Hearst and Whalen, 1963; Khavari, 1969; Vehave, 1958; and see review by Weiss and Laties, 1962), the drugs were administered immediately prior to the learning trials. Consequently, the behavioral change could be interpreted as an effect on performance, i.e., increased activity or alertness, rather than as an effect on the learning (consolidation) process itself. A cup of coffee, for instance, may alert one and make him more receptive to learning, but it would not increase one's learning ability.

During the 1950s and 1960s, McGaugh and his colleagues (reviewed by McGaugh and Petrinovich, 1965) conducted a series of experiments assessing the effects of strychnine and picrotoxin on maze learning by rats. They controlled for the possible facilitating effects on performance by administering the drugs after, rather than before, the learning trials. Even so, they consistently obtained improvement in acquisition rates. Objections that the drugs' learning enhancing-effects were of sufficient duration to persist into the next day's trials were met by showing that the closer the drug administration to the previous trial, the greater the improvement in the succeeding trial. The drug clearly must have been affecting some process occurring after the trial (consolidation?). The argument that the results reflected a rewarding effect of the drug[3] was countered by demonstrating that, when the drug was administered during "latent" learning,[4] subsequent rewarded learning without drug dosage was improved.

It seems that no matter in which direction brain activity is altered, the effect on learning is compatible with consolidation

---

3. Although there are no known strychnine or picrotoxin addicts.
4. The animal is placed in the learning situation (e.g., a maze), but no reward is provided. The conception is that some familiarity with the situation still develops and is utilized in subsequent rewarded learning.

theory. While many of these experiments seem to offer evidence for the fact of consolidation, they still contribute nothing to specifying the actual mechanisms by which it is accomplished or the anatomical locus of the changes. The engram remains nearly as vague today as it was for Lashley (1950).

Current status of the engram   In psychology, as in any other scientifically oriented area, there is frequently an inverse relationship between fact and theory; the fewer the facts available, the more theories there are. The current status of the learning engram reflects the truth of this homily.

Initial speculation (Hebb, 1949; Lashley, 1950), for instance, involved physical changes at the neuronal level, notably, the formation of new neuronal material. While nerve cells do not multiply, they do grow, particularly in response to stimulation. Kappers, Huber, and Crosby (1936) described *neurobiotaxis*, a process in which stimulation of embyronic nerve fibers causes them to grow towards the source of activity. Despite some evidence that postnatal environmental stimulation increases brain weight (Bennett et al., 1964; Rosenzweig, 1970; Rosenzweig, Love, and Bennett, 1968), no direct correlation between any kind of neural growth and learning has been established.

Other explanations of the engram process have involved changes in synaptic membrane permeability (Eccles and McIntyre, 1951), alteration of neuronal threshold levels (Morrell, 1963), changes in the glial cells (Galambos, 1961), qualitatively selective chemical sensitization of neurons (Deutsch, 1971; Milner, 1961, and see page 251), and selective sensitization to specific activation patterns (Burns, 1958). None of these theories has withstood all the shafts of objection.

The protein hypothesis and RNA

The proposal that has captured the greatest amount of contemporary research attention is known as the protein hypothesis. It was first stated by Katz and Halstead:

We wish to suggest that an essential feature in the genesis of the memory trace is the formation, as a result of individual experience, of geometrically ordered protein molecules in the neurons of the cerebrum (1950, p. 4).

They were not exactly sure how this came about, but they did suggest:

The mechanisms of racial and individual memory have in common . . . the formation of ordered protein molecules from a template; they differ in that the template in the genetic apparatus is a natural endowment, whereas in individual memory the template molecules arise from external stimuli (1950, p. 5).

Considering that these speculations were made before there was any knowledge of the RNA-DNA nucleoprotein basis of genetics, the statement now seems prophetic.

In the late 1950s, the American and British biochemists, James Watson and Francis Crick (see Watson, 1968), were beginning to make the discoveries that led to a new understanding of the role of the nucleic acids, *DNA, deoxyribonucleic acid* and *RNA, ribonucleic acid,* in fundamental life processes. It was concluded that DNA, which is found in cell nuclei, directs the synthesis of proteins. DNA contains the "genetic code" which provides the evolutionary memory that determines what characteristics an organism will have when it matures. RNA carries on the day-to-day job of complying with the directions of the genetic code. With this background, empirical elaboration of the Katz-Halstead notion of a memory molecule of protein was not long in coming.

Experiments linking RNA to learning and memory   Actually, the molecular basis of learning was hinted at before the great discoveries of the 1950s. In 1945 Hamberger and Hydén and Hydén (1943) had reported that neural RNA concentrations varied as a function of neural stimulation. Later, Riesen (1961) found that absence of stimulation resulted in reduction of neural RNA; and Morrell (1961a) correlated cerebral interhemispheric transfer of chemically-induced excitation with RNA concentration.

The first direct link between RNA levels in the nervous system and experience was established by Hydén and Egyhazi in 1962. They trained a group of rats to walk up a tight-wire to obtain food from an elevated platform, a behavior requiring use of the neural vestibular or balance organs. The average rat took four days to master the behavior. When the animals achieved asymptotic performance levels, they were sacrificed. The vestibular nuclei of the brainstem (Deiters' cells) were removed and analyzed for RNA content. Compared to control groups of untrained rats, the RNA level in the test group was significantly higher. Nerve cells from the trained rats averaged 751 micrograms of RNA per cell, compared to 683 micrograms in the untrained rats. With that finding,[5] and with elaboration of the role of RNA in protein synthesis, the protein hypothesis for the learning engram was on its way.

During those same years, a Canadian physician, Ewan Cameron, was reporting some related clinical studies (1958; Cameron and Solyom, 1961; Cameron et al., 1963). He and his colleagues administered large daily doses of yeast-manufactured RNA to senile patients. Doses were administered both orally and intravenously. They found favorable changes in memory, adjustive performance, and learning. The results led Cameron to conclude that RNA may well provide the organic substrate for the memory trace. Unfortunately, Cameron's studies could not be replicated (Nodine et al., 1967). They did, however, generate further interest in the protein hypothesis, and they introduced the intriguing notion that exogenous RNA could be active in the formation of the memory substrate.

Cook and his colleagues (1963) attempted to test Cameron's concept by administering yeast RNA to rats prior to conditioning them to avoid footshock by running up a pole at the sound of a buzzer. They compared this group of rats, which were given large doses of yeast RNA daily for thirty days, with a control group in regard to acquisition of the pole-climbing response. The rats were tested until 100 percent of the group jumped in each trial. As shown in Figure 12-3, the RNA-treated rats reached 100 percent avoidance with significantly fewer trials than the control group. Strangely, the RNA-treated animals also took more trials than the controls to reach extinction, that is, the point of no response after the shock was removed from the experiment.

5. There were numerous replications and variations as well; see reviews by Byrne, 1970; Fjerdingstad, 1971; Gurowitz, 1969; Pribram and Broadbent, 1970; Sweet, 1969.

This latter finding is very important because extinction is a learned behavior (learning to not respond) so its acquisition should be reflected by decreased extinction rates. Since the extinction rate increased, the experiment appeared to have created a paradox; it actually compromised any conclusion suggesting a role of RNA in learning. The question became why RNA facilitated one kind of learning and not another. Cook and his colleagues simply contended that the effects they obtained are dependent upon numerous specific behavioral and pharmacological variables, implying different types of learning and associated physiological mechanisms (Cook and Davidson, 1968). At best, that is merely begging the question.

RNA as a behavioral stimulant   The more parsimonious view is that the differential effects on acquisition and extinction

Figure 12-3. Effect of yeast RNA on acquisition and extinction of an avoidance response. (Redrawn and modified from Cook et al., 1963.)

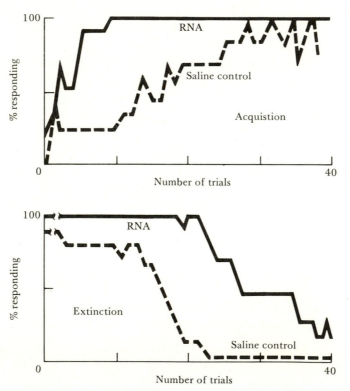

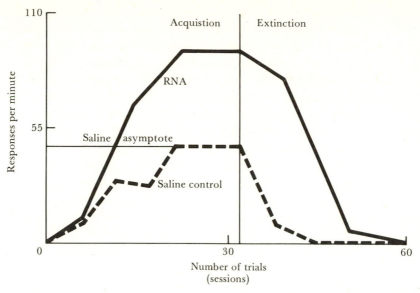

Figure 12-4. Effect of yeast RNA on performance of rats. (Redrawn and modified from Brown, 1966 *b*.)

reflect nothing more than a behavioral stimulant action of RNA, an effect on performance; that RNA really has no direct role in learning. RNA has indeed been found in subsequent experimentation to have behavioral stimulant actions.

Brown (1966*a*), for instance, carried out experiments in which a group of pigeons were administered RNA for thirty days, then compared with a control group with respect to their ability to learn to differentially peck food-rewarded blue and yellow keys. The pigeons were trained to perform in a 70:30 probability-of-reward situation.[6] The RNA-treated pigeons needed significantly fewer trials to achieve asymptotic responding than those that were untreated. However, when the odds in the probability situation were reversed and the pigeons were measured on how long they took to readjust, the RNA-treated pigeons took considerably longer. This result is compatible with

6. Pecking on one key was rewarded 70 percent of the time, pecking on the other only 30 percent of the time. Most animals (including humans) *maximize,* or respond every time to the key having the higher probability. A few species (including pigeons) "play the odds," or distribute responding proportionately between the two keys (Bitterman, 1965).

stimulation in that stimulant drugs characteristically produce perseverative errors.[7] Brown concluded from these experiments that the RNA affected behavior like any other stimulant. Another type of experiment by Brown (1966*b*), using rats, substantiated the conclusion. Measuring learning in terms of rate, both RNA-treated and untreated rats took the same number of trials to reach asymptote. Only the response rate was different, being higher for the RNA-stimulated animals (see Figure 12-4).

From a biochemical perspective, Enesco (1967) reviewed the literature concerning the metabolism of RNA and concluded: 1) RNA cannot pass the blood-brain barrier and thus does not reach the brain, and 2) uric acid (or related substances in nonprimates), the primary metabolite of RNA, acts as a behavioral stimulant. Thus, Brown's behavioral conclusions also have biochemical compatability.

From these studies, Sweet, in a recent review paper, was able to conclude:

> The Brown findings seriously questioned the validity of a theory which views RNA as a unique substrate or enhancer of learning and memory . . . Enesco suggested that RNA may react like a central nervous system stimulant with its final action being mediated possibly by uric acid, a major breakdown product of RNA . . . (1969, pp. 633–634).

Drugs which might raise RNA levels   Despite this doubt, the notion of an exogenous substance facilitating learning was pragmatically intriguing because it led to hopes that a "learning pill" could be developed. The temptation proved too great for one major pharmaceutical company which, announced in both the popular and scientific media, that its research staff had found a substance, magnesium pemoline (cylert), that improved learning capacity. Offered as proof were studies which indicated that magnesium pemoline stimulated brain synthesis of RNA (Glasky and Simon, 1966) and facilitated acquisition of avoidance responding in rats (Plotnikoff, 1966*a*).

Numerous studies quickly followed, but, unfortunately, it

---

7. Perseverative errors, it will be recalled (Chapter 11), are instances where organisms continue to respond in a set way even though the response is no longer appropriate. Responding during extinction is also a type of perseverative error.

proved impossible to replicate the biochemical finding that levels of RNA increased with the injection of the drug (Morris, Aghajanian, and Bloom, 1967; Stein and Yellin, 1967) or to demonstrate learning enhancement in humans through the use of the drug.[8] For the most part, except for Plotnikoff himself (1966*b;* Plotnikoff and Meekma, 1967; Stein, Brink, and Patterson, 1968), the animal findings could not be replicated and extended either.[9] The drug now appears to be clearly no more than a behavioral stimulant.

The magnesium pemoline episode once again demonstrates the danger of inferring learning from performance. Another mistake proponents made was to assume the existence of a physiological action from observation of a behavioral change alone, then to conclude that the former "caused" the latter. Even verifiable RNA-synthesizing substances, such as tricyanoaminopropene (TCAP) and vitamin B_{12}, have been similarly investigated, albeit more conservatively, but with essentially the same result (Gurowitz, 1969; Sweet, 1969).

Transfer effects of RNA   While positive results from the administration of exogenous RNA would lend validity to the existence of a protein engram of learning, negative results do not necessarily preclude the hypothesis completely. Accordingly, attempts at more direct implication of RNA have centered around transfer effects. That is, RNA from the brain of an animal after learning is injected into another animal that is untrained. Then a determination is made as to whether the second animal has "received" the learning.

McConnell and his colleagues, generally credited with initiating this approach, published their initial reports in the late 1950s (McConnell, 1962; McConnell, Jacobson, and Kimble, 1959). Their experimental subject was the flatworm, planaria, the small primitive invertebrate that neurophysiologically represents one of the earliest forms of encephalization and differentiation (Chapter 2). When these animals are subjected to

8. See the studies done by Burns et al., 1967; Gelfand et al., 1967; Orzack, Taylor, and Kornetsky, 1968; Smith, 1967; Talland, 1966; Talland and McGuire, 1967 among others.

9. Beach and Kimble, 1967; Bowman, 1966; Cyert, Moyer, and Chapman, 1967; Frey and Polidora, 1967; Goldberg and Ciofalo, 1967; Gurowitz et al., 1967; Lubar et al., 1967; Powell, Martin, and Kamano, 1967*a,b;* Soumirew-Mourat and Cardo, 1968; Yuwiler, Greenough, and Geller, 1968.

electroshock by way of electrodes placed in their water medium, they display characteristic, stereotyped, hyperactive twisting movements; they coil and contract reflexively.

McConnell and his colleagues attempted to condition this response by pairing electroshock with the flash of a light (planaria have primitive photoreceptors called eyespots that respond selectively to illumination). After a large number of pairings with shock, the planaria responded to the light alone with twisting contractions at a rate significantly higher than that of various controls. They could be said to have learned, or to have been conditioned, to respond to the light.[10]

The training procedure was then employed in experiments concerned with testing the RNA engram hypothesis. Planaria have the capacity to regenerate when cut in half crosswise; the head half grows a new tail and the tail end grows a new head. McConnell's group (1959) found that regenerated planaria retained the conditioned response. They assumed that the retention involved RNA, but the first experimental data suggesting implication of RNA in the process came only when Corning and John (1961) maintained regenerating worms in a solution of ribonuclease, an enzyme that destroys RNA. The tail ends did not, in that case, retain the response.

Also, McConnell and his group (1959) performed their famous "cannibal" experiments by grinding up trained planaria and feeding them to experimentally naive worms which were then subjected to conditioning. The naive worms acquired the response in significantly fewer trials than the original cannibalized group or comparable controls who were not fed a meal of trained worms. This result, the first demonstration of physically induced transfer of training, was accomplished with the RNA molecule as the hypothesized carrier of learning. One byproduct of this work was the prevalence on campuses of student urging that retired professors be ground up and fed to the students.

As for the work itself, the battle was soon joined again. A host of confounding variables, everything from slime trails to differential photosensitivity, were reported, with numerous studies to demonstrate their compromising influences. This situation

10. Naturally, argument as to whether the behavior was "real learning" or "only" sensitization came up, and, as always, it remains irrelevant.

led Corning and Riccio, who reviewed the entire situation (1970), to ask whimsically, in the worm-runner tradition, "Can a flatworm find happiness in memory research?"

While they did not answer their question, they did point out:

> We cannot blame the flatworm, the roach or any other animal for the debate over what we mean by "learning"— after all, they didn't invent the word (1970, p. 145).

In other words, all the criticism reduced once again to the old issue of "semantic nitpicking," totally ignoring the point that the planaria studies do, with relative consistency, show that animals are physiologically altered as a function of experience. The significant issue remains to define the mechanism of the change in terms of whether it involves RNA or some other substance. RNA was directly implicated in flatworm transfer by Zelman and his colleagues (1963) when they extracted RNA from trained worms and injected it into naive animals who then developed the avoidance response more rapidly than uninjected naive worms.

The logical extension of these findings, of course, involved carrying out transfer tests in vertebrate species. This came about in an unusual way. As Jacobson recently described the circumstances:

> Several years ago, Frank Babich, then a student in my course in physiological psychology, announced to me that he and his cousin, Suzanne Bubash, had successfully transferred a learned habit from one rat to another by injection of a brain extract. Although I had in that very class been discussing experiments on cannibalistic transfer in planarians, I was skeptical that similar effects could be obtained in more complex organisms. Nevertheless, imbued with a scientific daring that several years of association with the intrepid James McConnell had given me, I joined Babich and Bubash in further investigations of their rat transfer phenomenon. After some modifications in their original procedure, we succeeded in replicating, somewhat less dramatically, their pilot results, and we then performed several additional experiments which confirmed and extended the basic finding (Jacobson and Schlecter, 1970, p. 123).

Thus began a series of experiments that further exacerbated the RNA engram controversy.

In the first experiment (Babich et al., 1965), two groups of rats were trained to approach a food cup whenever a click was sounded (one group), or a light flashed (the other group). When asymptotic performance was obtained, the animals were sacrificed. Their brains were removed, and the RNA was extracted and intraperitoneally injected into naive rats.[11] The injected animals were then tested at four and twenty-four hours for the number of approach responses, following presentation of the click and light flash. Rats injected with RNA from click-trained animals averaged 5.75 approach responses per 25 clicks and 1.87 approach responses per 25 light flashes. Those injected from light-trained rats averaged 3.75 responses per 25 light presentations and 1.00 responses per 25 clicks. The differences are statistically significant.

Systematic replications by Jacobson's group and also by a number of other investigators[12] established the validity of the effect. One replication by Braud (1970) is of particular interest because it established transfer of extinction, thereby allowing him to conclude:

> My results suggest that extinction is a learned reaction to the conditional stimulus which opposes the original reaction conditioned to the conditional stimulus, rather than a simple weakening of the originally acquired reaction. Were the latter the case, one would expect extinction to be characterized by a gradual decrease in the chemical substrate of the conditioned response; it is difficult to conceive of such a lack of substrate from a donor producing a similar lack in a recipient (1970, p. 1236).

The paradox surrounding the Cook et al. (1963) extinction data with yeast RNA should be recalled.

There were, as would be expected, numerous negative re-

---

11. The rats were actually not totally naive since they had been habituated to, but never fed, in the chamber.
12. See Dyal, Golub, and Marrone, 1967; Golub et al., 1970; McConnell, Shigehisa, and Salive, 1970; Nissen, Røigaard-Petersen, and Fjerdingstad, 1965; Rosenblatt, Farrow, and Herblin, 1966; Ungar and Oceguera-Navarro, 1965; and a review of over fifty positive reports in Byrne, 1970.

ports (Beaulieu, 1966; Branch and Viney, 1966; Gordon et al., 1966; Gross and Carey, 1965; Halas et al., 1966; Luttges et al., 1966). Twenty-three investigators even went so far as to write a letter to the editor of a leading scientific journal, proclaiming the magnitude of negativity involved (Byrne et al., 1966). The present situation seems to be that the transfer is real but elusive, due to numerous parametric variables (Chapouthier, 1973; Fjerdingstad, 1971), not the least of which is that RNA may not even be the actual substrate involved.

For instance, Frank, Stein, and Rosen (1970) found that brain and liver homogenates from donor mice who had been footshocked or rolled about in a jar improved the learning of avoidance behavior in recipient mice. They concluded that the transfer did not involve specific information. Rather, some general stress substance was transfered that made recipient mice more wary. Again, as with yeast RNA, the RNA transfer data may be more compatible to a stimulant substance hypothesis.

Behavioral effects of decreased RNA levels   So far, discussion has centered entirely on assessment of the behavioral effects of increased RNA in attempts to establish it as the learning substrate. As was the case with stimulant drugs and convulsions, definitive experimentation requires demonstration that the dependent variable (learning) varies systematically as a function of changes in the independent variable (RNA). Thus, it is also necessary to consider studies in which the behavioral effects of decreased RNA levels were analyzed.[13] The general method is to treat animals with one or another of various RNA antimetabolites, substances that inhibit neural formation of RNA, and attempt to detect decrements in learned behaviors. The substances usually employed are either puromycin, actinomycin-D, ribonuclease, 8-azagnanine, or acetoxycycloheximide. All except ribonuclease and 8-azagnanine are antibiotics. The results of these studies have not been any more consistent or less con-

13. Such studies include Agranoff and Klinger, 1964; Agranoff et al., 1967; Barondes and Cohen, 1967; Barondes and Jarvik, 1964; Dingman and Sporn, 1961; Flexner, Flexner, and Roberts, 1966, 1967; Goldsmith, 1967; Jaffard and Cardo, 1968; and Stevens and Tapp, 1966.

troversial than those involving increased RNA content. They have contributed further complication to the controversy. Some investigators have found profound impairment, others no effect at all.

Overall, it would seem that the evidence for biochemical localization of the engram is confounded by the same problems involved in attempting any other kind of localization (see Chapter 11). That is, the integrative nature of neurobehavioral relationships is not taken into account. What has taken place, as mentioned earlier, is revival, in another form, of the isolated reflex arc, complicated by making a pseudoissue of the definition of learning (to be discussed further at the end of the present chapter).

Dissociation studies

While the protein hypothesis, primarily in the form of an RNA molecule of learning, has received most of the contemporary emphasis in the engrammic search, efforts have been directed at other possibilities. One area of some interest, because it has served to reveal clearly the ubiquitous nature of whatever goes on physiologically in regard to learning, involves *dissociation studies*. These are anatomical or chemical studies which sever or separate out one part of the nervous system to determine whether learning can occur without it. The part is not removed or ablated but disconnected or rendered inoperable. Such studies have emphasized the plasticity of the nervous system, helping (as the electrophysiological studies also have) to pull conceptualization away from temptations to localize learning. Dissociation studies suggest that learning is a whole nervous system-whole environment interaction.

Anatomical dissociation   The initial studies originated in the 1930s around an issue relevant to Pavlovian notions of conditioning. Pavlov (1927) believed that the cortex was necessary for learning; the bigger the cortex, the more advanced the organism and the better its learning capacity. As mentioned earlier, the primacy of the cortex to learning was a major theoretical issue of the time. The early dissociation experiments were designed to test Pavlov's contention that the cerebral cortex was essential to the establishment of conditioned reflexes. The idea was to separate the brain from the rest of the organism and then determine if the animal could still learn. One technique involved so-called spinal conditioning because spinal dogs were utilized. Various types of tactile stimuli and motor responses were employed. Both were restricted entirely to the spinal end of the preparation. That is, attempts were made to develop classically conditioned stimulus-response associations at the spinal level independent of any brain involvement (Kellogg, 1947; Kellogg et al., 1947; Shurrager and Culler, 1938, 1940). Again, despite the usual arguments about pseudoconditioning and sensitization, there were a number of positive results. These results suggested that conditioned spinal reflexes could be established independently of (dissociated from) brain involvement, thus implying that Pavlov might be wrong.

The most dramatic anatomical dissociation studies are those of Sperry (1952, 1962) involving the so-called "split-brain" operation in cats and monkeys. He found that midline sectioning of the optic chiasm, corpus callosum and anterior commissure (in effect anatomically isolating the cerebral hemispheres from each other) also divided learning capacity. After surgery, for example, animals could not perform visual discriminations with one eye if they had been trained to make the discriminations with the other eye. It seemed that the splitting prevented the transfer of learned information from one hemisphere to another; the "untrained" hemisphere had to "learn" of its own accord. Humans following surgery or brain damage of a nature similar to Sperry's operation likewise manifest dissociative behaviors.

Drug-induced dissociation   In 1933 Harlow and Stagner performed a number of drug-induced dissociation studies that involved shock-buzzer conditioned leg withdrawal and pupillary responses in dogs and cats under the influence of curare.[14] Pupillary dilation, being a smooth muscle response, occurred despite curarization. Leg withdrawal, being a skeletal muscle response, did not occur. When tested in the nondrugged state,

14. This drug, it will be recalled from Chapter 6, blocks transmission at the skeletal neuromuscular junction.

the pupillary conditioned response was active, but leg withdrawal was absent. Two interpretations were possible: 1) if learning of leg withdrawal did occur in the drugged state, it was dissociated from the nondrugged state; or 2) learning did not occur because no response was ever actually made. The investigators favored the latter conclusion.

Girden and Culler (1937) used Shurrager and Culler's (1938) technique (shown in Figure 12-5) of conditioning the exposed semitendonosus muscle of dogs in an attempt to extend Harlow and Stagner's (1933) findings. In this case, of course, the animals were not spinal. While the dogs were under the effect of curare, muscle contraction could still be induced by stimulating the muscle directly (remember that only the neuromuscular junction is blocked by curare). Such shock-induced muscle contractions, when paired with the sound of a bell, did become conditioned and carried over to the nondrugged state. They did not dissociate. Conversely, if the response was conditioned in the nondrugged state, it did not carry over to the drugged state. Still, the positive results suggested that muscles could learn independently of the rest of the organism!

In the late 1940s, the pure, active, neuromuscular blocking component of curare, *d-tubocuranine,* was isolated and established as having absolutely no effect on the CNS (Smith et al., 1947). Essentially, the same conditioning experiments of Girden and Culler and Harlow and Stagner were repeated, using pure *d*-tubocuranine (Solomon and Turner, 1962). There was perfect transfer of learning between the drugged state and undrugged state or vice versa, and it even occurred when the response could not be made during conditioning.

Since the earlier crude forms of curare contained substances that depressed cortical activity (Koelle, 1965), the dissociation in the earlier studies was not exclusively nerve-muscle, but also brain-cord. In the drugged state, the cord "did the learning." So, as is now well established, Pavlov was wrong because learning can occur without cortical involvement.[15] It is also interesting to note that it was not necessary for the response to occur in order for learning to occur.

Drug-induced dissociation has been demonstrated with a

15. See Hernández-Peón and Brust-Carmona, 1961, and recall interoceptive conditioning and Lashley's studies as discussed in Chapter 10.

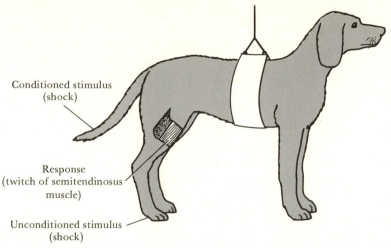

Conditioned stimulus
(shock)

Response
(twitch of semitendinosus
muscle)

Unconditioned stimulus
(shock)

Figure 12-5. Shurrager and Culler's (1938) method for spinal conditioning of a dog. The unconditioned stimulus applied to the foot causes the exposed semitendinosus muscle to twitch. That response could become a conditioned response by pairing its occurrence with a shock to the tail.

number of other drugs, such as phenobarbital, morphine, and amphetamine (Belleville, 1964; Overton, 1964). In some instances, transfer is unilateral; that is, it will only occur in one direction. In others, transfer is bilateral. This means that the learning will transfer in either direction—drug to nondrug state or nondrug to drug state. The drugs involved, unlike curare, have complex actions both centrally and peripherally which, while explaining the variable effects, contribute little to anatomical or mechanistic specificity. The results do serve to emphasize once again that learning, as any behavior, is an integrative activity involving the relationship of many diverse intra- and extra-organismic factors.

Intrahemispheric transfer Other dissociation studies have been concerned with a circumstance called *intrahemispheric transfer*. The method involves depression of a discrete area of the brain by topical application of a local anesthetic, such as potassium chloride or ethyl chloride. The animals are trained with one hemisphere depressed by the anesthetic and then later tested with the same or opposite hemisphere depressed. When the same hemisphere is again depressed, the behavior is retained. If the opposite hemisphere (the one undepressed during learning) is depressed, no evidence of learning is seen. Apparently, the originally undepressed hemisphere "did the learning" (Bureš and Burešova, 1963; Bohdanecky et al., 1963). In addition, Russell and Ochs (1963) found that if initial learning occurred with one hemisphere depressed, only one trial was necessary with both undepressed for the behavior to be retained when the originally trained hemisphere was again depressed. That suggests the engram was transferred as soon as it was physiologically possible. Morrell (1961*b*) has defined some of the electrical correlates involved in these transfers; and Sperry (1962) and Sechzer (1964) verified involvement of the corpus callosum.

LEARNING AND NEURONAL MODELING

Despite the failure to find a neuronal engram in the 1950s, the logic of looking into its activity for the source of the learning substrate remains valid from another respect. That is, the individual neuron, as the smallest functional unit of the nervous system, could be looked at as a prototype or model preparation —if the experience-induced changes that a single neural cell undergoes could be traced, then perhaps the changes that a total organism undergoes during learning could be more readily established.

Methodological limitations, primarily in terms of devising microelectrodes and other miniature apparatus small enough to work with individual neurons, prevented exploitation of this approach until recently. However, despite the fact that, due to the newness of the technique, only a small amount of research is currently available, some interesting insights have been provided. The following examples illustrate this point.

One line of research has involved the isolation of monosynaptic reflex arcs (or, at most, polysynaptic reflexes involving only one or two internuncial neurons) so that a single sensory neuron can be stimulated and a recording can be made from a single motor unit. For example, Kandel and Spencer (1966), using the sea slug (*aplysia*), found individual cells in the abdominal ganglion which, when electrically stimulated, resulted in EPSP activity in motor cells concerned with such behaviors as gill withdrawal. They were able to develop up to thirty minutes habituation to repetitive stimulation of the arc; i.e., the motor cell EPSP would decrease with repeated activation of the sensory cell. Habituation in intact organisms, it will be recalled, is considered a learned behavior; learning to not respond.

As well, these investigators demonstrated sensitization that also would last for several minutes. Repeated activation of a sensory cell would sensitize it, in the sense that a previously ineffective level of stimulation delivered to the cell via a different synapse would produce an EPSP. The circumstance has been regarded by some observers (see Kupfermann and Pinsker, 1969) as a model for classical conditioning in that pairing the two stimuli increased the rate at which sensitization developed (i.e., the initial stimulation was the unconditioned stimulus, the second stimulation the conditioned stimulus.) Typically, the contention remains controversial. Are these events "real" learning?

Morrell (1963) recorded the electrical activity of individual neurons evoked by a flashing light. As is typical under such circumstances, he achieved *driving*—the cells came to respond synchronously with the flashing light (e.g., if the light flashed five times per second, the driven cell would respond in bursts of five per second). Most significantly, the cells seemed to "learn" and "retain" the driving frequency for twenty to thirty minutes—a cell driven to fire at five bursts per second would later respond at that same rate to even a single light flash.

These, and other experiments, do show that single neuronal stimulation can bring about time-based functional changes analogous to the behavioral changes called learning at the organismic level. Still, the extrapolation problem remains to be resolved. As Kupfermann and Pinsker aptly point out:

It cannot be overemphasized that there is an enormous gap between knowledge of the plastic properties of neurons studied in simple preparations, and knowledge of the physiological basis of reinforcement and learning in intact animals (1969, p. 382).

Nonetheless, an increasing number of investigators are continuing to focus on neuronal events in an attempt to localize learning. As mentioned earlier, Deutsch (1971) has accumulated experimental evidence to support his hypothesis that experience increases the sensitivity of post-synaptic cholinergic receptor sites. By pharmacologically manipulating acetylcholine levels (with anticholinergic and anticholinesterase drugs) in animals engaged in various learning tasks (primarily rats running in Y-mazes), he has developed correlational data temporally and spatially linking acetylcholine levels in the body to learning and extinction rates.

More recently, Horn and his colleagues (1973), on the basis of biochemical analyses of the brains of chicks subjected to an imprinting[16] experience, carried the protein hypothesis to the neuronal level. They postulate that experience-induced electrical activity in neuronal membranes can lead to chemical changes. These chemical changes result in activation of an enzyme called RNA polymerase which functions to enhance synthesis of messenger-RNA, the type responsible for protein formation. The resultant proteins, the hypothesis maintains, then either directly modify the synapse by producing structural changes in it, or indirectly influence synaptic transmission by enzyme actions.

So, while neuronal modeling may in itself be subject to serious reservations, it has brought attention to bear on the neuron and has stimulated new conceptual possibilities. More importantly, the neuron may become the locus for a much needed synthesis of the different levels from which the neurophysiology of learning has been approached. For example, as the postulations of Horn and his colleagues show, membrane electrical activity can be considered in terms of the protein hypothesis.

THE LEARNING DILEMMA

Even though the foregoing review is extensive, it by no means covers all the attempts to find a physical basis for learning. Nonetheless, the discussion is sufficiently representative of the

16. Imprinting is an innately based learning process, characteristic of many species, in which stimulus selections become limited; e.g., imprinting is how newly-hatched ducklings learn to follow their mother as opposed to other moving objects. (See Chapter 14 for a further discussion of imprinting.) In the present experiment, the chicks were imprinted to a flashing orange light, a commonly used stimulus in imprinting research.

major trends in the area[17] to allow elucidation of the basic difficulty all such attempts so far share—namely, the definition of learning. As was repeatedly seen, the failure to define learning makes it impossible to describe any correlated physiological events, simply because there is no way of knowing what is being correlated.

In other words, there are few instances of conceptions about learning substrates where a careful distinction has been maintained between the *behavior* called learning and the *process* called learning. For example, notice how easy and tempting it is to assume that the habituation following repetitive electrical stimulation of a single neuron is equivalent to a person living near a busy street learning to sleep through traffic sounds. As was seen, the trend to treat the two as equivalent was started by James, exacerbated by Pavlov, and carried on until the most recent of studies, largely without question.

Efron has pointed out:

The terms "conditioning" and "conditioned reflex" have achieved such widespread usage, since their introduction by Pavlov, that the behavioral scientist presumably thinks that he "knows what he means" when he uses these words to describe, identify, or "explain" aspects of animal or human behavior.

And, as a consequence, such situations as the following arise:

The recent vitriolic arguments between McConnell who argues that worms can be "conditioned" and James and Halas who argue that McConnell does not know the difference between "true conditioning" and "pseudo-conditioning" should immediately suggest that the arguments are not concerned with the scientific observations (facts) but with the different meanings and implications which each author attaches to the concept "conditioned reflex" (1966, p. 488).

Attempted resolution has, as was implied at the beginning of this chapter, typically taken the form of developing new seman-

---

17. And it must not be forgotten that learning is a complex environmental interaction involving processes such as motivation, arousal, attention and sensory input. Thus, much of the discussion in Chapters 5, 8, and 10 are relevant to the present considerations of learning.

tic systems. Predictably, however, substituting one poorly defined set of words for another only increases confusion. The solution must go further. Psychology must first provide a *rigorous operational classification of learning*. With such a classification, it will be possible to look for the neural processes involved—the confusion will perforce disappear. Until then, however, any efforts to explore the physical dimensions of learning will remain futile. Piaget recently concluded a long book on the biological basis of knowledge with the statement: "This book has many shortcomings, the principle one being that it proves nothing . . ." (1971). Until learning can be made a specifiable dependent variable, nothing about it will be proven.

SUGGESTED READINGS

Byrne, W. L., ed. *Molecular Approaches to Learning and Memory*. New York: Academic Press, 1970. An assembly of papers, primarily on the protein hypothesis, by leading researchers in the area.

Hill, W. F. *Learning: A Survey of Psychological Interpretations*. (rev. ed.) Scranton, Pa.: Chandler, 1971. Concise summary descriptions and interpretations of major modern learning theories.

Piaget, J. *Biology and Knowledge*. Chicago: University of Chicago Press, 1971. A difficult book, but presents a brilliant attempt to reconcile the physical aspects of learning.

13 Personality

PERSONALITY

One of the oldest persistent myths is that personality is revealed through unmistakable signs in the body. In the time of Hippocrates, the Greeks related personality to fluids or humors in the body. They listed four different types. There was the sanguine personality, whose rich flow of blood made the individual warm-hearted, generous, and friendly. The phlegmatic person was one who was slow and sluggish due to an excess of phlegm, a cold, moist substance that coursed with the blood through his body. The choleric person had an excess of yellow bile, which showed up in bad temper. And the melancholy personality was full of black humor, which accounted for his dark, depressed moods.

Today, many laymen, while no longer using the old theoretical construct, do feel that the physiological basis of personality is not just a Greek myth. People speak of "rising bile" in cases of temper tantrum and "heaviness of heart" in the case of melancholy. Even more precise are the descriptions of personality that relate wide-spaced eyes to honesty, or close-set eyes to shiftiness. A protruding jaw is still connected with strength and courage, and a high forehead with intelligence and scholarship. "Yond' Cassius has a lean and hungry look"[1] still applies,

1. William Shakespeare, *Julius Caesar*, I, ii, 191.

in the minds of many people, to the mien of greed and ambition.

Over the years, some scientific attempts to correlate physical characteristics with personality types have been made, with mixed results. The first major study was carried out in the 1920s by Kretchmer (1921). He divided people into three categories: *pyknic*, or short and fat; *athletic*, or vigorous and muscular; and *asthenic*, or tall and thin. Kretchmer concluded that pyknics were extrovertive and sociable, athletes were aggressive and active, and asthenics were introverted and withdrawn. In the 1940s, Sheldon (Sheldon and Stevens, 1942) reviewed this work and added his own typology. He divided people into *endomorphs* (the short, fat, jolly types), *mesomorphs* (athletes whose personalities were assertive), and *ectomorphs* (fearful, introvertive, and artistic). Attempts to verify this work (Tyler, 1965) have not shown an objective basis to these classifications.

How much of the physical body is involved in the creation of that elusive assembly of human traits and reactions known as personality? To what extent is personality shaped by inherited or acquired physical aspects and attributes? These questions fall in the domain of physiological psychology and are of particular interest to that group of investigators who study the biology of personality. The present chapter attempts to analyze the role of biological processes, including genetics, in the development of personality. Considerable emphasis will be placed on studies of the physiological bases of abnormal personality for two reasons. First, analyzing the causes and characteristics of deviations from the normal can shed light on the normal. Second, the bulk of available research is concerned with abnormal behavior.

DEFINITION OF PERSONALITY

Even more than most other terms in psychology, personality has almost as many definitions as definers. Modern psychologists have apparently given up trying to agree upon a definition. Hall and Lindzey, in a recent edition of their textbook, *Theories of Personality,* state: ". . . it is our conviction that no substantive definition of personality can be applied with any generality" (1970). Personality is therefore ". . . defined by the particular empirical concepts which are a part of the theory of personality employed by the observer" (1970).

Yet, despite its vagueness, the term *personality* continues to be applied to a number of behaviors which have two things in common: 1) the behaviors are usually human (descriptions of animal personality are generally anthropomorphic), and 2) these behaviors are taken to represent some sort of baseline of typical adaptive actions to environmental change a given person will employ with high probability, his so-called normal or everyday behavior.

An individual's personality is characterized by the typical responses he makes to his environment to maintain successful heterotrophic functioning. In that sense, it might seem that the term personality is synonymous with behavior and, therefore, unnecessary. Actually, however, personality is only a part of one's behavior spectrum, a segment like the infrared band in the electromagnetic spectrum. Interestingly, the term personality derives from the Greek word *persona*, meaning a stage actor's mask; it is behavior one sees. In the tradition of Freudian subconsciousness (Chapter 10), some theorists speak of the so-called "true" personality of an individual as often being hidden. But, in general, behaviors that are called such are not labelled personality until they emerge into view.

However, in psychology the study of personality is not merely a matter of compiling a roster of observable behavioral characteristics. In practice, psychologists usually do not become interested in the behaviors they identify as typical of personality until they start dealing with a clinical deviation from the normal. Consequently, it is only in terms of attempting to define the abnormal that they turn with interest to the normal.

That this is the case is evident from the fact that physiological psychology has concerned itself almost exclusively with attempts at finding structural counterparts in the nervous system to the occurrence of one or another type of abnormal behavior. Even some of the early attempts at localization of behavioral control in the brain (Chapter 11) involved the types of behavior usually labelled as personality. Recall that the interest in phrenology and in Phineas P. Gage, the man who lived with the hole in his head, was almost exclusively a clinical one, expressed in terms of how physical factors had altered the individual's personality. In essence, the discussion of personality, from the viewpoint of physiological psychology, is really a discussion of abnormal behavior. Thus, this chapter looks mainly at studies concerning psychopathology and its reflection in biological changes that distinguish the abnormal from the normal.

BEHAVIORAL CLASSIFICATIONS OF ABNORMAL BEHAVIOR

To determine the physiological basis of abnormal behavior, it is first important to define abnormal. Unfortunately, somewhat as with learning (see Chapter 12), behavioral definitions of abnormal are, to a large extent, judgmental. Also, as with learning, abnormal behaviors have different levels of complexity. Kantor (1962), among others, has suggested a very simple classification to reflect the range of behavior involved. He distinguishes three divisions of abnormality: *unusual* (eccentric), *unadaptable* (ability to function impaired, as in phobias), and *pathological* (generally requiring institutionalization to protect self and society). The behaviors involved progress successively toward less and less social facility on a scale, or continuum, as follows:

Mowrer agrees with the concept of continuity, but sees normal as a center point rather than an end point. He states:

. . . the normal person may be thought of as occupying a kind of middle ground, with the criminal on his left as an undersocialized person, and the neurotic on his right as an oversocialized person (1965, p. 29).

Thus:

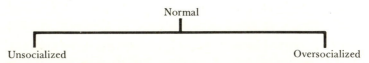

It can clearly be seen that any classification is quite arbitrary. Also, as with learning, for many scientists the concern with the classification of abnormal personality represents a pseudoissue (O'Kelley and Muckler, 1955; Szasz, 1960). So, as with many of the other behavioral labels already discussed, no attempt at a concise definition of abnormal behavior will be made. Instead, in the spirit of Hall and Lindzey, this chapter will examine whatever behaviors physiological psychologists look at when they address themselves to the question of the relationship of abnormal behavior to physiological functioning. No matter how the behavior is labelled, if it unequivocally varies in an orderly relationship with a physiological change, then, if nothing else, another link between mind and brain will have been established.

PSYCHOPHYSIOLOGIC OR PSYCHOSOMATIC REACTIONS

Almost everyone is familiar with ailments that seem to have no organic basis. Physicians have long known that a number of organic pathologies, "physical diseases," seem to have a correlative relationship with behavioral-environmental stress factors, rather than with infection or tissue trauma. The behavioral-environmental factors are usually emotional, and the organic changes usually involve tissues highly integrated with autonomic nerve activity. Disease conditions of this type are referred to as *psychophysiologic* or *psychosomatic*. They include some forms of asthma, obesity, peptic ulcers, migraine headaches, skin warts, high blood pressure, and arthritis, among others.

A fuller understanding of psychosomatic illnesses has profound clinical implications relevant to successful therapy. Further, the dynamics of psychosomatic illness have important theoretical implications in that they reveal a direct mind-body interaction. For these reasons, considerable research effort continues to be directed to psychosomatic diseases.

Physiological effects of emotional and environmental stress

One line of research goes back to the aspect of the Cannon-Bard "emergency" theory of emotion (Chapter 9; Cannon, 1929) which emphasizes that threatening situations result in acute (autonomically mediated) bodily changes, such that the organism is prepared for "fight or flight." For example, when an organism is frightened, blood vessels to the internal organs constrict, those to the skeletal muscles dilate, blood sugar increases (supplying more energy), heart rate increases, and piloerection occurs (increasing cooling efficiency).

Selye's formulation of the general adaptation syndrome   Using these types of observations, Hans Selye (1956, 1969), a Canadian biologist, suggested that a relatively constant environmental threat, or *stress*, might come to effect a relatively chronic, autonomically mediated, physiological alertness which could eventually produce organic pathology. He tested this hypothesis by exposing animals to a variety of stresses—including near-freezing temperatures, confinement in a small cage, forced exercise, drugs, and infections—and observing the development of pathologic states as the stress was prolonged. He concluded:

Experiments on animals have clearly shown that each exposure leaves an indelible scar, in that it uses up reserves of adaptability which cannot be replaced. It is true that immediately after some harassing experience, rest can restore us almost to the original level of fitness by eliminating acute fatigue. But the emphasis is on *almost*. Since we constantly go through periods of stress and rest during life, just a little deficit of adaptation energy every day adds up—it adds up to what we call aging (1956, p. 274).

To consider Selye's last point, it should be indicated that there is a reasonable doubt as to whether wear and tear is the basis for aging. For one thing, organisms are constantly metabolizing worn structures to replace lost substance; the half-life of human protein is about eighty days (Bender, 1953). Further, all species have a relatively fixed life span, and all members age at a relatively constant rate. That would suggest that aging is genetically, not environmentally, determined (Hayflick, 1968).

Nevertheless, maintained stress, while it may not cause aging, does clearly induce tissue deficits. Again, on the basis of his observations, Selye defined the stages of physiological decompensation that occur in conjunction with maintained emotionality. He called the progression of physiological deterioration the *general adaptation syndrome* or *GAS*. As shown in Figure 13-1, it

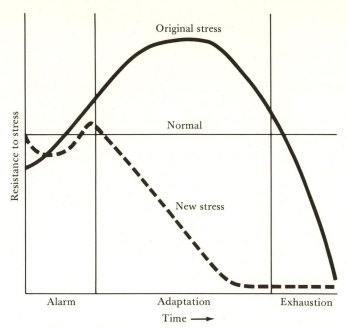

Figure 13-1. Stages of physiological reaction to chronic stress. (Redrawn and modified from Selye, 1956.)

occurs in three sequential steps as the stress is continued over a period of time: 1) the *alarm reaction,* simply the fight or flight syndrome; 2) *adaptation,* here the organism endures the stress as best it can; and 3) *exhaustion,* disintegration, even death in some cases. If the animal survives, its tolerance for further stress is markedly reduced, as shown by the dotted line in Figure 13-1. Studies of combat soldiers, prisoners in concentration camps, and other stressful situations have shown the development of these three components of the GAS.

The reactions themselves, Selye found, were accompanied by clear physiological changes. For instance, in the alarm reaction the adrenal glands become enlarged and produce more epinephrine. The body also discharges a stored up supply of steroids. The effects range throughout the body; tissue is broken down into sugar for increased energy, and salt content falls. As the animal adjusts to the stressful situation, the epinephrine returns to normal, but this is temporary. With continued stress, the glands grow enlarged again and damaging changes occur in the kidneys. The animal dies of exhaustion, or what looks like exhaustion—"knocked out" by the excess of hormone produced in its own defense.

Selye, as just mentioned, found that stresses can have an additive effect; if a stress is added to one to which the animal has adjusted, the amount of further adjustment is reduced. By compiling and rating the stresses individuals underwent immediately prior to suffering various illnesses, Holmes and his colleagues (Holmes and Masuda, 1972) have been able to quantify the relationship. As Table 13-1 shows, an accumulation of many stresses typical of everyday life is related to disease states.

Peptic ulcers: an illness resulting from the general adaptation syndrome Chronic physiological changes due to stress can bring about pathology, presumably as a result of the GAS, and affect the entire personality. One example involves hydrochloric acid secretion into the stomach. Wolf and Wolff (1942, 1946) demonstrated that stress will increase the secretion above normal levels to the point that the acid will eventually irritate and ulcerate the stomach lining. The condition is clinically referred to as peptic ulcer. As long ago as the 1820s, it was identified as a disease characteristic of young females (Tidy, 1944), but there was no suspicion of possible psychological causes until the early 1900s when a shift in the pattern of incidence occurred and the condition became more common in males, as it is today. The suspicion of a psychological cause was further confirmed by findings such as that of Steigmann (1936) who found that the incidence of ulcers among southern United States blacks was low until they migrated to large northern cities, where the incidence increased to that of whites.

Experimental verification of these clinical observations and impressions was eventually accomplished in animals by studies such as those of Sawrey and his colleagues (Conger, Sawrey, and Turrell, 1958; Sawrey, 1961; Sawrey and Weisz, 1956; Sawrey, Conger, and Turrell, 1956). These investigators maintained rats in conflict situations for periods of thirty days and compared results with a control group allowed to live normally. They found that most of the test animals developed peptic ulcers, whereas none of the similarly maintained but unstressed controls did. Subsequently, French and his colleagues (1957) reported that chronic hypothalamic stimulation to an area that

Table 13.1.   Rank impact of stressful events

Life Event	Impact Value
Death of spouse	100
Divorce	73
Jail term	63
Personal injury or illness	53
Marriage	50
Fired from work	47
Pregnancy	40
Death of close friend	37
Change of job	36
Son or daughter leaving home	29
Outstanding personal achievement	28
Begin or end school	26
Change in residence	20
Change in schools	20
Change in social activities	18
Change in eating habits	15
Vacation	13
Christmas	12
Minor law violation	11

Notes: Modified from Holmes and Masuda, 1972.

Persons who accumulate more than 300 units over two years risk development of a major illness.

produced fear and agitation behavior resulted in stomach ulcers.

Further support of this thesis has come from a number of other investigators. Brady's group reported the famous "executive" monkey studies (Brady, 1958*b*; Mason, Brady, and Sidman, 1957; Porter et al., 1958), which gave parametric specification to some of the environmental factors involved in the etiology of peptic ulcers in monkeys. They placed pairs of monkeys in a shock avoidance situation, such that only one of the pair could depress a lever to postpone the shock. If the lever was not pressed at least once every twenty seconds, a shock would be administered. The other monkey could do nothing but suffer a shock if the lever-pressing monkey (executive) failed to accomplish avoidance. In every instance, the decision-making monkey succumbed to a peptic ulcer, whereas the passive animal never did. Further, the incidence of ulceration depended on the schedule of stress, occurring maximally when six hours of stress alternated with six hour of rest. This was found to be due to the fact that pepsinogens, the substances that facilitate irritation of the stomach lining, reached their peak of secretion after six hours of rest. There was no increase during stress periods.

More recent studies by Weiss (1971, 1972) suggest that the etiology of peptic ulcers is even more complicated. In these studies, three rats were tested at a time; one (the executive) that could press a lever to avoid a tail-shock, a yoked control that was helpless in avoiding the shock, and a nonshocked control. Unlike the Brady experiments, the onset of shock was preceded by either a single uniform warning signal or a series of stimuli functioning as a "countdown" clock.

Under such circumstances, Weiss obtained results that were the opposite of Brady's results—the passive, helpless rats suffered much more stomach ulceration than did the lever-pressing rats. The critical difference seems to be the presence of a warning signal, which Weiss refers to as "relevant feedback." He postulates that if the animal obtains some tangible[2] consequence from its responding (something other than just control over the stressor) the situation will remain relatively unstressful. Manipulation of the feedback signal resulted in orderly correlations between ulceration and signal parameters, thereby lending validity to the relationship.

Empirical specification in relation to the behavioral-environmental aspects of other psychophysiologic conditions is not as extensive as that for peptic ulcers. Nonetheless, it seems reasonable to conclude that the psychological state of the organism can indeed influence the body adversely and cause physical pathology. In fact, the word "disease" itself originally meant lack of ease, implying recognition of psychological aspects. Psychosomatic illnesses, then, represent one of the clearest instances of the functional relation between body and mind.

BIOCHEMICAL ASPECTS OF PSYCHOPATHOLOGY

As both Kety (1959) and Lundin (1964) have pointed out, the notion that abnormal behavior has a biochemical basis was expressed as long ago as 1884 by Thudichum when he wrote:

2. It must be remembered that an avoidance response keeps a stimulus (the shock) absent from the environment and is thus intangible, in that the organism experiences no definable consequence of its response.

Many forms of insanity are unquestionably the external manifestation of the effects upon the brain substance of poisons fermented within the body, just as mental aberrations accompanying chronic alcoholic intoxication are the accumulated effects of a relatively simple poison fermented out of the body. These poisons we shall, I have no doubt, be able to isolate after we know the normal chemistry to its uttermost detail (cited by Kety, 1959, p. 1528).

In effect, the approach here is much like the search for the biochemical substrate of learning; namely, to find a substance, the amount of which shows an orderly correlation with the occurrence of a given psychopathologic behavior. Obviously the pragmatic implications of such a discovery would be profound. If mental illness could be reduced to a chemical problem, it could be cured more easily than the presently available psychotherapeutic methods allow.

The biochemical basis of schizophrenia

Blood studies   The most common method employed in the search for a biochemical basis of abnormal behavior involves comparing blood samples from sick and healthy individuals in the hope of turning up differences in one or another of various constituents. The disease most commonly studied is *schizophrenia* since it represents a major public health problem. Factors such as blood glucose, urea, creatine, minerals, salt, hormones, and blood proteins have all been suspected at one time or another and subjected to investigation.

From the very beginning, such studies have been conflicting and inconclusive, and the question of which, if any, factor is involved still has not been resolved. So far, no substance normally present in the blood of schizophrenics shows any marked or consistent deviation from the blood of nonschizophrenics. In the 1950s, however, Heath and his colleagues (Heath et al., 1958; Heath et al., 1957) caused considerable excitement when a protein they called *taraxein* was isolated from the blood of schizophrenics and administered to volunteer nonpsychotics who then demonstrated schizophreniclike behaviors. Animals injected with this protein also behaved abnormally. Unfortunately, it was not possible to systematically replicate or extend their findings (Kety, 1959). Since then, numerous other blood factors have been investigated (Mirsky, 1969; Pauling, 1968; Siva Sankar, 1962), but none has been decisive. The only general conclusion is that the blood of schizophrenics does consistently and adversely affect animal behavior to the point where it can be labelled abnormal (Ferguson and Fisher, 1963).

Studies of other chemical factors   Many other factors have had their moment in the search for the chemical basis of schizophrenia. Various nutritional deficiencies, such as vitamins, have occasionally been held suspect (Brozek and Vaes, 1961; Brozek and Erickson, 1948; Kety, 1960; Pauling, 1968; Pitts and McClure, 1967). Endocrine hormones, particularly the adrenocorticals, have been indicted (Bunney, Mason, and Hamburg, 1965; Friedhoff and vanWrinkle, 1962; Roessler and Greenfield, 1961; Sachar et al., 1970). Antibodies have been considered (Heath and Krupp, 1967; Heath et al., 1967). Yet, every contention remains compromised by negative follow-up studies or other contradictions. It is historically unfortunate that the findings relevant to endocrine function were not substantiated (Hollister and Friedhoff, 1966; Shagass and Schwartz, 1962) because they are what the pioneer psychiatrist Emil Kraepelin[3] (1900) predicted would be the physical basis of schizophrenia, and historical vindication is always satisfying.

One problem that any consideration of schizophrenia shares is the difficulty of precise diagnosis. The present status of the term in psychiatry is as a class designation, covering a whole host of behavior disorders. That circumstance, of course, somewhat as was the case with learning, makes it difficult to determine precise brain-behavior relationships.

The problem has been circumvented to some extent by recent studies which focus on the physiological concomitants of specific symptoms of mental illness rather than the whole syndrome. For example, Weiss, Glazer, and Pohorecky (1974) have been tracing the possible relationship between brain norepi-

---

3. Kraepelin was the first to describe the symptoms of schizophrenia and thereby characterize it as a disease. He called the condition dementia praecox (Latin for "premature mental deterioration"). In 1911, another psychiatric pioneer, Eugen Bleuler (1950) coined the term schizophrenia from the Greek for "split mind."

nephrine levels and a symptom commonly characteristic of schizophrenia—helplessness, the inability to react (or, to cope) under stress.

Weiss and his colleagues found that after exposing rats to various methods for depleting their norepinephrine levels (exposure to inescapable electroshock, a swim in cold water, or injection of antiadrenergic drugs), their subsequent ability to cope with even simple stress (escape from footshock by jumping a low hurdle) was impaired. The animals would always recover in about forty-eight hours, the time it takes for norepinephrine levels to re-establish. The researchers also found a drug that prevents breakdown of norepinephrine (a monoamine oxidase inhibitor) blocked the behavioral effects of the depleting methods. Following administration of a monoamine oxidase inhibitor, the ability to cope was not affected by stress. The animals would readily escape the footshock, despite a cold swim. The relationship is experimentally orderly and, therefore, it must be considered a viable possibility as the chemical basis for at least one aspect of the schizophrenia syndrome.

Study of hallucinogenic drugs   In an attempt to understand the chemical basis of schizophrenia, hallucinogenic substances have drawn a lot of research attention. These are a class of drugs that produce sensory and perceptual experiences in the absence of receptor activation by exogenous energy sources i.e., hallucinations. The sensory and perceptual experiences are also usually accompanied by profound emotionality (Madow and Snow, 1971). The mind-altering effects of hallucinogens seemed to some investigators very like the subjective experiences of schizophrenia (Hordern, 1968; Wikler, 1957). This was especially the case with the best known of the hallucinogens, *LSD,* the acronym for *d-lysergic acid diethylamide.* Soon after the discovery of LSD in the 1930s, it and related substances were often referred to as *psychotomimetics* ("psychoses-mimickers," Barron, Jarvik, and Bunnell, 1964).

Gaddum (1953) found that LSD antagonized serotonin in smooth muscle which led to speculation that serotonin was also a central nervous system neurohumoral transmitter (Brodie and Shore, 1957) and that LSD influenced behavior by antagonizing its function (Woolley, 1957, 1958). When that conclusion was combined with the alleged schizophreniclike behavioral influence of LSD, it seemed that the chemical basis of the disease had finally been found.

However, additional investigations soon revealed that, in some instances, LSD increased brain serotonin (Freedman and Giarman, 1962) and that, while it antagonized the hormone in smooth muscle, it did not do so in cerebral tissue (Bradley and Hance, 1956; Haley, 1957). Further, it soon became clear that the subjective experiences following LSD ingestion were different from the experiences of schizophrenia, primarily in that individuals who have taken LSD can recognize their experiences as due to the drug and not "real"[4] (Fischer, 1971; Hollister, 1962). The psychotomimetic hypothesis is no longer considered viable.

Dopamine as the biochemical substrate of schizophrenia   Another pharmacologic approach, one potentially more promising than the use of psychotomimetics, involves the employment of drugs that modify schizophrenic states (block or accelerate symptoms). Analyses of the mechanism of action of such drugs as the phenothiazines (tranquilizers that diminish schizophrenic symptoms) and the amphetamines (stimulants that worsen schizophrenic symptoms) implicate dopamine in the etiology of schizophrenia.

Dopamine is a catecholamine (Chapter 3). While it is the direct precursor in the synthesis of norepinephrine, dopamine itself is thought to be a neurohumoral transmitter in the CNS. A lot of recent evidence has been accumulated to suggest it may be the chemical basis of schizophrenia (Snyder et al., 1974). For instance, it is postulated that schizophrenics have lower levels of brain dopamine than nonschizophrenics. The phenothiazine drugs are thought to block dopamine receptor sites. The nervous system, the reasoning goes on to suggest, attempts to overcome this by increasing the output of dopamine, thereby raising its level and relieving the schizophrenic symptoms.

On the other hand, it is also postulated that excessive activity in dopamine pathways can result in schizophreniclike symptoms such as stereotyped compulsive behaviors. Amphetamines

4. This led some observers to suggest that a more accurate name for these drugs would be "illusionogens" rather than "hallucinogens."

in sufficiently high doses produce the same kinds of behavioral changes, presumably by stimulating dopamine activity. Thus, a relationship may exist between high dopamine levels and schizophrenia.

These kinds of speculations would suggest that the bio-chemical substrate of schizophrenia may be a defect in the nervous system's ability to properly regulate dopamine levels. The proposition is enticing but tentative and needs much more research elaboration, not the least of which is considerably more definition of the nature of neurotransmission in the CNS. The dopamine hypothesis, however, is currently the most promising chemical explanation of schizophrenia.

OTHER PHYSIOLOGICAL SUBSTRATES OF ABNORMAL BEHAVIOR

In addition to biochemicals, other types of physical bases have been investigated in terms of their relation to abnormal behavior. As well, behavioral disorders other than schizophrenia have been studied in terms of their physiogenic aspects. The range of possibilities is immense, being limited only by researchers' imaginations. The following gives a sampling of those possibilities.

As has already been discussed in Chapter 11, gross brain damage can bring about marked personality changes. Some of these changes are behaviorally dysfunctional in nature and thereby become characterized as abnormal. There are many ways brain damage can occur, the most obvious being trauma such as that suffered by Phineas P. Gage. Diseases such as encephalitis and syphilis can also cause brain damage. Hormone imbalances (such as hyperthyroidism or cortisone insufficiency), toxic substances (lead, carbon monoxide), and circulatory dysfunctions (thrombosis, hemorrhage) can all result in brain damage and concomitant behavioral disturbances.

One source of brain damage, of increasing importance as world population increases faster than food supplies, is nutritional deficiency. For example, a type of memory impairment called Korsakoff's psychosis often occurs as a consequence of vitamin B deficiency which, in turn, results in lesions in the thalamus, pons, and cerebellum (Talland and Waugh, 1969). Chronic protein deficiencies in children's diets produce irreversible brain damage that correlates with subsequent impaired intellectual and social adjustment (Eichenwald and Fry, 1969).

Brain tumors and degeneration due to aging are also common causes of brain damage and associated abnormal behavior. One such circumstance is Parkinson's disease, a severe tremorous motor disorder usually accompanied by withdrawal and apathy. The disease is neurologically characterized by deterioration of dopamine-producing areas in the motor pathways[5] (DeJong and Sugar, 1972). Since dopamine, as mentioned earlier, is the norepinephine precursor, adrenergic activity in the motor pathways is impaired, thereby disrupting proper function. Fortunately, as also mentioned earlier (Chapter 3), the disease can now be managed with dopamine's precursor, *l*-dopa.

Attempts have also been made to correlate variances in brain activity with abnormal behavior. For example, Hughes, Means, and Stell (1965) found that adjudicated delinquents, who characteristically manifested destructive impulsive behavior, had a significantly high incidence of EEG positive spikes (transient, large-amplitude, short-duration deflections). These are thought to be related to some underlying structural defect.

Pitts (1969) has found a relation between anxiety neuroses and body lactate (lactic acid) levels. He observed that patients suffering from anxiety neuroses have high blood lactate values and determined that the infusion of lactate can precipitate the anxiety condition. Anxiety involves unfocused feelings of apprehension and fear, increased heartbeat, labored breathing, and a conviction that death is imminent. Lactate is the end product of glucose breakdown, most commonly when muscles are utilizing glucose for energy (Chapter 6). Since epinephrine stimulates lactate production, it was concluded that anxiety neuroses occur because of overactive adrenal glands.

In addition to the foregoing, disruption of excitatory and inhibitory pathways (Voronin, 1962; Wortis, 1962), and imbalance between hypothalamic pain and pleasure centers

---

5. The specific area of deterioration is the substantia nigra, a nucleus in the cerebral peduncle, a major motor pathway between the cerebrum and spinal cord.

(Meehl, 1962) have been among the more provocative suggestions to explain the physiological basis of abnormal behavior. As with the biochemical studies, most of the other efforts to physically localize personality defects have problems of inconsistency, lack of extension, and an inability to systematically replicate findings. The physical substrates of mental illness still largely remain an enigma.

GENETICS AND PSYCHOPATHOLOGY

Behavior itself cannot be inherited. All that can be genetically transmitted from generation to generation are the protein templates of structure. In view of these facts, if any behavior is suspected of having a physical basis, one way to demonstrate it would be to show that the behavior conforms to the laws of genetic transmission and thereby must have a structural component. The methods used to determine if a behavior is genetically transmitted are varied, and all have been extensively applied to many types of abnormal behaviors, ranging from homosexuality to schizophrenia (Rosenthal, 1971). However, a few examples will suffice to illustrate the approach.

Numerous consanguinity studies, tracing traits through generations of blood relatives, have shown a clear correlation between the degree of blood relationship and the incidence of schizophrenia. One of the most extensive of these investigations is Kallmann's (1946) study of a thousand schizophrenics and their relatives. His data show that, while schizophrenia occurs in only eight out of a thousand of the general population, one out of ten parents or siblings of schizophrenics had the disease and forty out of a thousand of more distant relatives. The morbidity risk for siblings was found to be 14.3 percent. Most other studies report lower values, one as low as 3.3 percent. But, in every case, the incidence is significantly higher than in populations of unrelated individuals. These studies, then, suggest a genetic component in the disease.

Identical or monozygotic twins, those who developed from a single zygote,[6] are ideal subjects for studying the genetic basis of traits because both individuals carry exactly the same genetic material. Thus, if both twins have a given trait, this would indi-

6. A zygote is the fertilized egg cell formed by the union of a sperm and ovum.

cate that the trait is genetically influenced. Studies have been made of the concordance rates between schizophrenic identical twins, i.e. the number of instances where both twins suffer the disease. But no firm conclusion can be made since the rates range with great variability from no concordance at all to 86 percent (Rosenthal, 1971).

Adoption studies eliminate the possible influences of being reared in a deviant environment, i.e., if children of parents suffering behavioral disorders are raised in normal homes and show abnormal behavior patterns, that would be evidence for abnormal behavior being genetically transmitted. For example, Heston (1966) kept histories on forty-seven individuals who had been born to schizophrenic mothers and adopted soon after birth. Twenty-six suffered psychiatric problems as adults (five were actually schizophrenic). In the control group (adoptees not born to schizophrenic mothers), only nine became mentally ill, with none being schizophrenic. Other similar studies (Rosenthal and Kety, 1968) report similar findings. Thus, adoption studies support the contention that abnormal behavior may be genetically transmitted and thereby physically based.

Structural defects in genetic materials, such as chromosomes, have been correlated with various abnormal behaviors. Many types of mental retardation are due to such anomalies as the absence of all or part of a chromosome, the presence of an extra chromosome, or a structural irregularity in a chromosome (Levitan and Montagu, 1971).

Many of the above studies and numerous others like them are suggestive of a genetic, and hence physical, basis for abnormal behavior. However, the issue remains highly controversial due to the inability to totally isolate the behavior involved from potential environmental influences. These studies are thus all compromised by the learning-instinct problem (already discussed in Chapter 2 and further elaborated in Chapter 14).

SUMMARY

Because it has been subjected to so many definitions and interpretations, the term personality has become almost useless for describing behavior. Nonetheless, from the early Greeks right up to the most modern research, many attempts have been made to link behaviors that are referred to as personality with one or another physiochemical substrate.

Most contemporary effort has been directed at various dysfunctional behavioral states generally labelled as abnormal, mental illness, psychopathologic, or whatever. Research interest in these aspects of personality is pragmatic in that, if a physical basis for them could be defined, more efficient cures could be developed.

Some success has been achieved. Psychosomatic illnesses have been traced to the chronic strains imposed on organs by stress-induced sympathetic nervous system activity. Much remains to be learned, however, about the physiogenesis of functional diseases such as schizophrenia. In fact, because of its high prevalence, efforts to isolate the physiological concomitants of schizophrenia have been extensively pursued for many years. Numerous factors, such as blood proteins, neurotransmitters, hormonal imbalances, brain damage, and genetic trends, have been investigated without definitive conclusions.

Other psychiatric disorders have been similarly investigated with some positive consequences resulting. Parkinson's disease, for example, has been linked to neurohumoral depletion; Korsakoff's psychosis to nutritional deficiencies. As a result, these conditions are now clinically manageable. In most instances, however, the physiochemical aspects of mental illness remain enigmatical and a cogent problem for physiological psychologists.

SUGGESTED READINGS

Coleman, J. H. *Abnormal Psychology and Modern Life*. (4th ed.) Glenview, Ill.: Scott Foresman, 1972. A standard textbook on abnormal psychology; intermediate level.

Corah, N. L., and Gale, E. N., eds. *The Origins of Abnormal Behavior*. Reading, Mass.: Addison-Wesley, 1971. Very useful collection of articles relating to the causes, including biological, of abnormal behavior.

IV
Physiological aspects of social behavior

Probably no other area of psychology has as much immediate applied significance to the human condition as social psychology. Marriage, parents and children, student-professor relations, business, and all game-playing activities are examples of the fact that most human behavior is social and that all important issues of civilized life—legal, moral, political and philosophic—arise out of social interaction and conduct.

Since social behavior is so omnipresent, it is no surprise that it is the first class of behavior encountered so far in this book, perhaps the only class of behavior, that can be defined with some assurance of agreement among psychologists. McGinnies says that "social behavior is evidenced wherever two or more organisms, either directly or indirectly, serve both to prompt and to reinforce one another's performances" (1970). Agreeing fully, Lindgren states:

The term social as used by psychologists and other behavioral scientists refers to interaction among individuals and/or groups as well as the influence of individuals and/or groups on one another (1969, p. 3).

A fascinating consequence of this agreement as to definition is that the authors thereupon take very different approaches to elaborating the determinants of social behavior.

Despite the pervasive importance of social conduct, most of physiological psychology, and indeed psychology in general, has concentrated on the behavior of isolated individual organisms without much concern for the more realistic circumstances of living—the social milieu. To say that this has helped put psychology, as so much of contemporary academia, out of touch with general humanity would be an understatement.

What behavior, for example, more cogently needs the combined effort of all psychologists than does aggression? In a contemporary world marked by political assassination, skyjacking of peaceful commercial planes, astronomical increases in crime rates, not to mention the overriding danger of the threat of nuclear devastation, there is no social behavior that needs better understanding than the show or act of violence. Failure to come to terms with it may ultimately render the pursuit of all other knowledge futile. Thus, it is appropriate to begin the first chapter of this section of the book with a consideration of how physiological psychology has come to grips with what may, in the long run, be its most important problem, aggression. As well, its opposite, togetherness will be discussed. The remainder of Part IV considers another contemporary major social issue, the use and effects of behavior-modifying drugs.

14 Physiology of aggression and togetherness

AGONISTIC BEHAVIOR (AGGRESSIVENESS)

Definition of aggression

To clarify the term *aggression* at the outset, consider Kaufmann's statement:

In order for a behavior to be classified as "aggressive"—
1. It must be transitive; that is, directed against a living target (as opposed to being purely autistic).

and:

2. The attacker must have an expectation or subjective probability greater than zero of reaching the object and of imparting a noxious stimulus to it . . . (1970, pp. 10–11).

This definition has some obvious weaknesses. Not everyone believes that aggression is limited to a living target. Is it not aggression if the impulse to destroy is directed at school property, as in vandalism? On the other hand, is it aggression for the soldier to kill a foe or the homeowner to shoot a prowler? Is aggression necessarily violent, and is violence only the product of aggression? Answers are not readily available. For present purposes, however, the discussion will deal with the overt

277

behaviors from which the process of aggression is inferred. The behaviors involved usually take the form of fighting, attack, withdrawal, or surrender. These and other related postures are collectively referred to as *agonistic* (or combative) behavior (Scott and Fredericson, 1951), as distinguished from positive aggregation, or togetherness, behavior.

Is aggression learned or instinctive?

Early studies revealed that agonistic behavior may be inheritable (Fredericson et al., 1955; Keeler, 1942; Scott, 1942) and sex-linked (Fredericson et al., 1955; Noble and Borne, 1940), suggesting an underlying structural mechanism. A number of theorists have taken this possibility to mean that agonistic behavior cannot be significantly modified by learning, even in man (Lorenz, 1966; Tinbergen, 1968) and, hence, must be instinctive. "Man is an aggressive animal," says Aronson. "With the exception of certain rodents, no other vertebrate so consistently and wantonly kills other members of his own species." (1972).

Some recent popularizers of social science themes[1] state bluntly that man is an aggressive animal by nature and, therefore, that war is a normal state of affairs and cannot be prevented. Much of this argument is based on observations of non-human primate behavior and the discovery of such humanlike characteristics in apes as "the territorial imperative," and the dominance of a leader or "executive monkey." Since the apes come closest to man phylogenetically, this view of their behavior underlines the notion that man's own aggressive behavior may have arisen from genetic factors carried through the process of evolution.

Conversely, other research suggests aggression is a learned response developed by negative circumstances. For example, Azrin, Hutchinson, and Hake (1966) found that a pigeon pecking a key for food learned to attack another nearby pigeon

1. Some books expounding these themes have become "best sellers." For example, see Ardrey (1961); Lorenz (1966); Morris (1967).

when extinction[2] was implemented. The attacks were vicious and furious, sometimes lasting up to ten minutes.

The learning contention has also received popularization. Various social scientists have suggested that human violence can be better controlled by manipulating the environmental contingencies that contribute to eliciting aggression. A range of proposals, from limiting displays of violence on television (Eron, 1963) to totally restructuring human society (Skinner, 1971), have been put forth.

Putting aggression into a learning-instinct dichotomy, and the resultant consequences in contemporary rhetoric, have largely been brought about by behavioristic influences on psychology (Hall, 1961). Actually, the argument over the determinants of aggression affords another excellent example of the fallibility of differentiating the nature of behavior as learned or instinctive by association with an underlying inherited physiological substrate. As was pointed out earlier (Chapter 13), all that any organism inherits is a set of protein templates, from which subsequent physical structure is developed. The organism's heterotrophic functions do not appear until they are needed in environmental intercourse and then only to the extent that there is a physical capacity for such interaction. Thus, it is futile to attempt to classify behavior on a "nature-nurture" basis.

Aggressiveness is clearly a heterotrophic function in that it is essential to maintaining the viability of the organism by giving it a capacity to compete for food, sex, and other environmental factors essential to self and species preservation. Whether that can be considered instinctive or learned seems like much ado about nothing, except for those who need this kind of substantiation for their social or political views.

Sources of aggression

Nonetheless, many experiments have been conducted to determine whether agonistic behavior is instinctive or not by searching for the sources of aggression and attempting to isolate and

---

2. Extinction, it will be recalled, is removal of a reward.

manipulate them. Ethologists,[3] for instance, have determined that visual cues can be a source of aggression. Studies of the robin show that the male robin identifies another male robin to attack in defense of its territory by the bird's red feathers. Lack (1943) used dummy birds built exactly like robins; the subject robin did not respond to them. But a few red feathers caused the robin to attack. Similarly, Tinbergen (1951) studied the red-bellied stickleback, a fresh and salt water fish found in northern regions. He found that the stickleback defends its territory in breeding time by attacking any other red-belly-like object that enters its territory. Evidently these forms of aggression are oriented toward the species only and innate thereto.

Deets and Harlow (1971) tried to demonstrate the instinctive nature of aggression in rhesus monkeys by rearing them from birth in isolation from other monkeys, to see whether they would be aggressive. They found that, when threatened, these isolated monkeys showed aggressive behavior against humans and against themselves. Some even tore their own flesh and flailed their heads against the cage. The investigators concluded that aggressive behavior requires time to mature, but that it is definitely instinctive.

Deets and Harlow went further by suggesting that aggression is the third component in a three part developmental sequence. The organism, they said, is born with the capacity to affiliate, that is, to form social attachments to its mother and peers. In the first few weeks of life no fear or aggression is apparent. Then, after a few months, the organism begins to show signs of fear towards any novel stimuli, both animate and inanimate, social and nonsocial. This fear is later followed by aggressive behavior, which arises perhaps a year after birth.

One of the most extensive series of aggression experiments with rats was carried out by Azrin (1967). He wanted to determine if two rats could be conditioned to interact with each other with negative stimulation (escape from electric foot shock) instead of positive reward (food). The experimental design involved shocking the feet of two rats through an electrified grid until they moved toward each other and then to cut off the current so that the stopping of the shock treatment would be pleasantly associated with proximity. However, the opposite

3. Scientists who study animals behaving in their natural habitats.

reaction resulted; instead of coming together, the animals frequently attacked each other before the shock could be terminated. There was a direct relation between the intensity, duration, and frequency of the shock and the amount of aggression.

Azrin then addressed himself to the question of whether the pain-attack reaction was innate or learned. He found that isolating rats from one another did not eliminate the shock-attack response. Also, rats that lived together attacked one another just as often as rats caged separately. Sex was not involved, nor was the predatory reaction. Hunger had no effect on the number of attacks. It was concluded that shock-attack was a reflexive reaction to pain, relatively independent of learning experiences.

Even more significantly, it was found that the reaction occurred across species lines. Mice, hamsters, monkeys, alligators, and even boa constrictors exhibited the same behavior. Oddly, fighting cocks and Siamese fighting fish, which are known for aggressive behavior against their own species, were not appreciably affected by the shocks. Was the aggression triggered by the physical attributes of the target? This was answered with a series of experiments in which various species of animals were caged with other species—for instance, a rat caged with a guinea pig, a monkey with a rat, a rat with a rooster. It was found that, in every instance, under shock the animal attacked its neighbor. The type of target made no difference. Shocked animals attacked stuffed dolls, tennis balls, and small miscellaneous objects as quickly as other rats. "It seems therefore," Azrin concluded, "that under the stimulus of pain animals will attack and try to destroy almost any 'attackable' object in the environment . . ." (1967)

Nor was electric shock the sole motivator of aggression; other kinds of pain did just as well. As was just mentioned, withdrawal of expected rewards from certain animals would provoke them to attack nearby objects just as though they were foot shocked. It thus appears that the withdrawing of reward, or frustration, is the equivalent of physical pain in provoking aggression. The relationship to man is an easy step. Everyone is familiar with the human reaction of irritation and even violence at being fired from a job, being jilted, running out of gas on the highway, having one's salary cut down, or losing money in a vending machine or telephone coin box.

Avoidance behavior, Azrin found, would eliminate the attack reaction or, ". . . in everyday terms, it seems that pain evoked aggression can be controlled or eliminated by establishing effective, peaceful means for avoiding the pain" (1967).

The foregoing studies suggest that aggression has a genetic and, thus, a physical basis. However, the expression of aggression can be modified by environmental circumstances and, in that sense, also has a learned component. Consequently, as already stated, the distinction has little conceptual value.

The physical basis of aggression

The search for the physical basis of aggression has concentrated on two organismic aspects, hormone systems and brain areas. These have been studied by the usual techniques: hormone or drug injections and gland removal in the first instance; ablation and stimulation in the second instance.

Hormones and aggression   Looking at the humoral aspects, both neurohormones and sex hormones have been investigated. In regard to neurohormones, both adrenergic and cholinergic substances have been implicated in aggression. In the former case, the evidence shows that drugs that antagonize adrenergic action also depress fighting behavior (Janssen, Jageneau, and Niemegeers, 1960; Tedeschi et al., 1959), while adrenergiclike drugs that stimulate the adrenergic system increase aggressiveness (Thiessen, 1964). In the latter case, stimulation of the cholinergic centers produces fighting behavior (King and Hoebel, 1968). Although both evidence and logic might favor the influence of adrenergic substances on aggression over cholinergic substances (Remember that the sympathetic nervous system, which regulates the fight or flight syndrome, is adrenergically mediated.), once again, no definitive biochemical localization has been demonstrated relevant to fighting behavior. Besides, the adrenergic-cholinergic systems, as was explained in Chapter 10, are not necessarily antagonistic.

Sex hormones seem somewhat more clearly related to agonistic behavior. Males, for instance, are usually more aggressive than females, and the difference has been experimentally

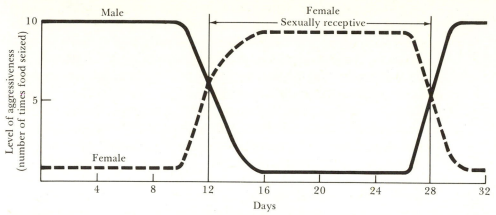

Figure 14-1. Changes in relative level of aggressiveness between male and female chimpanzees as a function of the female's period of sexual receptivity. (Reconstructed from Yerkes, 1939, data.)

related to the male sex hormones, the androgens. Castration of males reduces aggressiveness (Beaman, 1947; Tavolga, 1955); administration of androgens to either males or females increases aggressiveness (Allee, Collias, and Lutherman, 1939; Ball, 1940; Clark and Birch, 1945); while administration of estrogens (female sex hormones), under some conditions, reduces aggressiveness (Kislack and Beach, 1955). During estrus, however, females are often more aggressive than males (Yerkes, 1939, 1940). As shown in Figure 14-1, when food was introduced into the cage of a male and female monkey, the male almost always got it first. With onset of estrus the behavior was reversed—the female seized the meal before the male.

The physiological effects of the sex hormones on aggression are dependent on various other factors such as maturation (Bronson and Desjardin, 1968; Uricht, 1938) and on other types of social behavior such as dominance hierarchies (Crawford, 1940). Once again, it appears that multifactor integration, rather than any one substance (even a sex hormone) or condition, is involved in agonistic behavior.

Areas of the brain and aggression Almost all gross brain areas that have been implicated in agonistic behavior are either paleocortical or subcortical. They include the reticular formation,

283

cingulate gyrus, septum, thalamus, hypothalamus, and amygdala (Delgado, 1966; Flynn et al., 1970; MacDonnell and Flynn, 1964; Smythies, 1970). Of these, the amygdala seems to be a primary integrating center for aggressiveness, since stimulation or ablation of one or another part of the structure increases or decreases agonistic behavior (Goddard, 1964; Pribram, 1962; Rosvold, Mirsky, and Pribram, 1954; Smythies, 1970). In fact, Pribram (1962) found that destroying part of the amygdala of monkeys living in a colony dramatically changed the existing hierarchy of the monkey society. A monkey that was lowest on the social scale began to compete with his superiors and soon worked his way to the top. Conversely, when the dominant monkey totally lost his amygdala, the picture was reversed; he could no longer control the colony and dropped to the bottom of the hierarchy.

These data suggest the existence of two antagonistic aggression centers, a "stop" and "go" area (Pribram, 1971) similar to that discussed in connection with consummatory behavior (Chapter 8). In fact, inhibition of attack behavior has been dramatically demonstrated in an experiment in which a charging bull was stopped in its tracks by radio-controlled electrodes implanted in the bull's brain (Delgado, 1971). It should be pointed out, however, that this concept has been challenged by Valenstein (1973) who suggests that the bull's reaction may have been one of confusion, rather than of inhibited aggression.

The classification of agonistic behaviors according to source

One promising approach that may help clarify the relationship between brain mechanisms and aggression involves the realization that agonistic behavior stems not from a single source but from a variety of causes or stimuli. Moyer (1971) has noted that aggressive behavior is often a response to a specific stimulus. He has been able to differentiate seven patterns of aggressive behavior according to the stimuli that produce them. Predatory aggression, he points out, is elicited by the presence of the object of prey. Inter-male aggression results from the appearance of a competitive male to which the attacker has not become habituated. Other stimulus-bound aggressions are classified as fear-induced, irritable, territorial, maternal and instrumental.

Fear-induced aggression is characterized by destructive behavior that is linked to the attempt to escape. Irritable aggression is the result of an available nearby object, living or not, on which the organism can vent its frustration and anger. Maternal aggression is the response of the female to threats against her offspring, while territorial aggression is the response of the organism to invasion of its domain. Finally, instrumental aggression is learned through reward of an early aggressive response to a given situation. It does not require dominance or injury as a goal.

Clearly there is considerable interaction among these aggressive stimuli in the behavior of the organism. But, according to Moyer, each pattern of aggression has its own physiological substrate. On the basis of brain stimulation or ablation, and gland removal or hormone injection experiments, it appears that one group of aggressions—maternal, territorial, and inter-male—are primarily humorally integrated; while the second group—fear-induced, irritable, and predatory aggression—are mostly neurally integrated. Table 14-1 shows the specific substrates in the nervous system apparently involved in each aggressive behavior.

The need for a greater understanding of aggression

That these relatively few paragraphs sum up the essence of what is known about the physiology of aggression is a social tragedy since there is a great potential for developing the

Table 14.1.   Relation between types of aggressive behavior and physiological substrates

Aggressive behavior	Substrate
Predatory	Lateral hypothalamus; amygdala
Fear-induced	Amygdala; septum; ventro-medial nucleus of hypothalamus
Maternal	Estrogens
Territorial	Androgens
Inter-male	Androgens, septum
Irritable	Ventro-medial hypothalamus; amygdala; caudate nucleus
Instrumental	Based on history of reward

Note: Moyer, 1971.

means for a more peaceful existence through a fuller understanding of aggression. The challenge is clearly directed to
physiological psychology but it is not being met. A recent review
article (Shapiro and Schwartz, 1970), entitled "Psychophysiological Contributions to Social Psychology," does not even take
up the question of aggression.

Perhaps one reason why physiological psychologists are re-
luctant to approach the issue of aggression is that many observers fear that relevant studies might lead society to adopt
mind control by chemical means, by psychosurgery, or by en-
forced electrode implantation. Unfortunately, behaviorists fan
the fires of such thinking with their constant emphasis on the
benefits of behavioral control. The public apparently is not
ready for such an approach. A proposal by Kenneth Clark
(1971), former President of the American Psychological Association, urging development of a drug to curb man's violent
impulses resulted in a flood of protest by press and public, as
well as by some psychologists.

There has even been opposition to proposals suggesting early
identification and care of those who might become violent. In
their book, *Violence and the Brain* (1970), neurologists Vernon
Mark and Frank Ervin, after reviewing the neurophysiological
basis of agnostic behavior, concluded that there was strong
evidence for believing that some forms of violence arise
through defects of the limbic system. They suggested the need
to develop an early warning test of limbic brain function for
detecting and treating those people who have a low threshold
of violence.

This proposal drew considerable criticism. Protests were
made at UCLA, where Ervin wanted to set up a center for the
study of violent behavior, and at Boston City Hospital, where
Mark is head of neurosurgery. The opponents stressed the
difficulty of relating a given part of the brain to violent behavior. They further argued that attempts to pick out potentially violent individuals might result in harassment of political
dissidents. As a result, Mark and Ervin's suggestion never
even reached the study stage.

Such public reactions may work to the disadvantage of the
best interests of society. Realistically, in view of the built-in controls both in medical ethics and in a democratic society, there is

little danger that greater understanding of aggressive impulses will lead to medical or electronic manipulation of people. On the contrary, there is every possibility that further studies of aggression will lead to epistemological advances which could provide greater freedom from violence. At the very least, knowing the mechanisms of aggression and how they turn into unacceptable violence would certainly give society one more chance to survive than it has now.

POSITIVE AGGREGATE BEHAVIOR (TOGETHERNESS)

While agonistic behavior keeps organisms apart, *aggregate behavior* serves to bring them together. Aggregate behavior is a basic heterotrophic function. Organisms may aggregate without interaction, such as birds taking to flight at the sound of a gun or strangers sitting together at a bar. Ducks travel in coveys, sheep in flocks, and insects live their own kind of aggregated lives throughout their short life cycle. Aggregate behavior has even been observed in some species of amoeba, where the primary physical mechanism inducing aggregation involves chemical clues which draw the one-celled animals together (Bonner, 1963).

More relevant to this discussion, most animals have social systems and their aggregation involves social interaction. Such interaction is frequently in the interests of self and species preservation. This behavior facilitates defense against enemies and regulation of population size. A form of aggregate behavior, sometimes called affiliative behavior, involves mating and rearing of young—activities obviously necessary to continue the species. Aggregated animals maintain better physical health because of their social closeness and mutual helpfulness than do individuals on their own (Thiessen and Rodgers, 1961).

Aggregation may also create problems. Overcrowding, for instance, can have markedly deleterious pathological effects on a variety of animals, including man. In the case of man, overcrowding may even be an important variable in the incidence of psychosomatic conditions (Calhoun, 1962; Galle, Gove, and McPherson, 1972; and see Chapter 13). Further, overcrowding may represent a major social problem if it proves true that man has circumvented the natural regulatory mechanisms that maintain his optimal population size and dispersion for survival as a species (Wynne-Edwards, 1962). Unfortunately, as with aggression, these considerations remain hypothetical because of the dearth of experimental psychological research into aggregate behavior.

One type of aggregate behavior that has been widely studied in lower animals, where it has many humoral and anatomical aspects, is sex behavior (Beach, 1947). Relative to other aspects of social behavior, the physiology of sexual actions, as well as the neurological and endocrinological correlates, is well understood. Ironically, the one area of social behavior that has been extensively investigated physiologically has little direct applicability to man because human sexual behavior is primarily governed by psychological factors rather than physiological ones (Beach, 1969). It is obvious that knowledge of the actions of gonadal hormones or amygdaloid neurotransmitters will not counsel the bashful groom on the night of his honeymoon or answer the question of what you always wanted to know but were afraid to ask.

Physical bases of aggregation

Recognizing the limited research available, this section explores what is known about the physical bases of aggregate behavior. What brings living things together and makes them recognize their own kind? Visual signs are the most obvious single factor of recognition. As noted earlier, robins recognize fellow robins by their red feathers, and certain fish recognize other fish of their species by their red bellies. In addition, Lorenz (1970) has shown that newborn ducklings will respond to and follow any large moving object—not necessarily a mother duck. He has tested them with large mobile wooden animals or other contraptions, and even with himself. This process, it will be recalled (Chapter 12), is known as imprinting. It refers to an inborn capacity which apparently emerges as a result of a specific releasing-stimulus, such as size, shape, color, or motion.

Similarly, the Harlows' famous experiments (1971) demonstrate the early need for affiliation on the part of newborn monkeys. They found that neonate monkeys will cling to all kinds of wire contraptions if the objects are covered by something reasonably soft and warm. Apparently, clinging to the wire object relieves the infant's distress and provides contact comfort, as did the living mother.

Distress signals are another form of cue for aggregation. The dolphin is said to utter a high-pitched cry when in trouble in order to draw other dolphins to its side (Lilly, 1961). Many other animals have cries that distinctly call to their rescue available members of the same species. A chick's call will bring the mother hen running, just as a human infant's cry of pain will bring its mother (Maier, 1962).

A biochemical basis for some types of human interpersonal attraction has recently been postulated. Schachter (1964), it will be recalled, suggested that any emotion is a function of two factors: 1) physiological arousal, such as would be mediated by epinephrine; and 2) an appropriate stimulus object, such as another person. Walster and Berscheid (1971) reason that these conditions underlie individuals affectionately drawing together. Love, they maintain, arises under circumstances (such as stress) which precipitate increased levels of epinephrine, in conjunction with the availability of another person. Presumably, other emotionally based social contact (such as aggression) could similarly arise.

THE ROLE OF CHEMICALS IN SOCIAL COMMUNICATION

It will be remembered from Chapter 4 that a large part of the brain of most animals is concerned with olfactory sensation.[4] Man, who has a relatively poor sense of smell, is apparently an exception, although Doty (1972) postulated that air pollution may be restoring man's awareness of the importance of his olfactory organs.

In any case—with the exception of perfumes, colognes, and deodorants—man has, until recently, largely ignored the role of exogenous chemicals in social behavior. Yet the importance of chemical reception to much of social behavior, including agonistic and aggregate behavior, can be appreciated from the

---

4. It is interesting to note, as Doty (1972) pointed out, that psychologists use visually poor, olfactorily rich animals to study the *visual* aspects of learning!

elaboration by Whittaker and Feeny (1971), who organized the type of substances involved in terms of their behavioral consequences (summarized in Table 14-2).

Table 14-2.   Classes of interorganismic chemical effects

I. **Allelochemic effects**
   A. *Allomones* (+/), which give adaptive advantage to the producing organism.
      1. *Repellents* (+/), which provide defense against attack or infection (many secondary plant substances, chemical defenses among animals, probably some toxins of other organisms).
      2. *Escape* substances (+/) that are not repellents in the usual sense (inks of cephalopods, tension-swimming substances).
      3. *Suppressants* (+/), which inhibit competitors (antibiotics, possibly some allelopathics and plankton ectocrines).
      4. *Venoms* (+/), which poison prey organisms (venoms of predatory animals and myxobacteria, aggressions of parasites and pathogens).
      5. *Inductants* (+/), which modify growth of the second organism (gall, nodule, and mycorrhiza producing agents).
      6. *Counteractants* (+/), which neutralize as a defense the effect of a venom or other agent (antibodies, substances inactivating stinging cells, substances protecting parasites against digestive enzymes).
      7. *Attractants* (+/)
         a) Chemical lures (+−), which attract prey to a predator (attractants of carnivorous plants and fungi).
         b) *Pollination attractants,* which are without (+0) or with (++) advantage to the organisms attracted (flower scents).
   B. *Kairomones* (/+), which give adaptive advantage to the receiving organism.
      1. *Attractants* as food location signals (/+), which attract the organism to its food source, including those attracting to a food organism (−0) (use of secondary substances as signals by plant consumers, of prey scents by predators, or chemical cues by parasites), pollination attractants when the attracted organism obtains food (++), and those attracting to nonliving food (0+) (response to scent by carrion feeder, chemotactic response by motile bacteria and by fungal hyphae).
      2. *Inductants* (/+), which stimulate adaptive development in the receiving organism (hyphal loop factor in nematode-trapping fungi, spine-development factor in rotifers).
      3. *Signals* (/+) that warn of danger or toxicity to the receiver, such as repellent signals (Allomones) that have adaptive advantage to the receiver, scents and flavors that indicate unpalatability of nonliving food, predator scents.
      4. *Stimulants* (/+), such as hormones, that benefit the second organism by inducing growth.

C. *Depressants* (0−), wastes, and so forth, that inhibit or poison the receiver without adaptive advantage to releaser from this effect (some bacterial and parasite toxins, allelopathics that give no competitive advantage, some plankton ectocrines).

II. **Intraspecific chemical effects.**

A. *Autotoxins* (−/), repellents, wastes, and so forth, that are toxic or inhibitory to individuals of the releasing populations, with or without selective advantage from detriment to some other species (some bacterial toxins, antibiotics, ectocrines, and accumulated wastes of animals in dense culture).

B. *Adaptive autoinhibitors* (+/) that limit the population to numbers that do not destroy the host or produce excessive crowding (stalling substance of fungi).

C. *Pheromones* (+/), chemical messages between members of a species that are signals for:
Reproductive behavior
Social regulation and recognition
Control of caste differentiation
Alarm and defense
Territory and trail marking
Food location

Notes: Reproduced from Whittaker and Feeny (1971)
Adaptive advantage is indicated by +, detriment by −, and adaptive indifference by 0, for the releasing organism first and the receiving organism second. The virgule (/) indicates that adaptive advantage or detriment is not specified for one side of the relationship.

SUMMARY

In summary, it can only be said that the relative brevity of the present chapter demonstrates a gap in knowledge that is appalling. In terms of the need to know, the physiological aspects of social behavior should have made this the longest chapter in the book, not one of the shortest. Future students will have abundant opportunities for meaningful research.

SUGGESTED READINGS

Aronson, E. *The Social Animal.* San Francisco: Freeman, 1972. Insightful, thought-provoking discussion of human sociability.
Beach, F. A., ed. *Sex and Behavior.* New York: Wiley, 1965. Assemblage of papers by numerous authorities on the parameters of sex behavior.

Brown, R. *Social Psychology.* New York: Free Press, 1965. Best textbook on social psychology; comprehensive, interesting, and interpretive.

Lorenz, K. *On Aggression.* London: Methuen, 1967. Elaborate espousal of the ethnological point-of-view on the development of aggressive behavior.

Tinbergen, N. *The Study of Instinct.* New York: Oxford University Press, 1951. The classic description of ethnological theory.

15 Drugs and behavior

Psychologists, philosophers, and others concerned with the human condition have always taken delight in listing the attributes, from the obvious to the obscure, that distinguish man from other animals. For example, it has been suggested that man is the only animal that cooks his food, has a language, practices religion, kills for pleasure, can alter his environment, has self-awareness, knows he's going to die, and is preoccupied with sex.

While these are extremely important behaviors, there is one other human behavior, not on the list, that is of particularly profound interest to the physiological psychologist. More than any other human behavior, it gives realization to the phenomenon of mind in man. Simply, man is the only animal that intentionally takes chemical substances into himself for other than nutritional reasons.[1] These substances, called *drugs,* are taken by man for two primary reasons: 1) to treat disease, and 2) to alter his body or mind. The latter is the one of major concern to physiological psychology. Specifically, man employs drugs on himself to alter one or another of the various psychological processes discussed up to now: sensation, perception, emotion,

1. The contention that other animals do is compromised by two facts: 1. Almost all the evidence is anecdotal and anthropomorphically interpreted, and 2. There is not even the remotest indication of a phylogenetic progression or orderliness in the occurrence of the behavior. See Brown, 1974; Siegel, 1973.

motivation, consciousness, personality, and sociability. In effect, man chemically manipulates, to suit himself, all the experiential facets of heterotrophic functioning or operations relevant to his integrating with his environment. He changes reality, particularly stressful reality, to suit his innermost needs.

Since all that drugs do in the body is to enter into basic physiochemical relationships with ongoing biological processes, some questions arise. How can simple alterations of neural activity give rise to such profound subjective experiences as those reported by drug users? What power does this kind of chemical (for a drug is a chemical and nothing more) hold over the brain? Clearly, the answers to these questions would be directly relevant to the mind-body problem and of enormous use to society. To get at these answers, one must first examine what *pharmacology* (the science of drugs) has been able to determine about the physical effects of drugs in the nervous system and then attempt to relate those effects to changes in the behavior of the organism.

DRUG ACTION IN THE NERVOUS SYSTEM

Two broad types of chemical activity go on in the nervous system: *metabolism* maintains the viability and functioning (such as impulse conduction) of neural tissue, and *neurohumoral actions* facilitate transmission of impulses across synaptic junctions (Chapter 3). Some drugs affect the metabolism. For example, local anesthetics affect membrane polarization and cyanides interfere with neuronal respiration, but both produce little or no direct mind alteration. The drugs that are primarily utilized for their behavior-modifying or mind-altering effects are those that affect synaptic transmission. These drugs include LSD, marijuana, barbiturates, caffeine, nicotine, amphetamines, alcohol, and heroin, among others. It was partly because of the effect of hallucinogenic drugs on the synapse that Eccles (1953) termed the synapse "the locus of mind."

Drugs and neurohumoral actions

A review of neurohumoral transmission (Chapter 3) will reveal that there are at least six ways in which a drug can modify the relation between neurohormones and their receptor sites and, thus, alter the usual progression of synaptic events (Koelle, 1965). It can be accomplished by:

1. Interference with the synthesis of the neurotransmitter,

2. Interference with the release of the neurotransmitter,

3. Facilitation of release of the neurotransmitter,

4. Interference with enzymatic deactivation of the neurotransmitter,

5. Activation of the postsynaptic membrane, and

6. Inhibition of the neurotransmitter's action on the postsynaptic membrane.

Most of the drugs that affect the nervous system involve the last three types of action. Drugs that inhibit enzymatic neurotransmitter deactivation are referred to as *anticholinesterases* or *monoamine oxidase inhibitors,* depending on whether the synapse is cholinergic or adrenergic. Drugs that mimic the postsynaptic membrane activation of the neurotransmitter are called *mimetics* (*parasympatho-* or *sympatho-*). Those that inhibit postsynaptic neurotransmitter action are either *anticholinergics* or *antiadrenergics.*[2] It should be emphasized that definitive empirical verification of these effects comes from studies with peripheral synapses, but it is reasonable to assume that similar events due to drug action occur in the central nervous system (Krnjevic, 1969; Karczmar, 1969).

Ways in which drugs alter subjective experience

There are two broad ways in which drugs affect subjective experience. Some drugs can expand the experience across a range of inner states from simply increasing alertness to actually supplying sensations, perceptions, and, some claim, cognitions that are not available by the usual sensory and perceptive mechanisms. Other drugs restrict experience, again throughout a range of states from mere elevation of sensory thresholds to total unconsciousness. Usually, a nonmedical user will prefer

2. These are also known as adrenergic blocking agents.

one or the other type of alteration.[3] Table 15-1 lists some of the more commonly used of each of these types of drugs.

DRUG ACTION AND BEHAVIOR OF ORGANISMS

Although pharmacologists often refer to drugs that activate cellular processes as stimulants and those that decrease or inhibit cellular activity as depressants, there is no correlation between the action of a drug on neurons and its effect on the behavior of an organism. To take just one example, the amphetamines are drugs that stimulate cellular activity, but depress appetite (Brown, 1963, 1965; Brown and Richards, 1966; Harris, Ivy, and Searle, 1947).

Thus, correlations between drug actions and behavioral consequences have to be treated with considerable caution. The appearance of a well-defined mood in different people may look the same but may actually be the result of different patterns of cellular activity. For example, alcohol alters emotionality, causing a person to act silly, by depressing cortical inhibi-

---

3. But this is not always the case. Some users only want to achieve any kind of mind alteration and will use any mind-altering drug available. The state is called *polypsychopharmacotoximania.*

Table 15-1.   Drugs commonly employed for mind alteration.

	Type	*Examples*
Experience expanding	Hallucinogens	LSD
		Mescaline
		Marijuana
	Stimulants	Amphetamines
		Cocaine
		Caffeine
Experience restricting	Opiates (narcotics)	Heroin
		Morphine
		Methadone
	Depressants	Barbiturates
		Alcohol
		Nicotine
		Tranquilizers
		Solvents
		Methaqualone

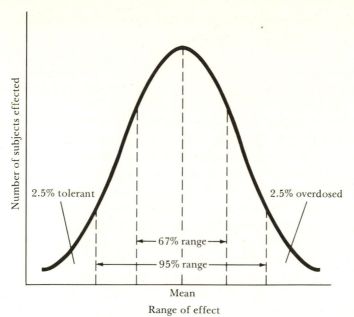

Figure 15-1. Distribution of the effect of a specific dose of a drug across a population of subjects.

tory systems. Amphetamines produce an essentially identical behavioral pattern by stimulating subcortical facilitory systems.

Another consideration is *dose,* the amount of drug administered to an organism (generally in mg) relative to the weight of the organism (in kg). When it comes to specifying the variance of effect as a function of dose, the dose-effect relationship, complications arise because the relationship depends on such physiological factors as body size, age, sex, species, health, previous drug use, and biological rhythms as well as on a host of psychological factors collectively called drug-behavior interactions (discussed later in this chapter).

As a consequence of such variability, if a given dose of a given drug is administered to a population of organisms, any effect measured will characteristically follow a normal distribution curve (Figure 15-1). The majority of individuals, those in the middle of the range, will show a similar magnitude of effect to a slightly greater or lesser degree. A few at the lower end of the range will be unaffected by the dose. They are said to be *drug tolerant.* Another group at the upper end of the range will show an exaggerated reaction to the dose. They are said to suffer from the effects of *overdose*.

Drug effects on an organism are also relative in another sense. Most drugs affect several systems simultaneously or successively, causing a variety of actions which are reflected at the organismic level as a diversity of symptoms. In measuring drug-induced changes, only one particular alteration is considered to be the effect. The other changes are referred to as *side-effects*. Since side-effects frequently compromise the desired effect, they are usually considered undesirable. To use the amphetamines once again as an example, they are used clinically for elevation of mood and for appetite control in dietary regimens, among other things. As is obvious, the use to which the physician puts the drug determines which reaction is considered the effect; while the other reaction is an undesirable side-effect.

Drug effects on an organism are modified when two or more drugs are simultaneously present in the system. The drugs can interact to achieve one of two possible results. First, one drug can offset or modify the action of the other in a process called *drug antagonism*. Second, two or more substances can complement each other in a process called *drug synergism*. In general, depressants and stimulants are antagonistic, whereas two depressants or two stimulants given together are synergistic.

However, here as elsewhere, caution must be exercised in expressing what is being stimulated and what is being depressed. For example, the central nervous system depressant, chlorpromazine, usually depresses the lever-pressing response of rats. Yet it antagonizes the appetite-depressing action of amphetamine, which itself is measured by cessation of food-rewarded lever pressing. So, chlorpromazine, a depressant, restores amphetamine-depressed lever pressing (Brown, 1963; Davis, 1965). Interestingly, the relationship does not hold for water rewarded behavior (Falk and Burnidge, 1970), but does hold for shock avoidance (Brown, 1966c).

Drug synergism examples are similar. Carlton and Didamo (1961) found that the stimulant effect of amphetamine on shock avoidance rewarded lever pressing was facilitated by atropine, an anticholinergic drug. Besides its other actions, amphetamine is also a sympathomimetic drug, so the relationship is not surprising. Nor, in that light, is Carlton's (1961) finding that imipramine, a monoamine oxidase inhibitor, also has a behavioral synergism with amphetamine. Probably the best known example of synergism occurs between two depressants— the barbiturates and alcohol. In combination the effect is often fatal. Both synergistic and antagonistic interactions have many important applications in the practice of medicine.

It can be seen that translation from the neural actions to the behavioral effects of drugs involves several considerations at both the structural and functional level; the relation is not direct. Any discussion of drug effects, including the one that follows, can only be meaningfully appreciated by maintaining such an integrative perspective.

DRUG-BEHAVIOR INTERACTION

Accepting the foregoing presumptions of complex and relative interactions between drugs and behavior, *psychopharmacologists,* scientists who study the relationship between drugs and behavior, have amassed large quantities of data correlating various synaptic drug actions with one or another type of behavior. This has been done in an attempt to define experience in terms of neurohumoral events (Russell, 1969; Reeves, 1966). Within the limitation of having to assume the nature of central synaptic transmission, they have established some evidence for such relationships. It seems that behavior can be regulated in an orderly fashion by manipulating adrenergic and cholinergic transmission. Carlton (1968), for example, has demonstrated that behavioral habituation can be abolished by anticholinergic intervention. He thereby concluded that such behaviors are cholinergically mediated (Recall Deutsch's contention about learning in Chapter 12.).

In addition to assessing the effects of drugs on behavior, psychopharmacologists have also found that behavior can alter the action of a drug. This circumstance is referred to as a *drug-behavior interaction.* Precisely stated, the organism's experiencing of environmental contingencies interacts with the physiological action of the drug. The psychological circumstances under which a drug is administered and its physiological actions are reciprocally integrated so that the resultant effect represents various combinations of both.

Placebo experiments

Historically, the earliest examples of drug-behavior interaction are found in the so-called placebo effect. A *placebo*[3] is a pharmacologically inert substance which is taken as a drug. Much of pre-nineteenth century drug therapy was actually conducted with such inactive substances, often quite successfully.

In many instances, the expectations of the user will endow the inactive substance with properties that have profound behavioral and physiological effects. To take one example, Frankenhaeuser and her colleagues (1963) gave various subjects sugar pills which were sometimes labelled depressants and at other times labelled stimulants. In the depressant instances, the respondents reported subjective depression and showed significant decreases in blood pressure, pulse rate, and reaction time. The stimulant instances produced just the opposite effects. It must be remembered that in neither instance was a real drug involved. In another circumstance, Volgyesi (1954) reported that 70 percent of a sample of peptic ulcer patients claimed significant improvement over a period of one year following injections of distilled water! Finally, direct proof of physiological actions by placebo comes from Wolf and Wolff's (1943) report. They gave three sugar capsules to their subject, Tom, whose stomach interior was visible because of an unhealed injury. The placebo not only caused Tom discomfort, but the causative inflammation of the stomach and increased acid secretion could be seen. In another instance they obtained a similar reaction following an injection of distilled water that Tom believed was a drug.

Placebo expectancy can also work against the therapeutic value of real drugs. Claridge (1970) calls this circumstance *negative placebo*. It commonly occurs with individuals who are knowledgable about placebos and have some reason to suspect, when they are in fact taking a real drug, that it is not. They simply dismiss as imaginary any effects they do experience.

3. Placebo is Latin for "I shall please."

The effect of environmental factors on drug action

The alteration of the action of real drugs as a function of environmental factors has a less extensive history, but equally profound implications. In 1940, Gunn and Gurd reported that the lethal effects of the amphetamines were markedly enhanced in mice that were maintained under conditions of social aggregation as opposed to those kept isolated. This is called the aggregate toxicity effect. Since then, numerous other experiments have demonstrated the influence of situational factors on drug effects in a variety of species under a diversity of circumstances.

As an example, Brown and Richards (1966) found that the depressant effect of amphetamines on eating behavior in pigeons could be partially eliminated by manipulating the social conditions relative to the expression of the behavior. A pigeon trained to cooperatively key peck with another bird in such a way that both could obtain food still did so under the effect of a dose of drugs that totally suppressed the behavior in a noncooperating bird. The drugged cooperating pigeon would aid in obtaining the food but would not eat its share when it became available.

In another instance, Brown (1965) was able to prevent the development of tolerance to the appetite-depressant effect of amphetamines in rats by altering environmental circumstances. Tolerance was measured by the resumption of food-rewarded lever pressing following its initial depression with daily doses of amphetamines. Groups of rats that were simply withheld from the experimental chamber during their daily dosage for a few days failed to ever develop tolerance when returned. Suitable controls demonstrated that their failure to lever press was not due to forgetting.

To take still another example, Weiss and Laties (1959) found that the lethal dose level of amphetamines was markedly lowered in rats subjected to shock-induced aversive conditioning. For rats not subjected to such conditioning, the lethal dose was 49.5 mg/kg; for animals exposed to shock, the lethal dose was 2.9 mg/kg. Nearly a 95 percent decrease was obtained simply by introducing stress.

Such findings, once again, reinforce the notion that the mind can and does affect the operation of the body. There is no unidirectional relationship between the physiological action of a drug and the behavioral results of that action. Rather, behavioral conditions can and do feedback on the interaction between drug and tissue. Indeed, the extent of this feedback is such that one can have profound drug experiences for which there is no physiological basis (placebo); or one can have experiences contrary to those which would ordinarily result from drug-induced simultaneous physiological events; or one can experience nothing, despite the physiological activity due to the drug. These interactions offer profound possibilities for resolving the mind-body problem, and it is hoped they will be appropriately exploited for that purpose.

DRUGS AND THE MIND

Man's unique desire to experience the subjective consequences of drug action reveals a good deal about the mind in the present-day world. With very few exceptions, primarily alcohol, caffeine and nicotine, mind-altering drugs used nonmedically are socially and legally disapproved in the Western World. Use of such substances is variously referred to as drug abuse, drug addiction, drug dependence, or drug habituation. Despite this attitude, illicit mind-altering drug use has increased enormously.

The psychological utility of drugs

Why has this come about? At times, man experiences his environment as being incompatible with his existence in it. Further, he finds his usual heterotrophic capacities inadequate to make the necessary adjustment to the environment or to himself that would serve to re-establish equilibrium. The disequilibrium and the inability to cope with it are, of course, aversive. Under such conditions, man has yet another behavioral adjustment at his disposal. When he cannot alter the environment or remove himself from it, a person, unlike any other animal, can ingest a substance that will alter his experience of the environment so that he can establish a less uncomfortable relationship. While perhaps not a highly adaptive behavior biologically, it certainly is psychologically adaptive, and that is, more often than not, sufficient to maintain the viability of the organism. Drug-induced mind alteration is an adaptive adjustment that promotes survival and, in that sense, is even becoming a medically feasible therapeutic goal. Consider the number of mind-altering drugs, such as tranquilizers, mood elevators, depressants, and stimulants, that are now available to physicians (Ban, 1969). In other words, treatment of behavioral dysfunction by chemically-induced mind alteration is becoming medically legitimate! The line between therapeutic and nontherapeutic drug usage is becoming difficult to distinguish and has given rise to major contemporary social/legal problems.

The medical utility of drugs

Indeed, it must not be forgotten that, although many mind-altering drugs are widely employed nonmedically, they also retain important medical utility. Some of today's most feared narcotics, for example, were once employed as cough suppressants (see Figure 15-2). Today, opiates and their derivatives still represent the best analgesics or pain-relieving drugs available to clinicians.

The effects of the opiates are of considerable psychopharmacological interest in the latter instance. While it is not precisely known how the opiates affect the nervous system, it is known that they do not inhibit impulse transmission in pain pathways (Jaffe, 1965). In fact, the patient still experiences pain, but his perception and attitude towards the pain are altered. He no longer perceives it as aversive and thus is unconcerned about its presence. The narcotics are also very popular among nonmedical users for the same reason. They alter the perception of, and attitude towards, psychologically induced pain in a manner similar to their action on physical pain. As was stated earlier, changing the experience of one's environment is a viable adjustment thereto, and it is nowhere better illustrated than in the instance of nonmedical opiate usage.

Drug dependence

The use of opiates for purposes of behavioral modification is considered an especially dangerous practice because of the ability of the drugs to produce what is called physical dependence. Continued use of narcotics and other drugs such as alcohol, nicotine, barbiturates, and methaqualone (quaaludes, sopors) effect metabolic changes in the nervous system such that abrupt removal of the drug from the system causes functional disruptions, behaviorally reflected as a characteristically unpleasant, medically dangerous syndrome known as *withdrawal.* The exact nature of the physiological changes are not known, although there are several theories (Goldstein, Aronow, and Kalman, 1965). It is generally contended that avoidance of withdrawal is a primary motivation for continued nonmedical opiate usage. The condition involving such an alleged motive is referred to as physical dependence, in opposition to psychological dependence, or instances where the drug is not taken to avoid withdrawal.

The fact is, however, that opiate withdrawal can be medically managed to the extent that it is relatively painless, and many opiate users have a history of having been repeatedly withdrawn. It would appear, then, contrary to general belief, that fear of withdrawal is not a major motivation for using narcotics. In that sense, there is no such condition as physical dependence. All mind-altering drug use is psychologically motivated representing, as explained above, a desire to alter experience. As Brown (1974) has pointed out, users "employ withdrawal producing drugs because they want to, not because they have to."

Behavioral aspects of drug dependence   Along with drug-behavior interaction, an investigation of the psychological dynamics of the use of drugs for mind-altering reasons would be of significant value to resolving the mind-body problem. Although not in that specific context, some investigation of the behavioral aspects of drug dependence has been accomplished.

A common procedure for experimentally studying dependence involves surgically implanting tubing in animals, usually rats or monkeys, such that they can self-administer drugs. The arrangement allows for the development of dependency and subsequent examination of its parameters. Figure 15-3 diagramatically represents a typical experimental set-up.

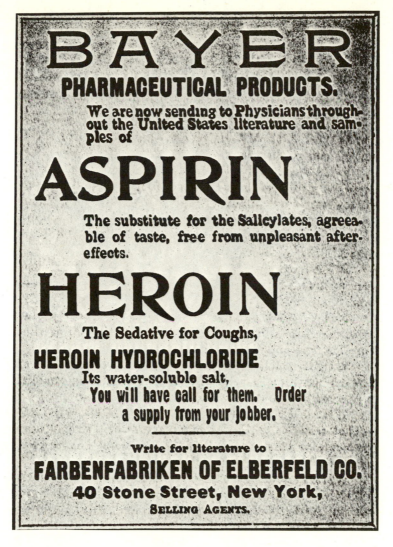

Figure 15-2. Turn-of-the-century medical journal ad.

Nichols (1965), however, used a somewhat different method to demonstrate that active self-administration of morphine is necessary for the establishment of dependency. He compared the development of opiate-directed behavior in rats under self-administration (active) with involuntary (passive) administration. Two groups of rats, predosed with morphine for several days, were employed. The first group, the active animals, were trained to initiate their own drug administration sequence by drinking a morphine solution at regular intervals. The second group, the passive animals, were given the same amount of morphine by injection. As shown in Figure 15-4, Nichols found that the active, self-dosing rats increased their voluntary mor-

Figure 15-3. One type of experimental arrangement used to study drug dependency. The rat, by pressing the lever, can self-administer the drug. The tubing in this case is surgically secured in the abdomen to provide intraperitoneal dosing. With larger animals, the tubing is often placed directly in a vein (Redrawn and modified from Nichols, 1965).

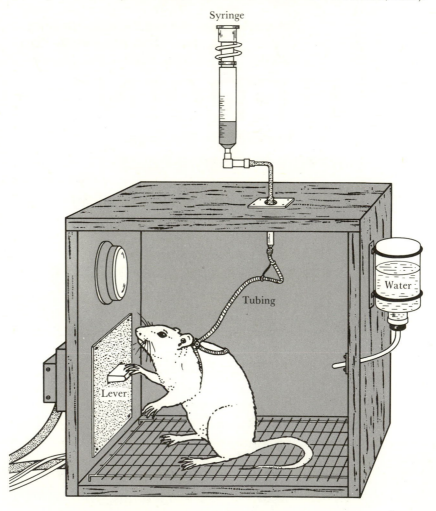

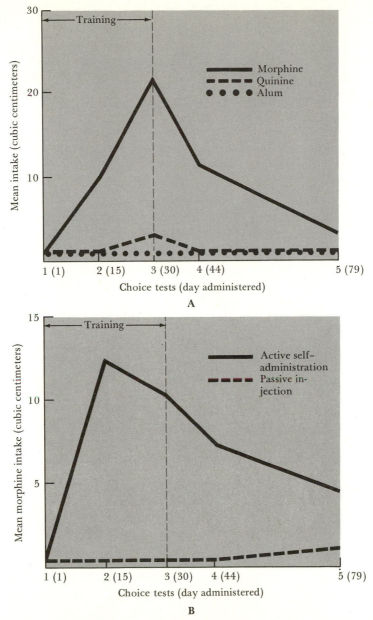

Figure 15-4. **A,** Consumption of a morphine solution by rats trained to drink it (solid line) as compared to those offered quinine (broken line) or alum (dotted line), solutions which are similarly bitter. **B,** Consumption levels of morphine solution by rats trained to self-administer it (solid line) as compared to rats that received morphine passively (broken line). (Redrawn and modified from Nichols, 1965).

307

phine consumption, and continued to do so even after withdrawal. In contrast, the passive rats continued to show no drug-seeking behavior even though they had received an amount equal to that of the active group. Evidently, drug dependency does involve, as implied above, a dynamic interaction between volition and physiological actions and thereby represents an issue of relevance to physiological psychology.

Even less is known regarding the physiological psychology aspects of other popular behavior-modifying agents, although a relatively large amount of research attention along those lines is being directed at marijuana because of a trend toward liberalization of its use. The drug appears to have cholinergic actions (Brown, 1971, 1972) and to be highly subject to expectancy factors (Hollister, 1971; Tart, 1971; Weil, Zinberg, and Nelsen, 1968). The hallucinogens, particularly LSD, have also received considerable research attention (Hoffer, 1965; Ostow, 1971) due, as explained earlier, to their alleged relation to schizophrenia (Chapter 13).

PSYCHOPHARMACOLOGY'S POTENTIAL CONTRIBUTION TO RESOLUTION OF MIND-BODY ISSUES

As was repeatedly pointed out in the preceding discussion, the potential of psychopharmacology for contributing to the resolution of mind-body issues is profound. With the advent of the tranquilizers in the 1950s and their tremendous success, the science and technology of chemically-induced mind alteration became highly viable; a psychopharmacological "revolution" occurred (Caldwell, 1970). Thus, the substances and techniques are on hand—and becoming constantly more sophisticated— for exploring the manner in which neurochemical events relate to experiencing.

It was seen in this chapter that drugs exert their effects by mimicking or interfering with normal chemical processes in the body. It was also seen that much subjective and overt behavior can be altered by drugs, suggesting that the normal operation of mind is, to a large extent, chemically mediated. Thus, it would follow that systematic investigation of the actions of mind-altering drugs would reveal much about the nature and processes involved in the relation between mind and body. Con-

"...IT'SH MY DAMN KIDSH AN' THEIR DOPE PROBLEM..."

Figure 15-5. Example of a present-day attitude toward mind-altering drug use. (Copyright © 1971 The Chicago Sun-Times. Reproduced by courtesy of Wil-Jo Associates, Inc. and Bill Mauldin.)

sider the insight that could be gained about volition, for example, by knowing the brain mechanisms that generate drug actions in the absence of a drug (placebo effects), or about hedonistic motivation ("pleasure" centers) from an understanding of the parameters of dependence.

Why has this potential not been exploited more? One factor is that modern psychopharmacology is a relatively new science. It has only been active for about twenty-five years, and that is not long as scientific advances go. Another factor is that resolution of mind-body issues does not appear to have the immediate clinical applicability that other psychopharmacological findings have. Psychopharmacology has been directing almost all of its effort to the development of therapeutic agents for mental illness (Chapter 13). Limited social acceptance is yet a third fac-

309

tor. The bulk of contemporary society still reacts negatively to the employment of most mind-altering drugs, even for research purposes. Figure 15-5 shows an example of the confused social attitudes that presently exist.

Nevertheless, with time, broadened scope, and changing attitudes, the use of drugs to explore the physiochemical dimensions of mind is coming into its own (Mandell, 1973; Mandell and Spooner, 1968; McGeer, 1971). With it, physiological psychology will have a powerful new tool to apply to its most enduring problem.

SUGGESTED READINGS

Brecher, E. M., ed. *Licit and Illicit Drugs.* Boston: Little Brown, 1972. Without exception the best book on nonmedical drug use; it should be read by every concerned citizen.

Caldwell, A. E. *Origins of Psychopharmacology from CPZ to LSD.* Springfield, Ill.: Thomas, 1970. Highly interesting and readable account of the history of the psychopharmacological revolution.

Group for the Advancement of Psychiatry. *Drug Misuse: A Psychiatric View of a Modern Dilemma.* New York: Scribner, 1971. An excellent account of the social factors relevant to drug dependence.

Joyce, C. R. B., ed. *Psychopharmacology.* Philadelphia: Lippincott, 1968. Collection of original writings by a number of authorities that serves as an excellent primer in psychopharmacology.

V

Finis coronat opus

The foregoing body of material, for better or worse, is a representative sample of the content of physiological psychology. Since physiological psychology's basic theoretical objective is the resolution of the mind-body problem, all that remains now is to see how the accumulated data have been applied to that problem.

16 Physiological theories of the mind

How well has contemporary scientific method done in determining whether such processes of mind as volition, thinking, and feeling are products of physical mechanisms or simply the unique characteristics of some sort of immaterial spirit? In making the evaluation it will be seen how much, if any, physiological psychology has contributed to resolution of the mind-body problem, one of the oldest issues in philosophy.

To make this judgment, it will first be necessary to review some of the philosophic arguments as they appeared in historic context. Then this chapter will look at current theories of mind which have arisen from the findings of physiological psychology or have been developed by contemporary physiological psychologists out of their own work and thought. Finally, the relationship between the philosophic issues and the concrete work done by physiological psychologists will be discussed.

HISTORICAL-PHILOSOPHIC BACKGROUND

Three possibilities have been established historically in regard to the mind-body relationship: 1. the mind is a product of body (or physiological) function, 2. the body is a product of mind (or psychological) function, and 3. mind and body are separate entities which relate in varying degrees and by various mechanisms.

The concept of dualism

The third concept, called *dualism*, is the oldest of the three, and since it continues to occupy a ranking position in Western philosophy, it will be considered first. Originating with Pythagorean speculations, and Platonic and Socratic elaboration and interpretations of them by St. Thomas Aquinas, dualism reached its peak of expression in the seventeenth century with René Descartes, the renowned French mathematician and philosopher, who is best known as the "father of modern philosophy." Descartes' concept, as expressed in his early works, was simple. He believed that there were two basic substances in the world—the mind, or thinking substance, and the body, an extended substance. Descartes specified that the mind took up no space but acted on the body through the pineal gland in the brain. Since it was believed that lower animals did not have a pineal gland,[1] they were thought to have no mind, and thereby were considered to be relatively nonvolitional automatons or reflexively responding organisms.

This philosophic idea has generally been interpreted to imply that Descartes believed in two distinct and separate worlds—that of mind and matter. Those who espouse this view are called *Cartesians* and the philosophy is known as *Cartesian dualism*.

The question that immediately arises is: How can two independent entities compose such a well integrated unity without some form of interrelation? If mind takes up no space, how can it move a particle of matter from one plane to another when it is clear that matter is affected only by other matter or by energy from matter obeying physical laws? One curious answer by an early Cartesian was to avoid the question by arguing that mind and matter were like two clocks wound up by God, one clock pointing to the hour and the other clock striking. This view of dualism is known as *parallelism*, and it has been said by some interpreters that Descartes believed in the

1. It is now known that most animals have pineal glands; they synthesize an important hormone, *melatonin,* which serves many functions in different species, from blanching the skin in frogs and fish (for camouflage) to regulating estrus in rats. The activity of the pineal is inhibited by light, e.g. rats kept in constant light exhibit persistent estrus, suggesting it may also be involved in the maintenance of circadian rhythms (see Axelrod, 1974).

notion that mind and matter were examples of independent, parallel worlds.

As is so often the case, the "classic" statement of Descartes' contentions is more a product of his interpreters than an accurate assessment of his own position. As Spicker recently contended:

> . . . "Cartesian philosophy" is not quite applicable as a description of Descartes' own position. It is simply one of the ironies of the history of European philosophy that Descartes is not a "Cartesian" (1970, p. 9).

Descartes' position was, in fact, closer to that of Aristotle, who rejected the pre-Socratic notion that body and mind are separate and relatively independent entities and instead regarded the mind as unique to, and inseparable from, the body. Descartes also believed that body and mind were two distinct but totally interdependent aspects of a living being, interacting as one. The position is sometimes referred to as *interactionism*.

How did the confusion over Descartes' position arise? It began with Aquinas' reinterpretation of Aristotle's position in an attempt to bridge the then existing schism between Greek rationalism and Christian emotionalism (Watson, 1968). The latter required an immortal soul separated from the body. Aquinas' restatement of Aristotle's position brought it into philosophic conformity with the church's position, and, in the process, established what was later to become a convenient position for validating psychology as the "science of the mind."

With that precedent, it was natural for Cartesian philosophy to develop as it did in conformity with the theologically convenient view of the time. Even Descartes initially yielded to the contemporary pressures and helped advance the classic interpretation of his own work, the complete separation of mind and body, which some of his disciples have since maintained as the only Cartesian dualism, despite Descartes' own later modifications. Pictures of Aristotle, Aquinas, and Descartes, philosophers important in the development of the concept of dualism, are presented in Figure 16-1.

The importance to Christianity of maintaining Cartesian dualism, or what should be more properly called Thomistic (Aquinas') dualism was, as just stated, the need to maintain the concept of a separate, immortal soul. Some insight into the significance of classic dualism as it relates to the development of psychology as a separate discipline can be obtained from Boring's statement:

> When Descartes established the scientific dichotomy between mind and body, he provided both the *raison d'être* of modern psychology and the mystery which it has never completely dissolved. Descartes cut the world in two, into mind and matter, just at the time when science was about to begin the course of development which has made it the dominating influence in modern civilization. We all know how successful the physical sciences have been and we can also see that biology has prospered in abandoning a vitalism and identifying itself with the physical side of the Cartesian dichotomy. If Descartes was right, if there are these two worlds, then the success of science in attacking the one forms a challenge for the creation of a science of the other. This view is common in psychology (1963, p. 3).

To establish itself as a science, psychology felt it needed the notion of a separate, nonphysical mind, either to give it a viable subject matter for investigation or to give it something to reject, so it could get on with being "objective." For psychology to have accepted an interactionistic dualism, on the other hand, would have compromised those ends by reducing the study of behavior to just a branch of biology. So, as is often done with inconvenient views, interactionistic dualism was simply dropped. Modern psychology reflects the consequences of this decision, notably, in saddling itself with the mind-body problem, without, as Lohr points out (1971), providing a way to accommodate the forces of mind with the same systems used to study physical forces acting on substance.

Monism: body or mind as the basic reality

The two remaining concepts of the mind-body relationship, rejection of either body or mind, results in a position called *monism.* The view that mind is the primary reality has been advocated by philosophers such as Berkeley (1910) and Kant (1929). This type of monism has not been extensively dealt with by psychologists.

A

B

C

Figure 16-1. **A,** Greek philosophers Plato and Aristotle as depicted in Raphael's fresco "The School of Athens." (The Vatican Museum), **B,** St. Thomas Aquinas (1225–74) Sicilian Christian theologian, (The New York Public Library), and **C,** French philosopher René Descartes (1596–1650), painted by Jan Weenix. (Centraal Museum der Gemeente, Utrecht.) All the foregoing were major influences in the formation of the dualistic theory of mind-body relationships.

The other side of the dichotomy, body as the only reality, has had its expression primarily in Russian reflexology. In an effort to dispose of will and volition and thus to make the action of environment on neural tissue the only cause of behavior, Ivan Sechenov, the pioneer of Russian reflexology, concluded:

... the question of whether the most voluntary of all voluntary actions of man depend on external and internal conditions has been answered in the affirmative. From this it inevitably follows that *given the same internal and external conditions the activity of man will be similar.* Choice of one of the many possible ends of the same physical reflex is absolutely impossible; its apparent possibility is merely a delusion of self-consciousness. The essence of this complex act is that apparently one and the same reflex with the same psychical content is reproduced in man's consciousness in the form of thought; however, this reflex takes place in more or less different conditions and is, therefore, expressed in different ways (1965, p. 105).

The compleat materialist view of behavior is expressed in the "man, a machine" concept, which is usually considered to have originated with Descartes' antagonist, Julien La Mettrie, and his book (*Man a Machine,* 1961), wherein La Mettrie regarded all of man's actions as mechanical, as analogs of the functions of machines. Spicker (1970) suggests that La Mettrie's views were actually similar to those of Descartes, especially in regard to the man-animal distinction. In its modern form, strict monism (other than Russian reflexology) finds expression in cybernetics (Wiener, 1948) and in computer models of brain function (Kemeny, 1968).

SOME CONTEMPORARY VIEWPOINTS

The foregoing has briefly summarized the context in which contemporary expositions of mind-body interactions are cast and has described the development of the philosophical contentions against which the empirical data from the physiological psychology laboratories must be considered. It is now appropriate to address attention to some major contemporary physiologically oriented points of view concerning the theory of mind to see whether research data have shed any light on this elusive construct.

The principle of emergence: the mind is greater than the sum of the parts

Lewes (1879) made a fundamental and inductive-empirical distinction between *resultants*, or events predictable from their constituent parts, and *emergents*, or events not predictable from their parts. Emergence refers to the development of a system in a way that would not be explainable from its antecedent conditions. The example most often given is that of water. One could not predict the development of water from a knowledge of the properties of hydrogen and oxygen, since the properties of water are more than the sum of the properties of its elements. This concept has been applied to evolutionary theory, especially in regard to the phylogenesis of behavior (Hobhouse, 1926; Morgan, 1909), where it is still considered a tenable variable (Teilhard de Chardin, 1959). It has also been an important principle in the development of Gestalt psychology, although it was not explicitly expressed as such.

In 1969, R. W. Sperry revived the emergent principle in another of its earlier areas of application, brain functions. He suggested that the conscious properties of brain excitation are something distinct and special, and that "They are 'different from and more than' the collected sum of the neuro-physicochemical events out of which they are built" (1969).

How are they "different from and more than"? Going further than the earlier emergent proponents, Sperry tried to answer the question as follows:

Just as the holistic properties of the organism have causal effects that determine the course and fate of its constituent cells and molecules, so in the same way, the conscious properties of cerebral activity are conceived to have analogous causal effects in brain function that control subset events in the flow pattern of neural excitation. In this holistic sense the present proposal may be said to place mind over matter, but not as any disembodied or supernatural agent.

thus:

The subjective mental phenomena are conceived to influence and to govern the flow of nerve impulse traffic by virtue of their encompassing emergent properties. Individual nerve impulses and other excitatory components of a cerebral activity pattern are simply carried along or shunted this way and that by the prevailing overall dynamics of the whole active process (in principle—just as drops of water are carried along by a local eddy in a stream or the way the molecules and atoms of a wheel are carried along when it rolls down hill, regardless of whether the individual molecules and atoms happen to like it or not) (1969, pp. 533–534).

Sperry's view, an atempt to combine the specifics of neural activity with the specifics of philosophical deduction, holds that the mind is not set aside or apart from the brain but is an essential directive force or property of the brain process; "it actively influences the course of brain events rather than just being a passive by-product," says Sperry (1969). Body and mind are united; one could not exist without the other; but, within this union, mind predominates. The result is a hierarchical interdependence which has appeared to some critics to be similar to interactionistic dualism.

Bindra (1970), for instance, suggested that Sperry's proposal was only a variant of the Cartesian concept of dualism. Sperry replied:

In the proposed scheme, the mental phenomena and the physical brain processes are seen to be mutually interdependent. Neither is primary nor ultimate to the exclusion of the other. In this sense . . . the present scheme represents a compromise between the older philosophies of mentalism and materialism . . . I can only disagree with Bindra regarding his pronouncement that such a compromise is impossible—even in the form in which he reinterprets it to imply degrees of dualism (1970, p. 588).

This compromise was reached 2000 years ago by Aristotle.

The concept of triadism: the mind as integrator of experience

From the Sperry-Bindra interchange, one could get the impression that traditional dualism is scientifically unacceptable; that, in the mechanistic world of objective analysis, the title "dualist" is something all scientists apparently wish to avoid. This is not so. Sherrington's famous student, neurophysiologist Sir John Eccles, unabashedly admitted that he has been a dualist most of his life:

> There have been many philosophical developments related to the two-world postulate of *Descartes,* that is generally called dualism. I myself until recently believed that this two world concept provided an adequate explanation of all our experience and knowledge (1970, pp. 163–164).

Eccles' change of heart was not conversion to some scientifically respectable compromise with monism. Instead, Eccles expanded his view in the opposite direction—into a three-world concept which he calls *triadism.*

The construct, represented in Table 16-1, divides experience into three categories called *Worlds.* World 1 is material, structural, and physical; World 2 is the totally subjective aspects of experience. World 3 is the historical accumulation of thought, primarily as transmitted by language; it consists of what is variously called knowledge, history, culture, and intellectual heritage, among other things; and it is unique to man.

World 1 and 3 can only relate by way of World 2. The human brain (itself part of World 1) serves as no more than an integrator (World 2) of the input from World 1 and World 3.

Table 16-1.   Content of Eccles' triadic worlds

World 1. Physical objects and states	World 2. States of consciousness	World 3. Knowledge in objective sense
1. Inorganic matter and energy of cosmos	Subjective knowledge Experience of:	1. Records of intellectual efforts:
2. Biology structure and actions of all living things, human brains	perception thinking emotions dispositional intentions memories dreams creative imagination	philosophical theological scientific historical literary artistic technological
3. Artifacts material substrates of human creativity: tools machines books works of art music		2. Theoretical systems: scientific problems critical arguments

Note: From Eccles (1970)

World 3 is not directly sensed but is encoded and stored (memory). It is uniquely human because its generation, accumulation, and transmission depends on a language system. The mind-body problem in this formulation becomes the mind-body-language problem.

Eccles then goes on to declare:

> I have now presented a scientific-philosophical basis on which to develop what I believe to be the only tenable position with respect to the brain and the soul. I submit that the Aristotelian-Thomist view that "the soul is the form of the body" is no longer tenable as was realized already by Descartes. However, in the historical surveys of the theological and philosophical disputations . . . I find compatibility with the suggestion that the subjective component of each of us in World 2, the conscious self, may be identified as the soul.
>
> The component of our existence in World 2 is non-material and hence is not subject in death to the disintegration that affects all components of the individual in World 1—both the body and the brain, though of course it is deprived of all communication with World 1 and World 3, and hence, for each of us, all experience as we know it must cease in oblivion . . . It will be recognized that this identification of World 2 as the soul is essentially the Cartesian position, but without commitment to any explanation of how the soul is "attached" to the brain (1970, pp. 173–174).

In direct contrast to Sperry's formulation, Eccles takes the classic position that mind exists as an entity separate from the body. Despite his lifelong devotion to the collection of precise neural data, he does not even accept the premise that neural mechanisms per se are a sufficient condition for experience. He concludes that there is some type of transcendent level that is beyond human understanding.

The Biologist view: mind is a structure of neural data

Man's behavioral uniqueness in the World 3 sense of language has also intrigued Karl Pribram. But, in contrast to Eccles, Pribram attempts to resolve the mind-body problem in terms of available empirical data, excluding subjective experience.

Since the data described are totally overt, the Biologist view is strictly structural. Pribram says that:

The biologist's data everywhere show him that structure becomes embodied in a variety of forms through processes and transformations that must be laboriously described. That mental structure (e.g., a phrase of music) can be embodied in brain rhythms, in the score of sheet music, on a long playing record, or on tape does not especially shock him. Everyday he views his wife, that strange embodiment he extends to himself to know, only to realize that she can be encoded in a DNA molecule—how else did his daughter turn out to be such an amazing replica? *In the Biologist view, multiple "aspects" turn out to become multiple "realizations," multiple embodiments achieved in what is often a long drawn out stepwise process* (1971, pp. 383–384).

Purely and simply, in Pribram's view, the mind has a structure that is developed step by step from brain processes. The primary structures that form the mind are what he calls "Communicative Acts"—language and culture. The process giving rise to the elements of the mind is manipulation of sensory inputs within a holographic context.

Holograms are reconstructions of images by an optical spatio-temporal distribution of energy patterns, usually laser beams (Stroke, 1969). They have form but no substance.[2] Van Heerden (1970) has speculated that their formation may represent the basis of perceptual processes in the brain. Pribram merely extended the process to cognition, which could be considered as simply the manipulation of percepts. As Lohr stated:

All knowledge begins with the senses and can be thought of as the result of the tendency of the mind to give order to the limitless array of incoming sensation. Roughly speaking, this is done by grouping bits of information, sorting these into categories, finding relationships among the categories and abstracting features that several of them have in common (1971, p. 11).

That, according to Pribram, is carried out in the brain by holographic relationships. The idea is also similar, on a conceptual level, to the notions of Piaget involving the development of

---

2. They can be seen but not touched, they are chimerical.

schemata (mind structures) by assimilation (experience) to form knowledge (Piaget and Inhelder, 1969) and compatible with his desire to define a biological substrate for the process (Piaget, 1971). In any case, Pribram's notion is indeed empirically based and very intriguing, although Pribram himself says it is not an exceptionally profound conclusion. Biologists, he says, wonder why there is all the fuss over the mind-body problem in the first place since biologists simply accept the mind-body dichotomy as a biological fact.

The concept of parallelism: coexistence of mind and body on two planes

The concept of parallelism, originated by Leibniz, was given experimental substance as psychophysical parallelism by Wundt and elaborated specifically in the context of physiological psychology by Bain. Essentially, parallelism regards the mind as coexisting with the physical environment on a separate plane, level, or universe. There is interdependence, but the two realms remain exclusive. Both are equally real and are related in terms of physiochemical neural events. For every experiential action, there is a correlative neurophysiological event that parallels its occurrence.

The notion has recently been revived and expanded by Arturo Rosenblueth (1970). He offered the following seven postulates and substantiated each empirically.

1. Although I can be directly aware of only my own mental states and events, other organisms, human and animal, have similar experiences, of which they in turn are directly aware.

2. Our sensations are causally related to events that occur in a material universe of which our bodies are a part.

3. There are regularities in the temporal succession of the events that occur in the material universe and in some measurable features of relatively isolated material systems when they are at equilibrium.

4. The following methods of inference are accepted as valid for the elaboration of scientific theories: deduction, probabilistic induction, analogy, and retroduction.

5. The physical correlates of our mental events are neurophysiological phenomena that develop in our brains.

6. Each specific mental event has as a correlate a specific spatiotemporal pattern of neuronal activity.

7. The laws of physics are applicable to all the material universe, including our bodies and nervous systems; furthermore, neither the neuronal nor the mental processes are subject to any determinism, causal or probabilistic, different from that of physics.

Rosenblueth then concluded:

The foregoing postulates lead to the view that a mental process and the neurophysiological phenomena that underlie it represent two different aspects of a single event. The mental aspect is that of which we are directly aware; the neurophysiological aspect is that which the event acquires when we interpret it as an occurrence in the material universe. There are not and cannot be any physical interactions between the mental and cerebral processes. . .

My philosophy is dualistic, in that I assert on the one hand the existence of our mental processes and on the other that of a material universe which determines the physical processes that develop in our brains. I start with mental processes because, like Descartes, I believe that they are the only events of which we can be directly aware and certain.

thus:

We invent or postulate a material universe in order to rationalize our perceptions. The universe is necessarily anthropomorphic in the sense that it has to adjust to the mental processes (perceptions and inferences) through which we judge its structure (1970, pp. 114–115).

Cognito ergo sum.

The behaviorist position

Behaviorism is often said to be an example of monism, but that is inaccurate. Behaviorism actually rejects the influence of both mind and body in behavior, putting the determinants of behavior totally outside the organism. As Boring described the behaviorist position:

> At first Skinner was concerned to rule out of psychology the events in the nervous system as well as those alleged to be in consciousness. Behavior, he held, is to be understood in terms of reflexes, but a reflex is a correlation between stimulus and response and concern with any neural connection between the two is irrelevant. That was a new kind of pure reflexology and, although Skinner could make use of the Pavlovian conditioned reflexes in which a secondary stimulus is substituted for the original one, he regarded these functional relations as mere observed correlations, ignoring the physiological connection between them. (1964, pp. 452–453).

Behaviorists do allow that organisms have an "internal environment" as distinct from the "external environment," the division occurring at the surface of the skin (Skinner, 1953). One cannot help but wonder, in view of that, where the organism that responds to these environments is. It is not an important question to behaviorism because behaviorists, as was just mentioned, consider the mind-body problem a psuedoissue and, by implication, physiological psychology a pseudoscience (Skinner, 1953). Nonetheless, the relationship of behaviorism to physiological psychology must be understood because, as was seen on numerous occasions in earlier chapters, behaviorism, directly or indirectly, does influence much contemporary psychological thinking.

FUTURE OF THE MIND

Sperry's, Eccles', Pribram's, and Rosenbleuth's reflections are by no means the total of contemporary notions about the mind and body, but they are representative of the current major approaches of physiological psychologists to achieving some resolution of the problem. Clearly, none of these approaches is better than any other in the state of the present evidence.

Insofar as physiological psychology is concerned, the primary difference in the contemporary points of view is the extent to which empirical data are considered important; that is, whether physiological events can or cannot be employed as explanatory constructs for the occurrence of mind. For instance, Sperry and Pribram rely heavily on research data. Sperry, in particular, draws strongly on his own work with split-brain animals and humans. He asserts that, by cutting the corpus callosum, two brains and two minds appear in the same individual. Similarly, Pribram's extensive experimental work with primate brains—and Lashley's data accrued from the effort to find the engram—provide a physical base for the holographic conceptions of the mind. For them, the empirical data of the neurosciences have provided resolution of the mind-body problem.

On the other hand, Eccles and Rosenblueth are not so rigorously bound to physiological data and use philosophic techniques to a greater extent in determining the relationship between mind and body. For them, empirical data are of limited value to understanding the nature of mind.

With such a divergency of opinion, it would have to be concluded that physiological psychology has so far not offered much towards resolution of the mind-body problem. Why? It may be that science and philosophy have become incompatible—as Benjamin said, ". . . most scientists write bad philosophy, and most philosophers write bad science" (1937). It may be that there is simply not enough experimental data yet—a hundred years or so is not very long as scientific advances go. In actual fact, the basic problem seems to be the apparent inability of man's mind to realize its own states and deal with them objectively. What experiments does one do to resolve the mind-body problem once and for all? Most of the empirical findings of physiological psychology, as detailed throughout the present book, appear irrelevant to the issue. They provide correlations between brain mechanisms and specific behaviors but do not show whether the mind controls the body or vice versa, or even whether there is a mind. The absence of any evidence on these issues has led some observers to question if there is such a thing as physiological psychology as defined in the opening chapter, i.e., a science which sets, as one of its goals, resolution of the mind-body problem (Bannister, 1968; Kantor, 1947). Is experimentation even the way to approach the problem or could it be better handled by epistemological deduction (Piaget, 1971)? Perhaps the so-called scientific approach, so appropriate to physics, is not going to work with the phenomena psychology has to contend with (Bakan, 1972), or perhaps it is not being applied rigorously enough (Skinner, 1971). Perhaps physiological psychology should first resolve the issue of the appropriateness of its own methodology before it takes on broader decisions such as whether the mind must forever remain unknown (as Eccles contends), whether it is already clearly and obviously defined in a structure without mass (Pribram), whether it is somewhere in between these notions (Sperry, Rosenblueth), or whether its existence is even a valid issue for psychology (Skinner).

Finally, since it is strange that something as conceptually simple as the transformation from autotrophic to heterotrophic functioning should be so mechanically difficult to understand and resolve, perhaps one should conclude somewhat gloomily that man, as presently constituted, is still a primitive heterotroph whose limited behavioral capacities do not allow understanding of his own being. This view could be temporary. After all, as was pointed out before, there is no evidence that *Homo Sapiens* is the final expression of evolution. All these issues are provocative and should provide students with a wealth of ideas which they can pursue and mine as deeply as their resolve and talents allow.

Even in the absence of a breakthrough in understanding the underpinnings of the science, one should not approach brain research with an entirely negative viewpoint. Although some areas of brain research have been as stubborn as they were in the time of Aristotle, there has been extraordinary progress in the understanding of the mechanisms of the mind and brain. Many of the elements have been isolated, examined, and placed in hierarchical order. While a unifying concept with which everyone can agree has not yet emerged, it can be said that physiological psychology is on the verge of relating the elements of the brain and may be at the same stage in this process as physics was at the turn of the century. At that time, many scientists thought physics was played out and there was nothing new to discover; a few years later there was a vast outburst of theory and findings that led to the modern era.

In reviewing the history of science, Kuhn (1970), Flesch

(1970), and Sidman (1960), among others, have emphasized the serendipitous nature of much of scientific discovery and advancement. Physics, for instance, has grown on the basis of such conceptual achievements as Newtonian gravity and Einsteinian relativity, both the result of happy accidents. It may well be that physiological psychology is still waiting for its accident to happen, which will hurtle the relatively young science out of its preparadigmatic stage and give it a unity of structure.

More significantly perhaps, there may be a burst of practical discovery that could go a long way toward resolving many applied problems, such as those of the mentally disturbed, and thus help individuals like Donald L. and Charles Whitman, who will be the clinical inheritors of the advance of physiological psychology.

SUGGESTED READINGS

Eccles, J. C. *Facing Reality: Philosophical Adventures by a Brain Scientist.* New York: Springer-Verlag, 1970. Best account of Eccles' position on the mind-body problem.

Pribram, K. H. *Languages of the Brain: Experimental Paradoxes and Principles in Neuropsychology.* Englewood Cliffs, N.J.: Prentice-Hall, 1971. Comprehensive, up-to-date description of Pribram's notions about mind-body relationships.

Rosenblueth, A. *Mind and Brain: A Philosophy of Science.* Cambridge: M.I.T. Press, 1970. Rosenblueth's statement of the mind-body problem.

Spicker, S. F., ed. *The Philosophy of the Body: Rejections of Cartesian Dualism.* Chicago: Quadrangle, 1970. A collection of papers by various philosophers which attempts to clarify the true nature of Descartes' position.

Young, J. Z. *An Introduction to the Study of Man.* New York: Oxford University Press, 1971. A heroic effort to unify all accumulated knowledge about man as a biological species; helps the reader overcome disciplinary barriers to obtain improved perspective on the nature of scientific findings.

References

Adrian, E.D. 1914. The "all-or-none" principle in nerve. *Journal of Physiology* *47*:450–474.

Agranoff, B.W., and Klinger, P.D. 1964. Puromycin effect on memory fixation in the goldfish. *Science 146*:952–953.

Agranoff, B.W.; Davis, R.E.; Casola, L.; and Lim, R. 1967. Actinomycin-D blocks formation of memory of shock-avoidance in goldfish. *Science 158*:1600–1601.

Airapetyantz, E., and Bykov, K. 1945. Physiological experiments and the psychology of the subconscious. *Philosophy and Phenomenological Research 5*:577–593.

Allee, W.C.; Collias, N.E.; and Lutherman, C.Z. 1939. Modification of the social order in flocks of hens by the injection of testosterone propionate. *Physiological Zoology 12*:412–440.

Allen, W. F. 1932. Formatis reticularis and reticulo spinal tracts: their visceral functions and possible relationships to tonicity and clonic contractions. *Journal of the Washington Academy of Sciences 22*:490–495.

Altman, J. 1966. *Organic foundations of animal behavior.* New York: Holt, Rinehart and Winston.

Amoore, J.E. 1962. The stereochemical theory of olfaction. I. Identification of the seven primary odours. *Proceedings of the Scientific Section of the Toilet Goods Association 37*:1–12.

Anand, B.K., and Brobeck, J.R. 1951a. Hypothalamic control of food intake in rats and cats. *Yale Journal of Biology and Medicine 24*:123–140.

Anand, B.K., and Brobeck, J.R. 1951b. Localization of a feeding center in the hypothalamus of the rat. *Proceedings of the Society for Experimental Biology and Medicine 77*:323–324.

Anand, B.K., and Dua, S. 1955. Blood sugar changes induced by electrical stimulation of the hypothalamus of the cat. *Indian Journal of Medical Research 45*:113–122.

Anderson, B; Gale, C.; and Sundsten, J. 1964. Preoptic influences on water intake. In: *Thirst: first international symposium on thirst in the regulation of body water,* ed. M.J. Wayner, pp. 361–379. Oxford: Permagon.

Andersson, S., and Gernandt, B.E. 1954. Cortical projection of vestibular nerve in cat. *Acta oto-laryngologica 116*:10–18.

Anokhin, P.K. 1961. Electroencephalographic analysis of cortico-subcortical relations in positive and negative conditioned reactions. *Annals of the New York Academy of Sciences 92*:899–938.

Ardrey, R. 1961. *African genesis.* New York: Atheneum.

Aronson, E. 1972. *The social animal.* San Francisco: Freeman.

Aserinsky, E., and Kleitman, N. 1955. A motility cycle in sleeping infants as manifested by ocular and gross bodily activity. *Journal of Applied Physiology 8*:11–18.

Asimov, I. 1972. *Asimov's guide to science.* New York: Basic Books.

Axelrod, J. 1974. The pineal gland: a neurochemical transducer. *Science 184*: 1341–1348.

Azrin, N.H. 1967. Pain and aggression. *Psychology Today 1*:27–33.

Azrin, N.H.; Hutchinson, R.R.; and Hake, D.F. 1966. Extinction-induced aggression. *Journal of the Experimental Analysis of Behavior 9*:191–204.

Babich, F.R.; Jacobson, A.L.; and Bubash, S. 1965. Cross-species transfer of learning: effect of ribonucleic acid from hamsters on rat behavior. *Proceedings of the National Academy of Sciences of the United States of America 54*:1299–1302.

Babich, F.R.; Jacobson, A.L.; Bubash, S.; and Jacobson, A. 1965. Transfer of a response to naive rats by injection of ribonucleic acid extracted from trained rats. *Science 149*:656–657.

Bain, A. 1885. *The senses and the intellect.* 3rd ed. New York: Appleton.

Bakan, D. 1972. Psychology can now kick the science habit. *Psychology Today 5*:26–27 and 86–88.

Baker, P.F. 1966. The nerve axon. *Scientific American 214*:74–82.

Ball, J. 1940. The effects of testosterone on the sex behavior of female rats. *Journal of Comparative Psychology 29*:151–165.

Ban, T. 1969. *Psychopharmacology.* Baltimore: Williams and Wilkins.

Bannister, D. 1968. The myth of physiological psychology. *Bulletin of the British Psychological Society 21*:229–231.

Barber, T.X. 1965. Physiologic effects of "hypnotic suggestions": a critical review of recent research, 1960–1964. *Psychological Bulletin 63*:201–222.

Bard, P. 1928. A diencephalic mechanism for the expression of rage with special reference to the sympathetic nervous system. *American Journal of Physiology 84*:490–515.

Bard, P. 1939. Central nervous mechanisms for emotional behavior patterns in animals. *Research Publications of the Association for Research of Nervous and Mental Disease 19*:190–218.

Barlow, H.B. 1956. Retinal noise and the absolute threshold. *Journal of the Optical Society of America 46*:634–639.

Barondes, S.H., and Cohen, S.D. 1967. Delayed and sustained effect of ace-toxycycloheximide on memory in mice. *Proceedings of the National Academy of Sciences of the United States of America 59*:157–164.

Barondes, S.H., and Jarvik, M.E. 1964. The influence of actinomycin-D on brain RNA synthesis and on memory. *Journal of Neurochemistry 11*:187–195.

Barron, F.; Jarvik, M.E.; and Bunnell, S. 1964. The hallucinogenic drugs. *Scientific American 210*:29–37.

Bash, K.W. 1939. An investigation into a possible organic basis for the hunger drive. *Journal of Comparative Psychology 28*:109–134.

Bazett, H.C.; McGlone, B.; Williams, R.; and Lufkin, H.M. 1932. Sensation. I. Depth, distribution, and probable identification in the prepuce of sensory end-organs concerned in sensations of temperature and touch; thermometric conductivity. *Archives of Neurology and Psychiatry 27*:489–517.

Beach, F.A. 1947. A review of physiological and psychological studies of sexual behavior in mammals. *Physiological Reviews 27*:240–307.

Beach, F.A. 1969. It's all in your mind. *Psychology Today 3*:33–35 and 60.

Beach, G., and Kimble, D.P. 1967. Activity and responsivity in rats after magnesium pemoline injections. *Science 155*:698–701.

Beaman, E.A. 1947. The effect of the male hormone on the aggressive behavior in male mice. *Physiological Zoology 20*:373–405.

Beaulieu, C. 1966. Ribonucleic acid and learning. *Bulletin of the Maritime Psychological Association 15*:1–8.

Belleville, R.E. 1964. Control of behavior by drug-produced internal stimuli. *Psychopharmacologia 5*:95–105.

Bender, A.E. 1953. Recent advances in protein synthesis. *Lancet 265*:1142.

Benjamin, A.C. 1937. *An introduction to the philosophy of science.* New York: Macmillan.

Bennett, E.L.; Diamond, M.C.; Krech, D.; and Rosenzweig, M.R. 1964. Chemical and anatomical plasticity of brain. *Science 146*:610–619.

Berger, B.D.; Wise, C.D.; and Stein, L. 1971. Norepinephrine: reversal of anorexia in rats with lateral hypothalamic damage. *Science 172*:281–284.

Berger, H. 1929. Über das elektrenkephalogramm des menschen. *Archiv fur Psychiatrie Nervenkrankheiten 87*:527–570.

Berkeley, G. 1910. *A new theory of vision and other writings.* London: Dent.

Bernard, C. 1858. *Leçons sur le système nerveux.* Paris: Balliere.

Bindra, D. 1970. The problem of subjective experience: puzzlement on reading R.W. Sperry's "a modified concept of consciousness." *Psychological Review 77*:581–584.

Bishop, M.P.; Elder, S.T.; and Heath, R.G. 1963. Intracranial self-stimulation in man. *Science 140*:394–396.

Bitterman, M.E. 1965. Phyletic differences in learning. *American Psychologist 20*:396–410.

Blakemore, E.; Iversen, S.D.; and Zangwill, O.L. 1972. Brain functions. *Annual Review of Psychology 23*:413–456.

Bleuler, E. 1950. *Dementia praecox or the group of schizophrenias.* New York: International Universities Press.

Blum, J.S.; Chow, K.L.; and Pribram, K.H. 1950. A behavior analysis of organization of parieto-temporo-preoccipital cortex. *Journal of Comparative Neurology 93*:53–100.

Bohdanecký, Z.; Bureš, J.; Burešova, O.; Nečina, J.; and Weiss, T. 1963. The use of spreading depression in neuropharmacology. In: *Psychopharmacological methods,* eds. Z. Votava, M. Horváth, and O. Vinař, pp. 191–196. New York: Macmillan.

Bonner, J.T. 1963. How slime molds communicate. *Scientific American 209*: 84–93.

Boring, E.G. 1916. Cutaneous sensation after nerve division. *Quarterly Journal of Experimental Physiology 10*:1–95.

Boring, E.G. 1957. *A history of experimental psychology.* 2nd ed. New York: Appleton-Century-Crofts.

Boring, E.G. 1960. Lashley and cortical integration. In: *The neuropsychology of Lashley: selected papers,* eds. F.A. Beach, D.O. Hebb, C.T. Morgan, and H.W. Nissen, pp. xi–xvi. New York: McGraw-Hill.

Boring, E.G. 1963. *The physical dimensions of consciousness.* New York: Dover.

Boring, E.G. 1964. The trend toward mechanism. *Proceedings of the American Philosophical Society 108*:451–454.

Bowman, R. 1966. Magnesium pemoline and behavior. *Science 153*:962.

Bradley, P.B. 1958. The central action of certain drugs in relation to the reticular formation of the brain. In: *Reticular formation of the brain,* ed. H.H. Jasper, pp. 123–149. Boston: Little-Brown.

Bradley, P.B., and Hance, A.J. 1956. The effects of intraventricular injections of LSD-25 and 5HT (serotonin) on the electrical activity of the brain of the conscious cat. *The Journal of Physiology 132*:50–51.

Brady, J.V. 1958*a*. The paleocortex and behavioral motivation. In: *Biological and Biochemical Bases of Behavior,* eds. H.R. Harlow and C.N. Woolsey, pp. 193–235. Madison, Wis.: University of Wisconsin Press.

Brady, J.V. 1958*b*. Ulcers in "executive" monkeys. *Scientific American 199*:95–100.

Brady, J.V. 1960. Emotional behavior. In: *Neurophysiology.* vol. 3. *Handbook of Physiology,* sec. 1, eds. J. Field, H.W. Magoun, and V.E. Hall, pp. 1529–1552. Washington D.C.: American Physiological Society.

Brady, J.V. 1962. Psychophysiology of emotional behavior. In: *Experimental foundations of clinical psychology,* ed. A.J. Bachrach, pp. 343–385. New York: Basic Books.

Brady, J.V., and Hunt, H.F. 1951. A further demonstration of the effects of electroconvulsive shock on a conditioned emotional response. *Journal of Comparative and Physiological Psychology 44*:204–209.

Brady, J.V., and Nauta, W.J.H. 1953. Subcortical mechanisms in emotional behavior: affective changes following septal forebrain lesions in the albino rat. *Journal of Comparative and Physiological Psychology 46*:339–346.

Brady, J.V., and Nauta, W.J.H. 1955. Subcortical mechanisms in emotional behavior: the duration of affective changes following septal and ha-benular lesions in the albino rat. *Journal of Comparative and Physiological Psychology 48*:412–420.

Brady, J.V.; Schreiner, L.; Geller, I.; and Kling, A. 1954. Subcortical mechanisms in emotional behavior: the effect of rhinencephalic injury upon the acquisition and retention of a conditioned avoidance response in cats. *Journal of Comparative and Physiological Psychology 47*:179–186.

Branch, J.C., and Viney, W. 1966. An attempt to transfer a position discrimination habit via RNA extracts. *Psychological Reports 19*:923–926.

Braud, W.G. 1970. Extinction in goldfish: facilitation by intracranial injection of RNA from brains of extinguished donors. *Science 168*:1234–1236.

Brazier, M.A.B. 1959. The historical development of neurophysiology. In: *Neurophysiology*. vol. 1. *Handbook of Physiology*, sec. 1, eds. J.H. Field, H.W. Magoun, and V.E. Hall; pp. 1–58. Washington, D.C.: American Physiological Society.

Bremer, F. 1935. Cerveau isolé et physiologie de sommeil. *Comptes Rendus de la Sociétié de Biologie 118*:1235–1242.

Brobeck, J.R. 1948. Food intake as a mechanism of temperature regulation. *Yale Journal of Biology and Medicine 20*:545–552.

Brobeck, J.R.; Tepperman, J.; and Long, C.N.H. 1943. Experimental hypothalamic hyperphagia in the albino rat. *Yale Journal of Biology and Medicine 15*:831–853.

Broca, P. 1861. Remarques sur le sièg de la faculté du langage articulé, suivies d' une observation d' aphémie (perte de la parole). *Bulletin de la Société Anatomique de Paris 6*:330–357.

Brodie, B.B., and Shore, P.A. 1957. On a role for serotonin and norepinephrine as chemical mediators in the central autonomic nervous system. In: *Hormones, brain function and behavior,* ed. H. Hoagland, pp. 161–180. New York: Academic Press.

Bronson, F.H., and Desjardins, C. 1968. Aggression in adult mice: modification by neonatal injections of gonadal hormones. *Science 161*:705–706.

Brown, B.S.; Wienckowski, L.A.; and Bivens, L.W. 1973. *Psychosurgery: perspective on a current issue.* Washington, D.C.: U.S. Dept. of Health, Education and Welfare.

Brown, H. 1963. *d*-Amphetamine-chlorpromazine antagonism in a food reinforced operant. *Journal of the Experimental Analysis of Behavior 6*:395–398.

Brown, H. 1965. Drug-behavior interaction affecting development of tolerance to *d*-amphetamine as observed in fixed ratio behavior of rats. *Psychological Reports 16*:917–921.

Brown, H. 1966*a*. Effect of ribonucleic acid (RNA) on reversal of a probability matching problem in pigeons. *Psychological Record 16*:441–448.

Brown, H. 1966*b*. Effect of ribonucleic acid (RNA) on the rate of lever pressing in rats. *Psychological Record 16*:173–176.

Brown, H. 1966*c*. Chlorpromazine-methamphetamine antagonism in a non-discriminated avoidance schedule. *Psychonomic Science 6*:95–96.

Brown, H. 1967. Behavioral studies of animal vision and drug action. In:

International review of neurobiology, vol. 10, eds. C.C. Pfeiffer and J.R. Smythies, pp. 277–322. New York: Academic Press.

Brown, H. 1971. Some anticholinergic-like behavioural effects of trans(−) −Δ^8 tetrahydrocannabinol. *Psychopharmacologia 21*:294–301.

Brown, H. 1972. Possible anticholinesterase-like effects of trans(−)−Δ^8 and −Δ^9 tetrahydrocannabinol as observed in the general motor activity of mice. *Psychopharmacologia 27*:111–116.

Brown, H. 1974. Can we rationalize drug abuse? In: *Drug perspectives: a handbook of readings on drug abuse,* eds. H. Brown and T.J. Cahill, pp. 179–183. Washington, D.C.: National Institute on Drug Abuse.

Brown, H., and Richards, R.K. 1966. An interaction between drug effects and food reinforced "social" behavior in pigeons. *Archives internationales de Pharmacodynamie et de Thérapie 164*:286–293.

Brozek, J., and Erickson, N.K. 1948. Item analysis of the psychoneurotic scales of the Minnesota Multiphasic Personality Inventory in experimental semistarvation. *Journal of Consulting Psychology 12*:403–411.

Brozek, J., and Vaes, G. 1961. Experimental investigation on the effects of dietary deficiencies on animal and human behavior. *Vitamin and Hormone 19*:43–94.

Buday, P.V. 1960. Neurohormone-phrenotropic drug activity correlates. *American Journal of Pharmacy 132*:355–361.

Bulatao, E., and Carlson, A.J. 1924. Influence of experimental changes in blood sugar level on gastric hunger contractions. *American Journal of Physiology 69*:107–115.

Bunney, W.E.; Mason, J.W.; and Hamburg, D.A. 1965. Correlations between behavioral variables and urinary 17-hydroxy-corticosteroids in depressed patients. *Psychosomatic Medicine 27*:299–308.

Bureš, J., and Burešova, O. 1963. Cortical spreading depression as a memory disturbing factor. *Journal of Comparative and Physiological Psychology 56*: 268–272.

Burn, J.H. 1963. *The autonomic nervous system.* Philadelphia: Davis.

Burns, B.D. 1958. *The mammalian cerebral cortex.* London: Arnold.

Burns, T.; House, R.F.; Fensch, F.C.; and Miller, J.G. 1967. Effects of magnesium pemoline and dextroamphetamine on human learning. *Science 155*:849–851.

Burt, C. 1962. The concept of consciousness. *British Journal of Psychology 53*: 229–242.

Bush, R.R., and Mosteller, F. 1951. A mathematical model for simple learning. *Psychological Reviews 58*:313–323.

Butter, C.M. 1968. *Neuropsychology: the study of brain and behavior.* Belmont, Calif.: Brooks/Cole.

Bykov, K.M. 1957. *The cerebral cortex and the internal organs.* New York: Chemical.

Byrne, W.L., ed. 1970. *Molecular approaches to learning and memory.* New York: Academic Press.

Byrne, W.L. and 22 others. 1966. Memory transfer. *Science 153*:658–659.

Cadoret, R.J. 1953. The effect of amytal and dexedrine on ESP performance. *Journal of Parapsychology 17*:259–274.

Calder, N. 1970. *The mind of man.* New York: Viking.

Caldwell, A.E. 1970. *Origins of psychopharmacology from CPZ to LSD.* Springfield, Ill.: Thomas.

Calhoun, J.B. 1962. Population density and social pathology. *Scientific American 206*:139–150.

Cameron, D.E. 1958. The use of nucleic acid in aged patients with memory impairment. *American Journal of Psychiatry 114*:943.

Cameron, D.E., and Solyom, L. 1961. Effects of ribonucleic acid on memory. *Geriatrics 16*:74–81.

Cameron, D.E.; Sved, S.; Solyom, L.; Wainrib, B.; and Barik, H. 1963. Effect of ribonucleic acid on memory defect in the aged. *American Journal of Psychiatry 120*:320–325.

Cannon, W.B. 1927. The James-Lange theory of emotions: a critical examination and an alternative theory. *American Journal of Psychology 39*:106–124.

Cannon, W.B. 1929. *Bodily changes in pain, hunger, fear and rage.* New York: Appleton-Century-Crofts.

Cannon, W.B., and Rosenblueth, A. 1937. *Autonomic neuroeffector systems.* New York: Macmillan.

Cannon, W.B., and Washburn, A.L. 1912. An explanation of hunger. *American Journal of Physiology 29*:441–454.

Carlton, P.L. 1961. Potentiation of the behavioral effects of amphetamine by imipramine. *Psychopharmacologia 2*:364–376.

Carlton, P.L. 1968. Brain-acetylcholine and habituation. In: *Progress in brain research,* eds. P.B. Bradley and M. Fink, pp. 48–60. Amsterdam: Elsevier.

Carlton, P.L., and Didamo, P. 1961. Augmentation of the behavioral effects of amphetamine by atropine. *Journal of Pharmacology and Experimental Therapeutics 134*:91–96.

Casey, K.L. 1973. Pain: a current view of neural mechanisms. *American Scientist 61*:194–200.

Chapouthier, G. 1973. Behavior studies of the molecular basis of memory. In: *The physiological basis of memory,* ed. J.A. Deutsch, pp. 1–17. New York: Academic Press.

Chaves, J.F., and Barber, T.X. 1973. Needles and knives. *Human Behavior 2*:19–24.

Chorover, S.L. 1974. The pacification of the brain. *Psychology Today 7*:59–69.

Chow, K.L. 1954. Effects of temporal neocortical ablation on visual discrimination learning sets in monkeys. *Journal of Comparative and Physiological Psychology 47*:194–198.

Claridge, G. 1970. *Drugs and human behaviour.* New York: Praeger.

Clark, G., and Birch, H.G. 1945. Hormonal modification of social behavior. I. The effect of sex hormone administration on the social status of a male castrate chimpanzee. *Psychosomatic Medicine 7*:321–329.

Clark, K.B. 1971. The pathos of power: a psychological perspective. *American Psychologist 26*:1047–1057.

Clark, W.E.L. 1941. Observations on the associative fibre system of the visual cortex and the central representation of the retina. *Journal of Anatomy 75*:225–236.

Cobb, S. 1958. *Foundations of neuropsychiatry.* 6th ed. Baltimore: Williams and Wilkins.

Cole, K.S., and Curtis, H.J. 1939. Electric impedance of the squid giant axon during activity. *Journal of General Physiology 22*:649–670.

Conger, J.J.; Sawrey, W.L.; and Turrell, E.S. 1958. The role of social experience in the production of gastric ulcers in hooded rats placed in a conflict situation. *Journal of Comparative and Physiological Psychology 51*:214–220.

Cook, L. and Davidson, A.B. 1968. Effects of yeast RNA and other pharmacological agents on acquisition, retention and performance in animals. In: *Psychopharmacology: a review of progress 1957–1967,* eds. D.H. Efron, J.O. Cole, J. Levine, and J.R. Wittenborn, pp. 931–946. Washington, D.C.: American College of Neuropsychopharmacology.

Cook, L.; Davidson, A.B.; Davis, D.J.; Green, H.; and Fellows, E.J. 1963. Ribonucleic acid: effect on conditioned behavior in rats. *Science 141*:268–269.

Cooper, J.R.; Bloom, F.E.; and Roth, R.H. 1970. *The biochemical basis of neuropharmacology.* New York: Oxford University Press.

Corning, W.C., and John, E.R. 1961. Effect of ribonuclease on retention of conditioned response in regenerated planarians. *Science 134*:1363–1365.

Corning, W.C., and Riccio, D. 1970. The planarian controversy. In: *Molecular approaches to learning and memory,* ed. W.L. Byrne, pp. 107–150. New York: Academic Press.

Crawford, M.P. 1940. The relation between social dominance and the menstrual cycle in female chimpanzees. *Journal of Comparative Psychology 30*:483–513.

Cyert, L.A.; Moyer, K.E.; and Chapman, J.A. 1967. Effect of magnesium pemoline on learning and memory of a one-way avoidance response. *Psychonomic Science 7*:9–10.

Dale, H.H. 1934. Chemical transmission of the effects of nerve impulses. *British Medical Journal 1*:835–841.

Dana, C.L. 1921. The anatomic seat of the emotions: a discussion of the James-Lange theory. *A.M.A. Archives of Neurology and Psychiatry 6*:634–639.

Darwin, C. 1872. *The expression of the emotions in man and animals.* London: Murray.

Davenport, L.D., and Balagura, S. 1971. Lateral hypothalamus: reevaluation of function in motivated feeding behavior. *Science 172*:744–746.

Davis, J.L. 1965. Antagonism of a behavioral effect of *d*-amphetamine by chlorpromazine in the pigeon. *Journal of the Experimental Analysis of Behavior 8*:325–327.

Dean, E.D., and Nash, C.B. 1967. Coincident plethysmograph results under controlled conditions. *Journal of the Society of Psychical Research 44* : 1–14.

Deets, A.C., and Harlow, H.F. 1971. Early experience and the maturation of the agonistic emotion. Paper presented to the American Association for the Advancement of Science, 28 December 1971, Washington D.C.

DeJong, R.N., and Sugar, O. 1972. *The yearbook of neurology and neurosurgery.* Chicago: Yearbook Medical Publishers.

Delgado, J.M.R. 1966. Aggressive behavior evoked by radio stimulation in monkey colonies. *American Zoologist 6* : 669–681.

Delgado, J.M.R. 1971. *Physical control of the mind: towards a psychocivilized society.* New York: Harper and Row.

Delgado, J.M.R., and Anand, B.K. 1953. Increased food intake induced by electrical stimulation of the lateral hypothalamus. *American Journal of Physiology 172* : 162–168.

Delgado, J.M.R., and Hamlin, H. 1956. Surface and depth electrography of the frontal lobes in conscious patients. *Electroencephalography and Clinical Neurophysiology 8* : 371–384.

Delgado, J.M.R.; Roberts, W.W.; and Miller, N.E. 1954. Learning motivated by electrical stimulation of the brain. *American Journal of Physiology 179* : 587–593.

Dement, W., and Kleitman, N. 1955. Incidence of eye motility during sleep in relation to varying EEG pattern. *Federation Proceedings 14* : 216.

Dement, W., and Kleitman, N. 1957. Cyclic variations in EEG during sleep and their relation to eye movements, body motility and dreaming. *Electroencephalography and Clinical Neurophysiology 9* : 673–690.

Denny-Brown, D. 1958. The nature of apraxia. *Journal of Nervous and Mental Diseases 126* : 9–32.

Denny-Brown, D., and Chambers, R.A. 1958. The parietal lobe and behavior. *Research Publications of the Association of Nervous and Mental Diseases 36* : 35–117.

De Robertis, E.D. 1964. *Histophysiology of synapses and neurosecretion.* New York: Macmillan.

De Robertis, E.D. 1971. Molecular biology of synaptic receptors. *Science 171* : 963–971.

Deutsch, J.A. 1971. The cholinergic synapse and the site of memory. *Science 174* : 788–794.

Deutsch, J.A., and Deutsch, D. 1973. *Physiological psychology.* rev. ed. Homewood, Ill.: Dorsey.

DeValois, R.L. 1965. Behavioral and electrophysiological studies of primate vision. In: *Contributions to sensory physiology,* vol. 1, ed. W.D. Neff, pp. 137–178. New York: Academic Press.

Dingman, W., and Sporn, M.B. 1961. The incorporation of 8-azaguanine into rat brain RNA and its effect on maze learning by the rat: an inquiry into the biochemical basis of memory. *Journal of Psychiatric Research 1* : 1–11.

Doty, R.I. 1972. The role of olfaction in man: sense or nonsense. In: *Perception in everyday life,* ed. H.S. Bartley, pp. 143–157. New York: Harper and Row.

Duncan, C.P. 1949. The retroactive effect of electroshock on learning. *Journal of Comparative and Physiological Psychology 42*:34–44.

Dunlap, K. 1922. Editor's preface to *The emotions,* by C.G. Lange and W. James, pp. 5–7. Baltimore: Williams and Wilkins.

Durell, J.; Garland, J.T.; and Friedel, R.O. 1969. Acetylcholine action: biochemical aspects. *Science 165*:862–866.

Durup, G., and Fessard, A. 1935. L'électroencephalogramme de l'homme. *Année Psychologique 36*:1–32.

Dyal, J.A.; Golub, A.M.; and Marrone, R.L. 1967. Transfer effects of intraperitoneal injection of brain homogenates. *Nature 214*:720–721.

Eccles, J.C. 1953. *The neurophysiological basis of mind.* New York: Oxford University Press.

Eccles, J.C. 1957. *The physiology of nerve cells.* Baltimore: Johns Hopkins Press.

Eccles, J.C. 1964. *The Physiology of Synapses.* New York: Academic Press.

Eccles, J.C. 1969. Historical introduction. *Federation Proceedings 28*:90–94.

Eccles, J.C. 1970. *Facing reality: philosophical adventures by a brain scientist.* New York: Springer-Verlag.

Eccles, J.C., and McIntyre, A.K. 1951. Plasticity of mammalian monosynaptic reflexes. *Nature 167*:466–468.

Eckstein, G. 1970. *The body has a head.* New York: Harper and Row.

Efron, R. 1966. The conditioned reflex: a meaningless concept. *Perspectives in Biology and Medicine 9*:488–514.

Eichenwald, H.F., and Fry, P.C. 1969. Nutrition and learning. *Science 163*: 664–648.

Enesco, H.E. 1967. RNA and memory: a re-evaluation of present data. *Journal of the Canadian Psychiatric Association 12*:29–33.

English, H.B., and English, A.C. 1958. *A comprehensive dictionary of psychological and psychoanalytical terms: a guide to usage.* New York: Longmans, Green.

Erickson, R.P. 1963. Sensory neural patterns and gustation. In: *Olfaction and taste,* vol. 1, ed. Y. Zotterman, pp. 205–213. New York: Permagon Press.

Erlanger, J., and Gasser, H.S. 1937. *Electrical signs of nervous action.* Philadelphia: University of Pennsylvania Press.

Eron, L.D. 1963. Relationship of TV viewing habits and aggressive behavior in children. *Journal of Abnormal and Social Psychology 67*:193–196.

Evans, R.I. 1968. *B.F. Skinner: the man and his ideas.* New York: Dutton.

Falk, J.L., and Burnidge, G.K. 1970. Drug antagonism and water intake. *Physiology and Behavior 5*:193–198.

Fechner, G. 1851. *Zend-Avesta, on the things of heaven and the hereafter.* Leipzig: Voss.

Fechner, G. 1860. *Elemente der psychophysik.* Leipzig: Breitkopf and Hartel.

Fehr, F.S., and Stern, J.A. 1970. Peripheral physiological variables and emotion: the James-Lange theory revisited. *Psychological Bulletin 74*:411–424.

Ferguson, D.C., and Fisher, A.E. 1963. Behavior disruption in Cebus monkeys as a function of injected substances. *Science 139*:1281–1282.

Ferrier, D. 1886. *The functions of the brain.* 2nd ed. London: Smith, Elder.

Finan, J.L. 1942. Delayed response with pre-delay reinforcement in monkeys after removal of the frontal lobes. *American Journal of Psychology 55*: 204–214.

Fischer, R. 1971. A cartography of the ecstatic and meditative states. *Science 174*:897–904.

Fjerdingstad, E.J., ed. 1971. *Chemical transfer of learned information.* New York: Elsevier.

Flesch, R. 1970. The more or less scientific method. In: *Selected readings in psychology,* eds. D.E. Gibbons and J.F. Connelly, pp. 3–8. St. Louis: Mosby.

Flexner, L.B.; Flexner, J.B.; and Roberts, R.B. 1966. Stages of memory in mice treated with acetoxycycloheximide before or immediately after learning. *Proceedings of the National Academy of Sciences of the United States of America 56*:730–735.

Flexner, L.B.; Flexner, J.B.; and Roberts, R.B. 1967. Memory in mice analyzed with antibiotics. *Science 155*:1377–1383.

Flourens, J.P.M. 1842. *Researches expérimentales sur les propriétés et les fonctions du systèm nerveux dans les animaux vertébrés.* 2nd ed. Paris: Ballière.

Flynn, J.P.; Vanegas, H.; Foote, W.; and Edwards, S. 1970. Neural mechanisms involved in cat's attack on a rat. In: *The neural control of behavior,* eds. R.W. Whalen, R.F. Thompson, M. Verzeano, and N.M. Weinberger, pp. 135–173. New York: Academic Press.

Frank, E.; Stein, D.G.; and Rosen, J. 1970. Interanimal "memory" transfer: results from brain and liver homogenates. *Science 169*:399–402.

Frank, M., and Pfaffmann, C. 1969. Taste nerve fibers: a random distribution of sensitivities to four tastes. *Science 164*:1183–1185.

Frankenhaeuser, M.; Järpe, G.; Svan, H.; and Wansjö, B. 1963. Psychophysiological reactions to two different placebo treatments. *Scandinavian Journal of Psychology 4*:245–250.

Franz, S.I. 1902. On the functions of the cerebrum: the frontal lobes in relation to the production and retention of simple sensory-motor habits. *American Journal of Physiology 8*:1–22.

Fredericson, E.A.; Story, A.W.; Gurney, N.L.; and Butterworth, K. 1955. The relationship between heredity, sex and aggression in two inbred mouse strains. *Journal of Genetic Psychology 87*:121–130.

Freedman, D.X., and Giarman, N.J. 1962. LSD-25 and the status and level of brain serotonin. *Annals of the New York Academy of Sciences 96*:98–107.

Freeman, W., and Watts, J.W. 1950. *Psychosurgery in the treatment of mental disorders.* Springfield, Ill.: Thomas.

French, G.M., and Harlow, H.F. 1962. Variability of delayed-reaction performance in normal and brain-damaged rhesus monkeys. *Journal of Neurophysiology 25*:585–599.

French, J.D.; Porter, R.W.; Cavanaugh, E.B.; and Longmire, R.L. 1957. Experimental gastroduodenal lesions induced by stimulation of the brain. *Psychosomatic Medicine 19*:209–220.

Freud, S. 1965. *New introductory lectures on psychoanalysis.* New York: Norton.

Frey, P.W., and Polidora, V.J. 1967. Magnesium pemoline: effect on avoidance conditioning in rats. *Science 155*:1281–1282.

Friedhoff, A.J., and vanWinkle, E. 1962. The characteristics of an amine found in the urine of schizophrenic patients. *Journal of Nervous and Mental Disease 135*:550–555.

Fritsch, G., and Hitzig, E. 1870. Über die elektrische erregbarkeit des grosshirns. *Archiv fur Wissenschaftliche Medizin 37*:300–332.

Gaddum, J.H. 1953. Antagonism between lysergic acid diethylamide and 5-hydroxytryptamine. *The Journal of Physiology 121*:15.

Galambos, R. 1961. A glia-neural theory of brain function. *Proceedings of the National Academy of Sciences of the United States of America 47*:129–136.

Galle, O.R.; Gove, W.R.; and McPherson, J.M. 1972. Population density and pathology: what are the relations for man? *Science 176*:23–30.

Gasnier, A., and Mayer, A. 1939. Récherches sur la régulation de la nutrition. *Année physiologie Physiochimie Biologie 15*:145–214.

Gawronski, R., ed. 1971. *Bionics: the nervous system as a control system.* Amsterdam: Esevier.

Gelber, B. 1964. Learning and associated phenomena in invertebrates. *Animal Behavior 12*:21–29.

Gelfand, S.; Clark, L.D.; Herbert, E.W.; Gelfand, D.M.; and Holmes, E.D. 1967. Magnesium pemoline: stimulant effects on performance of fatigued subjects. *Clinical Pharmacology and Therapeutics 9*:56–60.

Geller, I.; Sidman, M.; and Brady, J.V. 1955. The effect of electroconvulsive shock on a conditioned emotional response: a control for acquisition recency. *Journal of Comparative and Physiological Psychology 48*:130–131.

Ghent, L.; Mishkin, M.; and Teuber, H.-L. 1962. Short-term memory after frontal-lobe injury in man. *Journal of Comparative and Physiological Psychology 55*:705–709.

Gilbert, G.J., and Glaser, G.H. 1961. On the nervous system integration of water and salt metabolism. *Archives of Neurology 5*:179–196.

Girden, E., and Culler, E. 1937. Conditioned responses in curarized striate muscle in dogs. *Journal of Comparative Psychology 23*:261–274.

Glasky, A.J., and Simon, L.N. 1966. Magnesium pemoline: enhancement of brain RNA polymerases. *Science 151*:702–703.

Goddard, G.V. 1964. Functions of the amygdala. *Psychological Bulletin 62*:89–109.

Goldberg, M.E., and Ciofalo, V.B. 1967. Failure of magnesium pemoline to enhance acquisition of the avoidance response in mice. *Life Sciences 6*:733–737.

Goldsmith, L.J. 1967. Effect of intracerebral actinomycin-D and of electroconvulsive shock on passive avoidance. *Journal of Comparative and Physiological Psychology 63*:126–132.

Goldstein, A.; Aronow, L.; and Kalman, S.M. 1969. *Principles of drug action: the basis of pharmacology.* New York: Hoeber-Harper.

Goldstein, K. 1939. *The organism.* New York: American Book.

Goldstein, K. 1963. *Human nature in the light of psychopathology.* New York: Schocken.

Goldstein, L. and Beck, R.A. 1965. Amplitude analysis of the electroencephalogram. In: *International review of neurobiology,* vol. 8, eds. C.C. Pfeiffer and J.R. Smythies, pp. 265–312. New York: Academic Press.

Golub, A.M.; Masiarz, F.R.; Villars, T.; and McConnell, J.V. 1970. Incubation effects in behavior induction in rats. *Science 168*:392–395.

Gordon, M.W.; Deanin, G.G.; Leonhardt, H.L.; and Gurjnn, R.H. 1966. RNA and memory: a negative experiment. *American Journal of Psychiatry 122*:1174–1178.

Granit, R. 1970. *The basis of motor control.* New York: Academic Press.

Gross, C., and Carey, F.M. 1965. Transfer of learned response by RNA injection: failure of attempts to replicate. *Science 150*:1749.

Grossman, M.I., and Stein, I.F. 1948. Vagotomy and the hunger-producing action of insulin in man. *Journal of Applied Physiology 1*:263–269.

Grossman, S.P. 1960. Eating or drinking elicited by direct adrenergic or cholinergic stimulation of the hypothalamus. *Science 132*:301–302.

Grossman, S.P. 1967. *A textbook of physiological psychology.* New York: Wiley.

Gunn, J.A. and Gurd, M.R. 1940. The action of some amines related to adrenaline: cycloherylalkylamines. *Journal of Physiology, 97*:453–470.

Gurowitz, E.M. 1969. *The molecular basis of memory.* Englewood Cliffs, N.J.: Prentice-Hall.

Gurowitz, E.M.; Lubar, J.F.; Ain, B.R.; and Cross, D.A. 1967. Disruption of passive avoidance learning by magnesium pemoline. *Psychonomic Science 8*:19–20.

Guthrie, E.R. 1959. Association by contiguity. In: *Psychology: a study of a science,* vol. 2, ed. S. Koch, pp. 158–195. New York: McGraw-Hill, 1959.

Halas, E.S.; Bradfield, K.; Sandlie, M.E.; Theye, F.; and Beardsley, J. 1966. Changes in rat behavior due to RNA injection. *Physiology and Behavior 1*:281–283.

Haley, T.J. 1957. 5-Hydroxytryptamine antagonism by LSD after intracerebral injection into conscious mice. *Journal of the American Pharmaceutical Association (Scientific Edition) 46*:428–430.

Hall, C.S., and Lindzey, G. 1970. *Theories of personality.* 2nd ed. New York: Wiley.

Hall, J.F. 1961. *Psychology of motivation.* Philadelphia: Lippincott.

Hall, M. 1850. *Synopsis of the diastaltic nervous system.* London: Croonian Lectures.

Hamberger, C.A., and Hydén, H. 1945. Cytochemical changes in the cochlear ganglion caused by acoustic stimulation and trauma. *Acta Otolaryngia.* Supp. 61.

Harlow, H.F. 1971. *Learning to love.* San Francisco: Albion.

Harlow, H.F., and Stagner, R. 1933. Effect of complete striate muscle paralysis upon the learning process. *Journal of Experimental Psychology 16*:283–294.

Harlow, J.M. 1869. *Recovery from the passage of an iron bar through the head.* Boston: Clapp.

Harris, S.C.; Ivy, A.C.; and Searle, L.M. 1947. The mechanism of amphetamine induced loss of weight. *Journal of the American Medical Association 134* : 1468–1475.

Hartline, H.K., and Graham, C.H. 1932. Nerve impulses from single receptors in the eye. *Journal of Cellular and Comparative Physiology 1* : 277–295.

Hayflick, L. 1968. Human cells and aging. *Scientific American 218* : 32–37.

Head, H. 1920. *Studies of neurology.* London: Oxford University Press.

Hearst, E., and Whalen, R.E. 1963. Facilitating effects of *d*-amphetamine on discriminated-avoidance performance. *Journal of Comparative and Physiological Psychology 56* : 124–128.

Heath, R.G. 1962. Brain centers and control of behavior—man. In: *Psychosomatic medicine,* eds. J.H. Nodine and J.H. Moyer, pp. 228–240. Philadelphia: Lea and Febiger.

Heath, R.G. 1963. Electrical self-stimulation of the brain in man. *American Journal of Psychiatry 120* : 571–577.

Heath, R.G. 1964. *Role of pleasure in behavior.* New York: Hoeber-Harper.

Heath, R.G., and Krupp, I.M. 1967. Schizophrenia as an immunological disorder. I. Demonstration of antibrain globulins by fluroescent antibody techniques. *A.M.A. Archives of General Psychiatry 16* : 1–9.

Heath, R.G.; Krupp, I.M.; Byers, L.W.; and Liljekvist, J.I. 1967. Schizophrenia as an immunologic disorder. II. Effects of serum protein fractions on brain function. *A.M.A. Archives of General Psychiatry 16* : 10–23.

Heath, R.G.; Martens, S.; Leach, B.E.; Cohen, M.; and Angel, C. 1957. Effect on behavior in humans with the administration of taraxein. *American Journal of Psychiatry 114* : 14–24.

Heath, R.G.; Martens, S.; Leach, B.E.; Cohen, M.; and Feigley, C.A. 1958. Behavioral changes in nonpsychotic volunteers following the administration of taraxein, the substance obtained from serum of schizophrenic patients. *American Journal of Psychiatry 114* : 917–920.

Hebb, D.O. 1949. *The Organization of behaviour.* New York: Wiley.

Hebb, D.O. 1966. *A textbook of psychology.* 2nd ed. Philadelphia: Saunders.

Hebb, D.O., and Penfield, W. 1940. Human behavior after extensive bilateral removals from the frontal lobes. *A.M.A. Archives of Neurology and Psychiatry 44* : 421–438.

Hefferline, R.F., and Perera, T.B. 1963. Proprioceptive discrimination of a covert operant without its observation by the subject. *Science 139* : 834–835.

Henkin, R.I.; Graziadei, P.P.G.; and Bradley, D.S. 1969. The molecular basis of taste and its disorders. *Annals of Internal Medicine 71* : 791–821.

Hernández-Peón, R., and Brust-Carmona, H. 1961. Functional role of subcortical structures in habituation and conditioning. In: *Brain mechanisms and learning,* ed. J.F. Delafresnaye, pp. 393–408. Springfield, Ill.: Thomas.

Hess, W.R. 1954. *Diencephalon: autonomic and extrapyramidal functions.* New York: Grune and Stratton.

Heston, L.L. 1966. Psychiatric disorders in foster home reared children of schizophrenic mothers. *British Journal of Psychiatry 112*:819–825.

Hetherington, A.W., and Ranson, S.W. 1939. Experimental hypothalamico-hypophysial obesity in the rat. *Proceedings of the Society of Experimental Biology 41*:465–466.

Hilgard, E.R. 1973. The domain of hypnosis. *American Psychologist 28*:972–981.

Hilgard, E.R. 1974. Hypnosis is no mirage. *Psychology Today 8*:121–128.

Hitzig, E. 1884. Zür Physiologie des Grosshirns. *Archiv für Psychiatrie und Nervenheilkunde 15*:270–275.

Hobhouse, L.T. 1926. *Mind in evolution.* 3rd ed. London: Macmillan.

Hodgkin, A.L. 1964. *The condition of the nervous impulse.* Springfield, Ill.: Thomas.

Hodgkin, A.L., and Huxley, A.F. 1939. Action potentials recorded from inside nerve fiber. *Nature 144*:710–711.

Hodgkin, A.L., and Katz, B. 1949. The effect of sodium ions on the electrical activity of the giant axon of the squid. *Journal of Physiology 108*:37–77.

Hodos, W., and Campbell, C.B.G. 1969. Scala naturae: why there is no theory in comparative psychology. *Psychological Review 76*:337–350.

Hoebel, B.G., and Teitilbaum, P. 1962. Hypothalamic control of feeding and self-stimulation. *Science 135*:375–377.

Hoffer, A. 1965. *d*-Lysergic acid diethylamide (LSD): a review of its present status. *Clinical Pharmacology and Therapeutics 6*:83–255.

Hokanson, J.E. 1969. *The physiological bases of motivation.* New York: Wiley.

Hollister, L.E. 1962. Drug-induced psychoses and schizophrenic reaction: a critical comparison. *Annals of the New York Academy of Science 96*:10–92.

Hollister, L.E. 1971. Marijuana in man: three years later. *Science 172*:21–29.

Hollister, L.E., and Friedhoff, A.J. 1966. Effects of 3,4-dimethoxyphenyl-ethylamine in man. *Nature 210*:1377–1378.

Holmes, T.H., and Masuda, M. 1972. Psychosomatic syndrome. *Psychology Today 5*:71–72 and 106.

Hordern, A. 1968. Psychopharmacology: some historical considerations. In: *Psychopharmacology: dimensions and perspectives,* ed. C.R.B. Joyce, pp. 95–148. London: Tavistock.

Horn, G.; Rose, S.P.R.; and Bateson, P.P.G. 1973. Experience and plasticity in the central nervous system. *Science 181*:506–514.

Horsley, V., and Clarke, R.H. 1908. The structure and functions of the cerebellum examined by a new method. *Brain 31*:45–124.

Hubel, D.H., and Wiesel, T.N. 1959. Receptive fields of single neurons in the cat's striate cortex. *Journal of Physiology 148*:574–591.

Hubel, D.H., and Wiesel, T.N. 1962. Receptive fields, binocular interaction and functional architecture in the cat's visual cortex. *Journal of Physiology 160*:106–154.

Hubel, D.H., and Wiesel, T.N. 1965. Receptive fields and functional architecture in two nonstriate visual areas (18 and 19) of the cat. *Journal of Neurophysiology 28*:229–289.

Huby, P.M., and Wilson, C.W.M. 1961. The effects of centrally acting drugs on ESP ability in normal subjects. *Journal of the Society for Psychical Research 41*:60–67.

Hughes, J.R.; Means, E.D.; and Stell, B.S. 1965. A controlled study of the behavior disorders associated with the positive spike phenomenon. *Electroencephalography and Clinical Neurology 18*:349–353.

Hull, C.L. 1935. The influence of caffeine and other factors on certain phenomena of rate learning. *Journal of General Psychology 13*:249–274.

Hull, C.L. 1943. *Principles of behavior.* New York: Appleton-Century-Crofts.

Hydén, H. 1943. Protein metabolism in the nerve cell during growth and function. *Acta Physiologica Scandinavica 6*:Supp. 17.

Hydén, H. 1955. Nucleic acids and proteins. In: *Neurochemistry: the chemical dynamics of brain and nerve,* eds. K.A.C. Elliott, I.H. Page, and J.H. Quastel, pp. 204–233. Springfield, Ill.: Thomas.

Hydén, H., and Egyhazi, E. 1962. Nuclear RNA changes of nerve cells during a learning experiment in rats. *Proceedings of the National Academy of Sciences of the United States of America 48*:1366–1373.

Jacobsen, C.F. 1935. Functions of the frontal association area in primates. *A.M.A. Archives of Neurology and Psychiatry 33*:558–569.

Jacobsen, C.F. 1936. Studies of cerebral function in primates. I. The functions of the frontal association areas in monkeys. *Comparative Psychology Monographs 13*:3–60.

Jacobson, A.L., and Schlecter, J.M. 1970. Chemical transfer of training: three years later. In: *Biology of memory,* eds. K.H. Pribram and D.E. Broadbent, pp. 123–128. New York: Academic Press.

Jaffard, R., and Cardo, B. 1968. Influence de l'injection intracorticale de ribonucléase sur l'acquisition et la rétention d'un apprentissage alimentaire chez le rat. *Journal de Physiologie 60*:470.

Jaffe, J.H. 1965. Narcotic analgesics. In: *The pharmacological basis of therapeutics,* 3rd ed., eds. L.S. Goodman and A. Gilman, pp. 247–284. New York: Macmillan.

James, W. 1890. *The principles of psychology.* New York: Holt.

James, W. 1894. The physical basis of emotion. *Psychological Review 1*:516–529.

Janssen, P.A.J.; Jageneau, A.H.; and Niemegeers, C.J.E. 1960. Effects of various drugs on isolation-induced fighting behavior of male mice. *Journal of Pharmacology and Experimental Therapeutics 129*:471–475.

Jarvik, M.E. 1970. The role of consolidation in memory. In: *Molecular approaches to learning and memory,* ed. W.L. Byrne, pp. 15–26. New York: Academic Press.

Jarvik, M.E. 1972. Effects of chemical and physical treatments on learning and memory. *Annual Review of Psychology 23*:457–486.

Jasper, H.H., and Tessier, J. 1971. Acetylcholine liberation from cerebral cortex during paradoxical (REM) sleep. *Science 172*:601–602.

Jensen, D.D. 1965. Paramecia, planaria and pseudo-learning. *Animal Behavior 13*:9–20.

Jerison, H.J. 1973. *Evolution of the brain and intelligence.* New York: Academic Press.

John, E.R., and Killam, R.F. 1959. Electrophysiological correlates of avoidance conditioning in the cat. *Journal of Pharmacology and Experimental Therapeutics 125*:252–274.

Jouvet, M. 1967a. The states of sleep. *Scientific American 216*:62–72.

Jouvet, M. 1967b. Neurophysiology of the states of sleep. *Physiological Reviews 47*:117–177.

Jouvet, M. 1968. Neuropharmacology of sleep. In: *Psychopharmacology: a review of progress 1957–1967,* eds. D.H. Efron, J.O. Cole, J. Levine, and J.R. Wittenborn, pp. 523–540. Washington, D.C.: American College of Neuropsychopharmacology.

Kallman, F.J. 1946. The genetic theory of schizophrenia: an analysis of 691 twin index families. *American Journal of Psychiatry 103*:309–322.

Kamiya, J. 1968. Conscious control of brain waves. *Psychology Today 1*:56–60.

Kandel, E.R., and Spencer, W.A. 1968. Cellular neurophysiological approaches in the study of learning. *Physiological Reviews 48*:65–134.

Kant, I. 1929. *Critique of pure reason.* London: Macmillan.

Kantor, J.R. 1947. *Problems of physiological psychology.* Bloomington, Ind.: Principia.

Kantor, J.R. 1962. *Principles of psychology.* Bloomington, Ind.: Principia.

Kappers, C.U.A.; Kuber, G.C., and Crosby, E.C. 1936. *The comparative anatomy of the nervous system of vertebrates including man.* New York: Macmillan.

Karczmar, A.G. 1969. Is the central nervous system overexploited? *Federation Proceedings 28*:147–157.

Kast, E.C., and Collins, V.J. 1966. A theory of human pathologic pain and its measurement: the analgesic activity of methotrimeprazine. *Journal of New Drugs 6*:142–148.

Katz, B. 1966. *Nerve, muscle and synapse.* New York: McGraw-Hill.

Katz, J.J., and Halstead, W.C. 1950. Protein organization and mental function. *Comparative Psychology Monographs 20*:1–38.

Kaufmann, H. 1970. *Aggression and altruism.* New York: Holt, Rinehart and Winston.

Keeler, C.M. 1942. The association of the black (non-agouti) gene with behavior in the Norway rat. *Journal of Heredity 33*:371–384.

Kellogg, W.N. 1947. Is "spinal conditioning" conditioning? *Journal of Experimental Psychology 37*:263–265.

Kellogg, W.N.; Deese, J.; Pronko, N.H.; and Feinberg, M. 1947. An attempt to condition the chronic spinal dog. *Journal of Experimental Psychology 37*:99–117.

Kemeny, J.G. 1968. Man viewed as a machine. In: *Mathematical thinking in behavioral sciences,* ed. D.M. Messick, pp. 112–119. San Francisco: Freeman.

Kety, S.S. 1959. Biochemical theories of schizophrenia. *Science 129*:1528–1532.

Kety, S.S. 1960. Recent biochemical theories of schizophrenia. In: *The etiology of schizophrenia,* ed. D.D. Jackson, pp. 120–145. New York: Basic Books.

Khavari, K.A. 1969. Effects of central versus intraperitoneal *d*-amphetamine administration on learned behavior. *Journal of Comparative and Physiological Psychology 68*:226–234.

Kimble, G.A. 1967. *Foundations of conditioning and learning.* New York: Appleton-Century-Crofts.

Kimble, G.A., and Perlmuter, L.C. 1970. The problem of volition. *Psychological Review 77*:361–384.

King, M.B., and Hoebel, B.G. 1968. Killing elicited by brain stimulation in rats. *Communications in Behavioral Biology 2*:173–177.

Kislack, J.W., and Beach, F.A. 1955. Inhibition of aggressiveness by ovarian hormones. *Endocrinology 56*:684–692.

Kleitman, N. 1963. *Sleep and wakefulness.* Chicago: University of Chicago Press.

Kluver, H., and Bucy, P.C. 1937. "Psychic blindness" and other symptoms following bilateral temporal lobectomy in rhesus monkeys. *American Journal of Physiology 119*:352–353.

Koelle, G.B. 1965. Neurohumoral transmission and the autonomic nervous system. In: *The pharmacological basis of therapeutics,* 3rd ed., eds. L.S. Goodman and A. Gilman, pp. 399–440. New York: Macmillan.

Kohler, W. 1925. *The mentality of apes.* New York: Harcourt, Brace and World.

Kraepelin, E. 1900. *Psychiatrie: ein Lehrbuch für Studierende und Arate.* Leipzig: Barth.

Kravitz, E.A.; Kuffler, S.W.; and Potter, D.D. 1963. Gamma-aminobutyric acid and other blocking compounds in Crustacea. III. Their relative concentration in separated motor and inhibitory axons. *Journal of Neurophysiology 26*:739–751.

Kretchmer, E. 1921. *Korperbau und Charakter.* Berlin: Springer.

Krnjevic, K. 1969. Central cholinergic pathways. *Federation Proceedings 28*:113–120.

Kuffler, S.W. 1953. Discharge patterns and functional organization of mammalian retina. *Journal of Neurophysiology 16*:37–68.

Kuhn, T.S. 1970. *The structure of scientific revolutions.* 2nd ed. Chicago: University of Chicago Press.

Kulikowski, J.J. 1971. Information channels of the senses. In: *Bionics: the nervous system as a control system,* ed. R. Gawronski, pp. 97–142. Amsterdam: Elsevier.

Kupfermann, I., and Pinsker, H. 1969. Plasticity in *Aplysia* neurons and some simple neuronal models of learning. In: *Reinforcement and Behavior,* ed. J.T. Tapp, pp. 356–386. New York: Academic Press.

Lack, E. 1943. *The life of the robin.* London: Witherby.

La Mettrie, J.O. 1961. *Man a machine.* LaSalle, Ill.: Open Court.

Lange, C.G., and James, W. 1922. *The emotions.* Baltimore: Williams and Wilkins.

Lanier, L.H. 1934. An experimental study of cutaneous innervation. *Proceedings of the Association for Research on Nervous and Mental Diseases 15*:437–456.

Larsell, O. 1937. The cerebellum: a review and interpretation. *A.M.A. Archives of Neurology and Psychiatry 38*:580–607.

Lashley, K.S. 1917. The effects of strychnine and caffeine upon the rate of learning. *Psychobiology 1*:141–170.

Lashley, K.S. 1948. The mechanism of vision. XVIII. Effects of destroying the visual "associative areas" of the monkey. *Genetic Psychology Monographs 37*:107–166.

Lashley, K.S. 1950. In search of the engram. In: *Society of experimental biology symposium no. 4: physiological mechanisms in animal behavior*, pp. 454–482. New York: Cambridge University Press.

Lashley, K.S. 1963. *Brain mechanisms and intelligence.* New York: Dover.

LeShan, L. 1974. *The medium, the mystic, and the physicist.* New York: Viking.

Levin, S.S. 1970. *Adam's rib: essays on biblical medicine.* Los Altos, Calif.: Geron-X.

Levitan, M., and Montagu, A. 1971. *Textbook of human genetics.* New York: Oxford University Press.

Lewes, G.H. 1879. *Problems of life and mind.* London: Trubner.

Lichtenstein, P.E. 1971. A behavioral approach to "phenomenological data." *Psychological Record 21*:1–16.

Lilly, J. 1961. *Man and dolphins.* Garden City, N.Y.: Doubleday.

Lindgren, H.C. 1969. *An introduction to social psychology.* New York: Wiley.

Lindsley, D.B. 1958. The reticular system and perceptual discrimination. In: *Reticular formation of the brain*, ed. H.H. Jasper, pp. 513–534. Boston: Little-Brown.

Lindsley, D.B.; Schreiner, L.H.; Knowles, W.B.; and Magoun, H.W. 1950. Behavioral and EEG changes following chronic brain stem lesions in the cat. *Electroencephalography and Clinical Neurophysiology 2*:483–498.

Lindsley, D.B.; Schreiner, L.H.; and Magoun, H.W. 1949. An electromyographic study of spasticity. *Journal of Neurophysiology 12*:197–216.

Linseman, M.A., and Olds, J. 1973. Activity changes in rat hypothalamus, preoptic area, and striatum associated with Pavlovian conditioning. *Journal of Neurophysiology 36*:1038–1050.

Lisk, R.D. 1962. Diencephalic placement of estradiol and sexual receptivity in the female rat. *American Journal of Physiology 203*:493–496.

Livingston, R.B. 1959. Central control of receptors and sensory transmission systems. In: *Neurophysiology*. vol. 1. *Handbook of Physiology*, sec. 1, eds. J. Field, H.W. Magoun, and V.E. Hall, pp. 741–760. Washington, D.C.: American Physiological Society.

Lockard, R.B. 1971. Reflections on the fall of comparative psychology: is there a message for us all? *American Psychologist 26*:168–179.

Loeb, J. 1900. *Comparative physiology of the brain and comparative psychology.* New York: Putnam.

Loewi, O., and Navratil, E. 1926. Über humorale Übertragbarkeit der Herznervenwirkung. X. Mitteilung. Über das Schicksal des Vagusstoffs. *Pflugers Archiv Gesamte Physiologie 214*:678–688.

Lohr, T.F. 1971. *The mechanics of the mind*. Coopersburg, Pa.: Venture.

Lorenz, K. 1966. *On aggression*. London: Methuen.

Lorenz, K. 1970. *Studies in animal and human behavior*. vol. 1. London: Methuen.

Loucks, R.B. 1933. Preliminary report of a technique for stimulation or destruction of tissues beneath the integument and the establishing of a conditioned reaction with faradization of the cerebral cortex. *Journal of Comparative Psychology 16*:439–444.

Loucks, R.B. 1936. The experimental delimitation of neural structures essential for learning: the attempt to condition striped muscle responses with faradization of the sigmoid gyri. *Journal of Psychology 1*:5–44.

Loucks, R.B. 1938. Studies of neural structures essential for learning. II. The conditioning of salivary and striped muscle responses to faradization of cortical sensory elements, and the action of sleep upon such mechanisms. *Journal of Comparative Psychology 25*:315–332.

Lubar, J.F.; Boitano, J.J.; Gurowitz, E.M., and Ain, B.R. 1967. Enhancement of performance in the Hebb-Williams maze by magnesium pemoline. *Psychonomic Science 7*:381–382.

Luce, R.D. 1972. What sort of measurement is psychophysical measurement? *American Psychologist 27*:96–106.

Luckhardt, A.B., and Carlson, A.J. 1915. Contributions to the physiology of the stomach. XVII. On the chemical control of the gastric hunger mechanism. *American Journal of Physiology 36*:37–46.

Lundin, R.W. 1964. *Principles of psychopathology*. Colombus, O.: Merrill.

Luria, A.R. 1966a. *Higher cortical functions in man*. London: Tavistock.

Luria, A.R. 1966b. *Human brain and psychological processes*. New York: Harper and Row.

Luria, A.R. 1970. The functional organization of the brain. *Scientific American 222*:66–78.

Luria, A.R. 1973a. *The working brain*. New York: Basic Books.

Luria, A.R. 1973b. The frontal lobes and the regulation of behavior. In: *Psychophysiology of the frontal lobes*, eds. K.H. Pribram and A.R. Luria, pp. 3–26. New York: Academic Press.

Luria, A.R., and Homskaya, E.D. 1964. Disturbance in the regulative role of speech with frontal lobe lesions. In: *The frontal grandular cortex and behavior*, eds. J.M. Warren and K. Akert, pp. 353–371. New York: McGraw-Hill.

Luttges, J.; Johnson, T.; Buck, C.; Holland, J.; and McGaugh, J. 1966. An examination of "transfer of learning" by nucleic acid. *Science 151*:834–837.

McCleary, R.A., and Moore, R.Y. 1965. *Subcortical mechanisms of behavior: the psychological functions of primitive parts of the brain*. New York: Basic Books.

McConnell, J.V. 1962. Memory transfer through cannibalism in planarians. *Journal of Neuropsychiatry 3*:542–548.

McConnell, J.V. 1966. Comparative psychology: learning in invertebrates. *Annual Review of Physiology 28*:107–136.

McConnell, J.V.; Jacobson, A.L.; and Kimble, D.P. 1959. The effects of regeneration upon retention of a conditioned response in the planarian. *Journal of Comparative and Physiological Psychology 52*:1–5.

McConnell, J.V.; Shigehisa, T.; and Salive, H. 1970. Attempts to transfer approach and avoidance responses by RNA injections in rats. In: *Biology of memory*, eds. K.H. Pribram and D.E. Broadbent, pp. 129–159. New York: Academic Press.

McGaugh, J.L., and Petrinovich, L.F. 1965. Effects of drugs on learning and memory. In: *International review of neurobiology*, vol. 8, eds. C.C. Pfeiffer and J.R. Smythies, pp. 139–196. New York: Academic Press.

McGeer, P.L. 1971. The chemistry of mind. *American Scientist 59*:221–229.

McGinnies, E. 1970. *Social behavior: a functional analysis*. Boston: Houghton Mifflin.

McKenzie, K.G., and Kaczanowski, G. 1964. Prefrontal leukotomy: a five-year controlled study. *Canadian Medical Association Journal 91*:1193–1196.

MacDonnell, M.F., and Flynn, J.P. 1964. Attack elicited by stimulation of the thalamus of cats. *Science 144*:1249–1250.

MacLean, P.D. 1949. Psychosomatic disease and the "visceral brain": recent developments bearing on the Papez theory of emotion. *Psychosomatic Medicine 11*:338–353.

MacNichol, E.F. 1964. Retinal mechanisms of color vision. *Vision Research 4*:1, 119–133.

Madow, L., and Snow, L.H., eds. 1971. *The psychodynamic implications of the physiological studies on psychotomimetic drugs*. Springfield, Ill.: Thomas.

Magendie, F. 1826. *Lehrbuch der physiologie*. Tubingen: Ostlander.

Maier, N.R.F., and Schneirla, T.C. 1964. *Principles of animal psychology*, enlarged ed. New York: Dover.

Maier, R.A. 1962. Maternal behavior in the domestic hen. Unpublished Ph.D. dissertation, Kansas State University.

Maier, R.A., and Maier, B.M. 1970. *Comparative animal behavior*. Belmont, Calif.: Brooks/Cole.

Malmo, R.B. 1942. Interference factors in delayed response in monkeys after removal of frontal lobes. *Journal of Neurophysiology 5*:295–308.

Mandell, A.J. 1973. Neurological barriers to euphoria. *American Scientist 61*: 565–573.

Mandell, A.J., and Spooner, C.E. 1968. Psychochemical research studies in man. *Science 162*:1442–1453.

Manning, A. 1971. Evolution of behavior. In: *Psychobiology*, ed. J.L. McGaugh, pp. 3–7. New York: Academic Press.

Marañon, G. 1924. Contribution à l'étude de l'action émotive de l'adrénaline. *Revue Française d'Endocrinologie 2*:301–325.

Mark, V.H., and Ervin, F.R. 1970. *Violence and the brain*. New York: Harper and Row.

Mason, J.W.; Brady, J.V.; and Sidman, M. 1957. Plasma 17-hydroxycorticosteroid levels and conditioned behavior in the rhesus monkey. *Endocrinology 60*:741–752.

Mason, J.W.; Mangan, J.G.; Brady, J.V.; Conrad, D.; and Rioch, D.M. 1961.

Concurrent plasma epinephrine, norepinephrine and 17-hydroxy-corticosteroid levels during conditioned emotional disturbances in monkeys. *Psychosomatic Medicine 23*:344–353.

Matthews, B.H.C. 1931. The response of a single end organ. *Journal of Physiology 71*:64–110.

Mayer, A. 1901. *Essai sur la soil.* Paris: Felix Alcan.

Mayer, J., and Thomas, D.W. 1967. Regulation of food intake and obesity. *Science 156*:328–337.

Meehl, P.E. 1962. Schizotaxia, schizotypy, schizophrenia. *American Psychologist 17*:827–838.

Melzack, R. 1961. The perception of pain. *Scientific American 204*:28 and 41–49.

Melzack, R. 1970. Phantom limbs. *Psychology Today 4*:63–68.

Melzack, R., and Wall, P.D. 1965. Pain mechanisms: a new theory. *Science 150*:971–979.

Meyer, D.R. 1958. Some psychological determinants of sparing and loss following damage to the brain. In: *Biological and biochemical bases of behavior,* eds. H.F. Harlow and C.N. Woolsey, pp. 173–192. Madison, Wis.: University of Wisconsin Press.

Meyer, D.R. 1972. Access to engrams. *American Psychologist 27*:124–133.

Millenson, J.R. 1967. *Principles of behavioral analysis.* New York: Macmillan.

Miller, N.E. 1957. Experiments on motivation. *Science 126*:1271–1278.

Miller, N.E. 1969. Learning of visceral and glandular responses. *Science 163*:434–445.

Milner, B. 1954. Intellectual function of the temporal lobes. *Psychological Bulletin 51*:42–62.

Milner, B. 1963. Effects of different brain lesions on card sorting. *Archives of Neurology 9*:90–100.

Milner, B. 1964. Some effects of frontal lobectomy in man. In: *The frontal grandular cortex and behavior,* eds. J.M. Warren and K. Akert, pp. 313–334. New York: McGraw-Hill.

Milner, J.S.; Nance, D.M.; and Sheer, D.E. 1971. Effects of hypothalamic and amygdaloid chemical stimulation on appetitive behavior in the cat. *Psychonomic Science 23*:25–26.

Milner, P.M. 1961. The application of physiology to learning theory. In: *Current trends in psychological theory,* ed. R.A. Patton, pp. 111–133. Pittsburgh, Pa.: University of Pittsburgh Press.

Milner, P.M. 1970. *Physiological psychology.* New York: Holt, Rinehart and Winston.

Mirsky, A.F. 1969. Neuropsychological bases of schizophrenia. *Annual Review of Psychology 20*:321–348.

Mohr, B. 1840. Hypertrophie der Hypophyse cerebri und dadurch bedingter Druck auf die Hoehengrundflaeche insbesondere alf die Schnerven, dass Chiasma derselben, und dem laengseitigen Hoehenschenkel. *Wochenschrift gesamte Heilkunde, 6*:pp. 565–574.

Moniz, E. 1956. How I succeeded in performing the prefrontal leucotomy. In: *The great physiodynamic therapies in psychiatry,* ed. A.M. Sackler, pp. 131–137. New York: Hoeber-Harper.

Morgan, C.L. 1909. *Introduction to comparative psychology.* 2nd ed. London: Scott.

Morgan, C.T. 1965. *Physiological psychology.* 3rd ed. New York: McGraw-Hill.

Morison, R.S., and Dempsey, E.W. 1942. A study of thalamo-cortical relations. *American Journal of Physiology 135*:280–292.

Morrell, F. 1961*a*. Lasting changes in synaptic organization produced by continuous neuronal bombardment. In: *Brain mechanisms and learning,* ed. J.F. Delafresnaye, pp. 375–392. Oxford: Blackwell.

Morrell, F. 1961*b*. Electrophysiological contributions to the neural basis of learning. *Physiological Reviews 41*:443–494.

Morrell, F. 1963. Information storage in nerve cells. In: *Information storage and neural control,* eds. W.S. Fields and W. Abbott, pp. 189–229. Springfield, Ill.: Thomas.

Morris, D. 1967. *The naked ape.* New York: McGraw-Hill.

Morris, N.R.; Aghajanian, G.K.; and Bloom, F.E. 1967. Magnesium pemoline: failure to affect in vivo synthesis of brain RNA. *Science 155*:1125–1126.

Moruzzi, G. 1954. The physiological properties of the brain stem reticular system. In: *Brain mechanisms and consciousness,* ed. J.F. Delafresnaye, pp. 21–53. Springfield, Ill.: Thomas.

Moruzzi, G., and Magoun, H.W. 1949. Brain stem reticular formation and activation of the EEG. *Electroencephalography and Clinical Neurophysiology 1*:455–473.

Mountcastle, V.B.; Poggio, G.F.; and Werner, G. 1963. The relation of thalamic cell response to peripheral stimuli varied over an intensive continuum. *Journal of Neurophysiology 26*:807–834.

Mowrer, O.H. 1965. What is normal behavior? In: *Human values and abnormal behavior,* ed. W.D. Nunokawa, pp. 10–31. Chicago: Scott Foresman.

Moyer, K.E. 1971. *The physiology of hostility.* Chicago: Markham.

Müller, J. 1842. *Elements of physiology.* London: Taylor and Walton.

Munn, N.L. 1971. *The evolution of the human mind.* New York: Houghton Mifflin.

Murphree, H.B. 1966. Methodology for the clinical evaluation of analgesics. *Journal of New Drugs 6*:15–22.

Murphy, G. 1949. *Historical introduction to modern psychology.* rev. ed. New York: Harcourt, Brace and World.

Myers, R.D.; Bender, S.A.; Krstic, M.K.; and Brophy, P.D. 1972. Feeding produced in the satiated rat by elevating the concentration of calcium in the brain. *Science 176*:1124–1125.

Newsweek. 29 April 1974. Healing: mind over matter, pp. 67–68.

Nichols, I.C., and Hunt, J.M. 1940. A case of partial bilateral frontal lobectomy. *American Journal of Psychiatry 96*:1063–1087.

Nichols, J.R. 1965. How opiates change behavior. *Scientific American 212*:80–88.

Nissen, T.; Røigaard-Petersen, H.H.; and Fjerdingstad, E.J. 1965. Effect of ribonucleic acid (RNA) extracted from the brain of trained animals on learning in rats. II. Dependence of RNA effect on training conditions prior to RNA extraction. *Scandinavian Journal of Psychology 6*:265–272.

Noble, G.K., and Borne, R. 1940. The effect of sex hormones on the social hierarchy of *Xiphophorus helleri. Anatomical Record 78*:147.

Nodine, J.H.; Shulkin, M.W.; Slap, J.W.; Levin, M.; and Freiberg, K. 1967. A doubleblind study of the effect of ribonucleic acid in senile brain disease. *American Journal of Psychiatry 123*:1257–1259.

Oatley, K. 1972. *Brain mechanisms and the mind.* New York: Dutton.

O'Connell, R.J., and Mozell, M.M. 1969. Quantitative stimulation of frog olfactory receptors. *Journal of Neurophysiology 32*:51–63.

O'Kelley, L.I., and Muckler, F.A. 1955. *Introduction to psychopathology.* Englewood Cliffs, N.J.: Prentice-Hall.

Olds, J. 1958. Self-stimulation of the brain. *Science 127*:315–324.

Olds, J. 1962. Hypothalamic substrates of reward. *Physiological Reviews 42*: 554–604.

Olds, J. 1974. The creation of learning and memory. *Engineering and Science 37*:12–17.

Olds, J., and Milner, P. 1954. Positive reinforcement produced by electrical stimulation of septal area and other regions of rat brain. *Journal of Comparative and Physiological Psychology 47*:419–427.

Orzack, M.H.; Taylor, C.L.; and Kornetsky, C. 1968. A research report on the anti-fatigue effects of magnesium pemoline. *Psychopharmacologia 13*:413–417.

Ostow, M. 1971. Psychophysiology of hallucinogenic drug action. In: *The psychodynamic implications of the physiological studies on psychotomimetic drugs,* eds. L. Madow and L.H. Snow, pp. 52–66. Springfield, Ill.: Thomas.

Overton, D.A. 1964. State dependent or "dissociated" learning produced with pentobarbital. *Journal of Comparative and Physiological Psychology 57*:3–12.

Papez, J.W. 1937. A proposed mechanism of emotion. *A.M.A. Archives of Neurology and Psychiatry 38*:725–744.

Patton, H.D. 1960. Reflex regulation of posture and movement. In: *Medical physiology and biophysics,* eds. T.C. Ruch and J.F. Fulton, pp. 167–198. Philadelphia: Saunders.

Pauling, L. 1968. Orthomolecular psychiatry. *Science 160*:265–271.

Pavlov, I.P. 1927. *Conditioned reflexes.* New York: Oxford University Press.

Penfield, W. 1958. *The excitable cortex in conscious man.* Springfield, Ill.: Thomas.

Penfield, W., and Rasmussen, T. 1950. *The cerebral cortex of man.* New York: Macmillan.

Pfaffmann, C. 1959. The afferent code for sensory quality. *American Psychologist 14*:226–232.

Phoenix, C.H. 1961. Hypothalamic regulation of sexual behavior in male guinea pigs. *Journal of Comparative and Physiological Psychology 54*:72–77.

Piaget, J. 1971. *Biology and knowledge.* Chicago: University of Chicago Press.

Piaget, J., and Inhelder, B. 1969. *The psychology of the child.* New York: Basic Books.

Pines, M. 1973. *The brain changers.* New York: Harcourt, Brace, Jovanovich.

Pitts, F.N. 1969. The biochemistry of anxiety. *Scientific American 220*:69–75.

Pitts, F.N., and McClure, J.N. 1967. Lactate metabolism in anxiety disorders. *New England Journal of Medicine 277*:1329–1336.

Plotnikoff, N. 1966*a*. Magnesium pemoline: enhancement of learning and memory of a conditioned avoidance response. *Science 151*:703–704.

Plotnikoff, N. 1966*b*. Magnesium pemoline: enhancement of memory after electroconvulsive shock in rats. *Life Sciences 5*:1495–1498.

Plotnikoff, N., and Meekma, P. 1967. Pemoline and magnesium hydroxide versus pemoline: enhancement of learning and memory of a conditioned avoidance response in rats. *Journal of Pharmaceutical Science 56*: 290–291.

Pool, J.L. 1973. *Your brain and nerves.* New York: Scribners.

Popper, K.R. 1963. Science: problems, aims, and responsibilities. *Federation Proceedings 22*:961–972.

Porter, R.W.; Brady, J.V.; Conrad, D.G.; Mason, J.W.; Galambos, R.; and Rioch, D. 1958. Some experimental observations on gastrointestinal lesions in behaviorally conditioned monkeys. *Psychosomatic Medicine 20*: 379–394.

Powell, B.J.; Martin, L.K.; and Kamano, D.K. 1967*a*. Magnesium pemoline: effects of training vs testing of an avoidance response. *Psychonomic Science 8*:205–206.

Powell, B.J.; Martin, L.K.; and Kamano, D.K. 1967*b*. More on magnesium pemoline: differential effects of advance and immediate injections on avoidance performance. *Psychonomic Science 8*:303–304.

Prescott, R.G.W. 1966. Estrous cycle in the rat: effects on self-stimulation behavior. *Science 152*:796–797.

Pribram, K.H. 1962. Interrelations of psychology and the neurological disciplines. In: *Psychology: a study of a science,* vol. 4, ed. S. Koch, pp. 119–157. New York: McGraw-Hill.

Pribram, K.H. 1971. *Languages of the brain: experimental paradoxes and principles in neuropsychology.* Englewood Cliffs, N.J.: Prentice-Hall.

Pribram, K.H., and Broadbent, D.E., eds. 1970. *Biology of memory.* New York: Academic Press.

Pribram, K.H., and Luria, A.R., eds. 1973. *Psychophysiology of the frontal lobes.* New York: Academic Press.

Razran, G. 1961. The observable unconscious and the inferable conscious in current Soviet psychophysiology: interoceptive conditioning, semantic conditioning, and the orienting reflex. *Psychological Review 68*:81–147.

Reeves, C. 1966. Cholinergic synaptic transmission and its relationship to behavior. *Psychological Bulletin 65*:321–335.

Reich, W. 1970. *The greening of America.* New York: Random House.

Renshaw, B. 1940. Activity in the simplest spinal reflex pathways. *Journal of Neurophysiology 3*:373–387.

Riesen, A.H. 1961. Stimulation as a requirement for growth and function in behavioral development. In: *Functions of varied experience,* eds. D.W. Fiske and S.R. Maddi, pp. 57–80. Homewood, Ill.: Dorsey.

Riopelle, A.J., and Ades, H.W. 1951. Discrimination following deep temporal lesions. *American Psychologist 6*:261–262.

Riopelle, A.J.; Alper, R.G.; Strong, P.N.; and Ades, H.W. 1953. Multiple discrimination and patterned string performance of normal and temporal-lobectomized monkeys. *Journal of Comparative and Physiological Psychology 46*:145–149.

Roberts, W.W. 1970. Hypothalamic mechanisms for motivational and species-typical behavior. In: *The neural control of behavior,* eds. R.E. Whalen, R.E. Thompson, M. Verzeano, and N.M. Weinberger, pp. 175–206. New York: Academic Press.

Robin, A.A. 1958. A controlled study of the effects of leucotomy. *Journal of Neurology, Neurosurgery and Psychiatry 21*:262–269.

Roessler, R., and Greenfield, N.S. 1961. Incidence of somatic disease in psychiatric patients. *Psychosomatic Medicine 23*:413–419.

Rogers, D.P., and Carpenter, J.C. 1966. The decline of variance of ESP scores within a testing session. *Journal of Parapsychology 30*:141–150.

Rose, S. 1973. *The conscious brain.* New York: Knopf.

Rosenblatt, F.; Farrow, J.T.; and Herblin, W.F. 1966. Transfer of conditioned responses from trained rats to untrained rats by means of a brain extract. *Nature 209*:46–48.

Rosenblueth, A. 1970. *Mind and brain: a philosophy of science.* Cambridge, Mass.: MIT Press.

Rosenthal, D. 1971. *Genetics of psychopathology.* New York: McGraw-Hill.

Rosenthal, D., and Kety, S.S., eds. 1968. The transmission of schizophrenia. *Journal of Psychiatric Research. 6*: supp. 1.

Rosenzweig, M.R. 1970. Evidence for anatomical and chemical changes in the brain during primary learning. In: *Biology of memory,* eds. K.H. Pribram and D.E. Broadbent, pp. 69–85. New York: Academic Press.

Rosenzweig, M.R.; Love, W.; and Bennett, E.L. 1968. Effects of a few hours a day of enriched experience on brain chemistry and brain weights. *Physiology and Behavior 3*:819–825.

Rosvold, H.E.; Mirsky, A.F.; and Pribram, K.H. 1954. Influence of amygdalectomy on social behavior in monkeys. *Journal of Comparative and Physiological Psychology 47*:173–178.

Ruch, T.C. 1965. The homotypical cortex—the "association areas." In: *Neurophysiology,* 2nd ed., eds. T.C. Ruch, H.D. Patton, J.W. Woodbury, and A.L. Towe, pp. 465–479. Philadelphia: Saunders.

Ruch, T.C.; Patton, H.D.; Woodbury, J.W., and Towe, A.L., eds. 1965. *Neurophysiology.* 2nd ed. Philadelphia: Saunders.

Rushton, W.A.H. 1958. Chemical basis of human colour vision. *Research 11*: 478–483.

Russell, I.S., and Ochs, S. 1963. Localization of a memory trace in one cortical hemisphere and transfer to the other hemisphere. *Brain 86*:37–54.

Russell, R.W. 1969. Behavioral aspects of cholinergic transmission. *Federation Proceedings 28*:121–131.

Sachar, E.J.; Kanter, S.S.; Buie, D.; Engle, R.; and Mehlman, R. 1970. Psychoendocrinology of ego disintegration. *American Journal of Psychiatry 126*:1067–1078.

Sarnat, H.B., and Netsy, M.G. 1974. *Evolution of the nervous system.* New York: Oxford University Press.

Sawrey, W.L. 1961. Conditioned responses of fear in relationship to ulceration. *Journal of Comparative and Physiological Psychology 54*:347–348.

Sawrey, W.L.; Conger, J.J.; and Turrell, E.S. 1956. An experimental investigation of the role of psychological factors in the production of gastric ulcers in rats. *Journal of Comparative and Physiological Psychology 49*: 457–461.

Sawrey, W.L., and Weisz, J.D. 1956. An experimental method of producing gastric ulcers. *Journal of Comparative and Physiological Psychology 49*:269–270.

Schachter, S. 1964. The interaction of cognitive and physiological determinants of emotional state. In *Psychobiological approaches to emotional behavior,* eds. P.H. Leiderman and D. Shapiro, pp. 138–173. Stanford, Calif.: Stanford University Press.

Schachter, S. 1971. Some extraordinary facts about obese humans and rats. *American Psychologist 26*:129–144.

Schachter, S., and Singer, J.E. 1962. Cognitive, social and physiological determinants of emotional state. *Psychological Review 69*:379–399.

Schachter, S., and Wheeler, L. 1962. Epinephrine, chlorpromazine, and amusement. *Journal of Abnormal and Social Psychology 56*:121–128.

Scharrer, B. 1941. Endocrines in invertebrates. *Physiological Reviews 21*:383–409.

Schildkraut, J.J., and Kety, S.S. 1967. Biogenic amines and emotion. *Science 156*:21–30.

Schiller, F. 1947. Aphasia studied in patients with missile wounds. *Journal of Neurology, Neurosurgery, and Psychiatry 10*:183–197.

Schmeidler, G., ed. 1969. *Extrasensory perception.* New York: Atherton.

Schneck, J.N. 1953. *Hypnosis in modern medicine.* Springfield, Ill.: Thomas.

Schreiner, L., and Kling, A. 1953. Behavioral changes following rhinencephalic injury in the cat. *Journal of Neurophysiology 16*:643–659.

Scott, J.P. 1942. Genetic differences in the social behavior of inbred strains of mice. *Journal of Heredity 33*:11–15.

Scott, J.P., and Fredericson, E. 1951. The causes of fighting in mice and rats. *Physiological Zoology 24*:273–309.

Sechenov, I. 1965. *Reflexes of the brain.* Cambridge, Mass.: MIT Press.

Sechzer, J.A. 1964. Successful interocular transfer of pattern discrimination in split brain cats with shock avoidance motivation. *Journal of Comparative and Physiological Psychology 58*:70–83.

Selye, H. 1956. *The stress of life.* New York: McGraw-Hill.

Selye, H. 1969. Stress: it's a G.A.S. *Psychology Today 3*:24–25 and 56.

Sem-Jacobson, C.W., and Torkildsen, A. 1960. Depth recording and electrical stimulation in the human brain. In: *Electrical studies on the unanesthetized brain,* eds. E.R. Ramey and D.S. O'Doherty, pp. 275–290. New York: Hoeber-Harper.

Shagass, C., and Schwartz, M. 1962. Cerebral cortical reactivity in psychotic depression. *A.M.A. Archives of General Psychiatry 6*:235–242.

Shapiro, D., and Schwartz, G.E. 1970. Psychophysiological contributions to social psychology. *Annual Review of Psychology 21*:87–112.

Sharpless, S., and Jasper, H.H. 1956. Habituation of the arousal reaction. *Brain 79*:655–680.

Sheehan, P.W. 1973. Escape from the ambiguous. *American Psychologist 28*: 983–993.

Sheldon, W.H., and Stevens, S.S. 1942. *The varieties of temperament: a psychology of constitutional differences.* New York: Harper and Row.

Sherrington, C.S. 1900. Experiments on the value of vascular and visceral factors for the genesis of emotion. *Proceedings of the Royal Society 336*:390–443.

Sherrington, C.S. 1947. *The integrative action of the nervous system.* 2nd ed. New Haven: Yale University Press.

Shurrager, P.S., and Culler, E. 1938. Phenomena allied to conditioning in the spinal dog. *American Journal of Physiology 123*:186–187.

Shurrager, P.S., and Culler, E. 1940. Conditioning in the spinal dog. *Journal of Experimental Psychology 26*:133–159.

Sidman, M. 1960. *Tactics of scientific research.* New York: Basic Books.

Siegel, R.K. 1973. An ethologic search for self-administration of hallucinogens. *International Journal of the Addictions 8*:373–393.

Singer, C.J. 1957. *A short history of anatomy and physiology from the Greeks to Harvey.* New York: Dover.

Siva Sankar, D.V., ed. 1962. Some biological aspects of schizophrenic behavior. *Annals of the New York Academy of Sciences 96*:1–490.

Skinner, B.F. 1953. *Science and human behavior.* New York: Macmillan.

Skinner, B.F. 1971. *Beyond freedom and dignity.* New York: Knopf.

Smith, R.G. 1967. Magnesium pemoline: lack of facilitation in human learning, memory, and performance tests. *Science 155*:603–605.

Smith, S.M.; Brown, H.O.; Toman, J.E.P.; and Goodman, L.S. 1947. The lack of cerebral effects of *d*-tubocurarine. *Anesthesiology 8*:1–14.

Smythies, J.R. 1970. *Brain mechanisms and behavior.* New York: Academic Press.

Snyder, S.H.; Banerjee, S.P.; Yamamura, H.I.; and Greenberg, D. 1974. Drugs, neurotransmitters and schizophrenia. *Science 184*:1243–1253.

Solomon, R.L., and Turner, L.H. 1962. Discriminative classical conditioning in dogs paralyzed by curare can later control discriminative avoidance responses in the normal state. *Psychological Review 69*:202–219.

Soumirew-Mourat, B., and Cardo, B. 1968. Activity and learning in rats after magnesium pemoline. *Psychopharmacologica 12*:258–262.

Spence, K.W. 1956. *Behavior theory and conditioning.* New Haven: Yale University Press.

Spencer, H. 1855. *The principles of psychology.* London: Longmans.

Sperry, R.W. 1952. Neurology and the mind-brain problem. *American Scientist 40*:291–312.

Sperry, R.W. 1962. Some general aspects of interhemispheric integration. In: *Interhemispheric relations and cerebral dominance,* ed. V.B. Mountcastle, pp. 43–49. Baltimore: Johns Hopkins University Press.

Sperry, R.W. 1969. A modified concept of consciousness. *Psychological Review 76*:532–536.

Sperry, R.W. 1970. An objective approach to subjective experience: further explanation of a hypothesis. *Psychological Review 77*:585–590.

Spicker, S.F., ed. 1970. *The philosophy of the body: rejections of Cartesian dualism.* Chicago: Quadrangle.

Spinelli, D.N., and Pribram, K.H. 1966. Changes in visual recovery function produced by temporal lobe stimulation in monkeys. *Electroencephalography and Clinical Neurophysiology 20*:44–49.

Steigmann, F. 1936. The peptic ulcer syndrome in negros. *American Journal of Diseases of Nutrition 3*:310.

Stein, D.G.; Brink, J.J.; and Patterson, A. 1968. Magnesium pemoline: facilitation of maze learning when administered in pure dimethylsulfoxide. *Life Sciences 7*:147–153.

Stein, H.H., and Yellin, T.O. 1967. Pemoline and magnesium hydroxide: lack of effect of RNA and protein synthesis. *Science 157*:96–97.

Stellar, E. 1954. The physiology of motivation. *Psychological Review 61*:5–22.

Stellar, E. 1967. Hunger in man: comparative and physiological studies. *American Psychologist 22*:105–117.

Stevens, C.F. 1966. *Neurophysiology: a primer.* New York: Wiley.

Stevens, D.A., and Tapp, J.T. 1966. The effects of ribonuclease on learned discrimination and avoidance tasks in the rat. A.D.I. Document No. 8757.

Stevens, L.A. 1971. *Explorers of the brain.* New York: Knopf.

Stevens, S.S. 1961. To honor Fechner and repeal his law. *Science 133*:80–86.

Stevens, S.S. 1970. Neural events and the psychophysical law. *Science 170*:1043–1050.

Stevens, S.S. 1972. A neural quantum in sensory discrimination. *Science 177*:749–762.

Stroke, G.W. 1969. *An introduction to coherent optics and holography.* 2nd ed. New York: Academic Press.

Sudd, J.H. 1967. *An introduction to the behavior of ants.* New York: St. Martin's.

Sweet, R.C. 1969. RNA "memory pills" and memory: a review of clinical and experimental status. *Psychological Record 19*:629–644.

Szasz, T.S. 1960. The myth of mental illness. *American Psychologist 15*:113–118.

Talland, G.A. 1966. Improvement of sustained attention with cylert. *Psychonomic Science 6*:493–494.

Talland, G.A., and McGuire, M.T. 1967. Tests of learning and memory with cylert. *Psychopharmacologia 10*:445–451.

Talland, G.A., and Waugh, N.C., eds. 1969. *The pathology of memory*. New York: Academic Press.

Tart, C.T. 1963. Physiological correlates of psi cognition. *International Journal of Parapsychology 5*:375–386.

Tart, C.T. 1971. *On being stoned*. Palo Alto: Science and Behavior Books.

Tavolga, W.N. 1955. Effects of gonadectomy and hypophysectomy on pre-spawning behavior in males of gobiid fish, *Bathygobius soporator*. *Physiological Zoology 28*:218–233.

Tedeschi, R.E.; Tedeschi, D.H.; Mucha A.; Cook, L.; Mattis, P.A.; and Fellows, E.J. 1959. Effects of various centrally acting drugs on fighting behavior of mice. *Journal of Pharmacology and Experimental Therapeutics 125*:28–34.

Teilhard de Chardin, P. 1959. *The phenomenon of man*. New York: Harper and Row.

Teitelbaum, P. 1964. "Appetite." *Proceedings of the American Philosophical Society 108*:464–472.

Teitelbaum, P. 1966. The use of operant methods in the assessment and control of motivational states. In: *Operant behavior: areas of research and application,* ed. W.K. Honig, pp. 565–608. New York: Appleton-Century-Crofts.

Teitelbaum, P. 1967. *Physiological psychology*. Englewood Cliffs, N.J.: Prentice-Hall.

Teuber, H.-L. 1959. Some alterations in behavior after cerebral lesions in man. In: *Evolution of nervous control from primitive organisms to man*, pp. 157–194. Washington, D.C.: American Association for the Advancement of Science.

Teuber, H.-L., and Mishkin, M. 1954. Judgment of visual and postural vertical after brain injury. *Journal of Psychology 38*:161–175.

Thiessen, D.D. 1964. Amphetamine toxicity population density and behavior: a review. *Psychological Bulletin 62*:401–410.

Thiessen, D.D., and Rodgers, D.A. 1961. Population density and endocrine function. *Psychological Bulletin 58*:441–451.

Thompson, R.F. 1967. *Foundations of physiological psychology*. New York: Harper and Row.

Thompson, R.F.; Patterson, M.M.; and Teyler, T.J. 1972. The neurophysiology of learning. *Annual Review of Psychology 23*:73–104.

Thorndike, E.L. 1898. *Animal intelligence*. New York: Macmillan.

Tidy, H. 1944. Peptic ulcer. *American Practitioner and Digest of Treatment 152*: 197–203.

Tinbergen, N. 1951. *The study of instinct*. New York: Oxford University Press.

Tinbergen, N. 1968. On war and peace in animals and man. *Science 160*: 1411–1418.

Tolman, E.C. 1966. *Behavior and psychological man*. Berkeley: University of California Press.

Tompkins, P., and Bird, C. 1973. *The secret life of plants*. New York: Harper and Row.

Tooth, G.C., and Newton, M.P. 1961. *Leucotomy in England and Wales*. London: Her Majesty's Stationery Office.

Tsang, Y.C. 1938. Hunger motivation in gastrectomized rats. *Journal of Comparative Psychology 26*:1–17.

Tyler, L.E. 1965. *The psychology of human differences.* New York: Appleton-Century-Crofts.

Ullman, M.; Krippner, S.; and Vaughan, A. 1973. *Dream telepathy.* New York: Macmillan.

Ungar, G., and Oceguera-Navarro, C. 1965. Transfer of habituation by material extracted from brain. *Nature 207*:301–302.

Uricht, J. 1938. The social hierarchy in albino mice. *Journal of Comparative Psychology 25*:373–413.

Valenstein, E.S. 1973. *Brain control.* New York: Wiley.

Valenstein, E.S.; Cox, V.C.; and Kakolewski, J.W. 1970. Reexamination of the role of the hypothalamus in motivation. *Psychological Review 77*:16–31.

van Heerden, P.J. 1970. Models for the brain. *Nature 227*:410–411.

Vaughan, E., and Fisher, A.E. 1962. Male sexual behavior induced by intracranial electrical stimulation. *Science 137*:758–760.

Verhave, T. 1958. The effect of methamphetamine on operant level and avoidance behavior. *Journal of the Experimental Analysis of Behavior 1*:207–219.

Verplanck, W.S. 1957. A glossary of some terms used in the objective science of behavior. *Psychological Review 64*: part 2.

Verplanck, W.S., and Hayes, J.R. 1953. Eating and drinking as a function of maintenance schedule. *Journal of Comparative and Physiological Psychology 46*:327–333.

Volgyesi, F.A. 1954. School of patients, hypnosis-therapy and psychoprophylaxis. *British Journal of Medical Hypnotism 5*:8–17.

von Békésy, G. 1960. *Experiments in hearing.* New York: McGraw-Hill.

von Euler, U.S. 1946. A specific sympathomimetic ergone in adrenergic nerve fibres (sympathin) and its relations to adrenaline and noradrenaline. *Acta Physiologia Scandanavia 12*:73–97.

von Euler, U.S. 1966. Twenty years of noradrenaline. *Pharmacological Reviews 18*:29–38.

von Frisch, K. 1950. *Bees, their vision, chemical senses, and language.* Ithaca, N.Y.: Cornell University Press.

von Holst, E., and von St. Paul, U. 1960. Vom wirkungsgefuge der treibe. *Die Naturwissenschaften 47*:409–422.

Voronin, L.G. 1962. Some results of comparative physiological investigations of higher nervous activity. *Psychological Bulletin 59*:161–195.

Wallace, R.K. 1970. Physiological effects of transcendental meditation. *Science 167*:1751–1754.

Wallace, R.K.; Benson, H.; and Wilson, A.F. 1971. A wakeful hypo-metabolic physiological state. *American Journal of Physiology 221*:795–799.

Walster, E., and Berscheid, E. 1971. Adrenaline makes the heart grow fonder. *Psychology Today 5*:47–50 and 62.

Wangensteen, O.H., and Carlson, A.J. 1931. Hunger sensations in a patient after total gastrectomy. *Proceedings of the Society for Experimental Biology and Medicine 28*:545–547.

Warren, J.M., and Akert, K., eds. 1964. *The frontal granular cortex and behavior.* New York: McGraw-Hill.

Watson, J.B. 1913. Psychology as the behaviorist views it. *Psychological Review 20*:158–177.

Watson, J.B. 1916. The place of the conditioned reflex in psychology. *Psychological Review 23*:89–116.

Watson, J.B., and Rayner, R. 1920. Conditioned emotional reactions. *Journal of Experimental Psychology 3*:1–14.

Watson, J.D. 1968. *The double helix.* New York: Atheneum.

Watson, L. 1973. *Supernature.* New York: Doubleday.

Watson, R.I. 1968. *The great psychologists from Aristotle to Freud.* 2nd ed. Philadelphia: Lippincott.

Weight, F.F. 1968. Cholinergic mechanisms in recurrent inhibition of motoneurons. In: *Psychopharmacology: a review of progress 1957–1967,* eds. D.H. Efron, J.O. Cole, J. Levine, and J.R. Wittenborn, pp. 69–75. Washington, D.C.: American College of Neuropsychopharmacology.

Weil, A.T.; Zinberg, N.E.; and Nelsen, J.M. 1968. Clinical and psychological effects of marijuana in man. *Science 162*:1234–1242.

Weinstein, S., and Teuber, H.-L. 1957. Effects of penetrating brain injury on intelligence test scores. *Science 125*:1036–1037.

Weiss, B., and Laties, V.G. 1959. Amphetamine toxicity in rats subjected to aversive stimulation. *Federation Proceedings 18*:457.

Weiss, B., and Laties, V.G. 1962. Enhancement of human performance by caffeine and the amphetamines. *Pharmacological Reviews 14*:1–36.

Weiss, J.M. 1971. Effects of coping behavior in different warning signal conditions on stress pathology in rats. *Journal of Comparative and Physiological Psychology 77*:1–30.

Weiss, J.M. 1972. Psychological factors in stress and disease. *Scientific American 226*:104–113.

Weiss, J.M.; Glazer, H.I.; and Pohorecky, L.A. 1974. Neurotransmitters and helplessness: a chemical bridge to depression. *Psychology Today 8*:58–62.

Weiss, K.M., and Strongman, K.T. 1969. Biochemical blockade of cholinergic thirst. *Psychonomic Science 15*:274–276.

Wen, H.L., and Chung, S.Y.C. 1973. How acupuncture helps addicts. *Drugs and Society 2*:18–20.

Werner, H. 1948. *Comparative psychology of mental development.* New York: International Universities Press.

Whittaker, R.H., and Feeny, P.P. 1971. Allelochemics: chemical interactions between species. *Science 171*:757–770.

Wiener, N. 1948. *Cybernetics.* New York: Wiley.

Wikler, A. 1957. *The relation of psychiatry to pharmacology.* Baltimore: Williams and Wilkins.

Wilder, R.L., and Schultz, F.W. 1931. The action of atropine and adrenaline on gastric tonus and hypermotility induced by insulin hypoglycemia. *American Journal of Physiology 96*:54.

Williams, M. 1970. *Brain damage and the mind.* Harmondsworth: Penguin.

Wolf, S., and Wolff, H.G. 1942. Evidence for the genesis of peptic ulcer in man. *Journal of the American Medical Association 120*:670–675.

Wolf, S., and Wolff, H.G. 1943. *Human gastric function: an experimental study of a man and his stomach.* New York: Oxford University Press.

Wolf, S., and Wolff, H.G. 1946. Psychosomatic aspects of peptic ulcers. *Scope 11*:4–9.

Woodbury, J.W. 1965. The cell membrane: ionic and potential gradients and active transport. In: *Neurophysiology,* 2nd ed., eds. T.C. Ruch, H.K. Patton, J.W. Woodbury, and A.L. Towe, pp. 1–25. Philadelphia: Saunders.

Woodbury, J.W.; Gordon, A.M.; and Conrad, J.T. 1965. Muscle. In: *Neurophysiology,* 2nd ed., eds. T.C. Ruch, H.D. Patton, J.W. Woodbury, and A.L. Towe, pp. 113–152. Philadelphia: Saunders.

Woolley, D.W. 1957. Manipulation of cerebral serotonin and its relationship to mental disorders. *Science 125*:752.

Woolley, D.W. 1958. Participation of serotonin in mental processes. In: *Chemical concepts of psychoses,* eds. M. Rinkel and H.C.B. Denber, pp. 176–189. New York: McDowell.

Woolley, D.W., and van der Hoeven, T. 1963. Alteration in learning ability caused by changes in cerebral serotonin and catechol amines. *Science 139*:610–611.

Wortis, J. 1962. Pavlovianism and clinical psychiatry. In: *Recent advances in biological psychiatry,* vol. 4, ed. J. Wortis, pp. 13–23. New York: Pleum Press.

Wynne-Edwards, V.C. 1962. *Animal dispersion in relation to social behaviour.* Edinburgh: Oliver and Boyd.

Yerkes, R.M. 1939. Social dominance and sexual status in the chimpanzee. *Quarterly Review of Biology 14*:115–136.

Yerkes, R.M. 1940. Social behavior of chimpanzees: dominance between mates in relation to sexual status. *Journal of Comparative Psychology 30*: 147–185.

Young, R.M. 1970. *Mind, brain and adaptation.* New York: Oxford University Press.

Youtz, R.P. 1968. Can fingers see color? *Psychology Today 1*:36–41.

Yuwiler, A.; Greenough, W.; and Geller, E. 1968. Biochemical and behavioral effects of magnesium pemoline. *Psychopharmacologia 13*:174–180.

Zelman, A.; Kabat, L.; Jacobson, R.; and McConnell, J.V. 1963. Transfer of learning through injection of "conditioned" RNA into untrained planarians. *Worm Runner's Digest 5*:14–21.

Glossary

Ablation   removal of all or part of an organ.

Acalculia   loss of ability to carry out arithmetical operations.

Accessory structure   nonsensory portion of a sense organ which facilitates input to the receptor proper.

Acetylcholine   neurohumoral transmitter at all parasympathetic post-ganglionic and all preganglionic peripheral synapses.

Actin   contractile protein in muscle fibrils; functions in conjunction with myosin.

Action commune   Fluorens' term for nonspecific nervous system functions.

Action potential   sequence of changes in potential associated with impulse conduction in nerves and muscles.

Action propre   Fluorens' term for specific nervous system functions.

Activation pattern   low-voltage, fast-wave EEG recording.

Acupuncture   Chinese method of healing involving insertion of fine needles in various body regions.

Adenosine triphosphate (ATP)   substance which provides energy for muscle contraction.

Adipsia   loss of thirst and drinking behavior.

Adrenal cortex   portion of the adrenal gland whose hormones regulate electrolyte and sugar balance.

Adrenal gland   endocrine gland on the surface of the kidneys; consists of two parts, cortex and medulla.

Adrenaline   epinephrine.

Adrenal medulla   portion of adrenal gland which secretes epinephrine.

Adrenergic   activity characteristic of norepinephrine or substances which act like it.

Adrenergic blocking agent   drug that blocks the action of norepinephrine or other adrenergic substances.

Adrenocorticotropic hormone (ACTH) pituitary hormone which regulates the activity of the adrenal glands.

Adrenohypophysis anterior portion of the pituitary gland.

Afferent nerves or neural conduction to the central nervous system; generally, conduction to or towards.

Aggression behavior directed at organisms or objects with intention to inflict injury.

Agonist (muscle) contracting muscle that initiates movement.

Agonistic behavior aggressive behavior.

Agraphia loss of ability to write.

Alexia loss of ability to read.

Allelochemicals chemicals which facilitate interspecies communication.

All-or-none principle maintains that the magnitude of the action potential is independent of stimulus amplitude; the potential will always be of maximum strength or not at all.

Alpha blocking shift from alpha to beta waves due to alerting.

Alpha innervation innervation of extrafusal muscle fibers by alpha efferent neurons.

Alpha waves medium voltage, medium frequency brain electrical activity.

Amphetamine sympathomimetic drug; in some instances a behavioral stimulant.

Ampulla area of the semicircular canal which contains hair cell receptors.

Amusia loss of ability to comprehend musical tones.

Androgens hormones secreted by the testes; male sex hormones.

Anerobic not requiring oxygen or air.

Annulospiral ending muscle spindle nerve ending that responds to changes in tension; also called primary, the ending winds around individual muscle fibers.

Anode positive electrode.

Anorexia decreased appetite and eating behavior.

Antagonist muscle muscle that apposes the action of an agonist muscle.

Anticholinergic drug that blocks the action of acetylcholine or other cholinergic substances.

Anticholinesterase drug that blocks the action of cholinesterases.

Antidiuretic hormone (ADH) pituitary hormone which regulates activity of the renal tubules to control water balance in body tissues.

Antidromic conduction conduction of nerve impulses in a direction opposite to the normal.

Aphagia loss of appetite and eating behavior.

Approach reflexes behaviors which bring organisms towards other organisms or objects.

Apraxia loss of ability to perform objective or purposeful movements.

Arachnoid fine, delicate, middle meningeal layer.

Association areas cortical areas other than sensory and motor; silent areas.

Association nuclei thalamic nuclei that project between cortical areas.

Asthenic Kretchmer's term for tall, thin persons having introverted withdrawn personalities.

Athletic Kretchmer's term for vigorous, muscular persons having aggressive, active personalities.

Atropine an anticholinergic drug.

Autonomic nervous system (ANS) ganglia, nerves, and plexuses which regulate activities of the viscera, heart, blood vessels, smooth muscle, and glands.

Autotrophs organisms that can utilize inorganic compounds such as carbon dioxide, minerals, and salts for their energy; only organisms that can accomplish photosynthesis.

Aversive conditioning conditioning using a negative reward such as electric shock.

Axon neuron fiber processes that generally conduct impulses away from the cell body; long neuron fibers.

Bands (muscle) transverse stripes in muscle fibers resulting from filaments of different thicknesses.

Basal ganglia group of cerebral nuclei involved in motor control.

Basilar membrane cochlear membrane containing auditory hair cells.

Basket cells cells comprising the outermost layer of the cerebellum; also called star cells.

Behaviorism school of psychology which maintains that only overt, measurable behavior which can be operationally defined can be the subject matter of psychology.

Bell-Magendie law states that dorsal roots are sensory; ventral roots are motor.

Beta-waves low-voltage, fast-wave brain electrical activity.

Biasing mechanism gain control mechanism.

Biogenic amines amines naturally present in organisms, primarily the catecholamines and serotonin.

Bipolar neurons neurons with two long fiber processes.

Blood-brain barrier (BBB) functional barrier between brain vascular system and brain tissue that selectively controls which substances can enter brain tissue; also regulates quantity and rate of entry.

Body righting reflex reflex which maintains the head in a normal position relative to the surface on which a body is standing.

Brain part of the central nervous system, from medulla to cerebrum, contained within the skull.

Brain stem portion of the brain remaining after the cerebrum and cerebellum have been removed.

Broca's area part of the inferior frontal gyrus (left, in right-handed people) important to proper speech functioning.

Brodmann's areas numbered regions of the cerebral cortex differentiated by underlying cell structure.

Bulbar of or pertaining to the medulla.

Cannon-Bard theory notion that emotion produces bodily changes, integrated via the hypothalamus, that prepare organism for "fight or flight" or positive adaptive interaction.

Cannon-Head theory earlier version of the Cannon-Bard theory.

Carbohydrate class of organic compounds commonly called sugars.

Catecholamines group of sympathomimetic amines including epinephrine, norepinephrine, and dopamine.

Catechol-o-methyl-transferase (COMT) enzyme that catabolizes norepinephrine.

Cathode negative electrode.

Centralization (neural) organization of neurons into ganglia, plexuses, nuclei, nerves, or tracts.

Central nervous system (CNS) brain and the spinal cord.

Cerebellar ataxia staggering, uncoordinated movements resulting from cerebellar damage.

Cerebellar cortex anterior portion of the cerebellum.

Cerebellar hypotonia loss of tonus in skeletal muscles resulting from cerebellar damage.

Cerebellum metencephalic brain structure primarily involved with motor coordination.

Cerebrospinal fluid fluid in the cerebral ventricles, the central canal of the cord, and the subarachnoid spaces.

Cerebrospinal fluid-brain barrier functional barrier between brain cerebrospinal fluid and brain tissue that selectively controls which substances can enter brain tissue; also regulates quantity and rate of entry.

Cerebrum telencephalic; largest and functionally highest part of the brain; associated with volition, cognition, intellect, learning, and other advanced behaviors.

Cerveau isolé neuraxial transection at the level of the thalamus.

Chemoreceptors sensory receptors to chemical energy.

Chlorpromazine tranquilizer drug which is also an adrenergic blocking agent.

Choline acetylase enzyme involved in synthesis of acetylcholine.

Cholinergic activity characteristic of acetylcholine or substances which act like it.

Cholinesterase enzyme that catabolizes acetylcholine.

Chorda tympani branch of the VII (facial) cranial nerve which innervates the tongue and is involved in taste reception.

Clairvoyance perception or sensing without sensory mediation.

Clasp-knife reflex when resistance of a muscle to extension is followed by sudden relaxation.

Classical conditioning pairing of an unconditioned stimulus with a neutral stimulus such that the latter becomes a conditioned stimulus.

Climbing fibers nerve fibers which synapse with cerebellar Purkinje cells.

Colliculus (pl. -i) small eminence or prominence in the brain stem.

Common receptors unspecialized receptors that respond to any type of energy source.

Complex cells higher levels of visual cortical cells.

Conditioned response (CR)   response to a conditioned stimulus.

Conditioned stimulus (CS)   neutral stimulus which, by classical conditioning, becomes effective in eliciting a response similar to that formerly elicited by an unconditioned stimulus.

Conduction   electrochemical transmission of excitation within or between cells.

Cones   retinal photoreceptor cells involved in wavelength (color) reception.

Consolidation   conception that when a learning experience is terminated, physiological activities continue which can effect permanent tissue changes.

Constructive apraxia   loss of ability to carry out constructive activities.

Consummatory behavior   action of seeking and consuming in response to reducing biological needs.

Cori cycle   process by which liver forms glucose from lactic acid.

Coronal   plane through a body that would divide it into front and rear portions.

Corpus callosum   fiber tract that connects the two cerebral hemispheres.

Cortical recruitment   serial discharge of cortical neurons following input from thalamic nuclei which receive RAS fibers.

Cranial nerves   nerves arising directly from the brain stem and entering the periphery through the skull.

Crossed reflex   reflex in which one or more of the synaptic junctions are contralateral to each other.

Curare   drug that produces skeletal muscle paralysis by blocking impulses at the neuromuscular junction.

Dale's principle   maintains that all synaptic junctions of a neuron utilize the same type of neurohumoral transmitter.

Decerebrate rigidity   exaggerated postural tone in the antigravity muscles.

Dendrite   neuron fiber processes that generally conduct impulses towards the cell body; short neuron fibers.

Deoxyribonucleic acid (DNA)   nucleic acid in chromosomes which serves as a genetic template.

Depolarization   reduction or neutralization of polarity; reducing differential ion distributions across polarized tissue membranes.

Dermatome   area of skin supplied with sensory fibers from a single spinal nerve.

Desynchronized pattern   low voltage, fast-wave EEG recording.

Diencephalon   the thalamus, hypothalamus and related structures.

Differentiated receptors   specialized receptors that provide discrete sensations when stimulated.

Differentiation (neural)   phylogenetic or ontogenetic increase in complexity and organization of tissues.

Diffuse thalamic projection system   corticothalamic pathway concerned with RAS projection to the cortex.

Doctrine of specific nerve energies   Müller's contention that each sensory nerve is only capable of reacting in a specific way regardless of the nature of the stimulation.

Dopamine   catecholamine and norepinephrine precursor thought to be a central neurohumoral transmitter.

Dorsal root   afferent component or branch of a spinal nerve.

Dorsal root ganglion   spinal nerve ganglion containing sensory neuron cell bodies.

Dose   quantity of drug administered to an organism.

Drive-reduction   principle that an organism behaves to reduce effects of deprivation.

Drug   nonnutritional, ingestible substance consumed to alleviate disease or alter the mind or body.

Drug antagonism   condition where one drug offsets or reduces the action of another drug.

Drug-behavior interaction (DBI)   instance where a drug's effect is modified by environmental influences.

Drug synergism   condition where two or more drugs produce a greater effect than one or the other alone.

Drug tolerance   state in which an organism is unaffected by a generally active dose of a drug.

Dualism   philosophical position which maintains that there is some type of distinction between mind processes and body processes.

Dura mater   outermost, thickest meninges.

Dysmetria   inability to accurately control range of movement.

Ectomorph   Sheldon's term for thin, introverted persons.

Effector   neuron innervating a muscle or gland.

Efferent   nerves or neural conduction to a muscle or gland; generally, conduction away from.

Electrode   conductor through which electricity enters or leaves a medium.

Electroencephalogram (EEG)   recording of brain electrical activity from electrodes attached to the surface of the scalp or inserted into the brain.

Electron   smallest unit of negative electricity.

Electrophysiology   study of the electrical characteristics of organismic function.

Emotion   perceived states (feelings) which give rise to nonrational adaptive reactions (approach or avoidance).

Encephale isolé   neuraxial transection at the level of the medulla.

Encephalization (neural)   evolutionary development of the brain; control of the nervous system by the brain.

End plate potential   localized nonpropagated potential developed in the motor end plate.

Endocrine system   system of ductless glands that secrete hormones directly into the bloodstream.

Endolymph   fluid which fills the cochlear canals.

Endomorph   Sheldon's term for short, fat, jolly persons.

Energy   capacity for action; power in action.

Enervation   removal of nerves or neural excitation.

Engram   permanent change of state in living tissue as a result of excitation.

Epinephrine (adrenaline)   hormone secreted by the adrenal glands which stimulates glucose production and activity mediated by the sympathetic nervous system.

Equipotentiality   Lashley's conception that any brain part has equal potential for subsuming any function.

Ergotrophic zone   posterior portion of the hypothalamus; functions as an integrating center for the sympathetic nervous system.

Estrogens   hormones secreted by the ovaries, the female sex hormones.

Ethology   comparative study of animal behavior as it occurs in its natural habitat.

Evolution   concept that contemporary organisms developed from earlier organisms by processes of natural selection.

Excitation   process of causing electrochemical changes in cells or tissue by stimulation.

Exocrine glands   glands having ducts.

Extensor muscle   muscle which extends or stretches a limb.

Exteroceptors   sensory receptors that receive input from sources in direct or very close contact with them.

Extrafusal fibers   striated muscle fibers that function as the contracting elements.

Extrapyramidal motor system   polysynaptic pathways of cortical motor fibers.

Extrasensory perception (ESP)   awareness of an event without mediation by any of the known senses.

Faculty psychology   school of psychology which suggests that the mind is made up of separate independent areas of power or faculties.

Fechner's law   contention that when stimulus intensity changes in a geometrical progression, sensations change in an arithmetical progression.

Fibril (muscle)   component of a muscle fiber.

Filament (muscle)   entities of actin and myosin molecules which are organized into muscle fibrils.

Final common path   lower motor neuron shared by many reflex pathways.

Fissure   shallow folds or grooves in the cerebral cortex.

Flexor muscle   muscle that bends or flexes a limb.

Flocculonodular lobe   posterior portion of the cerebellum.

Flowerspray ending   muscle spindle nerve ending that responds to changes in tension; also called secondary, the ending branches out across the surface of the muscle fibers.

Froelich's syndrome   condition of obesity resulting from damage to pituitary gland and/or hypothalamus.

Frontal lobe   part of the cerebrum anterior to the central fissure.

Functionalism   school of psychology which maintains that the primary task of psychology is to analyze the functions of mind; the processes by which organisms adjust to their environment.

Functional localization designating of parts of the nervous system as the source of specific functions (behaviors).

Fusimotor system gamma efferent system.

Gain control mechanism feedback loop that maintains the system optimally sensitive to change; also called a biasing mechanism.

Galvanometer device for measuring electrical potential.

Gamma innervation innervation of intrafusal muscle fibers by gamma efferent neurons.

Ganglion clustered group of peripheral neurons.

Ganglion cells retinal cells whose fibers constitute the optic nerve.

Gate hypothesis Melzack's concept of the neural basis of pain.

General adaptation syndrome (GAS) Selye's term for the course of body reactions to stress.

Genetic template pattern of DNA molecules which determines ultimate characteristics of organisms.

Gland organ which secretes substances.

Glucose simplest carbohydrate.

Glycogen complex carbohydrate, often called "animal starch," utilized in ATP formation.

Glycolysis conversion of carbohydrates to lactic acid.

Golgi tendon organ kinesthetic receptor in tendons that responds to changes in tension.

Gonadotropic hormone pituitary hormone which regulates the activity of the ovaries or testes.

Gonads endocrine glands in the sex organs whose hormones regulate sexual activity and characteristics.

Granular cells cells comprising the innermost layer of the cerebellum.

Granular cortex homotypical cortex.

Grasping reflex clutching movements of fingers or toes in response to stimulation of the palm or sole.

Gray matter (neural) center area of the spinal cord largely composed of neuron cell bodies.

Habituation diminution or cessation of responding to a stimulus as a result of repetitive or continuous exposure.

Hallucination perception in the absence of appropriate sensory stimulation.

Hallucinogen drug which produces hallucinations.

Hedonism principle that an organism behaves to gain pleasure.

Heterotrophs organisms that require organic compounds, such as glucose, for their energy.

High voltage slow-wave (HVS) pattern EEG recording characterized by large, infrequent, voltage changes.

Homeostasis maintenance of optimal steady organismic states by coordinated physiologic processes integrated by the autonomic nervous system.

Homotypical cortex   cortex which constitutes the association areas.

Homunculus   analogic representation of the human body.

Hormone   substance produced by one organ or cell which is transported to other organs or cells where it has a specific regulatory effect.

Hypercomplex cells   highest level of visual cortical cells.

Hyperphagia   excessive appetite and eating behavior.

Hypnosis   artificially induced state of increased suggestibility and decreased initiative.

Hypothalamus   group of diencephalic nuclei concerned with many autonomic and limbic system functions.

Imprinting (ethology)   rapid learning process in young organisms in which the range of stimuli eliciting a behavior becomes narrowed.

Impulse   active electrochemical change conducted along a nerve fiber.

Innervation   supplying of nerves or neural excitation to an organ or tissue.

Inorganic compounds   noncarbon containing substances.

Intentional tremors   coarse, irregular tremors of the limbs induced in conjunction with volitional movement.

Interactionism   position that body and mind are independent but inseparable from each other.

Internuncial (inter-) neurons   neurons which conduct impulses between other neurons.

Interoceptors   sensory receptors that receive input from body organs and tissues.

Intersegmental reflex   supersegmental reflex.

Intracranial self stimulation (ICSS)   brain stimulation, usually of pleasure or pain producing areas, under the control of the organism.

Intrafusal fibers   muscle fibers containing stretch receptors.

Intrahemispheric transfer   movement of neural information from one cerebral hemisphere to another.

Ion   atom which has lost or gained an electron and is thereby capable of conducting electricity.

Irritability   capacity of living matter to respond to stimulation.

Isometric contraction   increase in muscle tonus without shortening.

Isotonic contraction   shortening of a muscle without an increase in tonus.

James-Lange theory   notion that emotion is an organism's perception of bodily changes induced by an emotion-provoking situation.

Just noticeable difference (j.n.d.)   least difference between two stimuli that can be detected.

Kinesthesis   sense of body movement or movement of body parts.

Kluver-Bucy syndrome   a behavioral state following temporal lobe lesions that involves loss of fear and rage reactions, hypersexuality, memory defects, compulsive mouthing, and hyperphasia.

Labyrinthine righting reflex   righting reflexes activated by the vestibular organs.

Lactic acid   end product of anerobic glycolysis in muscle.

Latent learning   learning which reveals itself in later circumstances following activity which did not involve the behavior being measured or its reward.

Lateral geniculate body   thalamic area where the optic nerve synapses with brain neurons.

Lateral hypothalamic syndrome   pattern of changes in eating and drinking behaviors following lateral hypothalamic lesions.

Law of forward conduction   contention that impulse conduction between neurons can only be from the axon of one to the membrane of another.

Learning   relatively permanent change in behavior developed as a function of experience.

Learning-instinct dichotomy   categorizing of specific behaviors as either learned or inherited.

Learning set   generalized approach to problem solving; a general method by which specific instances of a type of problem can be solved.

Limbic lobe   ring of paleocortical structures involved with emotionality.

Limen   threshold.

Lobotomy   surgical severing of nerve pathways between the frontal lobes and the thalamus.

Local circuit theory of conduction   contention that neural impulse conduction is accomplished by current flow between resting and active areas of a nerve.

Locus coeruleus   brain stem areas having a high norepinephrine content; thought to be involved in producing sleep.

Low voltage fast-wave (LVF) pattern   EEG recording characterized by small, frequent, voltage changes.

***d*-lysergic acid diethylamide (LSD)**   potent hallucinogenic drug.

MAO inhibitor   drug that blocks the action of monoamine oxidase.

Mass function   Lashley's contention that behavior depends on the quantity of brain tissue available rather than its location.

Mechano receptors   sensory receptors responsive to mechanical energy.

Medial   in or near the middle.

Medulla   a cluster of mylencephalic nuclei associated with autonomic function and cranial nerve pathways.

Membrane theory of nervous conduction   conception that cell membranes are polarized and conduct excitation by sequential depolarization.

Meninges   protective tissue layers around the brain and spinal cord.

Mesencephalon   midbrain, containing mostly fiber tracts.

Mesomorph   Sheldon's term for athletic, assertive persons.

Metabolism   synthesizing simpler elements into complex compounds (anabolism) and reducing complex compounds to simpler ones (catabolism).

Metencephalon   cerebellum, pons, and related structures.

Microelectrode   very small electrode, often not visible except under magnification.

Mind   organized mental processes of an organism; the totality of structures which are alleged to account for the occurrence of behavior; all conscious experience; self; psyche; intellect.

Mitochondria   cell structures where metabolic activity is regulated in relation to energy production.

Monism   philosophical theory which maintains there is no distinction between mind and body processes; they are one and the same.

Monoamine oxidase (MAO)   enzyme that catabolizes norepinephrine.

Monosynaptic reflex   reflex in which only one synapse is involved.

Moro reflex   reflex characteristic of human infants in which the limbs become extended in response to changes in the plane between head and trunk.

Mossy fibers   nerve fibers which enter the cerebellum and synapse with granular and basket cells.

Motivation   awareness of bodily states (feelings) arising from needs; behavior directed toward reducing tissue deficits.

Motor end plate   point at which a motor neuron fiber contacts a muscle fiber; a neuromuscular synapse.

Motor unit   motor neuron and the muscle fibers it innervates.

Muscle   tissue composed of contractile fibers and cells.

Muscle action potential   sequence of changes of potential in muscle fibers.

Muscle fibers   ultimate element of muscle tissue.

Myelencephalon   most caudal portion of the brain, contains the medulla.

Myelin (sheath)   white, fatty substance that forms a sheath around some nerves.

Myosin   contractile protein in muscle fibers; functions in conjunction with actin.

Myotatic reflex   contraction of a muscle in response to its being stretched.

Natural selection   conception that organisms best able to adapt to environmental pressures survive to perpetuate while those less able to adapt become extinct.

Neck-righting reflex   reflex which orients body position relative to the head.

Negative placebo   circumstances in which a drug effect is voided by expectancy.

Neocerebellar lobe   posterior portion of the cerebellar cortex, also called the posterior lobe.

Neocortex   phylogenetically more recent cortex, primarily the cerebrum.

Nerve   bundle of neuron fibers in the peripheral nervous system.

Nervous system   complex of neural tissue.

Neural tube   embryonic structure that differentiates into the spinal cord and brain.

Neuraxial transection   surgical separation of various levels of the cerebrospinal axis.

Neuroanatomy   study of the structure of the nervous system.

Neurobiotaxis   contention that developing neural fibers will grow toward sources of stimulation.

Neurohormone   substance liberated from an axon which crosses a synapse and effects excitation of a postsynaptic membrane.

Neurohumoral transmission   transmittal of neural excitation across a synapse by a neurohormone.

Neurohypophysis   posterior portion of the pituitary gland.

Neuromuscular system   complex of nerves and muscles associated with movement of the body or its parts.

Neuron   nerve cell, the basic structural and functional unit of the nervous system.

Neuron theory   point of view which maintains neurons are structurally independent, being only functionally connected.

Neurosecretion   secretory activity of nerve cells.

Nociceptors   sensory receptors responsive to pain-inducing stimuli.

Node of Ranvier   local constriction in the myelin sheath.

Nonspecific thalamic projection system   diffuse thalamic projection system.

Norepinephrine (noradrenaline)   neurohumoral transmitter at all sympathetic postganglionic synapses.

Nuclei   group or cluster of neuron cell bodies in the central nervous system.

Nuclei of Raphe   brain stem areas having a high serotonin concentration; thought to be involved in producing sleep.

Nystagmus   oscillatory movement of the eyeballs.

Ontogenetic   development of an individual organism.

Operant conditioning   conditioning in which reward is contingent upon the occurrence of a response.

Operational definition (operationism)   contention that any phenomenon can only be defined in terms of the operations used to study it.

Optic agnosia   inability to form visual perceptions.

Optic chiasma   area in brain where optic nerve fibers cross to side opposite their origin.

Optic righting reflex   reflex which maintains body upright in relation to visual cues.

Organic compounds   substances containing carbon; so named because they were originally thought to be unique to living matter.

Orthodromic conduction   conduction of a nerve impulse from an axon to a dendrite; conduction in the normal direction.

Oscilloscope   device which graphically represents changes in electric potential as a function of time.

Oxidation   loss of electrons by an element.

Oxygen debt   amount of oxygen needed to metabolize lactic acid formed by anerobic metabolism in muscle during severe exercise.

Oxytoxin   pituitary hormone which regulates uterine contractions and mammary gland secretion.

Overdose   exaggerated reaction to a dose of a drug.

Paleocerebellar lobe   anterior portion of the cerebellar cortex; also called the anterior lobe.

Paleocortex   phylogenetically older parts of the cerebrum such as those that make up the limbic system and rhinencephalon.

Pancreas   endocrine gland below the stomach whose hormones regulate the body's glucose uptake.

Papez circuit   major connections of the limbic system.

Paradoxical sleep   stage of sleep during which an organism is behaviorally quiescent but manifests a desynchronized EEG.

Parallelism   position that body and mind are concomitant but have no causal connection.

Paralysis   impairment of the function of muscles.

Parapsychology   study of stimulus-response relationships which cannot be explained in terms of present conceptions of physical energies.

Parasympathetic nervous system (PNS)   craniosacral division of the autonomic nervous system; usually induces effects opposite those of the sympathetic nervous system.

Parasympathomimetic   drug that mimics the action of acetylcholine.

Parathyroid gland   endocrine gland adjacent to the thyroid gland whose hormones regulate body calcium and phosphate levels.

Perception   assigning value and meaning to sensations.

Peripheral nervous system (PNS)   all of the nervous system outside the central nervous system.

Permanent physiological gradients   specific areas of one-celled organisms having specialized functions.

Perseverative error   continuance of a behavior after it is no longer appropriate.

Personality   patterns of traits characterizing an individual person.

Pharmacology   study of drugs and drug effects.

Pheronomes   chemicals which facilitate intraspecies communication.

Photoreceptors   sensory receptors responsive to radiant energy.

Photosynthesis   process of converting solar energy into other forms; a capacity unique to autotrophs.

Phrenology   theory relating mental faculties to particular parts of the brain, and contending that the shape of the skull over a given area indicates the predominance of a particular faculty.

Phylogenetic   origin and development of a species.

Physiological psychology   science which studies how body structures and functions—especially the nervous system—affect and control the overt and subjective behavioral characteristics of an organism.

Pia mater   vascular innermost meninges.

Pineal gland (pineal body)   small endocrine gland on roof of third ventricle; where Descartes thought body and soul interacted.

Pinna   accessory apparatus of the ear, membranes which collect sound waves for passage into the ear; the external ear.

Pituitary gland   "master gland" whose hormones regulate the activities of all other endocrine glands.

Placebo   pharmacologically inert substance which produces a drug-like effect.

Planarian   free-swimming flatworm.

Plasticity   quality or state of being plastic; capable of being molded, re-shaped, reformed.

Plexus (pl. es)   network of interlacing nerve fibers, blood vessels, or lymphatic ducts.

Polarity   having poles or regions with opposite intensity; the electrically positive or negative condition of a substance.

Polysynaptic reflex   reflex involving two or more synapses.

Pons   metencephalic brain structure connecting cerebrum and cerebellum and the two halves of the cerebellum with each other.

Postsynaptic generator potential   localized, nonpropagated potential developed in a postsynaptic membrane by a neurohormone.

Potential   amount of electrical charge.

Precognition   ability to forecast future events—"fortune telling."

Primary ending   annulospiral ending.

Projection areas   regions of the cerebral cortex which receive impulses generated in sensory receptors; each is specific to a particular modality.

Propioceptors   sensory receptors that receive input from muscles, tendons, joints, and balance organs.

Psi   a sense other than those utilized by most organisms.

Psychic blindness   loss of sight in the absence of damage to the visual system.

Psychic healing   ability to effect cures for pathological conditions by will rather than medical intervention.

Psychokinesis (PK)   ability to influence movement or condition of an object without physical mediation.

Psychopathology   mental illness.

Psychopharmacology   study of drugs which affect behavior.

Psychophysics   study of the relationship between physical stimuli and sensory experience.

Psychosomatic reaction   organic pathology of psychogenic origin.

Psychosurgery   brain surgery to correct behavior disorders.

Psychotomimetic   drug which produces psychotic-like symptoms.

Purkinje cells   cells comprising the middle layer of the cerebellum.

Pyknic   Kretchmer's term for short, fat persons having extroverted, sociable personalities.

Pyramidal motor system   monosynaptic pathway of cortical motor fibers to primary spinal motor neurons.

Rapid eye movements (REM)   rhythmic, synchronized eye movements characteristic of paradoxial sleep.

Receptive field   area circumscribed by rods and cones which innervate a single ganglion cell.

Receptor generator potential   localized, nonpropagated potential developed in a receptor following stimulation.

Receptors   specialized cells differentially sensitive to stimulation; areas of a postsynaptic membrane specifically receptive to neurohormones.

Reciprocal organization (muscle)   arrangement of skeletal muscles in agonistic and antagonistic pairs.

Recruiting response   cortical recruitment.

Recurrent inhibition   inhibitory feedback of a neuron upon itself.

Red muscles   muscles which contract isometrically and are also called holding or slow.

Reflex   stereotyped response; the neural pathway of a stereotyped response; a stimulus-response connection; a mechanical unconscious act; the simplest unit of behavior; innate behaviors; inflexible gross behaviors.

Reflex arc   a neural circuit consisting of a receptor and an effector and may also involve one or more internuncials; the path an impulse travels in a reflex arc; the behavior resulting from activation of a reflex arc.

Reflex chain   reflex in which several neurons are involved; a sequence of reflexes.

Reflexology   school of psychology that conceives all behavior in terms of conditioned and unconditioned reflexes or combinations thereof.

Refractory   resisting stimulation.

Regulatory feedback system   automatic means of controlling performance by having reciprocal links between input and output.

Reinforcement   consequence of a behavior; reward.

Releasing stimulus (ethology)   highly specific stimulus which elicits species-specific behavior.

Renshaw arc   neural feedback circuit involving a motor neuron and an interneuron such that the motor neuron's impulses can damp its own activity.

Renshaw cell   interneuron of a Renshaw arc.

Reterocognition   having knowledge of past events that were not experienced.

Reticular activating system (RAS)   reticular formation, thalamus, hypothalamus, and related structures which function to maintain appropriate states of arousal.

Reticular formation   complex network of nerve fibers and cell bodies at the core of the brain stem.

Reticular theory   point of view which maintains neurons are structurally connected.

Retina   photosensitive lining of the eyeball.

Retrograde amnesia   loss of memory for events immediately preceding the cause of the amnesia.

Rhinencephalon   olfactory bulbs, hippocampus, fornix, and related structures concerned with olfactory perception.

Rhodopsin   photosensitive rod pigment.

Ribonucleic acid (RNA)   nucleic acid found in body cells which is involved in protein synthesis.

Righting reflexes   reflexes that maintain an organism in an upright position.

Rods   retinal photoreceptor cells involved in intensity reception.

Rooting reflex   head turning and mouth opening movements of human infant in response to tactile stimulation of facial region.

Rostral   towards the front or head end.

Saggital plane through a body that would divide it into right and left portions.

Saltatory conduction conduction of an action potential by skipping between adjacent nodes of Ranvier.

Schizophrenia group of psychotic reactions characterized by withdrawal and fundamental disturbances of reality.

Secondary ending flowerspray ending.

Segmental reflex reflex in which all synaptic junctions are in the same spinal cord segment.

Segmented (neural) natural division between homologous parts of the nervous system.

Semicircular canals type of labyrinthine receptor.

Sensation experience resulting from activation of a sensory system.

Sensory coding transformation of stimulus input to a receptor into a neural signal.

Serotonin (5-hydroxytryptamine) substance present in neural, intestinal and vascular tissue thought to have neurotransmitter functions.

Side-effect drug effect other than the one(s) desired.

Silent areas parts of the cerebrum which have no demonstrable function.

Simple cell first level of visual cortical cells.

Skeletal muscle striated muscles; attached to the skeleton and function to effect movement.

Skull bones of the head; bony cavity containing the brain.

Sleep complex behavioral state characterized by inhibition of voluntary activities, partial or total loss of consciousness, and dreaming.

Smooth muscle unstriped muscle for the most part located in visceral walls and blood vessels.

Sodium hypothesis notion that changes in sodium ion concentration is the basis of neural impulse conduction.

Soma refers to the cell body of a neuron exclusive of the fiber processes.

Somatotropic hormone growth regulating hormone secreted by the pituitary gland.

Spinal animal experimental preparation in which the brain and spinal cord are surgically separated.

Spinal cord part of the central nervous system contained within the spine.

Spinal nerves nerves arising in the spinal cord and passing peripherally through the spine to body parts.

Spine columnar assemblage of vertebrae which surrounds the spinal cord; the backbone.

Stevens' power law contention that both stimulus intensity and sensation change in a geometric progression.

Stimulation activation of a sense receptor or excitation of tissue by energy or energy change.

Stimulus bound behavior that only occurs in conjunction with the presence of a stimulus.

Stress application of or result of aversive stimulation.

Striated muscle skeletal muscles; has a cross striped appearance.

Structuralism   school of psychology which maintains that the primary task of psychology is to analyze the structure of the mind rather than its functioning.

Subarachnoid space   space between the arachnoid and pia mater filled with cerebrospinal fluid.

Subconsciousness   Freudian term referring to a type of unawareness in awake organisms.

Successive induction   facilitation of a reflex by an antagonistic reflex so that rhythmic actions, such as walking, result.

Sulcus (pl. -i)   deep folds or grooves in the cerebral cortex.

Supersegmental reflex   reflex in which one or more synaptic junctions are in different segments of the spinal cord.

Suprasegmental reflex   reflex in which one or more synaptic junctions are in the brain.

Sympathetic nervous system (SNS)   thoraciolumbar division of the autonomic nervous system; usually induces effects opposite those of the parasympathetic nervous system.

Sympathomimetic   drug that mimics the action of norepinephrine.

Synapse   the space or gap between continuous neurons.

Synaptic vesicle   areas of axons which contain neurohormones.

Synchronized pattern   high-voltage, slow-wave EEG recording.

Synergistic action (muscle)   facilitation of a muscle's action by other muscles.

Taraxein   protein fraction found in the blood of schizophrenics.

Tectum   dorsal portion of the midbrain.

Tegmentum   ventral portion of the midbrain.

Teleceptors   sensory receptors that receive input from sources spacially distant from them.

Telencephalon   most rostral part of the brain, primarily the cerebral cortex.

Telepathy   interorganismic communication exclusively by thought processes.

Temporal lobe   cerebral area ventral to the lateral fissure and anterior to the occipital lobe.

Tendon   tissue which attaches muscle to bone.

Thalamus   cluster of diencephalic nuclei which functions to relay impulses to and from the cortex and the rest of the nervous system and between areas of the cortex.

Thermoreceptors   sensory receptors responsive to thermal energy.

Threshold   minimum amount of energy or energy change needed to activate a receptor.

Thyroid gland   endocrine gland in the neck region whose hormones regulate several metabolic processes.

Thyrotropic hormone   pituitary hormone which regulates the activity of the thyroid gland.

Tinnitus   unpleasant ringing, roaring, or hissing sensations associated with temporal lobe damage.

T-neuron   transmission neuron.
Tonic labyrinthine reflexes   acceleratory and righting reflexes.
Tonic neck reflexes   reflexes which control the position of the limbs in rela-
   tion to the position of the head.
Tonic reflexes   reflexes which control and maintain proper muscle tone.
Tonus   degree of contraction or tension in muscles when not contracting.
Tract   bundle of neuron fibers in the central nervous system.
Transcendental meditation   self-induced, trance-like state in which the indi-
   vidual attempts to obtain greater knowledge or insight.
Transducer   device or organ capable of effecting transduction.
Transduction   process of transferring energy from one system to another;
   the transferred energy may remain in the same form or be changed to
   a different form.
Transmission neuron   spinal neuron which conducts pain impulses to the
   brain.
Transorbital lobotomy   partial ablation of the prefrontal lobes.
Tremor   purposeless rhythmic movements resulting from alternate contraction and relaxation of opposing skeletal muscles.
Tropotropic zone   anterior portion of the hypothalamus which functions
   as an integrating center for the parasympathetic nervous system.
d-**tubocuranine**   the active constituent of curare.

Uncinate fit   unpleasant, disagreeable, olfactory hallucinations associated
   with temporal lobe damage.
Unconditioned response (UR)   response to an unconditioned stimulus.
Unconditioned stimulus (US)   stimulus which can elicit a response without
   prior association.
Uncrossed reflex   reflex in which all synaptic junctions are ipsilateral.
Unilateral neglect   loss of sensory awareness for one half of one's body.

Ventral   referring to the belly; or in the direction of the belly.
Ventral root   efferent component or branch of a spinal nerve.
Vertebrae   bones which comprise the spine.
Vestibular sacs   type of labyrinthine receptor.
Visual purple   rhodopsin.

Weber's law   contention that there is a constant (K) ratio between change
   required to effect a j.n.d. (ΔR) and the existing stimulus (R);
$$K = \frac{\Delta R}{R}$$
White matter (neural)   peripheral areas of the spinal cord largely composed
   of myelinated nerve fibers.
White muscles   muscles which contract isotonically, and are also called moving or fast.
Withdrawal (drug)   adverse reactions following abrupt termination of
   chronic drug use.

Withdrawal reflexes behaviors which remove an organism from other organisms or objects.

Witzelsucht symptom of human frontal lobe damage involving silly, shallow, facetious behavioral episodes.

Young-Helmholtz theory notion that there are three receptors—one for each primary—involved in color vision.

Acknowledgments

de l'adrénaline. *Revue Française d'Endocrinologie,* 1924, *2*:301–325, Masson & Cie, Paris.   W. B. Cannon, The James-Lange theory of emotions: a critical examination and an alternative theory. *American Journal of Psychology,* 1927, *39*:106–124.   J. W. Papez, A proposed mechanism of emotion. *A.M.A. Archives of Neurology and Psychiatry,* 1937, *38*:725–744.   E. G. Boring, *The Physical Dimensions of Consciousness,* 1963, New York: Dover. K. S. Lashley, *Brain Mechanisms and Intelligence,* 1963, New York: Dover.   W. James, *The Principles of Psychology,* 1890, New York: Dover.   R. F. Thompson, M. M. Patterson, & T. J. Teyler, The neurophysiology of learning. *Annual Review of Psychology,* 1972, *23*:73–104.   K. S. Lashley, In search of the engram. In: *Society of Experimental Biology Symposium No. 4: Physiological Mechanisms in Animal Behavior,* 1950, 454–482, New York: Cambridge University Press.   J. J. Katz & W. C. Halstead, Protein organization and mental function. *Comparative Psychology Monographs,* 1950, *20*:1–38, University of California Press.   S. Rose, *The Conscious Brain,* 1973, New York: Knopf. L. A. Stevens, *Explorers of the Brain,* 1971, New York: Knopf. E. Airapetyantz & K. Bykov, Physiological experiments and the psychology of the subconscious. *Philosophy and Phenomenological Research,* 1945, *5*:577–593.   K. H. Pribram, *On the Biology of Learning,* Harcourt Brace Jovanovich, Inc.   G. Murphy, Historical introduction to modern psychology, 1949, Harcourt Brace Jovanovich.   J. P. M. Flourens, *Researches Expérimentales sur les Propriétés et les Fonctions du Systèm Nerveaux dans les Animaux Vertébrés.* 2nd ed., 1842, Paris: Ballière.   R. M. Young, *Mind, Brain and Adaptation,* 1970, by permission of The Clarendon Press, Oxford.   E. G. Boring, *A History of Experimental Psychology* (2nd ed.). Copyright © 1950, by permission of Appleton-Century-Crofts.   R. F. Thompson, *Foundations of Physiological Psychology,* 1967, Harper & Row.   A. R. Luria, *Human Brain and Psychological Processes,* 1966, Harper & Row. F. A. Beach, D. O. Hebb, C. T. Morgan, & H. W. Nissen (eds.), *The Neuropsychology of Lashley: Selected Papers.* Copyright 1960, used with permission of McGraw-Hill.   H. Selye, *The Stress of Life.* Copyright 1956, used with permission of McGraw-Hill. J. Loeb, *Comparative Physiology of the Brain and Comparative Psychology,* 1900, Putnam.   M. Pines, *The Brain Changers,* 1973, Harcourt Brace Jovanovich, Inc.   D. O. Hebb, *A Textbook of*

Psychology (2nd ed.), 1966, Saunders.   T. C. Ruch, H. D. Patton, J. W. Woodbury, & A. L. Towe, *Neurophysiology* (2nd ed.), 1965, Saunders.   R. C. Sweet, RNA "memory pills" and memory: a review of clinical and experimental status. *Psychological Record*, 1969, *19*:629–644.   W. C. Corning & D. Riccio, The planarian controversy. In: W. L. Byrne (ed.), *Molecular Approaches to Learning and Memory*, 1970, Academic Press.   A. L. Jacobson & J. M. Schlecter, Chemical transfer of training: three years later. In: K. H. Pribram & D. E. Broadbent, *Biology of Memory*, 1970, Academic Press.   J. Piaget, *Biology and Knowledge*, 1971, University of Chicago Press.   R. Efron, The conditioned reflex: a meaningless concept. *Perspectives in Biology and Medicine*, 1966, *9*:488–514, The University of Chicago Press.   C. S. Hall & G. Lindzey, *Theories of Personality* (2nd ed.), 1970, John Wiley & Sons, Inc.   H. C. Lindgren, *An Introduction to Social Psychology*, 1969, John Wiley & Sons, Inc.   O. H. Mowrer, *Learning Theory and Personality Dynamics*. Copyright © 1950, New York: The Ronald Press Company.   H. Kaufmann, *Aggression and Altruism*, 1970, Holt, Rinehart and Winston.   E. Aronson, *The Social Animal*. Copyright © 1972, W. H. Freeman.   N. Azrin, Pain and aggression. Reprinted from *Psychology Today*, May 1967. Copyright © Ziff Davis Publishing Company.   S. F. Spicker (ed.), *The Philosophy of the Body: Rejections of Cartesian Dualism*, 1970, Quadrangle.   I. Sechenov, *Reflexes of the Brain*, 1965, M.I.T. Press.   A. Rosenblueth, *Mind and Brain: A Philosophy of Science*, 1970, M.I.T. Press.   J. C. Eccles, *Facing Reality: Philosophical Adventures by a Brain Scientist*, Heidelberg Science Library, Vol. 13. Copyright © 1970, Springer-Verlag.   K. H. Pribram, *Languages of the Brain: Experimental Paradoxes and Principles in Neuropsychology*. Copyright © 1971, by permission of Prentice-Hall.   T. F. Lohr, *The Mechanics of the Mind*, 1971, Venture.   R. I. Evans, *B. F. Skinner: The Man and His Ideas*. Copyright © 1968 by R. I. Evans, used with permission of E. P. Dutton & Co., Inc.   E. McGinnies, *Social Behavior: A Functional Analysis*, 1970, Houghton Mifflin.   A. C. Benjamin, *An Introduction to the Philosophy of Science*, 1937, Macmillan. Copyright by A. C. Benjamin.   A. Manning, Evolution of behavior. In: *Psychobiology*, ed. J. L. McGaugh, 1971, 3–7, Academic Press.   I. Kupfermann & H. Pinsker, Plasticity in *Aplysia* neurons and some simple neuronal models of learning. In: *Reinforcement and Behavior,* ed. J. T. Tapp, 1969, 356–386, Academic Press.   D. E. Kelly, Anatomy Dept., University of Southern California.   M. A. Cahill, Dept. of Biological Structure, University of Miami.   R. C. Clark, Dept. of Biological Structure, University of Miami.   Warren Anatomical Museum, Harvard Medical School, Boston, Massachusetts.   Wil-Jo Associates, Inc. & Bill Mauldin.

Name Index

Subject Index